Instructor's Manual and
to accompany

Anthropology
The Exploration of Human Diversity
and
Cultural Anthropology
Both Ninth Editions

Conrad Phillip Kottak
The University of Michigan

Prepared by
Christopher P. Glew
The University of Michigan

Also Included:

**Test Bank for
Culture Sketches: Case Studies in Anthropology, 2/e
By Holly Peters-Golden**
The University of Michigan

and

**Instructor's Resourse for
Through the Looking Glass: Readings in Anthropology
By David L. Carlson and Vaughn M. Bryant, Jr.**
Texas A&M University

Boston   Burr Ridge, IL   Dubuque, IA   Madison, WI   New York   San Francisco   St. Louis
Bangkok   Bogotá   Caracas   Kuala Lumpur   Lisbon   London   Madrid   Mexico City
Milan   Montreal   New Delhi   Santiago   Seoul   Singapore   Sydney   Taipei   Toronto

McGraw-Hill Higher Education

*A Division of The **McGraw-Hill** Companies*

Instructor's Manual and Test Bank to accompany
ANTHROPOLOGY: THE EXPLORATION OF HUMAN DIVERSITY AND
CULTURAL ANTHROPOLOGY
Conrad Phillip Kottak

2 3 4 5 6 7 8 9 0 QSR/QSR 0 9 8 7 6 5 4 3 2 1

ISBN 0-07-242657-8

www.mhhe.com

TABLE OF CONTENTS

HOW TO USE THIS MANUAL

This Edition of the Instructor's Manual

This manual is an update version of the manual I prepared for the eighth edition of *Anthropology: The Exploration of Human Diversity*, which was based on the instructor's manual that David Brawn prepared for the seventh edition of the text. Changes have been made to accommodate the revisions found in the ninth of the text.

Chapter Outlines

Each chapter begins with an outline of the chapter in the Kottak text. These outlines are intended to provide instructors with the ability to review the information covered in the text with a minimum expenditure of time. These outlines are also available at the Online Learning Center as PowerPoint slides.

Lecture Topics and Suggested Films

Lecture topics have been suggested that correspond to and complement the points of emphasis in the text. The films come from a variety of sources, but the majority are available through *The University of Illinois Film and Video Center* and *Films for the Humanities and Sciences*. Many of the films may be available through your school's library (be sure to check interlibrary loan resources).

Questions

The questions in the test-bank have been added, revised, and updated to correspond with the ninth edition of the text. There are questions that are keyed directly to subject matter in the text and questions that require students to apply concepts from the text to hypothetical situations. There is only one most-correct answer for each multiple choice question (highlighted in boldface), although occasionally this correct answer is "all of the above" or--more rarely--"none of the above." In addition to the multiple-choice questions, each chapter has 20 "True or False" questions.

Resources for Supplementary Books

Included in this manual are two test banks/instructor's manuals which correspond to books sold as part of a set with Kottak's *Anthropology: The Exploration of Human Diversity*. These books are *Culture Sketches: Case Studies in Anthropology*, by Holly Peters-Golden, and *Through the Looking Glass: Readings in Anthropology*, edited by David L. Carlson and Vaughn M. Bryant, Jr. *Culture Sketches* is a series of synoptic case studies taken from the cultures of peoples who figure prominently in the Kottak text. *Through the Looking Glass* is a set of short readings selected to correspond with each of the Kottak text's chapters and to exemplify or expand upon some of the major issues found therein. These additional instructor's resources have been prepared by the books' author and editors, respectively, and are located in Appendices B and C.

CHAPTER 1
WHAT IS ANTHROPOLOGY?

CHAPTER OUTLINE

I. Adaptation, Variation, and Change

    A. Anthropology is the study of the human species and its immediate ancestors.
        1. Anthropology is holistic in that the discipline is concerned with studying the whole of the human condition: past, present and future, biology, society, language, and culture.
        2. Anthropology offers a unique cross-cultural perspective by constantly comparing the customs of one society with those of others.

    B. People share both society and culture.
        1. Society is organized life in groups, a feature that humans share with other animals.
        2. Cultures are traditions and customs, transmitted through learning that govern the beliefs and behaviors of the people exposed to them.
        3. While culture is not biological, the ability to use it rests in hominid biology.

    C. Adaptation is the process by which organisms cope with environmental stresses.
        1. Human adaptation involves interaction between culture and biology to satisfy individual goals.
        2. Four types of human adaptation (see the illustration of these with regard to adjustment to high altitude).
            a. *Cultural (technological)* adaptation.
            b. *Genetic* adaptation.
            c. *Long-term physiological* or *developmental* adaptation.
            d. *Immediate physiological* adaptation.

    D. Humans are the most adaptable animals in the world, having the ability to inhabit widely variant ecological niches.
        1. Humans, like all other animals use biological means to adapt to a given environment.
        2. Humans are unique in having cultural means of adaptation.

    E. Through time, social and cultural means of adaptation have become increasingly important for human groups.
        1. Human groups have devised diverse ways in order to cope with a wide range of environments.
        2. The rate of this cultural adaptation has been rapidly accelerating during the last 10,000 years.
            a. Food production developed between 12,000 and 10,000 years ago after millions of years during which hunting and gathering was the sole basis for human subsistence.
            b. The first civilizations developed between 6,000 and 5,000 years ago.
            c. More recently, the spread of industrial production has profoundly affected human life.

II. General Anthropology

    A. The fourth subdisciplines of American Anthropology.
        1. The academic discipline of American anthropology is unique in that it includes four subdisciplines: cultural anthropology, archaeological anthropology, biological or physical anthropology, and linguistic anthropology.

2. This four-field approach developed in the U.S., as early American anthropologists studying native peoples of North America became interested in exploring the origins and diversity of the groups that they were studying.
3. This broad approach to studying human societies did not develop in Europe (e.g. Archaeology, in most European universities, is not a subdiscipline of anthropology; it is its own department).

B. The four subdisciplines share a similar goal of exploring variation in time and space to improve our understanding on the basics of human biology, society, and culture.
1. Variation in "Time" (diachronic research): using information from contemporary groups to model changes that took place in the past; and using knowledge gained from past groups to understand what is likely to happen in the future (e.g. reconstructing past languages using principles based on modern ones).
2. Variation in "Space" (synchronic research): comparing information collected from human societies existing roughly at the same time, but from different geographic locations (e.g. the race concept in the U.S., Brazil, and Japan).

C. Any conclusions about "human nature" must be pursued with a comparative, cross-cultural approach.

III. Cultural Forces Shape Human Biology

A. Cultural traditions promote certain activities and abilities, discourage others, and set standards of physical well being and attractiveness.
1. Participation and achievement in sports is determined by cultural factors, not racial ones.
2. In Brazilian culture, women should be soft, with big hips and buttocks, not big shoulders; since competitive swimmers tend to have big, strong, shoulders and firm bodies, competitive swimming is not very popular among Brazilian females.
3. In the U.S., there aren't many African-American swimmers or hockey players, not because of a biological reason, but because those sports aren't as culturally significant as football, basketball, baseball, and track.

B. There is no conclusive evidence for biologically based contrasts in intelligence between the rich and poor, black and white, or men and women.
1. The best indicators of how any individual will perform on an intelligence test are environmental, such as educational, economic, and social backgrounds.
2. All standard tests are culture-bound and biased because they reflect the training and life experiences of those that develop and administer them.
3. Jensenism asserts that African-Americans are hereditarily incapable of doing as well as whites.
   a. Named for Arthur Jensen, the educational psychologist, who observed that on average African-Americans perform less well on intelligence tests that Euro-Americans and Asian-Americans.
   b. This racist notion of the inborn inferiority of African-Americans recently resurfaced in the 1994 book *The Bell Curve* by Richard Hernnstein and Charles Murray.

C. *The Bell Curve* (1994).
1. Like Jensen, Hernnstein and Murray disregard more convincing environmental explanations in favor of a genetic one to explain patterns observed in intelligence test scores.
2. An environmental explanation acknowledges that for many reasons, both genetic and environmental, some people are smarter than others, however these differences in intelligence **cannot** be generalized to characterize whole populations or social groups.
3. Psychologists have come up with many ways to measure intelligence, but there are problems with all of them.

4. Intelligence tests reflect the experiences of the people who write them.
    a. Middle-and upper-classed children do well because they share the test makers' educational expectations and standards.
    b. The SATs claim to measure intellectual aptitude but they also measure the type and quality of high school education, linguistic and cultural background, and parental wealth.
    c. Studies have shown that performance on the SATs can be improved by coaching and preparation, placing those students who can pay for an SAT preparation course at an advantage.
5. Cultural biases in testing, affect performance by people in other cultures, as well as different groups in the same nation.
    a. Native Americans scored the lowest of any group in the U.S., but when the environment during growth and development for Native Americans is similar to that of middle-class whites, the test scores tend to equalize (e.g. the Osage Indians).
    b. At the start of World War I, African-Americans living in the north, scored on average better than whites living in the south, due to the better public school systems in the north.

IV. The Subdisciplines of Anthropology

A. Cultural Anthropology combines ethnography and ethnology to study human societies and cultures for the purpose of explaining social and cultural similarities and differences.
    1. Ethnography produces an account (a book, an article, or a film) of a particular community, society, or culture based on information that is collected during fieldwork.
        a. Generally, ethnographic fieldwork involves living in the community that is being studied for an extended period of time (e.g. 6 months to 2 years).
        b. Ethnographic fieldwork tends to emphasize *local* behavior, beliefs, customs, social life, economic activities, politics, and religion, rather than developments at the national level.
        c. Since cultures are not isolated, ethnographers must investigate the local, regional, national, and global systems of politics, economics, and information that expose villagers to external influences.
    2. Ethnology examines, interprets, analyzes, and compares the ethnographic data gathered in different societies to make generalizations about society and culture.
        a. Ethnology uses ethnographic data to build models, test hypotheses, and create theories that enhance our understanding of how social and cultural systems work.
        b. Ethnology works from the particular (ethnographic data) to the general (theory).

B. Interesting Issues: Even Anthropologists Get Culture Shock
    1. "Culture shock" is alienation that results from stepping outside one's own cultural frame and into a different one.
    2. The example of Kottak's work among the Arembepe suggests that culture shock eases once we begin to grasp the logic of a culture that is new to us.

C. Archaeological anthropology reconstructs, describes, and interprets past human behavior and cultural patterns through material remains.
    1. The material remains of a culture include artifacts (e.g. potsherds, jewelry, and tools), garbage, burials, and the remains of structures.
    2. Archaeologists use paleoecological studies to establish the ecological and subsistence parameters within which given group lived.
    3. The archaeological record provides archaeologists the unique opportunity to look at changes in social complexity over thousands and tens of thousands of years (this kind of time depth is not accessible to ethnographers).

4. Archaeology is not restricted to prehistoric societies.
   a. Historical archaeology combines archaeological data and textual data to reconstruct historically known groups.
   b. William Rathje's "garbology" project in Tucson, Arizona.

D. Biological, or physical, anthropology investigates human biological diversity across time and space.
   1. There are five special interests within biological anthropology:
      a. Paleoanthropology: human evolution as revealed by the fossil record.
      b. Human genetics.
      c. Human growth and development.
      d. Human biological plasticity: the body's ability to change as it copes with stresses such as heat, cold, and altitude.
      e. Primatology: the study of the biology, evolution, behavior, and social life of primates.
   2. Biological anthropology is multidisciplinary as it draws on biology, zoology, geology, anatomy, physiology, medicine, public health, osteology, and archaeology.

E. Linguistic anthropology is the study of language in its social and cultural context across space and time.
   1. Some linguistic anthropologists investigate universal features of language that may be linked to uniformities in the human brain.
   2. Historical linguists reconstruct ancient languages and study linguistic variations through time.
   3. Sociolinguistics investigates relationships between social and linguistic variations to discover varied perceptions and patterns of thought in different cultures.

V. Applied Anthropology

A. Anthropology, as defined by the American Anthropological Association (AAA), has two dimensions: 1) theoretical/academic anthropology and 2) practicing or applied anthropology.
   1. Theoretical/academic anthropology includes the four subfields discussed above (cultural, archaeological, biological, and linguistic anthropology).
      a. Directed at collecting data to test hypotheses and models that were created to advance the field of anthropology.
      b. Generally, theoretical/academic anthropology is carried out in academic institutions (e.g. universities and specialized research facilities).
   2. Applied anthropology is the application of any of anthropological data, perspectives, theory, and techniques to identify, assess, and solve contemporary social problems.
      a. Some standard subdivisions have developed in applied anthropology: medical anthropology, environmental anthropology, forensic anthropology, and development.
      b. Applied anthropologists are generally employed by international development agencies, like the World Bank, United States Agency for International Development (USAID), the World Health Organization (WHO), and the United Nations.

B. Applied anthropologists assess the social and cultural dimensions of economic development.
   1. Development projects often fail when planners ignore the cultural dimensions of development.
   2. Applied anthropologists work with local communities to identify specific social conditions that will influence the failure or success of a development project.

VI. Anthropology and other Academic Fields

A. Anthropology's own broad scope has always lent it to interdisciplinary collaboration.
   1. Anthropology is a science, in that it is a systematic field of study that uses experiments, observations, and deduction to produce reliable explanations of human cultural and biological phenomena.
   2. Anthropology is also one of the humanities, in that it encompasses the study and cross-cultural comparison of languages, texts, philosophies, arts, music, performances and other forms of creative expression.

B. Cultural anthropology and sociology
   1. Formerly, sociology focused on "Western" societies while anthropology looked at "exotic" societies.
   2. Cultural anthropological methodologies have primarily been in-depth and qualitative (e.g. participant observation).
   3. Sociological methodologies tended to be mainly quantitative (statistically based).
   4. The trend toward increasing interdisciplinary cooperation (deconstruction) is causing these differences to disappear.

C. Anthropology, Political Science, and Economics
   1. While other disciplines have looked at such institutions as economics and politics as distinct and amenable to separate analysis, anthropology has emphasized their relatedness to other aspects of the general social order.
   2. Anthropology has tended to emphasize cross-cultural variation in such institutions, in contrast to the almost exclusively Western orientation of the other disciplines.

D. Anthropology and the Humanities
   1. The anthropological concept of "culture" has gained increasing influence in the humanities' treatment of human artifacts.
   2. In turn, cultural studies have brought a fuller recognition of the influence such artifacts may exert on human behavior.

E. Anthropology and Psychology
   1. Anthropology has contributed a cross-cultural perspective to concepts developed in psychology.
   2. The school of cultural anthropology known as culture and personality has emphasized child-rearing practices as the fundamental means for transmitting culture.

F. Box: "Margaret Mead, Public Anthropologist"
   1. Margaret Mead worked at the American Museum of Natural History in New York City, and at Columbia University.
   2. Mead was a student of Franz Boas, and her work followed his in emphasizing the importance of culture in shaping human behavior.
   3. Mead made a point of publishing her findings in the popular press and appearing on television, as well as producing work for scholarly purposes, only.

G. Anthropology and History
   1. The convergence between the disciplines of anthropology and history has been marked, particularly during the last decade.
   2. Recent treatments of colonial history have emphasized the importance of understanding the cultural contexts of historical texts.
   3. Kottak argues for some continued distinction between history and anthropology, based on history's focus on the movement of individuals through roles, as opposed to anthropology's focus on change in structure or form.

VII. Beyond the Classroom: The Utility of Hand and Foot Bones for Problems in Biological Anthropology

    A. Della Collins Cook studied hand and foot bones to determine the stature and sex of individuals that had been buried in a burial mound in west central Illinois.

    B. After taking a series of measurements, she used statistical methods to predict the sex of the individuals with accuracies of over 87%.

    C. Based on a series of skeletal anomalies on one of the skeletons, Ms. Cook argues that this individual suffered from a rare genetic syndrome called Rubinstein-Taybi Syndrome.

LECTURE TOPICS

1.   Discuss what it means when we say that anthropology is holistic. Provide examples of the pervasiveness of culture. Discuss why it is important to understand and preserve cultural diversity.

2.   Discuss the origins and development of anthropology. Be sure to discuss the rise of American anthropology and what distinguishes it from European anthropology.

3.   Bring anthropology out of the ivory tower and National Geographic. Discuss how anthropology is more than traveling to distant places, eating strange foods, and speaking foreign languages. Make anthropology relevant to the lives of your students.

SUGGESTED FILMS

In Her Own Time

VHS 60 min color 1986
Directed by Lynn Littman. This film portrays fieldwork done in a conservative Jewish community of Los Angeles by acclaimed anthropologist Barbara Meyerhoff, who learned she was dying of cancer as the research began. What results is a moving exegesis of the process of ethnographic understanding. Footage of Meyerhoff's discussions with the filmmaker concerning her work and her illness are combined with footage of her research in progress, providing insight into how her analysis is shaped and strengthened by her awareness of the changes in herself. The film is an excellent basis for discussion and lectures about reflexivity, work in complex societies, and many other aspects of ethnography in this era. Distributed by Direct Cinema, Ltd.

Eye of Empire

VHS 26 min color 1992
Directed by Geoff Smith, Barrie Gavin, Script by Valerie Lloyd. With the series title, *Images: a Celebration of 150 Years of Photography*, this program draws on the anthropological photographic collections of the Pitt-Rivers Museum, Oxford; Anthropological Institute and Museum of Mankind, the Cambridge University Museum of Anthropology and Archaeology. It also deals with the work of amateur archaeologist Gertrude Bell. Published by Princeton NJ: Films for the Humanities and Sciences.

How Man Discovers His Past

20 min   1970   color
A definition and justification of history as a discipline, with a frank presentation of its difficulties and shortcomings (lack of evidence, necessity of subjective choice regarding relative importance and interpretation of evidence) its methods (fact gathering, organizing, interpreting), and its resources, with special emphasis on new contributions of allied fields such as archaeology and anthropology. *History of Man Series.*

Ishi in Two Worlds

19 min   1967   general color
Presents a portrait of Ishi, Yahi Indian, believed to be the last person in North America to have spent most of his life leading a totally aboriginal existence. Chronicles the Yahis' fight against the white men and the eventual extermination of the tribe, except Ishi, who hid in the forest for 25 years. He suddenly appeared near the town of Orville, California in 1911, sick, starved, and middle-aged, and spent his remaining years as a guest of the University of California Museum of Anthropology. Rare photographs depict Ishi demonstrating his Yahi skills. Based on the book by Theodore Kroeber. Winner of a CINE Golden Eagle, 1968.

Human Relations Area Files: A Fund of Knowledge

16mm   1970   16 min
Covers the history, use, and key features of the human relations area files, a major data resource and retrieval system for the study of human behavior customs, and social life.

Masks

16mm   1962   12 min
A presentation of one of the world's greatest collections of masks, both primitive and modern. The film discusses the masks' importance in the performance of rituals, in the perpetuation of myths, in the dramatization of legends, and in the cultural and artistic life of all people.

MULTIPLE-CHOICE QUESTIONS

1.   What makes anthropology unique among disciplines that study humans?

    a.   It includes biology.
    b.   It is holistic and comparative.
    c.   It uses personal interviews of the study population.
    d.   It studies foreign places.
    e.   It studies only groups that are thought to be "dying."

2.   Anthropology is interested in human variation resulting from

    a.   genetic differences
    b.   differences caused by developmental influences
    c.   social factors
    d.   cultural factors
    e.   all of the above

3.   Four-field Anthropology _____.

    a.   was originally practiced in Europe, because of a particularly British interest in military behavior
    b.   stopped being useful when the world became dominated by nation-states
    c.   was largely shaped by early American anthropologists' interests in Native Americans
    d.   was replaced in the 1930's by the two-field approach
    e.   all of the above

4.   What are anthropologists concerned with?

    a.   the structure of societies
    b.   the functions of social institutions
    c.   the meanings that culture gives to experience
    d.   the change in structure that societies show over time
    e.   all of the above

5.   What is the world system perspective?

    a.   the viewpoint that emphasizes the linkages between the world's societies
    b.   the theory that cultures around the world share the same set of universal symbols
    c.   the idea that the world consists of a series of isolated, independent cultures
    d.   the perspective that emphasize cooperation between American and European anthropologists to better understand the system of cultures around the world
    e.   all of the above

6.   The fact that anthropology focuses on both cultural and biological evolution

    a.   allows it to address "nature vs. nurture" questions
    b.   is the reason it has traditionally studied primitive societies
    c.   is insignificant, since evolution is studied by biological anthropologists while culture is studied by cultural anthropologists
    d.   is a product of the participant observation approach
    e.   none of the above is true

7.   What do anthropological archeologists study?

    a.   garbage
    b.   potsherds
    c.   paleoecology
    d.   burials
    e.   all of the above

8.   Anthropological linguistics _____.

    a.   includes sociolinguistics, descriptive linguistics, and the study of the biological basis for speech
    b.   includes cultural anthropology and paleoecology
    c.   has definitively identified the origin date of hominid language
    d.   is a research strategy peculiar to the biological anthropologist
    e.   all of the above

9. An anthropologist who is consulting for a development project in northern Ohio is

    a.   doing paleoethnography
    b.   **an applied anthropologist**
    c.   a biological anthropologist
    d.   an ethnomarketer
    e.   doing glottochronology

10. Which of the following statements about Margaret Mead is true?

    a.   She was a feminist in the 1890's.
    b.   She was the advisor of Franz Boas.
    c.   She saw human behavior as determined more by biology than by culture.
    d.   **She did ethnographic fieldwork in Samoa and New Guinea, among other places.**
    e.   all of the above

11. Based on his observations that contact between neighboring tribes had existed since human beginnings and covered enormous areas, Franz Boas argued _____.

    a.   that even the earliest hunter-gatherers engaged in warfare
    b.   that language must have originated with Neanderthals
    c.   that biology, and not culture, was responsible for the vast majority of human diversity
    d.   that general anthropologists had the wrong idea, because they were interested in biology
    e.   **against treating cultures as isolated phenomena**

12. What are the four subdisciplines of anthropology?

    a.   medical anthropology, ethnography, ethnology, and cultural anthropology
    b.   archaeology, biological anthropology, applied linguistics and applied anthropology
    c.   **biological anthropology, linguistic anthropology, cultural anthropology, and archaeology**
    d.   genetic anthropology, physical anthropology, psychological anthropology, anthropology and linguistics
    e.   primatology, ethnology, cultural anthropology, and paleoscatology

13. Archaeologists study garbage because

    a.   the even decay rate of garbage yields more accurate dating estimates
    b.   they are no longer allowed access to human remains
    c.   artifacts are only useful in cross-cultural comparison, and so need some supporting data
    d.   **it contains information about patterns of consumption**
    e.   all of the above

14. Where do cultural anthropologists carry out fieldwork?

    a.   in the third world
    b.   **in all kinds of societies**
    c.   in the tropics
    d.   in former colonies
    e.   none of the above

15. According to the Kottak text, anthropology is a (n)

    a. humanity
    b. science
    c. avocation
    d. nuisance
    e. both a and b

16. What is ethnography?

    a. the field-work aspect of cultural anthropology
    b. the generalizing aspect of cultural anthropology
    c. the study of animal behavior
    d. the comparative component of cultural anthropology
    e. none of the above

17. Archaeological data from prehistoric populations can provide information about

    a. population densities
    b. settlement patterns
    c. trade networks
    d. political organization
    e. all of the above

18. What distinguishes anthropology from other social sciences?

    a. its holistic approach
    b. broad cross-cultural comparison
    c. participant observation
    d. ethnography
    e. all of the above

19. One basis for the increasing cooperation between the disciplines of anthropology and history is _____.

    a. that historians do not understand the world systems perspective
    b. a common interest in change through time
    c. that anthropology maybe holistic, but it does not include history
    d. that historians need help translating the written records left by Neanderthals
    e. typically, anthropology is relativist, while history is not

20. According to Kottak, anthropology may improve psychological studies of human behavior by contributing

    a. examples of primitive thinking from tribal societies
    b. nothing, since anthropology focuses on culture and psychology focuses on personality
    c. prehistoric analysis
    d. uncritical repletion
    e. cross-cultural perspective on models of "human" psychology

21. What is the process by which children learn a particular cultural tradition?

    a. acculturation
    b. ethnology
    c. enculturation
    d. ethnography
    e. biological adaptation

22. Which of the following kinds of adaptation is unique to human groups?

    a. short-term physiological adaptation
    b. long-term physiological adaptation
    c. biological adaptation
    d. cultural adaptation
    e. genetic adaptation

23. How are the four subfields of American anthropology unified?

    a. Each subfield studies human variation through time and space.
    b. Each subfield studies the human capacity for language.
    c. Each subfield studies human biological variability.
    d. Each subfield studies human genetic variation through time and space.
    e. The subfields really are not unified; their grouping into one discipline is an historical accident.

24. Which of the following is not one of the four subfields of academic anthropology?

    a. linguistic anthropology
    b. medical anthropology
    c. biological anthropology
    d. cultural anthropology
    e. archaeological anthropology

25. Forensic anthropology applies the data, perspectives, theory, and methods of which subfield of academic anthropology?

    a. archaeological anthropology
    b. cultural anthropology
    c. linguistic anthropology
    d. medical anthropology
    e. biological anthropology

ESSAY QUESTIONS

26. What themes and interests unify the subdisciplines of anthropology? In your answer, refer to historical reasons for the unity of anthropology.

27. State and discuss the major similarities and differences between:

    a. cultural anthropology and sociology
    b. anthropology and history
    c. anthropology and psychology

28. How do anthropologists study the past?

29. What is culture? How does it help human populations adapt to their environments? Has reading this chapter helped you come to a clearer understanding of culture or a murkier one?

30. Why do anthropologists differentiate the human capacity for culture from particular human cultures?

31. Any of the above multiple choice questions can be converted to an essay question by requiring that the students justify their responses. To do this, the student should explain why the correct response actually answers the question (providing examples where necessary and feasible) and explain why the incorrect responses are incorrect.

TRUE OR FALSE QUESTIONS

32. True or **False** Anthropologists study only non-Western cultures.

33. True or False Anthropology is unique in that it is both holistic and cross-cultural.

34. True or **False** Human adaptability is only biological, not cultural.

35. True or **False** Ethnomusicology is one of the main four subfields of anthropology.

36. True or **False** American anthropologists only study native groups in North America.

37. True or **False** Anthropologists would agree that a comparative, cross-cultural approach is unnecessary as long as you are diligent in your work.

38. True or False Cultural forces play an important role in determining how individuals score on tests of intelligence.

39. True or False The authors of *The Bell Curve* favor biological explanations for the variation in intelligence test scores.

40. True or **False** Although many tests of intelligence are biased, some are not.

41. True or False Ethnography involves the collection of data that is used to create and account of a particular community, society, or culture.

42. True or False During his first trip to Arembepe, Kottak was overwhelmed by all of the cultural differences he encountered, including the cuisine.

43. True or **False** Archaeologists only study prehistoric communities.

44. True or **False** Biological anthropologists only study human bones.

45. True or False Linguistic anthropologists study the ways in which language and culture influence each other, over time and space.

46. True or **False** Applied anthropologists are people who do anthropology in their free time.

47. True or False Applied anthropologists identify the social and cultural conditions that need to be addressed in order for a development project to be successful.

48. True or False Anthropology is both a science and a humanity.

49. True or False The distinctions between sociology and cultural anthropology are becoming increasingly blurred.

50. True or False Psychologists tend to study only people living in the industrialized Western world.

51. True or **False** Margaret Mead was a biological determinist, arguing that human biology was the source of cultural variation.

CHAPTER 2

IN THE FIELD

CHAPTER OUTLINE

I. Ethnography is the firsthand personal study of a local cultural setting.

   A. Ethnographers try to understand the whole of a particular culture, not just fragments (e.g. the economy).

   B. In pursuit of this holistic goal, ethnographers usually spend an extended period of time living with the group they are studying and employ a series of techniques to gather information.

   C. The early ethnographers conducted research almost exclusively among small-scale, relatively isolated societies, with simple technologies and economics.

II. Ethnographic Techniques

   A. Observation and Participant Observation
      1. Ethnographers are trained to be aware of and record details from daily events, the significance of which may not be apparent until much later.
      2. "Participant observation," as practiced by ethnographers, involves the researcher taking part in the activities being observed.
      3. Unlike laboratory research, ethnographers do not isolate variables or attempt to manipulate the outcome of events they are observing.

   B. Conservation, Interviewing, and Interview Schedules
      1. Ethnographic interviews range in formality from undirected conversation, to open-ended interviews focusing on specific topics, to formal interviews using a predetermined schedule of questions.
      2. Increasingly, more than one of these methods are used to accomplish complementary ends on a single ethnographic research project.

   C. The Genealogical Method
      1. Early anthropologists identified types of relatedness, such as kinship, descent, and marriage, as being the fundamental organizing principles of nonindustrial societies.
      2. The genealogical method of diagramming such kin relations was developed as a formalized means of comparing kin-based societies.

   D. Key Cultural Consultants are particularly well-informed members of the culture being studied that can provide the ethnographer with some of the most useful or complete information.

   E. Life Histories are intimate and personal collections of a lifetime of experiences from certain members of the community being studied.
      1. Life histories reveal how specific people perceive, react to, and contribute to changes that affect their lives.
      2. Since life histories are focused on how different people interpret and deal with similar issues, they can be used to illustrate the diversity within a given community.

F. Local Beliefs and Perceptions and the Ethnographer
   1. An emic (native-oriented) approach investigates how natives think, categorize the world, express thoughts, and interpret stimuli.
      a. Emic = "native viewpoint"
      b. Key cultural consultants are essential for understanding the emic perspective.
   2. An etic (science-oriented) approach emphasizes the categories, interpretations, and features that the anthropologist considers important.

G. The Evolution of Ethnography
   1. Bronislaw Malinowski is generally considered the father of ethnography.
      a. He did salvage ethnography, recording cultural diversity that was threatened by westernization.
      b. His ethnographies were scientific accounts of unknown people and places.
   2. Ethnographic realism
      a. The writer's goal was to produce an accurate, objective, scientific account of the study's community.
      b. The writer's authority was rooted in his or her personal research experience with that community.
   3. Malinowski believed that all aspects of culture were linked and intertwined, making it impossible to write about just one cultural feature without discussing how it relates to others.
   4. Malinowski argued that understanding the emic perspective, the native's point of view, was the primary goal of ethnography.
   5. Interpretive anthropologists believe that ethnographers should describe and interpret that which is meaningful to the natives.
      a. Geertz argues that cultures are texts that natives constantly "read" and that ethnographers must decipher.
      b. Meanings in a given culture are carried by public symbolic forms, including words, rituals, and customs.
   6. Experimental anthropologists, like Marcus and Fischer, have begun to question the traditional goals, methods, and styles of ethnographic realism and salvage ethnography.
      a. Ethnographies should be viewed as both works of art and works of science.
      b. The ethnographer functions as the mediator who communicates information from the natives to the readers.
   7. The early ethnographies were often written in the *ethnographic present*, a romanticized timelessness before westernization, that gave the ethnographies and eternal, unchanging quality.
      a. Today, anthropologists understand that this is an unrealistic construct that inaccurately portrayed the natives as isolated and cut off from the rest of the world.
      b. Ethnographers today recognize that cultures constantly change and that this quality must be represented in the ethnography.

H. Problem-Oriented Ethnography
   1. Ethnographers typically address a specific problem or set of problems, within the context of broader depictions of cultures.
   2. Variables with the most significant relationship to the problem being addressed are given priority in the analysis.

I. Longitudinal Research is the long-term study of a community, region, society, or culture based on a series of repeated visits.
   1. Longitudinal research study has become increasingly common among ethnographic studies, as repeat visits to field sites have become easier.
   2. Such studies may also encompass multiple, related sites.

J. Team Research involves a series of ethnographers conducting complimentary research in a given community, culture, or region.

III. Field Work in Archaeological Anthropology

  A. Systematic survey provides a regional perspective on the archaeological record.
   1. Survey collects information on settlement patterns (e.g. the location of cities, towns, villages, and hamlets) over a large area (e.g. a river valley).
   2. Survey is one of the ways in which archaeologists locate sites that might be excavated in the future.
   3. During a survey, the team records the location, size, and the approximate age of the site.
   4. Settlement patterns are important for making inferences regarding the social complexity of the prehistoric communities.
     a. Groups at lower levels of complexity generally have lower population densities than people living in small campsites or hamlets with very little variation in architecture.
     b. With greater complexity, comes higher population densities (more people living in the same space) and a variety of sites organized along a settlement hierarchy (e.g. cities, towns, villages, and hamlets) with increased architectural variation between sites.

  B. Excavation compliments the regional survey data with more fine-grained data collected at the level of a specific site.
   1. The layers or strata that make up a site help archaeologists establish a relative chronology for the material recovered (e.g. this pot is older than that pot).
     a. The principle of superposition states that in an undisturbed sequence of strata, the oldest is on the bottom and each successive layer above is younger than the one below.
     b. Artifacts from the lower strata are older than artifacts from higher strata and artifacts from the same strata are roughly the same age.
   2. Nobody digs a site without a clear reason, because there are so many sites and excavation is so expensive and labor intensive.
     a. Cultural Resource Management (CRM) or contract archaeology is concerned with excavating sites that are threatened by modern development.
     b. Most other sites are selected for excavation because they are well suited to address a series of specific research questions.
   3. Before a site is excavated, it is first mapped and the surface is collected so that the archaeologist can make an informed decision about where to dig.
     a. Using the map, the archaeologist lays an arbitrary grid of one-meter square across the site.
     b. This grid is used to record the location of the surface collection units as well as the excavation units on the surface of the site.
   4. Digging can be done in either arbitrary levels or by following the natural stratigraphy.
     a. Using arbitrary level is quicker, but less refined and important information can be lost.
     b. Following the natural stratigraphy is more labor intensive, but also a more precise way of excavating, as each layer (natural or cultural) is peeled off one by one.
   5. Archaeologists use a range of techniques to recover materials from the excavation.
     a. All of the excavated soil is passed through screen to increase the likelihood that small and fragmented remains are recovered.
     b. Flotation is used to recover carbonized and very small materials, like fish bones and seeds.

IV. Show Me the Money

    A. Anthropologists need funding to support their research in the field.
        1. There are a series of agencies that support anthropological research.
            a. National Science Foundation (NSF)
            b. National Institutes of Health (NIH)
            c. Social Science Research Council (SSRC)
            d. Wenner-Gren Foundation for Anthropological Research
        2. In order to receive funding from any of these institutions, anthropologists must write grant proposals that summarize what questions will be addressed, where the research will be conducted, and how it will be done.

    B. Why this topic and problem?
        1. The grant writer must present the topic or problem that they will address during the proposed research.
        2. More importantly, the writer needs to convince the agency that the topic is important and worthy of being funded.

    C. Why this place?
        1. The grant writer needs to demonstrate the connection between the research topic and the location where the research will be carried out.
        2. Some locations address certain topics better than others.

    D. Why this person?
        1. The grant writer needs to identify the special qualifications that he or she brings to the research topic.
        2. Proficiency in the local language, previous research experience in the area, and strong local contacts are important.

    E. How will the study be done?
        1. The grant writer needs to discuss, as specifically as possible, how this research will be carried out.
        2. This section can include a discussion of the techniques and methods as well as the logistics of living in the study community and gaining permission from the study community to perform the research.

V. Ethics (American Anthropological Association (AAA) Code of Ethics 1997)

    A. Research Ethics
        1. Responsibility to people and animals
            a. The primary ethical obligation of the anthropologist is to the people, species, or materials he or she studies.
            b. Researchers must respect the safety, dignity, and privacy of the people, species or materials we study.
            c. Researchers should determine in advance whether their hosts wish to remain anonymous or receive recognition.
            d. Researchers should obtain the informed consent of the people to be studied and of those whose interests may be affected by the research.
            e. Anthropologists who develop close relationships with individuals must adhere to the obligations of openness and informed consent.
            f. Anthropologists may gain personally form their work, but they must not exploit individuals, groups, animals, or cultural or biological materials.
        2. Responsibility to scholarship and science
            a. Anthropologists should expect to encounter ethical dilemmas during their work.
            b. Anthropologists are responsible for the integrity and reputation of their discipline, scholarship, and of science.
            c. Researchers should do all they can to preserve opportunities for future field-workers.

      d. To the extent possible, researchers should disseminate their findings to the scientific and scholarly community.
      e. Anthropologists should consider reasonable requests for access to their data for purposes of research.
   3. Responsibility to the public
      a. Researchers should make their results available to sponsors, students, decision-makers, and other non-anthropologists.
      b. Anthropologists may move beyond disseminating research results to a position of advocacy.

B. Teaching Ethics
   1. Anthropologists should conduct their programs in ways that preclude discrimination on the basis of sex, marital status, "race", social class, political convictions, disability, religion, ethnic background, national origin, sexual orientation, and age.
   2. Anthropologists should strive to improve their teaching and training techniques.
   3. Teachers should impress a concern with ethics on their students.
   4. Teachers should properly acknowledge student assistance in their research and in the preparation of their work.
   5. Teachers must avoid sexual liaisons with those for whose education and professional training they are way responsible for.

C. Ethics for Applied Anthropology
   1. Applied anthropologists should use and disseminate their work appropriately.
   2. With employers, applied anthropologists should be honest about their qualifications, capabilities, aims, and intentions.
   3. Applied anthropologists should be alert to the danger of compromising ethics as a condition for engaging in research or practice.

VI. Survey Research

A. Anthropologists working in large-scale societies are increasingly using survey methodologies to complement more traditional ethnographic techniques.
   1. Survey involves drawing a study group or sample from the larger study population, collecting impersonal data, and performing statistical analyses on these data.
   2. By studying a properly selected and representative sample, social scientists can make accurate inferences about the larger population.

B. Survey research is considerably more impersonal than ethnography.
   1. Survey researchers call the people who make up their study sample respondents.
   2. Respondents answer a series of formally administered questions.

C. See table 2.1 for a concise summary of the major differences between survey research and ethnography.

D. Anthropology in Complex Societies
   1. Anthropologists rely increasingly on a variety of different field methodologies to accommodate demand for a greater breadth of applicability of results.
   2. Kottak argues that the core contribution of ethnology remains the qualitative data that results from close, long-term, in-depth contact between ethnographer and subjects.

VII. Science, Explanation, and Hypothesis Testing

A. Science is a way of viewing the world.
   1. Science recognizes the tentativeness and uncertainty of our knowledge and understanding.
   2. To improve our knowledge, scientists test hypotheses, which are suggested explanations of things and events.

3. Explanations show how and why the thing to be understood is related to other things in some known way.
4. Explanations rely on associations, which are the observed relationships between two or more measured variables.
5. A theory is more general, suggesting and implying associations and attempting to explain them.

B. Social sciences
1. Associations are usually stated probabilistically: two or more variables *tend to be* related in a predictable way, but there are exceptions.
2. A theory is an explanatory framework that helps us understand why something exits.
3. Theories cannot be proved, we evaluate them through the method of falsification.
   a. If a theory is true, certain predictions should stand up to tests designed to disprove them.
   b. Theories that have not been disproved are accepted.

VIII. Beyond the Classroom: Stories from Women Domestics of the Yucatán

A. Allen F. Burns studied the relationship between domestic servants (empleadas) and their employers.
1. He was interested in gaining a fuller understanding of how the distinction between domestic servant and family member begins to blur.
2. He used a series of ethnographic techniques to conduct his research: auto-photography, unstructured and semi-structured interviews, and participant observation.

B. In writing his ethnography, Allen wanted to provide an identity to the domestic servants that are faceless numbers in survey research.
1. Through his writing, he attempted to let the women speak for themselves, make decisions, and control their story.
2. Allen uses some narrative ethnography (first-person accounts) that enable him to move his research away from a purely scientific project.

LECTURE TOPICS

1. By far the most engaging and effective introduction to research is a presentation of the anthropologist's own work, especially if it is accompanied by slides. Such a presentation will set a mood for the course and keep students involved long after the immediate occasion for the presentation has passed.

2. Give examples of networks with which students must deal. Explain how similar contingencies arise in non-Western societies and describe the alternative networks with which natives or ethnologists must deal.

3. The role of the anthropologist as ethnographic fieldworker has come under some scrutiny. Discuss the various political issues attached to the practice of researchers from industrialized nations studying peoples in for example, Third World nations. Give examples of both successful and unsuccessful field work, for example, from the work of Chagnon, Evans-Pritchard, Benedict, Briggs, Malinowski, and Radcliffe-Brown. Catalog some of the problems and experiences that anthropologists face during field work. The debate over anthropological involvement in the Vietnam War provides an interesting basis for the discussion of professional ethics. Describe the reaction to anthropological studies and published ethnographies by people who have been the subject of these.

4.	This chapter stresses the emerging synthesis of techniques that were once typically practiced separately, by anthropologists and sociologists. Discuss how quantitative and qualitative techniques compliment each other in anthropological research. How is qualitative data used to inform survey questionnaire formulation, for example?

5.	Applied anthropology has become increasingly important in the discipline. One way of addressing this is to invite guest lecturers from local cultural institutions (representing ethnic communities, for example) to speak about how they see their relationship with anthropological scholarship, describe how they deal with such anthropological models as culture, and the like. Similarly, there are other institutions (hospitals, shelters, and businesses) that are practically involved with many notions anthropology has contributed to public discourse.

SUGGESTED FILMS

Sir Walter Baldwin Spencer (1860-1929)

Field work

52 min   color
The series begins by showing the work of Sir Walter Baldwin Spencer with the Australian aborigines who had, up until then, been regarded as a step in the evolutionary ladder between Neolithic man and the "civilized" Victorian. In 1887, he went from England to Australia, where, after seeing the aborigines for the first time, he wrote: "The sight was not an appetizing one, and the savages looked more like wild beasts gnawing their prey than human beings." Spencer began to work with Frank Gillen, the operator of a telegraph station and an initiated elder of the Aranda tribe--a remarkable man who was befriending aborigines at a time when most whites were persecuting them. Gillen's special place in aboriginal society enabled both men to witness scenes that no white man had ever seen. But despite their extensive field work, it was left to others to capitalize on their discovery of just how complex and resilient aboriginal life really was. Spencer was knowledgeable, enlightened, and liberal, but constrained by the prevailing notions of the day, he never really saw Aboriginals other than as a prehistoric race doomed to extinction. However, the approach that the two men used to study the aborigines has remained valid, and strongly influenced the way that other cultures have been studied since. Their method came to be known as field work. From the Strangers Abroad series. Published by Princeton, NJ: Films for the Humanities and Sciences.

Bronislaw Malinowski (1882-1942)

Off the Verandah

52 min   color
Bronislaw Malinowski was the anthropologist who really changed the way that field studies were carried out. A Pole, who chose to live in England, he began to work on a remote group of Pacific islands-the Trobriands-and lived for long periods among the people he was studying. A brilliant linguist, he quickly learned their language and later published books which brought the islanders to life. In this way, he made their work and lives intelligible to the West. The idea that native peoples were primitive savages was altered for good with Malinowski's insight into their mastery of their world. From the Strangers Abroad series. Published by Princeton, NJ: Films for the Humanities and Sciences.

MULTIPLE-CHOICE QUESTIONS

1. As an academic discipline, anthropology _____.

    a. shares its roots with sociology, in the work of Emile Durkheim, among others
    b. began in the late eighteenth century, by the missionary Ruse Potvin, who studied the Winnebago
    c. became established under the sponsorship of Queen Victoria, who was fascinated by an early study of Hindus in India
    d. initially focused *only* on studies of the middle and lower classes in Europe's great cities
    e. all of the above

2. What is reflexive ethnography?

    a. The study of human responses to physical stimuli.
    b. The study of how cultures reflexively respond to westernization.
    c. The incorporation of the natives' points of view.
    d. The incorporation of the ethnographer's thoughts, experiences, and reactions to conducting fieldwork into their research.
    e. The study of how human reflexes vary through time and space.

3. How is survey research different from ethnography?

    a. It studies whole functioning communities.
    b. It based on firsthand fieldwork.
    c. It is more personal.
    d. It tends to focus on the behavior of fewer issues within a sample population.
    e. It has been traditionally conducted in nonindustrial, small-scale societies.

4. In survey research, what is sampling?

    a. The collection of a representative sample of a larger population.
    b. The interviewing of a small number of key cultural consultants.
    c. participant observation
    d. The collection of life histories of every member in a community.
    e. The collection of the emic perspective.

5. Which of the following strategies is unique to anthropology?

    a. comparison
    b. the biological perspective
    c. ethnography
    d. the evolutionary perspective
    e. working with skilled respondents

6. Which of the following statements about ethnography is true?

    a. It was initially practiced exclusively in small-scale societies.
    b. Bronislaw Malinowski was one of its earliest influential practitioners.
    c. It may involve participant observation and survey research.
    d. It is used as a basis for ethnology.
    e. all of the above

7. Which of the following is a significant change in ethnography?

   a. Ethnographers now use only quantitative techniques.
   b. Ethnographers have begun to work for colonial governments.
   c. Ethnographers have stopped using the standard four-member format, because it disturbs the informants.
   d. Larger numbers of ethnographies are being done about people in Western, industrialized nations.
   e. There are now women ethnographers.

8. What do ethnographers do?

   a. firsthand field work
   b. most of their own field work.
   c. establish direct relationships with the people being studied
   d. strive to establish rapport with informants
   e. all of the above

9. Which of the following is *not* a characteristic field technique of the ethnographer?

   a. the genealogical method
   b. participant observation
   c. conversation
   d. telephone questionnaires
   e. interview schedules

10. Which of the following is *not* a characteristic field technique of the ethnographer?

    a. structured interviewing
    b. life histories
    c. random sampling
    d. work with well-informed informants
    e. the genealogical method

11. Ethnographers

    a. study public and private styles of behavior.
    b. study individual and collective behavior in varied settings.
    c. should record what they see as they see it.
    d. often keep personal diaries.
    e. perform all of the above

12. What is the term for an expert on a particular aspect of native life?

    a. representative sample
    b. etic informant
    c. well-informed informant
    d. biased informant
    e. example of the life-history approach

13. What is the ethnographic style developed by Bronislaw Malinowski?

    a. ethnographic realism
    b. theory of cognitive dissonance
    c. interpretative anthropology
    d. practice anthropology
    e. structural Marxism

14. Which of the following is *not* an example of participant observation?

    a. **administering interviews according to an interview schedule**
    b. helping out at harvest time
    c. dancing at a ceremony
    d. buying a shroud for a village ancestor
    e. engaging in informal chit-chat

15. In survey research, a sample should _____.

    a. include the entire population in question
    b. include anyone who will let you talk to them
    c. target only one social, cultural, or environmental factor that influences behavior
    d. **be constituted so as to allow inferences about the larger population**
    e. be invariant

16. What are the two major components of fieldwork in archaeological anthropology?

    a. the genealogical method and excavation
    b. excavation and participant observation
    c. **systematic survey and excavation**
    d. systematic survey and the emic perspective
    e. all of the above

17. Why do anthropological anthropologists use flotation?

    a. To identify regional settlement patterns
    b. **To recover very small remains like fish bones and seeds**
    c. To control for the location of artifacts in three-dimensional space
    d. To establish relative chronologies
    e. all of the above

18. Which of the following techniques was developed specifically because of the importance of kinship and marriage relationships in nonindustrial societies?

    a. the life history
    b. participant observation
    c. **the genealogical method**
    d. the interview schedule
    e. network analysis

19. Why do anthropologists record genealogical information?

    a. To reconstruct history and to chart current relationships.
    b. In most nonindustrial, small-scale societies kinship ties are extremely important.
    c. Kin and marriage links within and between villages are the basis of social life.
    d. The rules of etiquette attached to particular kin relationships are basic to the conduct of everyday life.
    e. **all of the above**

20. Which of the following is one of the advantages an interview schedule has over a questionnaire-based survey?

    a. Interview schedules allow informants to talk about what *they* see as important
    b. Interview schedules rely on very short responses, and therefore are more useful when you have less time.
    c. Questionnaires are completely unstructured, so your informants might deviate from the subject you want them to talk about.
    d. Interview schedules are better suited to urban, complex societies where most people can read.
    e. Questionnaires are emic, and interview schedules are etic.

21. Why do anthropological archaeologists use the principle of superposition?

    a. To create a relative chronology for the materials uncovered during excavation
    b. To overlay various maps of a site to produce a composite map
    c. To superimpose motifs from one site onto designs found at another site
    d. To locate sites during a systematic survey
    e. none of the above

22. What should be included in a grant proposal?

    a. The methods that will be used in the research
    b. A justification for your study site
    c. The goals of your research
    d. A discussion of your qualifications for carrying out the research
    e. all of the above

23. American Anthropological Association's Code of Ethics is _____.

    a. too broad and encompassing for most anthropologists to find it useful
    b. designed to ensure that all anthropologists are aware of their obligations to the field of anthropology, the host communities that allow them to conduct their research, and to society in general
    c. designed to protect anthropologists who conduct field work in remote places and are subject to potentially hazardous working conditions
    d. mostly lip-service, as most researchers disregard most of its main points
    e. all of the above

24. What is a hypothesis?

    a. A hypothesis is a suggested explanation of things and events.
    b. A hypothesis is an observed relationship between two or more measured variables.
    c. A hypothesis is a general concept that explains the association between two or more measured variables.
    d. A hypothesis is an observed event that demonstrates a general principle.
    e. all of the above

25. What is an explanatory framework containing a series of statements?

    a. an association
    b. a hypothesis
    c. an observation
    d. a theory
    e. a perspective

26. How are theories evaluated?

    a. by proving them to be true
    b. through checks and balances
    c. through the method of ossification
    d. through the method of falsification
    e. all of the above

27. What is the ethnographic present?

    a. The period of time when the ethnographer conducted their research.
    b. The period of time when the ethnographer published their research.
    c. The period of time when represented in the memory of the key cultural consultants.
    d. The period of time just after the ethnographer conducted their research.
    e. The period of time before westernization, when the "true" native culture flourished.

ESSAY QUESTIONS

28. What advantages do you see in ethnographic research techniques? What are the advantages for survey techniques? Which one would you choose? Give the conditions of your choice.

29. What is the intent behind the reflexive style of ethnographic writing? What benefits and problems might come from this method?

30. What are the differences between questionnaires and interview schedules? What advantage might an ethnographer gain by using an interview schedule instead of a questionnaire?

31. Briefly describe the six characteristic field techniques of the ethnographer.

32. What, if anything, has Bronislaw Malinowski given to the study of populations in modern urban settings?

33. What advantages might a project that combines *both* quantitative and qualitative techniques have over one that utilizes *only* one or the other? What research situation might be best suited to such a combined strategy?

34. Explain participant observation, and contrast it with other research techniques.

35. What is the genealogical method and why did it develop in anthropology?

36. Describe the advantages for ethnography of life histories and working with well-informed informants.

37. Identify the problems and advantages of community study research.

38. Explain how urban social networks differ from those in nonurban societies. What implications does this have for network analysis?

39. What techniques do anthropologists use to study urban life?

TRUE OR FALSE QUESTIONS

40. True or False   Ethnography has been traditionally performed in small-scale, non-Western communities.

41. True or **False**   Compared to questionnaires, interview schedules tend to be more indirect and impersonal.

42. True or **False**   Really good key cultural consultants will actually end up recording most of the data you need to write an ethnography.

43. True or False   The emic perspective focuses on how the natives think.

44. True or **False**   Since there are so many anthropologists in the U.S., the distinction between emic and etic does not apply to American culture.

45. True or False   Ethnographic realism and the ethnographic present are both common features of Malinowski's ethnographies.

46. True or False   Longitudinal ethnographic research is the long-term study of a particular study unit, frequently based on repeated visits.

47. True or **False**   Archaeological anthropologists excavate sites to gain a better understanding of the regional patterning of the archaeological record.

48. True or **False**   Archaeologists use screens in the field to provide some protection from the sun and insects.

49. True of False   Digging according to arbitrary levels is quicker, but less refined than digging according to the site's stratigraphy.

50. True or False   Flotation is a technique used by archaeologists to recover very small remains from an excavation.

51. True or **False**   Grant proposals are used only by anthropologists who do not make enough money to pay for their own research.

52. True or False   It is important that a grant proposal summarize the research that is to be performed and explain why this research is important.

53. True or False   The main point of the American Anthropological Association's Code of Ethics is that anthropological research should not harm the study's community.

54. True or **False**   Survey research is ethnography with the addition of some statistical analyses.

55. True or **False**   A survey researcher must establish a rapport with the respondents.

56. True or **False**   Theory and hypothesis are synonymous terms.

57. True or **False**   Ethnography usually focuses on a small number of variables, rather than study all aspects of social life.

58. True or False   Survey research studies a small sample of a larger population.

59. True or **False**   Survey research is usually conducted with a tremendous amount of personal contact with the study subjects.

CHAPTER 3
EVOLUTION AND GENETICS

CHAPTER OUTLINE

I. Creationism and Evolution

    A. Creationism and Catastrophism
1. Creationism accounts for biological diversity by referring to the divine act of Creation as described in Genesis.
2. The discovery of fossil remains of creatures clearly unknown to modern humans was not accountable within the terms of simple Creationism.
3. Catastrophism is a modified version of Creationism. It accounts for the fossil record by positing divinely authored worldwide disasters that wiped out the creatures represented in the fossil record, who were then supplanted by newer, created species.
4. Both versions of creationism describe the different species of plants and animals as *essentially* different, having distinct, separate moments of creation.

    B. Evolution
1. An alternative term for early evolutionism was "transformism."
2. Darwin was influenced by the geological concept of uniformitarianism.
    a. Uniformitarianism states that past geological events can be best explained by observing the ongoing events of the present and generalizing backward through time.
    b. It further asserts that current geological structures are the result of long-term natural forces.
3. Transformism had posited the primordial relatedness of all life forms.
4. Darwin posited *natural selection* as the mechanism through which speciation takes shape (reaching this conclusion along with Alfred Russell Wallace).
5. "Natural selection is the gradual process by which nature selects the forms most fit to survive and reproduce in a given environment."
6. For natural selection to work on a given population there must be variety within that population and competition for strategic resources.
7. The concept of natural selection argues that organisms that have a better fit within their environmental niche will reproduce more frequently than those organisms that fit less well.

II. Genetics

    A. The science of genetics explains the origin of the variety upon which natural selection operates.

    B. Heredity is Particulate
1. The study of hereditary traits began in 1856 by Gregor Mendel, an Austrian monk.
2. By experimenting with successive generations of pea plants, Mendel came to the conclusion that heredity is determined by discrete particles, the effects of which may disappear in one generation, and reappear in the next.

3. Mendel determined that the traits he observed occurred in two basic forms: dominant and recessive.
   a. Dominant forms manifest themselves in each generation.
   b. Recessive forms are masked whenever they are paired with a dominant form of the same trait in a hybrid individual.
   c. It has since been demonstrated that some traits have more than these two forms-- human blood type, for example, has several forms, some of which are codominant.
4. The traits Mendel identified occur on chromosomes.
   a. Humans have twenty-three matched pairs of chromosomes, with each parent contributing one chromosome to each pair.
   b. Chromosomes contain several genes, or genetic loci, which determine the nature of a particular trait.
   c. A trait may be determined by more than one gene.
   d. Alleles are the biochemically different forms that may occur at any given genetic locus.
   e. Chromosome pairs' loci may be homozygous (identical alleles) or heterozygous (mixed).

C. Independent Assortment and Recombination
   1. Mendel also determined that traits are inherited independently of one another.
   2. The fact that traits are transmitted independently of one another, and hence may occur in new combinations with other traits is responsible for much of the variety upon which natural selection operates.
   3. Mitosis is ordinary cell division, wherein one cell splits to form two identical cells.
   4. Meiosis is the type of division particular to sex cells, wherein four cells are produced from one, each with half the genetic material of the original cell (i.e., twenty-three chromosomes instead of forty-six).
   5. Fertilization allows the products of meiosis from one parent to recombine with those from the other parent.
   6. Because genes sort independently during recombination, the number of possible combinations is exponentially high (2^{23}): a major source of variety.

III. Population Genetics

A. Population genetics looks at changes in gene frequencies at the level of the community or breeding population.
   1. Gene pool refers to all of the alleles and genotypes within a breeding population.
   2. Genetic evolution is defined as change in the frequency of alleles in breeding population from generation to generation.

B. There are four basic mechanisms which produce changes in gene frequency in a population (i.e., genetic evolution): natural selection, mutation, genetic drift, and gene flow.

IV. Mechanisms of Genetic Evolution

A. Natural Selection
   1. Genotype refers to the genetic makeup of an organism.
   2. Phenotype is the expression of the genotype as it has been influenced through development by interacting with its environment.
   3. Environmental influence in this interaction is extremely important, and lends great plasticity to human biology.
   4. Natural selection acts upon *phenotypes*.

B. Directional Selection
   1. Natural selection affects gene frequencies within a population.
   2. Adaptive genes are selected for (organisms containing them reproduce more frequently).

3. Maladaptive genes are selected against (organisms containing them reproduce less frequently).
4. When specific adaptive genes are selected for over a long time period, causing a major shift in gene frequency, this is called directional selection.
5. Directional selection continues until equilibrium is reached (due to the effects of contradictory selective forces, the base mutation rate, or both).
6. Directional selection, in favoring one gene, can reduce variation in a gene pool.

C. Sickle-Cell Anemia
1. Just as directional selection reduce varieties, it can also maintain genetic variety by favoring a situation in which the frequency of certain alleles remains constant between generations.
2. Hemoglobin in Africa
   a. Hb^A and Hb^S are two alleles for a gene that largely determines hemoglobin production in humans.
   b. Homozygous Hb^A produces normal hemoglobin, homozygous Hb^S produces lethal sickle cell anemia, heterozygosity for this gene produces the (in some circumstances) deleterious but non-lethal sickle-cell syndrome.
   c. It was discovered in certain populations in Africa, India, and the Mediterranean that Hb^S existed at surprisingly high frequencies.
   d. This is largely explained by the fact that the populations noted were in heavily malarial areas, and that the heterozygous form produced a phenotype that was resistant to malaria, and was thus the phenotype most fit for that environment.
3. It is important to note that traits that are maladaptive in one environment, such as the sickle cell would be in a malaria-free zone, can be adaptive in a different environment, and the reverse of this is also true.

D. Mutation
1. Mutation introduces genetic variation into a breeding population.
2. Chemical alterations in genes may provide a population with entirely new phenotypes, with possible concomitant selective advantages.
3. The spread of Hb^S in heavily malarial environments is one example.

E. Random Genetic Drift
1. Random genetic drift is the loss of alleles from a population's gene pool through chance.
2. There is no set form for this chance; it may simply occur through a statistical fluke in sexual reproduction patterns, or through the effects of a catastrophe on the population as a whole.

F. Gene Flow
1. Gene flow occurs through interbreeding: the transmission of genetic material from one population to another.
2. Gene flow inhibits speciation, the formation of new species.
   a. A species is an internally interbreeding population whose offspring can survive and are capable of reproduction.
   b. Speciation occurs when populations of the same species become isolated from each other (thus stopping gene flow) allowing natural selection and genetic drift to gradually produce gene pools that are different, to the extent that successful interbreeding is no longer impossible.

V. Human Biological Adaptation

A. Much of the human biological diversity is the result of human genetic adaptation to specific environments.
1. The high frequencies of the Hb^S heterozygote in malarial environments is a good example.

2. Some alleles that were once maladaptive can lose their disadvantage if the environment changes.
3. The Human Genome Project is working to map all of the genes and chromosomes found in humans.
    a. Many of today's incurable hereditary diseases someday may be rendered evolutionarily neutral through genetic therapies.
    b. One downside of this research is that it can also lead to genetic discrimination (eugenics).

B. In the News: Human Cloning: Yesterday's Never is Today's Why Not?
    1. Scientists and ethicists are debating whether human beings should be cloned, and if so, for what purposes.
    2. Most researchers see the medical utility of cloning while ethicists are more concerned with who would control the technology.

C. Genes and Disease
    1. Despite the advances in medical research over the last 100 years, diseases still pose a significant threat to the health of human populations all over the world.
    2. Human blood factors play an important role in resistance to some diseases.
        a. There is evidence that the various alleles producing human blood types interact with infectious and non-infectious ailments.
        b. For example, the presence of type A blood cells seems to make a person more susceptible to small pox.

D. Facial Features
    1. Thomson's nose rule asserts that noses tend to be longer in colder climates.
    2. The Australian Aborigines' sand-permeated diet has selected for larger teeth than seen in other populations.

E. Size and Body Build
    1. Different climates have selected for different body shapes.
    2. Bergmann's rule: because of the respective ratios between mass and surface area, smaller bodies dissipate heat faster, and larger bodies retain heat better; thus more larger animals are found in colder habitats, while smaller animals have been selected for in hotter habitats.
    3. Allen's Rule: slender bodies with long limbs dissipate heat more efficiently, and are selected for in tropical climates: heavy, short-limbed bodies retain heat better, and are selected for in colder climates.

F. Lactose Intolerance
    1. The term phenotypic adaptation refers to changes, which occur to an individual organism during its lifetime, which enhance its reproductive fitness.
    2. Individuals from herding populations in Northern Europe and parts of Africa maintain their ability to digest milk (continue to produce the enzyme, lactase) into adulthood, whereas people from other populations can digest milk (specifically, milk sugar, called lactose) only during childhood.
    3. The fact that descendents of these herding population who no longer herd continue to be lactose tolerant as adults indicates genetic adaptation to a milk-rich diet.
    4. The fact that lactose intolerance can vary during an individual's adult life, depending on how much milk is consumed, indicates that some phenotypic adaptation also takes place.

LECTURE TOPICS

1. Use the sources of diversity to explain the genetic mechanism and relationship between genotype and phenotype. List the types of diversity and the sources of diversity. Explain the relationships among diversity, adaptation, and selection.

2. Explain how natural selection is blind, not working toward a predetermined end. Explain the relationships among differential reproduction, key resources, key hazards, and natural selection.

3. Challenges to the teaching of evolutionary theory have become increasingly numerous and threatening to free speech in the classroom. The crux of many of these challenges has to do with the claim that evolution is "just a theory." Build on the discussion of the scientific method in Chapter 2 by using the theory of evolution as your case study. Give your students some indications about the necessary attributes of critical inquiry by telling them how to decide whether evidence supports or refutes a hypothesis. Stress to your students that acceptance of the validity of evolutionary theory is *not* essential to their grade, but understanding the arguments you describe *is*.

SUGGESTED FILMS

Patterns of Inheritance: Understanding Genetics

VHS   33 min   color
Presents Gregor Mendel's ideas and principles of genetics, and describes some advances since Mendel. Uses graphics and computer animation, and the principles of dominance, segregation and independent assortment are illustrated using Punnett squares. Insight Media. Produced by Human Relations Media.

Darwin's Revolution: Fit to Rule

VHS   52 min   color   1986
Part 8 of *The Day the Universe Changed* series. People believed in the 1700's that all forms of life were unchanged since creation. Then the study of geology and fossils produced new ideas about change in living things and the age of the earth. Wallace and then Darwin concluded that species evolved to survive in their environments over great periods of time. The concept of survival of the fittest was later adapted to justify Nazism, robber baron capitalism, and Communism. BBC TV. Distributed by Churchill Films.

Macroevolution

VHS   30 min   color   1997
Part eleven of the *Cycles of Life*. Paleontologists discuss their use of fossils and other techniques to understand macroevolution. Also looks at ways in which scientists reconstruct the events that led to the formation of amino acids and the first unicellular organisms. Annenberg/CPG Collection, Coast Telecoast Productions.

MULTIPLE CHOICE QUESTIONS

1. What did Charles Darwin propose as the mechanism driving evolution?

   a. independent assortment
   b. **natural selection**
   c. phenotypic adaptation
   d. inclusive fitness
   e. culpability

2. What role do recombination and independent assortment play in evolution?

   a. They work to limit the amount of variation in a population.
   b. They increase the frequencies of deleterious genes.
   c. They work to limit the number of potential phenotypes.
   d. **They act to create genetic variability in a breeding population.**
   e. They act to reduce the overall fitness of a breeding population.

3. Which of the following theories does *not* seek to explain the origin of species by referring to an outside agent?

   a. **evolution**
   b. catastrophism
   c. creationism
   d. extraterrestrial seeding
   e. creation science

4. What does the term gene flow refer to?

   a. A random pattern of chromosome mutations.
   b. The movement of alleles from one chromosome to another.
   c. **The transmission of genes between populations.**
   d. The random loss of genes through sampling error.
   e. none of the above

5. In evolutionary terms, what does fitness refer to?

   a. An organism's ability to displace natural predators from many different niches.
   b. An organism's ability to become as specialized as possible.
   c. An organism's ability to control the largest amount of resources in a particular niche.
   d. **An organism's ability to survive and reproduce viable young.**
   e. An organism's ability to mature more rapidly than other organisms.

6. Evolution can be most simply defined as

   a. natural selection
   b. mutations in a breeding population
   c. **descent with modification**
   d. the process of achieving a perfect fit to the environment
   e. competition over strategic resources

7.   Which of the following theoretical models did Darwin and Wallace simultaneously
      propose?

      a.   evolution
      b.   natural selection
      c.   creationism
      d.   uniformitarianism
      e.   transformism

8.   As outlined by Darwin, what does the theory of evolution involve?

      a.   natural selection
      b.   change in form over generations
      c.   variety in a population
      d.   competition for resources
      e.   all of the above

9.   Natural selection _____.

      a.   is the driving principle behind creationism
      b.   operates when there is competition for strategic resources
      c.   operates only on single-celled animals, since their genotypes are readily
            accessible to specific environments
      d.   was discovered by Gregor Mendel, the primatologist
      e.   all of the above

10.   Natural selection _____.

      a.   acts directly on genotype rather than on phenotype
      b.   was first scientifically described by Charles Darwin and A. R. Wallace
      c.   can lead to genetic evolution, only in the absence of variation within a
            population
      d.   is an evolutionary mechanism of less significance than a mixture and crossing
            over
      e.   is no longer operating on the members of highly industrialized societies because
            of access to modern medicine and technology

11.   What does natural selection directly act on?

      a.   the phenotypes of organisms
      b.   Mitochondrial DNA
      c.   the genotypes of organisms
      d.   DNA
      e.   none of the above

12.   Which of the following statements about natural selection is *not* true?

      a.   Natural selection operates directly on genetic variety.
      b.   Natural selection is the sum of environmental forces that conditions the survival
            of particular phenotypes.
      c.   Natural selection operates with respect to specific environments.
      d.   Natural selection is responsible for the maintenance of the sickle hemoglobin
            polymorphism.
      e.   Natural selection was first scientifically described by Darwin and Wallace.

13. Gregor Mendel's work with hereditary traits of pea plants _____.

    a.   confirmed the paint-pot theory of inheritance
    b.   was the basis for Darwin's theory of evolution
    c.   led to the formulation of the law of segregation
    d.   disconfirmed the phenomenon of balanced polymorphism
    e.   proved that natural selection operates on genotypes

14. What does the particulate nature of inheritance refer to?

    a.   The inheritance of more traits from one ancestor than from another.
    b.   The ability of DNA to build proteins.
    c.   The effects of random mutations on heredity.
    d.   The inheritance of discrete hereditary units from both parents.
    e.   all of the above

15. What is the relationship between the alleles that determine our blood type?

    a.   dominant and recessive
    b.   codominance
    c. F_2 directional selection
    d.   cogenotypes
    e.   corecombination

16. What does Mendel's law of segregation state?

    a.   Genetic traits are mixed together like paints in a paint pot.
    b.   Natural selection is the major cause of evolution.
    c.   Traits are inherited as discrete units that may reemerge in later generations.
    d.   Hybrids are more vigorous than purebred.
    e.   The offspring of tall pea plants and short pea plants are medium-sized plants.

17. What is the process by which sex cells are produced?

    a.   mitosis
    b.   recombination
    c.   meiosis
    d.   independent assortment
    e.   none of the above

18. What does Mendelian genetics study?

    a.   The changes in gene frequencies in breeding populations.
    b.   The ways in which chromosomes transmit genes across generations.
    c.   How nuclear DNA transmits information to other parts of the cell.
    d.   Evolution in pea plants.
    e.   Phenotypic mutations.

19. Which of the following does *not* increase the variety of a gene pool?

    a.   independent assortment
    b.   crossing over
    c.   mutation
    d.   gene flow from another population
    e.   directional selection

20. Natural selection cannot work without _____.

    a. a good lubricating oil
    b. basic similarity in the target organisms
    c. constant gene frequencies
    d. variation
    e. homeostasis

21. The allele Hb^S which codes for the type of hemoglobin associated with sickle-cell anemia

    a. is evenly distributed throughout all human populations
    b. confers resistance to malaria
    c. is always lethal when found in a human population
    d. has no effect on the viability of a population
    e. is never expressed in the phenotype when present in a heterozygous state

22. Which of the following statements about individuals with the Hb^S allele in homozygous form is true?

    a. They usually develop fatal cases of sickle-cell anemia.
    b. They usually develop fatal cases of sickle-cell anemia late in life.
    c. They rarely develop any form of sickle-cell anemia before reaching reproductive age.
    d. They are usually found in temperate regions of the world.
    e. all of the above

23. Which of the following statements about the Hb^S allele is *not* true?

    a. In homozygous individuals usually develop fatal cases of dysentery.
    b. It spreads through the tropics, as communities adopted slash and burn agriculture.
    c. It is found in higher gene frequencies, in regions where malaria is endemic.
    d. Heterozygous individuals have an increased immunity to malaria.
    e. none of the above are true

24. The study of sickle-cell anemia and its relation to malarial environments demonstrates that

    a. changes in cultural adaptation can result in changes in the selective pressures on a human population
    b. natural selection improves a gene pool by wiping out deleterious alleles
    c. selection removes recessive alleles from the gene pool faster than it does dominant alleles
    d. heterozygotes are not as selectively fit, as are dominant homozygotes
    e. both c and d are correct

25. What do gene flow and interbreeding act against?

    a. migration
    b. speciation
    c. natural selection
    d. mutations
    e. balanced polymorphisms

26. What is the term for the exchange of genetic material between populations of the same species through direct or indirect interbreeding?

   a. gene pool
   b. mutation
   c. genetic drift
   d. genetic evolution
   e. gene flow

27. What is the term for adaptive biological changes that take place during an individual's lifetime?

   a. genotypical adaptation
   b. cultural adaptation
   c. linguistic adaptation
   d. phenotypical adaptation
   e. species-level adaptation

28. Which of the following populations tends to be lactose intolerant?

   a. Israelis
   b. South American Indians
   c. Eskimos
   d. Japanese
   e. all of the above are lactose intolerant

29. What does Thomson's nose rule state?

   a. long noses are adaptive in cold environments
   b. short noses are adaptive in cold environments
   c. nose size is causally linked to skin color
   d. nose size is causally linked to cranial capacity
   e. long noses are adaptive in hot environments

30. What does Bergmann's rule state?

   a. Average body size tends to decrease at high elevations and increase in low ones
   b. Average body size tends to increase in cold climates and decrease in hot ones
   c. Average body size tends to decrease in cold climates and increase in hot ones
   d. Average body size tends to decrease at low elevations and increase in high ones
   e. all of the above

31. What does Allen's rule state?

   a. The relative size of protruding body parts decreases with temperature.
   b. The relative size of protruding body parts increases with altitude.
   c. The relative size of protruding body parts decreases with altitude.
   d. The relative size of protruding body parts increases with temperature.
   e. The relative size of protruding body parts increases with humidity.

32. What is the term for the belief that explanations for past events should be sought in ordinary forces that are at work today?

   a. uniformitarianism
   b. speciation
   c. creationism
   d. recombination
   e. catastrophism

ESSAY QUESTIONS

33. State and discuss Charles Darwin's major contribution to the study of life forms. What was new about Darwin's views, and what others had previously proposed?

34. How do population geneticists define evolution? What are the major mechanisms of genetic evolution?

35. Identify and discuss genetic sources of variety on which natural selection may operate.

36. What does it mean to say that a trait may be adaptive or maladaptive, depending on the environmental conditions affecting it? Give at least one example in your answer.

37. Discuss the differences between creationism, catastrophism, evolution, and uniformitarianism. Which does the best job of explaining human variation? The fossil record? Why?

38. What is the difference between phenotypic adaptation and genetic adaptation? What role does each play in human evolution?

39. Any of the above multiple choice questions may be converted to an essay question by requiring students to choose the correct answer and to justify their selection in essay form. Such justifications should include explanations, as to why the chosen answer is correct, and why those responses not chosen are incorrect.

TRUE OR FALSE QUESTIONS

40. True or **False**   The theory of creationism argues that all of the species present today were created as natural selection selected the fittest individuals.

41. True or **False**   The inheritance of acquired characteristics is central to Darwin's theory of evolution.

42. **True** or False   Uniformitarianism states that the natural forces at work today have more or less been the same as those at work in the past.

43. True or **False**   Mendelian genetics studies the ways in which gene frequencies vary in communities from generation to generation.

44. **True** or False   One of Mendel's contributions to genetics was that he discovered that traits were inherited as discrete units.

45. **True** or False   Recessive traits are expressed only in homozygous individuals.

46. True or **False**   The genotype is the expressed trait based on the genetic makeup.

47. **True** or False   Mendel's concept of independent assortment is based on the fact that individual traits are inherited independently of one another.

48. True or **False**   Mitosis is the special process by which sex cells are produced.

49. **True** or False   Genetic evolution involves changes in gene frequencies between generations within a given breeding population.

50. True or **False**   Natural selection is the only mechanism driving genetic evolution.

51. True or **False**   Natural selection operates directly on the genotype of an organism.

52. True or False   Directional selection works to reduce genetic variation by removing maladaptive traits from the gene pool.

53. True or **False**   Directional selection has eliminated sickle-cell anemia from all human populations, except those in regions where filariasis is endemic.

54. True or False   The Hb^S allele has been maintained in certain populations in Africa, India, and the Mediterranean because heterozygotes with this allele are less susceptible to malaria.

55. True or False   Mutations introduce genetic variation into a gene pool.

56. True or False   Gene flow between populations work to prevent speciation.

57. True or **False**   Genetic discrimination is the term for scientific racism in which geneticists have identified units of genes that accurately classify human populations into discrete races.

58. True or False   According to Thomson's nose rule, longer noses are more adaptive to colder climates than shorter ones.

59. True or **False**   Allen's rule states that protruding body parts get shorter as the temperature increases.

CHAPTER 4
THE PRIMATES

CHAPTER OUTLINE

I. Our Place in the Primate Order

    A. Definitions of key terms
        1. Taxonomy: the assignment of organisms to categories.
        2. Hominoidea (hominoids): the superfamily containing humans and apes.
        3. Phylogeny: genetic relatedness based on common ancestry.

    B. Phylogenetic Classification
        1. Organisms are placed in classifications, which are arranged hierarchically, according to the degree of genetic relatedness.
        2. Phylogenetic classification is a descending hierarchy of classifications, from the most inclusive to the least inclusive (see figure 4.1 in the textbook).
        3. Species are constituted by organisms whose mating produces viable and fertile offspring.
        4. See table 4.1 for a complete statement of the phylogenetic classification of modern humans.

II. Homologies and Analogies

    A. Homologies
        1. Similarities that organisms share because of common ancestry are called homologies.
        2. The presence of homologies is the principal factor in determining how organisms are assigned to taxonomic categories.

    B. Analogies
        1. Analogies are similarities between species that are the result of similar adaptation to similar selective pressures--analogies are not the result of common ancestry.
        2. The process, which leads to analogies, is called convergent evolution.

III. Primate Tendencies

    A. While the primate order is extremely diverse, its members share a significant number of homologies derived from common arboreal ancestors.

    B. Grasping (precision grip, thumb opposability, nails instead of claws).

    C. Smell to Sight (eye placement, brain organization, and color vision all reflect a primate's emphasis upon sight over smell--not that some of these features are not common to all primates in the same degree).

    D. Nose to Hand (increasing reliance on sense of touch as opposed to muzzle, whiskers for information).

    E. Brain Complexity (the brain areas devoted to thought, memory and association are more elaborate and proportionally larger).

    F. Parental Investment (single offspring births combined with longer development periods stemming from neotony).

G. Sociality (strongly associated with parental investment, cooperative social groups are selected for in part because of the needs arising from primate parenting).

IV. Prosimians

A. Prosimians vs. Anthropoids
  1. Prosimians and anthropoids constitute the two suborders of primates.
  2. 30 million years ago, prosimians were driven from niches by better adapted anthropoids.

B. Lemurs and Tarsiers
  1. Most of the remaining prosimians, by far, are lemurs.
  2. These live only in Madagascar, which separated from Africa prior to the development of anthropoids.
  3. Tarsiers survived in Asia, where there are monkeys, by adapting to night conditions (monkeys are not nocturnal).

V. Anthropoids

A. Vision
  1. Evolutionary changes in vision probably occurred in response to the pressures of an arboreal habitat.
  2. Binocular, stereoscopic vision and color vision may have been selected due to the improved depth perception it endows (locomotion, catching insects, identifying edible fruits).

B. The arboreal habitat (climbing, feeding) and the increasingly social environment (mutual grooming, tool making) were likely factors in selecting for increased manual tactility.

C. Proportionately larger than prosimians, brain mass and emphasis on memory and cognition were likely selected for by the social environment.

VI. Monkeys

A. Platyrrhines and Catarrhines
  1. There are two anthropoid infraorders: platyrrhines (flat-nosed, New World monkeys) and catarrhines (sharp-nosed, Old World monkeys, hominoids).
  2. Unlike hominoids, monkeys' rear and fore limbs articulate from their bodies as do dogs'.
  3. Most monkeys have tails.

B. New World Monkeys
  1. New World monkeys' traits: universally arboreal, some brachiate, some have prehensile tails (among primates, a trait exclusive to the New World).
  2. The brachiation of New World monkeys and the brachiation of gibbons constitute an analogy.

C. Old World Monkeys
  1. Old World monkeys are both terrestrial and arboreal.
  2. Significant distinctions existing between arboreal and terrestrial Old World monkeys include size (arboreal monkeys are smaller than terrestrial monkeys) and sexual dimorphism (terrestrial males are significantly larger and fiercer than terrestrial females, while little or no such differentiation existing among arboreal monkeys.

VII. Apes

    A. Old World Monkeys comprise the superfamily Cercopithecoidea, while humans and apes are in the superfamily Hominoidea.

    B. Hominoidea is subdivided into three families.
        1. Hominids (humans and their fossil ancestors).
        2. Pongids ("great apes": gorillas, chimpanzees, and orangutan).
        3. Hylobatids (gibbons and siamangs).
        4. Recent biochemical evidence suggests that gorillas and chimpanzees are almost as closely related to humans as they are to each other.

    C. Gibbons
        1. Gibbons are small, arboreal, mate for life and produce few offspring.
        2. Their principal mode of locomotion is brachiation.

    D. Orangutans
        1. Orangutans relatively large (up to 200 pounds), solitary, and markedly sexually dimorphic.
        2. Orangutans move between arboreal and terrestrial habitats.

    E. Gorillas
        1. Gorillas are large (up to 400 pounds), the most sexually dimorphic of all primates, and are primarily terrestrial.
        2. They live in relatively stable social groups, typically led by a mature silver-back male.

    F. Chimpanzees
        1. There are two kinds of chimpanzee: the common (*Pan troglodytes*) and the pygmy (*Pan paniscus*).
        2. Size range is up to 200 pounds, and sexual dimorphism is proportionally the same as in humans.
        3. The social organization of chimpanzees is relatively well-known, because of the longitudinal studies done by Goodall and other primatologists.

VIII. Endangered Primates

    A. Humans are the only hominoids that are not endangered.

    B. Deforestation, poaching, and the capture of primates have all contributed to the demise of wild primate populations.

IX. Human-Primate Similarities

    A. Adaptive Flexibility through Learning
        1. Neotony and life in cooperative social groups allow primates to learn behavior from their fellows, rather than relying only on genetically encoded behaviors.
        2. Learned behavior has been observed in monkeys as well as apes.

    B. Tools
        1. Tool use allows primates to adapt to a wider range of niches more quickly than physiological adaptation alone (although primates are not the only animals that use tools).
        2. Wild chimps have been observed constructing tools.

C. Predation and Hunting
    1. Hunting is a regular and normal component of wild chimpanzee behavior.
    2. Hunting by chimps is both opportunistic and planned.
    3. Wild chimpanzees have been observed hunting consistently, using cooperative techniques, with some sex specialization (males hunt more than females).

D. Aggression and Resources
    1. The capacity for hunting exists among many different primates, but expression of this capacity can depend upon environmental pressure and opportunity.
    2. Observations of chimps and orangutans indicate that aggressive behavior ("warfare," in some chimp cases) may increase when territorial encroachment occurs.

E. In the News: Carnivorous Chimps
    1. Studies (particularly those by Craig Stanford of the University of Southern California) of wild chimpanzees increasingly reveal that chimps eat a surprisingly large amount of meat.
    2. Hunting by chimpanzees is done most often by males, and they may offer meat to females in exchange for sex.
    3. The style and intensity of hunting varies from population to population as well as by season.
    4. It may be reasonable to infer from this data that hunting and meat consumption by hominids significantly antedates the oldest (2.5 million years ago) known stone tools.

X. Human-Primate Differences

A. Sharing, Cooperation, and Division of Labor
    1. Sharing and cooperation is common to most primates, however humans do it much more complexly.
    2. Human foraging bands tend to have a sexual division of labor (e.g., men hunt, women gather), other primates do not.
    3. *Homo sapiens* is the only primate species that engages in food sharing consistently on a large scale.

B. Mating and Kinship
    1. Human females do not experience estrus.
    2. Marriage and kinship are two exclusively, universally human systems that give identity and stability to certain types of human relationships in a way that is absent from other primate social systems.

XI. Sociobiology and Fitness

A. "Sociobiology is the study of the evolutionary basis for behavior."

B. Types of Fitness
    1. Individual fitness is the number of direct descendents an individual organism has.
    2. Inherent in this notion, as seen in terms of natural selection, is the implication that any individual's fitness competes with that of its conspecifics.
    3. A model attributing a drive to protect one's individual fitness to all organisms could not explain altruistic or self-sacrificing behavior.
    4. Inclusive fitness is a theoretical concept developed to account for unselfish behavior and is defined as "reproductive success measured by the representation [in succeeding generations] of genes one shares with other, related animals."

XII. Beyond the Classroom: Lemurs

    A. "A Behavioral Ecology Study of Two Lemur Species" by Jennifer Burns and Chris Howard

        1. Working with wild communities in the Ranomafana National Park in Madagascar, Burns and Howard recorded behavioral and ecological data on two species of lemurs over a six month period.

        2. Burns and Howard investigated the implications of "dominance," "leadership," "competition," "reproductive stress," and "male versus female roles" within lemur communities.

    B. "Feeding Behavior and Environmental Degradation in Lemurs" by Natalie Cummings

        1. Cummings compared the feeding habits of communities of the Eastern gray bamboo lemur in Madagascar living in different ecological settings.

            a. One community lived in a deforested region.

            b. The other community lived in a more pristine region within the Ranomafana National Park.

        2. Cummings found the field required for this research was daunting given the quickness and agility of the lemurs coupled with the dense vegetation and mountainous terrain.

LECTURE TOPICS

1. An illustration of homologies and analogies by using the various animals commonly familiar to undergraduates is most effective for demonstrating that difference. Such discussion also serves as the basis for explaining the importance of homologies in classification.

2. The variety of primate social groupings or organization should be categorized and presented in a simple tabular form for easy recall. The adaptive basis for the various forms should be made explicitly clear, particularly for the differences among the categories of mated couples, single male groups, groups in which relationships among female kin form the basis for social organization (female-bonded groups), and groups in which relationships among males form the basis for social organization (male-bonded groups; chimpanzees).

3. The adaptive roots of sexual dimorphism (competition among males for sexual access to females, in the case of most primates), both in external physical pressures and in social relations, should be explained carefully. How such adaptive pressures might or might not apply to humans should be considered.

4. The sociobiological concept of inclusive fitness has been used to explain human behavior (to widely varying extents). This continues to generate some controversy, and it is important that introductory students be introduced to the basic elements of this debate.

5. There have been a number of studies done which investigate the nature of sex relations among non-human primates and attempts to draw some conclusions about, for example, the origins of monogamy and marriage, sexual violence, and the origins of the sexual division of labor. Any of these issues is both interesting in its own right and useful as a case study illustrating the possibilities and limits for making generalizations across species. In particular, studies of male-to-female violence among non-human primates can be particularly useful for discussions on the "naturalness" of battering among humans.

SUGGESTED FILMS

The Family of Chimps

video 1987 55 min color
An excellent documentary on the social behavior of chimpanzees as exhibited by the zoo population studied by Frans de Waal for his acclaimed book, *Chimpanzee Politics*. This community is the largest group of chimpanzees ever brought together in captivity, and their behavior provides vivid examples of dominance, problem solving, sexuality, tool use, and a wide range of social interactions. Directed by Bert Haanstra. New York: Film Makers Library.

Monkey in the Mirror

video 1995 60 min color
From the BBC *Nature* series. Discusses the similarities between humans and other primates. Shows primates in the wild living in complex and varied societies in which they use tools, take herbal medicines, bargain, practice power and sexual politics, and sometimes suffer from stress. Shows primate communication/language experiments. New York: WNET.

Rock-a-bye Baby

16mm or video 1973 30 min
Shows using emotionally deprived children and primates, the importance of tactile, visual, and aural stimuli on the mental and emotional development of an infant. Demonstrates the analogous stereotyped movements and reactions of infants and monkeys deprived of maternal stimuli, illustrating that restoration of stimuli can overcome certain retardation. Emphasizes the value of prenatal and postnatal stimuli through experiments with premature infants. From the British Broadcasting Corporation and Time-Life Video.

Jane Goodall: My Life with the Chimpanzees

video 1990 28 min color
From the National Geographic *Explorer* series. This film is a fairly recent presentation of Jane Goodall's epoch-making research among the chimpanzees of Gombe. Narrated by Jack Lemmon. Stamford, Connecticut: Vestron Video.

Life in the Trees

video 58 min 1984 color
Deals with the evolution, physiology, and behavior of primates. Episode 12 from the acclaimed series, *Life on Earth*, with David Attenborough. BBC, WQLN, in association with Warner Bros. and Reiner Moritz Productions.

MULTIPLE-CHOICE QUESTIONS

1. Which of the following primate traits are believed to have been selected for life in trees?

    a. fewer offspring and bipedality
    b. meat-eating and aggression
    c. larger females and gentle males
    d. fingernails (instead of claws) and soft fingertips
    e. **stereoscopic vision and an opposable thumb**

2. Of the following primates, which are most likely to provide reasonable comparisons to humans?

   a. lemurs
   b. prosimians
   c. New World monkeys
   d. terrestrial primates
   e. arboreal primates

3. Which of the following are most closely related to chimpanzees?

   a. humans
   b. gibbons
   c. lemurs
   d. siamangs
   e. orangutans

4. Which of the following hominoids mate for life?

   a. gorillas
   b. gibbons
   c. chimpanzees
   d. baboons
   e. lorises

5. What is the term for the evolutionary process by which organisms as unrelated as birds and butterflies develop similar characteristics because of adaptations to similar environments?

   a. divergence
   b. brachiation
   c. convergence
   d. genetic drift
   e. gene flow

6. Which of the following is *not* a hominoid?

   a. gibbon
   b. spider monkey
   c. *Homo sapiens*
   d. orangutan
   e. siamang

7. Which of the following is shared by all anthropoids?

   a. the ability to knuckle-walk and carry tools
   b. bipedalism and one offspring born at a time
   c. prehensile tails
   d. a decrease in size of canines and an increase in size of molars
   e. an emphasis on vision

8.   Which of the following is used for putting organisms in the same taxon (zoological category)?

   a.   all phenotypic similarities
   b.   homologies
   c.   only similarities that have evolved since the time of their common ancestor
   d.   analogies
   e.   all of the above

9.   Which of the following conditions is the defining feature of speciation?

   a.   Groups that once belonged to the same species can no longer interbreed
   b.   Groups that formerly were very different have become similar enough to interbreed
   c.   Groups of formerly similar organisms show some phenotypic differences
   d.   Groups of formerly similar organisms show some genotypic differences
   e.   Groups of ancient primates began to walk upright

10.   Which of the following is an example of an analogy?

   a.   the mammary glands of dogs and cats
   b.   similarities in chromosomal DNA between apes and humans
   c.   pentadactyly (five-digits on hands and feet) among baboons and macaques
   d.   dolphin and fish fins
   e.   bony eye sockets in chimps and similar structures in gorillas

11.   Why are studies of baboons and macaques seen as particularly relevant to humans?

   a.   They are terrestrial and live in complex social groups
   b.   They are hominoids
   c.   Like humans, they exhibit great sexual dimorphism
   d.   They are bipedal
   e.   all of the above

12.   What is the term for a trait that organisms have jointly inherited from a common ancestor?

   a.   analogy
   b.   homology
   c.   phenotype
   d.   allele
   e.   meiosis

13.   Which of the following is *not* an adaptive trend in anthropoids?

   a.   stereoscopic vision
   b.   enhanced sense of touch
   c.   grasping hands and feet
   d.   having more offspring (increasing litter size)
   e.   increased brain complexity

14. What do the trends that *all* primates share (five fingers, opposable thumbs, and stereoscopic vision) indicate?

    a.   only after humans' ancestors began to walk upright
    b.   a socially complex environment
    c.   a common ancestral arboreal heritage
    d.   by the primitive "sexual division of labor," in which females gathered seeds while males hunted insects and small animals
    e.   all of the above

15. Which of the following is a general primate tendency?

    a.   stereoscopic vision
    b.   small litter size
    c.   five-fingered hands
    d.   relatively large brain size
    e.   all of the above

16. Ancient anthropoids began to have fewer offspring who required longer and more attentive care. What did this select for?

    a.   pair-bonding, which resembles the nuclear family, among 90% of present-day anthropoids
    b.   domestic, nurturing females and aggressive, protective males
    c.   increased social complexity
    d.   increased reliance on arboreality (living in trees), which protected the young from predators
    e.   all of the above

17. Which of the following traits is *not* associated with primates?

    a.   reliance on smell as the main sense
    b.   single births
    c.   social groupings
    d.   grasping adaptations
    e.   brain complexity

18. Recent research on chimpanzee eating habits confirms that _____.

    a.   chimps hunt and eat meat regularly
    b.   chimps are almost exclusively frugivorous
    c.   male chimps cooperate to kill and eat large game animals, such as giraffes
    d.   female chimps do most of the hunting, while male chimps try real hard but are too noisy
    e.   gorillas eat more meat (including chimpanzee meat) than chimps

19. Which of the following is *not* considered an anthropoid trend?

    a.   A shift from a moist muzzle and tactile hairs to fingers as the primary organs of touch
    b.   The evolution of a complicated visual system
    c.   An increase of cranial capacity relative to body size
    d.   An increase in hearing capacity at the expense of smell
    e.   A decrease in litter size

20. Which of the following was *not* one of the trends that distinguished anthropoids from other primates?

    a.   a shift from reliance on smell to reliance on sight
    b.   improved stereoscopic and color vision
    c.   increased number of offspring
    d.   a tendency toward being active during the day
    e.   none of the above; all were part of the anthropoid revolution

21. Recent research on chimpanzee eating habits indicates that _____.

    a.   chimpanzee hunting is the main reason New World monkeys are almost extinct
    b.   male chimps sometimes exchange meat for sex with females
    c.   chimpanzees have been observed "cooking" meat at volcanically heated springs
    d.   while chimps do hunt a little, they get most of their meat by stealing it from predators
    e.   all of the above

22. Ischial callosities and nonprehensile tails are characteristic traits of

    a.   Old World monkeys
    b.   New World monkeys
    c.   pongids
    d.   prosimians
    e.   tarsiers

23. Which of the following primates is arboreal, active during the day, and has a prehensile tail?

    a.   prosimian
    b.   New World monkey
    c.   Old World monkey
    d.   gibbon
    e.   extinct

24. Which of the following traits is *not* shared by humans and chimpanzees?

    a.   tool use
    b.   meat-eating
    c.   stereoscopic vision
    d.   high intelligence
    e.   estrus

25. Platyrrhines/catarrhines is the same as

    a.   prosimians/anthropoids
    b.   Old World monkeys/New World monkeys
    c.   New World monkeys/Old World monkeys
    d.   brachiates/non-brachiates
    e.   none of the above

26. What makes gibbons and siamangs unique among the apes?

   a. They are completely arboreal
   b. They are brachiators
   c. They exhibit little sexual dimorphism
   d. They live in primary groups consisting of one male, one female, and their preadolescent offspring
   e. **all of the above**

27. New World monkeys are the only anthropoids who _____.

   a. have ischial callosities
   b. exhibit sexual dimorphism
   c. **have prehensile tails**
   d. are capable of brachiation
   e. have orthograde posture

28. In terms of numbers and range, what is the most successful living hominoid species?

   a. the gorilla
   b. *homo sapiens*
   c. the baboon
   d. the gibbon
   e. the chimpanzee

29. Which of the following is true?

   a. The large size of the orangutan protects it from extinction
   b. Orangutans are sociable animals
   c. As is typical of arboreal species, the orangutan exhibits little sexual dimorphism
   d. Orangutans are less arboreal than are gorillas
   e. **Orangutans used to live over much of Asia, but now are found only on two islands in Indonesia**

30. Which of the following is *not* part of a uterine group of terrestrial monkeys?

   a. mothers
   b. daughters
   c. sisters
   d. juvenile males
   e. **all of the above**

31. How is individual fitness measured?

   a. By the gene an individual shares with relatives
   b. By the maximum lung capacity
   c. **By the number of direct descendents an individual has**
   d. By the amount of genetic diversity in a breeding population
   e. all of the above

32. According to sociobiologists, what is inclusive fitness?

    a.   The number of direct descendents an individual organism has
    b.   The idea that human behavior is unconnected to genetics by virtue of their having culture
    c.   **Reproductive success measured by the representation of genes one shares with other, related individuals**
    d.   The degree to which anaerobic fitness is included in certain behaviors
    e.   The ability of an individual to reproduce

33. Which of the following primates is the most capable of maker and user of tools?

    a.   lemur
    b.   **chimpanzee**
    c.   macaque
    d.   gibbon
    e.   orangutan

34. Which of the following statements about the social organization of terrestrial primates is true?

    a.   Among monkeys, adult females form the group core
    b.   Among monkeys, males tend to leave their birth group at puberty
    c.   Among chimpanzees and gorillas, females tend to leave their birth group
    d.   Among monkeys, males are larger than females and act to defend the group against predators
    e.   **all of the above are true**

35. Which of the following traits is unique to humans?

    a.   tool use
    b.   **kinship**
    c.   meat eating
    d.   food sharing
    e.   all of the above

36. Which of the following primate species exhibits the *smallest* degree of sexual dimorphism?

    a.   baboons
    b.   orangutans
    c.   chimpanzees
    d.   **humans**
    e.   gorillas

37. Which of the following traits are found among some nonhuman primates but are most fully developed among humans?

    a.   meat eating
    b.   food sharing
    c.   tool use
    d.   division of labor by sex
    e.   **all of the above**

38. Which of the following has a prehensile tail?

    a.   Old World monkeys
    b.   apes
    c.   New World monkeys
    d.   gibbons
    e.   siamangs

39. What is the greatest threat to endangered primates?

    a.   gene flow
    b.   directional selection
    c.   intra-group predation
    d.   loss of habitat
    e.   all of the above

40. Who is believed to have killed Dian Fossey?

    a.   Koko
    b.   poachers
    c.   Wahsoe
    d.   the Rwandan military
    e.   Digit

41. Which of the following is *not* a threat to endangered primates?

    a.   intra-species conflict
    b.   deforestation
    c.   capture for laboratory testing
    d.   capture for pets
    e.   poachers

42. Which of the following is unique to humans?

    a.   marriage
    b.   kinship
    c.   use of fire
    d.   incest taboo
    e.   all of the above

ESSAY QUESTIONS

43. Any of the above multiple choice questions may be converted to an essay question, by requiring students to choose the correct answer, and justify their selection in essay form. Such justifications should include explanations as to why the chosen answer is correct and why those responses not chosen are incorrect.

44. Is it possible to rate different primates on the basis of differential evolutionary success? How? Discuss the relative evolutionary success of different groups of hominoids.

45. Discuss trends that are characteristic of primate evolution. Indicate how these trends differentiate between the anthropoids and the prosimians.

46. Discuss two cases of confirmed or possible convergent evolution between different primate species, indicating similarities and differences in natural selective forces and means of adaptation.

47. Using your everyday activities as examples, discuss abilities that you share with monkeys and apes but not with prosimians. Then discuss differences and similarities between your activities and those of apes.

48. What are some primate evolutionary trends associated with an arboreal heritage?

49. Phylogenetically, who are our closest relatives? What evidence is used to support this relationship?

50. What do recent studies of primate social organization tell us about territorial behavior and aggression?

51. Discuss the role of dominance in the adaptations of baboons and macaques. Indicate differences between male and female macaque dominance hierarchies.

52. What are the differences between human and nonhuman primate mating patterns?

53. Based upon new evidence produced by studies of wild chimpanzees in various parts of Africa, what is the nature of chimpanzee hunting behavior? What are the implications of this behavior for such things as social organization and hypotheses about human origins?

TRUE OR FALSE QUESTIONS

54. **True** or False   Homologies are similarities between two species that have been jointly inherited from a common ancestor.

55. True or **False**   Analogies are similarities that are shared by organisms that belong to the same genus.

56. True or **False**   Lemurs are the most numerous members of the Anthropoidea suborder.

57. **True** or False   All primates share a common arboreal heritage.

58. True or **False**   Opposable thumbs evolved as the early primates adapted to terrestrial life.

59. **True** or False   Primates invest a lot of time and energy raising single offspring or small litters of offspring.

60. True or **False**   Since primates are highly social animals, less care over a shorter period of time is provided to offspring.

61. True or **False**   Prosimians are only found in Madagascar.

62. **True** or False   Platyrrhines are the New World monkeys.

63. True or **False**   Most New World monkeys have a tendency to use orthograde posture.

64. **True** or False   Old World monkeys include both arboreal and terrestrial species.

65. **True** or False   Sexual dimorphism tends to more pronounced in terrestrial species.

66. **True** or False   Gibbons are unlike gorillas in that they are agile brachiators.

67. True or **False**   Orangutans are found mostly in Madagascar.

68. True or **False**   Since they are predominantly terrestrial, gorillas exhibit only minor sexual dimorphism.

69. True or False   Chimpanzee social networks involve complex systems of dominance relationships.

70. True or **False**   The spread of sickle-cell anemia to primate populations has drastically reduced the number of primate communities in the world.

71. True or **False**   Learning, adaptive flexibility, and tool use are traits found only in the platyrrhines.

72. True or False   Aggressive and violent behavior is not restricted to human populations.

73. True or False   Sociobiologists define fitness as reproductive success measured by the genes one shares with relatives.

CHAPTER 5

PRIMATE EVOLUTION

CHAPTER OUTLINE

I. The Fossil Record

    A. Preservation
        1. The fossil record is not a representative sample of all species that have lived on earth.
        2. Some species and body parts preserve better than others.
        3. Taphonomy is the study of the processes that affect the remains of dead animals.

    B. Finding fossils
        1. Fossils are more likely to be found in areas with little vegetation and lots of erosion.
        2. Due to issues regarding the preservation and discovery of fossils, the fossil record of early primates is "limited and spotty".

II. Dating the Past

    A. Fundamental Concepts
        1. Paleontology is the study of ancient life through the fossil record.
        2. Anthropology and paleontology both are interested in establishing a chronology for primate and human evolution.
        3. Much dating depends upon stratigraphy, which is the study of the sequence of geographical layers.

    B. Relative Dating
        1. Relative dating uses the natural layers or strata to establish a relative chronology – material from this layer is older than the material from that layer.
        2. Association with known fossils is the most common method of fossil dating.
        3. Fluorine dating is another relative dating technique, and was used to expose the Piltdown Man hoax.

    C. Absolute Dating
        1. Whereas relative dating techniques allow you to say only what is older or younger, absolute dating techniques produce dates in years so differences in age can be quantified.
        2. Radiometric techniques are based on known rates of radioactive decay in elements found in or around fossils.
        3. Examples are: ^{14}C and potassium argon (K/A) dating (both of which are radiometric techniques), thermoluminescence (TL), and electron spin resonance (ESR) (see table 5.1).

III. Early Primates

    A. Arboreal theory
        1. Primates became primates by adapting to life in trees.
        2. Enhanced sight (depth perception)
        3. Grasping hands and feet

B. Visual predation hypothesis (Cartmill 1972, 1992)
1. Binocular vision, grasping hands and feet, and reduced claws developed because they facilitated the capture of insects.
2. Early primates first adapted to life in the bushy forest undergrowth and low tree branches.

C. Early Cenozoic Primates
1. The earliest primates date to the first part of the Cenozoic (65-54 m.y.a.).
2. The Eocene (54-38 m.y.a.) was the epoch of prosimians with at least 60 different genera in two families.
   a. The omomyid family lived in North America, Europe, and Asia and may be ancestral to all anthropoids.
   b. The adapid family was ancestral to the lemur-loris line.
3. Anthropoids branched off from the prosimians during the Eocene.
   a. Anthropoid eyes are rotated more forward compared to prosimians.
   b. Anthropoids have a fully enclosed bony eye socket.
   c. Anthropoids have a dry nose separate from the upper lip.
   d. Anthropoids have molar cusps.

D. Oligocene Anthropoids
1. During the Oligocene (38-23 m.y.a.), anthropoids were the most numerous primates.
2. The *parapithecid* family may be ancestral to the New World monkeys.
3. The *propliopithecid* family may be ancestral to Old World monkeys, apes, and humans.

IV. Miocene Hominoids

A. The earliest hominoid fossils date to the Miocene epoch (23-5 m.y.a.).

B. *Proconsul*
1. *Proconsul* was the most abundant anthropoid in the early Miocene.
2. Its teeth have similarities with modern apes, but below the neck the skeleton is more monkey-like.
3. Their teeth suggest that they ate fruits and leaves.
4. *Proconsul* probably contained the last common ancestor shared by Old World monkeys and the apes.
5. *Proconsul* was replaced by monkeys in the late Miocene.
   a. Monkeys probably were superior at eating leaves.
   b. Monkey molars developed lophs, which enhanced their ability to chew leaves.
6. Traits
   a. Primitive traits are those passed on unchanged from an ancestor.
   b. Derived traits are those that develop in a particular taxon after a split from a common ancestor.

C. *Afropithecus* and *Kenyapithecus*
1. *Afropithecus* is a large slow moving Miocene hominoid with large projecting front teeth from northern Kenya (18-16 m.y.a.)
2. Recent research suggests that the two species of *Kenyapithecus* should be reclassified as *Equatorius*.
3. *Equatorius* and *Afropithecus* are probable stem hominoids, species somewhere on the evolutionary line near the origins of the modern ape group that are too primitive to be considered direct ancestors of living apes and humans.

D. *Sivapithecus*
1. *Sivapithecus* belongs to the ramapithecid genera along with *Gigantopithecus*.
2. *Sivapithecus* is now believed to be ancestral to the modern orangutan.

E. *Gigantopithecus*
    1. *Gigantopithecus* is the largest primate that ever lived, some standing over 10 feet tall and weighing 1,200 pounds.
    2. Since it died out around 400,000 years ago, it coexisted with *Homo erectus*.
    3. Some people believe it is still alive today as the yeti and Bigfoot.

F. *Dryopithecus*
    1. *Dryopithecus* lived in Europe during the middle and late Miocene.
    2. This group probably includes the common ancestor of the lesser apes (gibbons and siamangs) and the great apes.
    3. *Dryopithecus* has the Y-5 arrangement of molar cusps typical of *Dryopithecus* and of hominoids.

G. *Oreopithecus*
    1. *Oreopithecus bambolii* lived between 9-7 m.y.a and spent much of its time standing upright and shuffling short distances.
    2. Its big toe splayed out 90 degrees from the other toes.

V. A Missing Link?

    A. Kottak refers to the last ancestral population held commonly by humans, gorillas, and chimpanzees as Hogopans (after the genus names of these three).

    B. The lines of the orangutans, gibbons and siamangs having split off several million years earlier, the hominid line almost certainly diverged from those of chimps and gorillas late in the Miocene epoch, between 7 and 5 m.y.a.

    C. Hogopans probably split into the three separate lines leading to gorillas, chimpanzees and humans no more than 8 m.y.a., with each group moving into separate niches: equatorial forest-dwelling and eating bulk vegetation (gorilla), Central African woodland-dwelling frugivores (chimpanzee), and open grassland (hominids).

VI. Beyond the Classroom: Maceration of a Canadian Lynx

    A. Barbara Hewitt studied how the condition of a lynx's bones reflected its former health.

    B. After preparing the skeleton, Hewitt was able to identify pathologies in the animal's bones.

LECTURE TOPICS

1. Discuss the differences between relative and absolute dating techniques. Be sure to demonstrate that they are not competing ways of dating the past. Rather, they are used together to establish more and more refined chronologies.

2. Discuss what a fossil is, how they form, and how people find them. It is important to discuss the nature of the fossil record. In particular, discuss its limits and its advantages (time depth).

3. Discuss the patterns of hominoid evolution during the Miocene.

4. Discuss the differences between primitive and derived traits. What kinds of relationships can be reconstructed based on each kind of feature?

5. Discuss the relationship between the advancement of thought and world view. Use the example of the Great Chain of Being as your starting point.

SUGGESTED FILMS

The Record of the Rocks

VHS 20 min color 1988
Discusses the process of sedimentation and gives examples from the Grand Canyon of the Colorado River, where life forms have been preserved through this process. Covers how to date rock samples and explains why fossils provide evidence for the theory of evolution. Films For The Humanities, Granada TV

Macroevolution

VHS 30 min color 1997
Part eleven of the *Cycles of Life*. Paleontologists discuss their use of fossils and other techniques to understand macroevolution. Also looks at ways in which scientists reconstruct the events that led to the formation of amino acids and the first unicellular organisms. Annenberg/CPG Collection, Coast Telecoast Productions.

How Old Is Old?

16mm 30 min color 1971
Methods for dating objects are reviewed historically and scientifically with illustrations. Includes thermoluminescence, dendrochronology, carbon 14, and potassium argon clock. Time Life Video.

MULTIPLE-CHOICE QUESTIONS

1.   Under what conditions are fossils most likely to form?

    a.   acidic soils
    b.   geologically inactive regions
    c.   region with lots of scavengers
    d.   in newly forming sediments
    e.   all of the above

2.   What term refers to the study of the processes that affect the remains of dead animals?

    a.   necrology
    b.   autopsy
    c.   degradation
    d.   osteology
    e.   taphonomy

3.   Radiometric dating techniques available to anthropologists _____.

    a.   work only for the australopithecines, because genus *Homo* had culture
    b.   have caused a wholesale reevaluation of the fossil record since their 1991 development
    c.   are virtually worthless, as they can only be used to date inorganic materials over 1 million years old
    d.   do not work well for hominid fossils, because hominid fossils are too young for the effective range of the techniques
    e.   establish a probable date for fossils by identifying the age of the rock strata that surround the fossils.

4.   Which of the following statements about techniques used in dating fossil remains is *not* true?

   a.   The potassium-argon (K/A) technique is used to date inorganic substances, such as rock.
   b.   Carbon-14 (^{14}C) techniques are used to date organic material.
   c.   Potassium-argon (K/A) dating is most accurate on specimens over 500,000 years old.
   d.   Carbon-14 (^{14}C) dating is most accurate on specimens *over* 70,000 years old.
   e.   all of the above are true

5.   The utility of stratigraphy for dating purposes is based on the fact that

   a.   all environmental forces leave behind the same kind of soil deposit
   b.   the depth and order of undisturbed soil strata reflect the age of their deposition
   c.   higher strata are usually older than lower strata in undisturbed soil
   d.   soil strata are uncluttered by bones, stones, and artifacts
   e.   none of the above

6.   What are both Carbon-14 and potassium-argon dating techniques are based on?

   a.   radioactive decay
   b.   stratigraphic associations
   c.   reversals of magnetic fields
   d.   accumulations of mineral salts
   e.   relative as opposed to absolute dating

7.   The Paleocene, Eocene, Oligocene, Miocene, and Pliocene are divisions of the
   _____.

   a.   Pleistocene epoch
   b.   Mesozoic era
   c.   hominid fossil record
   d.   Tertiary period
   e.   last million years

8.   What dating technique exposed the Piltdown fraud?

   a.   fluorine absorption analysis
   b.   potassium-argon
   c.   carbon-14
   d.   electron spin resonance
   e.   thermoluminescence

9.   What kind of dating technique is fluorine absorption analysis?

   a.   absolute
   b.   relative
   c.   radiometric
   d.   chronologic
   e.   radioactive

10. What kind of absolute dating technique is used to date volcanic rock?

     a.   fluorine absorption analysis
     b.   thermoluminescence
     c.   carbon-14
     d.   electron spin resonance
     e.   potassium-argon

11. What theory argues that primates, became primates, by adapting to life in the trees?

     a.   visual predation theory
     b.   terrestrial theory
     c.   deciduous theory
     d.   coniferous theory
     e.   arboreal theory

12. Which of the following shifts was a key feature of the first primate?

     a.   smell over sight
     b.   sight over smell
     c.   touch over sight
     d.   taste over sight
     e.   smell over touch

13. What hypothesis argues that binocular vision, grasping hands and feet, and reduced claws developed to facilitate the capture of insects in the bushy forest undergrowth?

     a.   visual predation hypothesis
     b.   arboreal hypothesis
     c.   opposable digit hypothesis
     d.   stereoscopic hypothesis
     e.   binocular hypothesis

14. What is the advantage of binocular vision?

     a.   better night vision
     b.   enhanced ability to recognize colors
     c.   better depth perception
     d.   enhanced peripheral vision
     e.   enhanced myopic vision

15. Which of the following statements about the omoyid family is *not* true?

     a.   They were squirrel-sized.
     b.   They may be ancestral to tarsiers and anthropoids.
     c.   They were distributed throughout Africa.
     d.   They had grasping hands and feet.
     e.   They lived during the Eocene.

16. Which of the following statements about the adapid family is true?

     a.   They are the only primates to lack binocular vision.
     b.   They are probably ancestral to the lemur-loris line.
     c.   They have a fully enclosed bony eye-socket.
     d.   They were diurnal.
     e.   all of the above

17. Which of the following traits is characteristic of anthropoids?

    a. fully enclosed bony eye-socket
    b. dry nose
    c. four or five molar cusps
    d. forward rotated eyes
    e. all of the above

18. Which of the following statements about the Oligocene epoch is *not* true?

    a. It was a time of major geological and climatic change.
    b. This period dates to 38-23 m.y.a.
    c. Most of what we know about primates from this period comes from fossils found in the Fayum.
    d. The parapithecid family was ancestral to the Old World monkeys.
    e. all of the above are true

19. When do the first hominoid fossils appear?

    a. during the Oligocene
    b. during the Miocene
    c. during the Pliocene
    d. during the Pleistocene
    e. during the Holocene

20. Which of the following statements about *Proconsul* is *not* true?

    a. It was the most abundant and successful of the anthropoids during the early Miocene.
    b. It is probably the last common ancestor shared by the Old World monkeys and the apes.
    c. It was a carnivore.
    d. It had marked sexual dimorphism.
    e. It lacked the capacity for brachiation.

21. Why did the Old World monkeys thrive as the Miocene apes faded?

    a. The Old World monkeys were superior at eating leaves.
    b. The Miocene apes lacked opposable thumbs.
    c. The Old World monkeys were bipedal.
    d. The Miocene apes were too large for the environmental setting of the Miocene.
    e. all of the above

22. What kinds of traits are passed unchanged from an ancestor?

    a. primitive traits
    b. acquired traits
    c. derived traits
    d. consequent traits
    e. ancient traits

23. What kinds of traits develop in a particular taxon after two taxa splits from a common ancestor?

    a. primitive traits
    b. acquired traits
    c. derived traits
    d. consequent traits
    e. ancient traits

24. Which of the following statements about *Afropithecus* and *Kenyapithecus* is true?

    a. They lived during the middle Miocene.
    b. They both had wet noses.
    c. They belong to different hominoid families.
    d. They were found in Europe.
    e. all of the above

25. What term is given to a species somewhere on the evolutionary line near the origin of the modern ape group, but is still too primitive to be the direct ancestor of living apes and humans?

    a. trunk hominoids
    b. core hominoids
    c. stem hominoids
    d. apical hominoids
    e. stalk hominoids

26. What species is believed to be ancestral to the modern orangutan?

    a. *Afropithecus*
    b. *Kenyapithecus*
    c. *Gigantopithecus*
    d. *Sivapithecus*
    e. *Dryopithecus*

27. What species coexisted with *Homo erectus* in Asia

    a. *Afropithecus*
    b. *Kenyapithecus*
    c. *Gigantopithecus*
    d. *Sivapithecus*
    e. *Dryopithecus*

28. Which of the following statements about *Dryopithecus* is true?

    a. It has been found in Europe and China.
    b. This taxon probably includes the common ancestor of the lesser apes and the great apes.
    c. It had the Y-5 five cusp fissure pattern on its molars.
    d. It lived during the middle and late Miocene.
    e. all of the above

29. Which of the following species was probable capable of walking upright with a short, shuffling stride over very short distances?

    a. *Oreopithecus*
    b. *Kenyapithecus*
    c. *Gigantopithecus*
    d. *Sivapithecus*
    e. *Dryopithecus*

30. What is the name of the theological belief that all living things could be placed in a progressive hierarchy?

    a. Divine Classification
    b. Great Chain of Being
    c. Heavenly Order
    d. Celestial Hierarchy of Life
    e. Binomial Nomenclature

ESSAY QUESTIONS

31. How are fossils formed? Where are they found? How representative is the fossil record?

32. Compare and contrast relative and absolute dating techniques. Is one better than the other?

33. What are the general trends in hominoid evolution during the Miocene? What derived hominoid traits appear during this time?

34. What is the Great Chain of Being? How did it influence the way in which people thought about out ancestors?

35. Any of the above multiple choice questions may be converted to an essay question by requiring students to choose the correct answer and justify their selection in essay form. Such justifications should include explanations as to why the chosen answer is correct and why those responses not chosen are incorrect.

TRUE OR FALSE QUESTIONS

36. **True** or False   Taphonomy is the study of the processes that affect preservation of organic remains.

37. True or **False**   Relative dating techniques use radiometric analyses to generate approximate ages that are relatively accurate within a few years.

38. **True** or False   Volcanic rock can be dated using the Potassium-Argon dating technique.

39. **True** or False   Carbon-14 dating cannot be used to accurately date organic remains older then 40,000 years old.

40. **True** or False   Fluorine absorption dating is used in relative dating.

41. True or **False**   Stratification refers to the science that studies the ways in which sediments accumulate in layers.

42. True or **False**   The Cenozoic era was the era of fish and reptiles.

43. True or **False**   The Piltdown hoax was exposed by the electron spin resonance technique.

44. True or False   Absolute dating techniques generates age estimates with dates in numbers of years before the present.

45. True or False   According to the arboreal theory, primates became primates by adapting to life in the trees.

46. True or **False**   The visual predation hypothesis argues that primates evolved elaborate ways of hiding themselves from their forest-based predators.

47. True or **False**   The Eocene was the age of the Old World monkeys.

48. True or **False**   Lemurs have a fully enclosed bony eye-socket.

49. True or False   It was during the Oligocene that anthropoids became the most numerous of the primates.

50. True or **False**   *Proconsul* had ape-like teeth and an ape-like body.

51. True or False   *Sivapithecus* belongs to the ramapithecid genera.

52. True or False   *Sivapithecus* is ancestral to modern orangutans.

53. True or **False**   Some people believe that *Dryopithecus* is still alive today and is known as Big Foot.

54. True or False   There is evidence that suggests that *Oreopithecus* may have been able to shuffle in an upright posture.

55. True or False   Kottak uses the term "hogopans" to refer to the ancestral population of late Miocene hominoids that eventually split three ways to produce chimps, gorillas, and humans.

CHAPTER 6

EARLY HOMINIDS

CHAPTER OUTLINE

I. Chronology of Hominid Evolution

    A. The Pleistocene (2 m.y.a. to 10,000 B.P.) is the epoch of human life.
        1. Lower Pleistocene (2 to 1 m.y.a.): *Australopithecus* and early *Homo*
        2. Middle Pleistocene (1 m.y.a. to 130,000 B.P.): Homo *erectus* and archaic *Homo sapiens*
        3. Upper Pleistocene (130,000 to 10,000 B.P.): modern *Homo sapiens*

    B. During the Pleistocene there were several ice ages, or glacials.
        1. The glacials were separated by warm periods called interglacials.
        2. The Würm was the last glacial (75,000 to 12,000 B.P.)

II. The Varied Australopithecines

    A. Introduction
        1. There are two major hominid genera: *Australopithecus* and *Homo*.
        2. However, in 1992 Berhane Asfaw, Gen Suwa, and Tim D. White discovered substantial remains considered to be from hominids ancestral to the australopithecines; these remains have been called *Ardipithecus ramidus* (thus establishing a third hominid genus) and dated a 4.4 m.y.a.
        3. A more recent (1995, by Maeve Leakey and Alan Walker) discovery has been named *Australopithecus anamensis* and been dated at 4.2 m.y.a.
        4. Kottak argues for the likelihood of *Ardipithecus ramidus* evolving directly into *A. anamensis*.

    B. The Five Species of *Australopithecus* (see table 6.2)
        1. *A. anamensis* (4.2 m.y.a.).
        2. *A. afarensis* (3.8? to 3.0 m.y.a.).
        3. *A. africanus* (3.0? to 2.5? m.y.a.).
        4. *A. robustus* (2.6 to 2.0 m.y.a.).
        5. *A. boisei* (2.6? to 1.2 m.y.a.).

    C. *Australopithecus afarensis*
        1. Earliest definite *afarensis* remains are dated at 3.8 m.y.a. and (with *Ardipithecus ramidus* and *A. anamensis*) strongly support a very recent (8 m.y.a. at the most) divergence from common ancestry with chimpanzees, because of the clearly apelike features found in all three species.
        2. Post-cranial remains, particularly the pelvis, leg, feet, and spinal entry into the skull, all indicate bipedalism, and are thus clearly hominid.
        3. *A. anamensis* remains (4.2 m.y.a.) also indicate bipedalism, and thus bipedalism predates *afarensis*.
        4. Cranial remains show that afarensis was still remarkably "apelike" is some respects, in that the brain capacity was only slightly larger than a modern chimpanzee's, and canines indicate considerable sexual dimorphism.
        5. Fossils of molars and jaws indicate the beginnings of adaptation to a coarse (seeds, lots of sand) savanna diet.
        6. *Afarensis* young probably depended on their parents for a relatively long time.

D. In the News: From 4 Legs to 2
1. The article discusses the various interpretations of new (in particular *Ardipithecus ramidus* and *A. anamensis*) data and addresses the question of how bipedalism evolved among hominids.
2. The most widely accepted theories stress the advantages provided by bipedalism in a habitat increasingly dominated by drier, savanna-like conditions.
   a. The ability to see over long grass.
   b. Bipedalism is more energy efficient and therefore advantageous in grassland, where resources are more dispersed than in forests.
   c. Bipedalism exposes less body surface area to solar radiation, which facilitates cooling and reduces moisture loss.

E. Gracile and Robust Australopithecines
1. There is some debate as to the nature of the distinction that existed between the gracile *A. africanus* and the robust *A. robustus*.
   a. One model has *africanus* and *robustus* as separate species, whose life-spans were at least partly contemporaneous.
   b. Another model has *africanus* and *robustus* as sequential, with *africanus* being ancestral to *robustus*.
   c. A third model has both groups as part of a single polytypic species, representing opposite extremes of variation within that species.
2. A similar debate obtains for *A. robustus* vs. *A. boisei*, but it is most likely that *boisei* developed from *robustus* into a separate, hyperrobust species, highly specialized (giant molars, sagittal crest, relatively small front teeth) for a savanna vegetation diet (cf., the discussion of the black skull, below).
3. Both *africanus* and *robustus* probably made tools from perishable material, which is not preserved in the fossil record.
4. There was only a slight increase in brain capacity throughout *Australopithecus*, but brain organization was basically human.

III. Australopithecines End, *Homo* Begins

A. *Homo* Begins
1. Contemporaneous (2 m.y.a.) sets of teeth, very different in size comprise the earliest evidence of a generic split: the larger set is attributed to *A. boisei*, the smaller to *H. habilis*, and the first species of the genus, *Homo*.
2. The distinctive early *Homo* trends are a rapid increase in brain size, increasingly elaborate tool making, and an increasing emphasis on hunting, but there remains considerable debate as to when and in what population these trends led to speciation (from an australopithecine to *Homo habilis*).
3. Johanson and White propose that *A. afarensis* effectively produced two populations, one of which evolved into the other australopithecines, the other evolving into *Homo habilis*.
4. The 1985 discovery of the black skull (dated 2.5 m.y.a.), apparently an early *A. robustus*, has made for more possible models of the divergence between *Homo* and *Australopithecus*.
   a. The black skull, so-called because of the coloration lent by the mineral content of the fossil itself, was a surprising mixture of australopithecine features, particularly given its relatively early date.
      i. An apelike jaw and relatively small brain (primitive features).
      ii. A sagittal crest on the top of the skull (previously associated with the relatively modern hyperrobusts, thus surprising to be found on a skull so old).
   b. One interpretation: on one branch of the split produced by the *afarensis* population there was another split, with one branch leading to the gracile species (*africanus*), the other branch leading to black skull's population (called *A. aethiopicus*), which in turn split to produce *robustus* on one branch and *boisei* on another.

      c. Another interpretation: on one branch of the split leading from *afarensis* there is a second split, with one branch leading to *robustus* and *africanus*, and the other leading to the black skull and, thence, to *boisei*.
    5. *H. Habilis* was transitional and co-existed with *A. boisei*.

B. *Homo erectus*
    1. Due to rapid changes in post cranial structure between 1.8 and 1.6 m.y.a., *Homo erectus* looks much more human than *Homo habilis* does, in both size and limb proportionality.
    2. *Homo erectus*' dentition differs from Australopithecines in that it is smaller overall, and the back teeth are smaller, proportionally, likely reflecting a move toward a diet including more meat.
    3. Tools made by *Homo erectus* were greatly refined over those associated with *Homo habilis*.
    4. Other *Homo erectus* features
        a. Smaller back teeth and larger front teeth, relative to the australopithecines.
        b. The *erectus* skull wall is thick, and was probably selected by increasing hunting activity, which required better protection against blows.
        c. Skeletal remains are robust, reflecting relatively massive musculature (for example, the ridge of spongy bone across the back of the skull supported large neck muscles).
        d. The cranial capacity of Homo erectus, on average, was 1000 cubic centimeters, as compared with australopithecine range of 450-550 cubic centimeters.

IV. Beyond the Classroom: Hydrodynamic Sorting of Avian Skeletal Remains

    A. Josh Trapani simulated the conditions of a stream channel to study how water currents sort bird bones.

    B. He was able to create a "sorting sequence" which can be used to determine if a particular assemblage of bird bones has been sorted by water.

V. Tools

    A. Tool-making as a Competitive Advantage
        1. The oldest known manufactured tools are dated at 2.6-2 m.y.a., were found in various parts of Africa, and are grouped under the name Oldowan pebble tools, given them by the Leakeys in 1931.
        2. There is some speculation that relatively advanced tool-making by *Homo* ancestors might have created the environment, which produced the generic, *Homo-Australopithecus* split.
        3. *H. habilis* may be as old as 2.4 m.y.a. which means it existed close to the time of the origin of stone tools.
        4. Kottak argues, based on circumstantial evidence, that it was likely that Australopithecines also made tools, if less well and of less permanent material than later *Homo* groups.
        5. 1.6-1.8 m.y.a. saw a dramatic increase in the hunting efficacy of *Homo* and during this period *A. boisei* may have been forced into an exclusively vegetarian niche, providing an example of competitive exclusion.
    B. *Homo erectus* remains indicate rapid cultural expansion.
        1. Cultural treatment of food began to select for smaller dentition.
        2. Cultural manipulation of the environment allowed *erectus* to exploit a wider array of environments.

LECTURE TOPICS

1. Students are often eager to know just what it is that started humans on a unique line. A lecture spent on the possible initial divergence usually sparks considerable interest. One possibility for this is a comparison of the various theories concerning the origin of bipedality (*e.g.*, "man the hunter" vs. "woman the gatherer" vs. "man the provisioner" vs. models based upon climate change, etc.). This works well because it gives you a chance to discuss what makes a good model, and how evidence supports (or does not) any particular model.

2. Why is tracing the exact line of human evolution so important? What difference does it make when *Homo habilis* first appeared? Presenting the importance of the distinctions, and their implications for alternative theories of social life, makes recall of the fossils easier.

3. The relationships among upright posture, the size of the birth canal, neotonous young, a large brain, the capacity for culture, and social complexity often difficult to understand. A lecture devoted to this topic is valuable.

4. The fact that the line of succession from Lucy to the other australopithecines is contested, as well as the various debates about Neandertals, frequently makes students wonder why they should believe any of the claims made about hominid evolution. Be explicit about the limits of implications that derive from debates about the exact sequence of hominid evolution. Let them know precisely what is being questioned and (perhaps more important) what is not.

5. If you have any available, casts of fossils representing the different stages of hominid evolution are an excellent aid in getting students to understand the distinctions being made and the trends that developed during the course of evolution. It also helps to compare the hominid skulls to those of other animals (particularly primate skulls).

SUGGESTED FILMS

In Search of Human Origins: 2--Surviving In Africa

video 60 min 1994 color
Famed paleoanthropologist Donald Johanson (the narrator and chief consultant on the film) argues against the model that hominid intelligence and culture resulted from hunting activity by scavenging his way across Africa. Originally produced for the PBS series, *Nova*. Boston: WGBH Educational Foundation.

The Making of Mankind: 1--In the Beginning

video 1981 55 min color
In this series, anthropologist Richard Leakey explores clues that lie buried in fossil records and interprets how humans developed over the millennia. Walking among the earliest-known fossil beds in Turkana, East Africa, Leakey explains our transformation from four-footed, tree-dwelling, vegetarian primates to upright, omnivorous tool makers. Series produced by the BBC, published New York: Ambrose Video Publishing.

The Making of Mankind: 2--One Small Step

video 1981 55 min color
Richard Leakey describes the discovery made by his mother Mary, of the oldest human footprints in the world. The 4-million-year-old footprints offer the earliest evidence of the shift from four legs to two. He also discusses the famous "Lucy" skeleton, Ethiopian fossils and the controversy over the nature of ancient upright creatures. Series produced by the BBC, published New York: Ambrose Video Publishing.

The Making of Mankind: 3--A Human Way of Life

video 1981 55 min color
Richard Leakey describes the work of archaeologists in piecing together a picture of human life 1.5 m.y.a. to explain subsistence modes and organization of society. This film is especially useful for its presentation in the treatment of archaeological evidence. Leakey also visits a 1980 Kung San camp on the Kalahari, raising aspects of comparability with early hominids, but also taking some pains to point out the dangers of direct comparisons of this kind. Series produced by the BBC, published New York: Ambrose Video Publishing.

Children of Eve

video 1987 57 min color
This films stresses the importance of the (at that time) new mitochondrial DNA evidence that strongly supported the "Out of Africa" model for the transition from *erectus* to *sapiens*. Unfortunately, it does not fully cover the controversial nature of that evidence. By John Groom. From the *Nova* series. New York: Coronet Film and Video.

MULTIPLE CHOICE QUESTIONS

1. When are hominids now thought to have differentiated from the ancestors shared with the African apes (Hogopans)?

    a. 20 to 15 m.y.a.
    b. 35 to 30 m.y.a.
    c. **no more than 10 m.y.a. and probably 8 to 5 m.y.a.**
    d. 1.8 to 1.2 m.y.a.
    e. 400,000 to 300,000 years ago

2. What is the name of the oldest hominid fossil yet discovered?

    a. ***Ardipithecus ramidus***
    b. *Australopithecus anamensis*
    c. *Australopithecus afarensis*
    d. *Australopithecus africanus*
    e. *Homo habilis.*

3. What was the Würm?

    a. The region of Kenya where the first australopithecine fossils were found.
    b. The time period during which the australopithecines lived.
    c. The time period when *Homo* first appeared.
    d. The earliest part of the Pleistocene.
    e. **The last glacial in the Pleistocene.**

4. Which of the following is *not* a location where australopithecine fossils have been found?

    a.   South Africa
    b.   Morocco
    c.   Kenya
    d.   Ethiopia
    e.   Tanzania

5. What is the most important difference between the australopithecines and the modern apes?

    a.   *Australopithecus afarensis* increased cranial capacity.
    b.   *Australopithecus afarensis* had better color vision than apes.
    c.   *Australopithecus afarensis* had a narrow chest while living apes have a barrel chest.
    d.   *Australopithecus afarensis* had lost its prehensile tail.
    e.   *Australopithecus afarensis* was bipedal.

6. How were Oldowan tools manufactured?

    a.   by chipping flakes off a core
    b.   by chipping blades off a prepared core
    c.   using deer antlers to pressure flake a core
    d.   by striking steel against a stone core
    e.   by grinding a coarser stone against a softer one

7. Who is credited with finding "Lucy?"

    a.   Dian Fossey
    b.   Timothy White
    c.   Meave Leaky
    d.   Jane Goodall
    e.   Donald Johanson

8. What is the trend regarding changes in the hominid birth canal?

    a.   It becomes longer
    b.   It becomes wider
    c.   It becomes less direct
    d.   It becomes narrower
    e.   all of the above

9. What do researchers know about *Ardipithecus ramidus*?

    a.   It was a knuckle-walking proto chimpanzee.
    b.   It was a bipedal hominid with strongly apelike characteristics.
    c.   It was really a male *Australopithecus anamensis*.
    d.   It is a Hogopan.
    e.   It is ancestral to Neandertals, but not to *Homo sapiens*.

10. How is bipedalism an adaptation to grassland environments?

    a. Bipedalism was an adaptation to heat stress caused by greater exposure to sunlight on the savanna.
    b. Bipedal posture increased the hominoids ability to spot food and predators, since they could see over the grass.
    c. Bipedalism freed the hands from locomotion allowing for increased tool use.
    d. Bipedalism is a more efficient means of traveling long distances.
    e. all of the above

11. Which of the following species was found in South Africa?

    a. *Australopithecus afarensis*
    b. *Australopithecus anamensis*
    c. *Australopithecus robustus*
    d. *Ardipithecus ramidus*
    e. *Australopithecus boisei*

12. What is the term for the bony crest found on top of the skulls of robust australopithecines?

    a. ischium
    b. foramen magnum
    c. sagittal crest
    d. masseter
    e. temporalis

13. Which of the following statements is true?

    a. *Australopithecus* was the most geographically widespread of all hominid genera.
    b. The australopithecines lived longer than any other hominid genus, so far.
    c. Australopithecines probably relied more on the use of tools than did the early *Homo*.
    d. *Australopithecus* had smaller molars than genus *Homo*.
    e. all of the above are true

14. What was the major hominid group that lived from about 4 million to 1 m.y.a?

    a. *Australopithecus*
    b. *Homo erectus*
    c. *Ramapithecu.*
    d. *Dryopithecus*
    e. *Homo sapiens*

15. What is the significance of the discovery of *Australopithecus afarensis*?

    a. It showed that humans evolved in Asia rather than in Africa.
    b. It is the oldest hominid fossil yet found in the New World.
    c. *Afarensis* remains are the oldest to be found in association with evidence of both stone tools and fire use.
    d. It was the first fossil evidence to confirm that bipedalism preceded the evolution of a human-like brain.
    e. It shows that the gracile australopithecines were not hominids after all.

16.   Which of the following most clearly identifies *Australopithecus afarensis* as a hominid?

      a.   pointed canines that project beyond the other teeth
      b.   molars larger than those of later *Australopithecus* remains
      c.   **postcranial (below the head) remains that confirm upright bipedalism**
      d.   curved or parabolic dental arcade
      e.   all of the above

17.   Which of the following statements about australopithecines is true?

      a.   They were the first hominids to migrate out of Africa.
      b.   They developed and used Acheulian stone tools.
      c.   They are well known for their cave paintings.
      d.   They have been found only in East Africa.
      e.   **none of the above are true**

18.   Which of the following statements about australopithecines is true

      a.   They were primarily carnivores.
      b.   They lived in the tropical forest.
      c.   **They were fully bipedal.**
      d.   They had a greater cranial capacity than did *Homo erectus.*
      e.   all of the above

19.   Of the following features belonging to *Australopithecus afarensis*, which is evidence of its adaptation to bipedal locomotion?

      a.   Its relatively large grinding surfaces on the back teeth, compared to earlier primate fossils.
      b.   Its cranial capacity.
      c.   **The position of its *foramen magnum* (point of entry of the spine) underneath the skull.**
      d.   The presence of crude stone tools.
      e.   all of the above

20.   What species made and used Oldowan tools?

      a.   *Homo erectus*
      b.   *Australopithecus afarensis*
      c.   *Australopithecus robustus*
      d.   *Australopithecus africanus*
      e.   **There are still many debates about who made the Oldowan tools**

21.   What aspect of the robust australopithecine fossils indicates a diet based on tough, gritty, fibrous grassland vegetation?

      a.   face
      b.   jaws
      c.   sagittal crest
      d.   molars
      e.   **all of the above**

22. Which of the following is *not* true about the australopithecines?

  a. They mainly ate savanna vegetation.
  b. They had greater sexual dimorphism than do modern humans.
  c. They are dated as having lived from 4.2 m.y.a. until 1.2 m.y.a., approximately.
  d. They started out (with *A. anamensis*) as knuckle walkers and ended up (with *A. boisei*) as bipedal.
  e. They lived in small bands.

23. The presence of very large molars and a sagittal crest on the top of the skull is evidence of

  a. a probable adaptation to a cold weather climate exhibited by Neandertals.
  b. the earliest hominid use of domesticated plants.
  c. the earliest australopithecine evidence of human-like brain organization.
  d. the dramatic increase in hunting activity starting with the earliest members of the genus *Homo*.
  e. hyperrobust australopithecines' adaptation to food sources dominated by hard-shelled seeds and grasses.

24. Which of the following has been suggested as the cause of the anatomical variety found in the australopithecine fossils?

  a. random genetic drift
  b. differences in natural selective forces operating in specific environments
  c. age and sex differences
  d. the long time span within which they existed
  e. all of the above

25. What are the anatomical features of australopithecines that reflect their savanna diet?

  a. massive posterior teeth
  b. sagittal crest
  c. large chewing muscles
  d. thick facial bones
  e. all of the above

26. Based on comparisons to chimpanzees, Kottak hypothesizes that the australopithecines probably _____.

  a. engaged in warfare
  b. made hunting camps
  c. nested in trees
  d. made simple tools of perishable materials
  e. all of the above

27. What do the brain casts of *Australopithecus africanus* indicate?

  a. Its brain was smaller than the brain of *Australopithecus afarensis*.
  b. Its brain was organized in a way that was essentially human.
  c. It had a brain organized in a way like the brains of prosimians.
  d. It probably became extinct as a result of warfare.
  e. It had a high incidence of epilepsy.

28. What do the skull, jaws, and teeth of the australopithecines indicate?

    a.   Warfare was commonplace, because we see much evidence of head trauma
    b.   They were carnivores
    c.   They used a fairly complex spoken language
    d.   **Their diet was vegetarian**
    e.   They were cannibals

29. Which hominid population is considered to be the *last* shared ancestor of both *Australopithecus boisei* and *Homo habilis*?

    a.   *Australopithecus africanus*
    b.   *Australopithecus robustus*
    c.   *Australopithecus anamensis*
    d.   *Ardipithecus ramidus*
    e.   ***Australopithecus afarensis***

30. Why did the "black skull" force a reappraisal of the early hominid fossil record?

    a.   **It has a relatively small brain capacity and apelike jaws, but a sagittal crest like the robust australopithecines, and is dated 300,000 years earlier than any other robust australopithecine.**
    b.   It is clearly an *Australopithecus afarensis* skull, but it is associated with a pre-bipedal skeleton.
    c.   It has very large molars for grinding, but in all other respects it is like Lucy, and came from roughly the same time.
    d.   It seems to be associated with tools far more advanced than anything previously credited to *Homo habilis* remains.
    e.   It is an *Australopithecus boisei* skull, but it was initially dated much later than any other *Australopithecus boisei* remains, suggesting that *Homo* came from *Australopithecus boisei*.

31. Which of the following is not considered to be a direct ancestor of *Homo sapiens*?

    a.   *Australopithecus afarensis*
    b.   *Homo habilis*
    c.   *Homo erectus*
    d.   ***Australopithecus boisei***
    e.   *Australopithecus africanus*

32. According to the recent assessment of the hominid tree provided in the Kottak text, which of the following statements is true?

    a.   The hyperrobust australopithecines (*Australopithecus boisei* and *Australopithecus robustus*) evolved directly into the Neandertals.
    b.   *Australopithecus boisei* is the most recent australopithecine thought to be a direct ancestor of the genus *Homo*.
    c.   *Australopithecus aethiopicus* (the "Black Skull") is ancestral to *Australopithecus Australopithecus africanus*.
    d.   ***Afarensis* is the most recent australopithecine thought to be a direct ancestor of the genus *Homo*.**
    e.   *Ardipithecus ramidus* established a separate hominid line which eventually evolved into *Homo habilis*.

33. Which of the following is *not* a trend in early hominid evolution?

   a. An emphasis of back teeth over front teeth
   b. The development of bipedal locomotion
   c. A decrease in cranial capacity
   d. A greater reliance on tools
   e. An elaboration of extrasomatic means of adaptation

34. Worldwide, what were the Middle and Upper Pleistocene characterized by?

   a. successive glacial advances and retreats
   b. a climate much warmer than at present
   c. widespread tropical rain forests
   d. massive extinctions of hominid populations
   e. all of the above

35. What does the extinction of the australopithecines suggest?

   a. They were in a short-lived, transitional stage between apes and humans.
   b. They were eventually unsuccessful in competing for available resources with early populations of *Homo*.
   c. They had no social organization.
   d. They are relatively unimportant to the study of human evolution.
   e. all of the above

36. Which of the following statements about the "black skull" is true?

   a. It belongs to a very early hyperrobust australopithecine.
   b. It dates at about 2.5 m.y.a. making it a contemporary of gracile australopithecines.
   c. It combines relatively small overall size with large chewing dentition.
   d. It has a sagittal crest.
   e. all of the above

37. When did the ancestors of *Homo* split off and become reproductively isolated from the later australopithecines?

   a. between 5 and 4 m.y.a.
   b. between 4 and 3 m.y.a.
   c. between 3 and 2 m.y.a.
   d. between 2 and 1 m.y.a.
   e. *Homo* never became reproductively isolated from the later australopithecines.

38. *Homo habilis* trends are marked by _____.

   a. a gradual shift away from predation to vegetarianism
   b. a relatively rapid expansion of cranial capacity
   c. a shift from knuckle walking to full bipedalism
   d. a move from an arboreal to a savanna environment
   e. all of the above

39. Which of the following is a difference between *Homo erectus* and the australopithecines?

   a.   *Homo erectus* exhibited full bipedalism.
   b.   The australopithecines' teeth suggest they ate a lot more meat.
   c.   *Homo erectus'* cranial capacity was much larger.
   d.   *Homo erectus* had the largest sagittal crest of any hominid.
   e.   *Homo erectus'* mortuary practices are less elaborate.

40. *Homo erectus* remains _____.

   a.   indicate increasing hunting proficiency
   b.   show increasing reliance on cultural adaptation
   c.   include stone tools
   d.   shows a thickening of the skull wall, probably as an adaptation to game hunting
   e.   all of the above

ESSAY QUESTIONS

41. Discuss the place of *Ardipithecus ramidus* and *Australopithecus anamensis* in hominid evolution.

42. If several physically different but clearly hominid fossils are found at the same site, deposited in a single stratum, what kinds of conclusions might anthropologists reach about the interrelationships between the hominids?

43. Identify and discuss the major features of australopithecine dentition. What do these teeth tell us about the australopithecine mode of adaptation?

44. Early humans probably lived in social groups on the savanna because they, like wolves and dogs, were primarily hunting carnivores and, therefore, pack animals. This is the source of contemporary human aggression and warfare. Discuss.

45. What are the major difficulties that arise in trying to interpret the hominid fossil record? How do these difficulties lead to conflicting interpretations of human evolution?

46. What are some advantages and disadvantages of bipedalism?

47. What selective pressures operated on the front teeth of the australopithecines, and what on their back teeth?

48. What are the most significant features of the split between the australopithecines and *Homo*? How does environmental specialization figure into the equation? What about cultural adaptation?

49. How might the change in climate, which caused a major expansion of savanna environments at the expense of woodlands, have selected for bipedalism among the early hominid species?

50. Any of the above multiple choice questions may be converted to an essay question by requiring students to choose the correct answer and justify their selection in essay form. Such justifications should include explanations as to why the chosen answer is correct and why those responses not chosen are incorrect.

TRUE OR FALSE QUESTIONS

51. True or False — The expansion of the birth canal is a trend in hominid evolution.

52. True or **False** — In apes, the thigh bone angles into the hip, permitting the space between the knees to be narrower than the pelvis.

53. True or **False** — Although the teeth suggest a vegetarian diet, the skulls of the australopithecines indicate a diet based on meat.

54. True or False — The expansion of brain size is a trend in hominid evolution.

55. True or **False** — The robust australopithecines had significantly larger chest cavities.

56. True or **False** — The footprints at the site of Laetoli in northern Tanzania were made by *Australopithecus africanus*.

57. True or False — The cranial features of *Australopithecus afarensis* were adapted to powerful chewing, grinding, and crushing.

58. True or **False** — Sexual dimorphism is more pronounce in modern *Homo sapiens* than in the australopithecines.

59. True or **False** — The dentition of *Australopithecus afarensis* exhibits no similarities to the dentition of modern chimpanzees.

60. True or False — One of the theories regarding why bipedalism evolved in primates asserts that upright two-legged posture enabled those primates to move more efficiently across open grasslands while looking out over the grass for food and predators.

61. True or **False** — Some researchers have argued that bipedalism evolved in response to global cooling, and that upright posture was more efficient at conserving heat, and as a result kept those primates warmer.

62. True or **False** — Robust australopithecines have been found only in east Africa.

63. True or False — A polytypic species is one in which there is a lot of phenotypic variation.

64. True or **False** — The oldest known stone tools date to roughly 1 million years ago.

65. True or **False** — The genus *Homo* did not appear until after all of the Australopithecines had died off.

66. True or False — Most paleoanthropologists argue that the "black skull" is a hyperrobust australopithecine.

67. True or False — Compared to the australopithecines, early *Homo* had smaller teeth and a larger cranial capacity.

68. True or False — Oldowan tools were made by striking flakes off the sides of cobbles.

69. True or **False** — The earliest known stone tools belong to the Acheulian tradition.

70. True or False — After 1 m.y.a. *H. erectus* was the only one hominid species still alive.

CHAPTER 7

MODERN HUMANS

CHAPTER OUTLINE

I. Early *Homo*

    A. Finds in east Africa indicate the *Homo habilis* was not very different from the australopithecines in terms of body size and shape.

    B. The earliest *Homo erectus* remains indicate rapid biological change.
       1. The fossil record for the transition from *H. habilis* to *H. erectus* supports the punctuated equilibrium model of evolution.
       2. *H. erectus* was considerably taller and had a larger brain than *H. habilis*.

II. Gradual and Rapid Change

    A. Gradualism is a model of evolution proposing that most species were produced by the gradual, steady effects of natural selection operating on whole populations.

    B. Punctuated equilibrium is a model proposing that most species were produced by genetic drift, occurring in relatively quick leaps (of 50,000 years, or so) interspersing long periods of relative stasis (of several million years).

    C. Transitional fossils, such as those documenting the development of heavy grinding structures among the australopithecines, are thought to support gradualism.

    D. An absence of transitional fossils, despite the presence of sequentially related species, is used as evidence supporting punctuated equilibrium.

    E. The early *Homo* fossil sequence displays rapid change and therefore supports punctuated equilibrium.
       1. One possible key to explanation such rapid change may lie in *H. erectus*' greater reliance on cultural means of adaptation.
       2. With the emergence of *H. erectus* there is a rapid proliferation in the number and diversity of tools being made.
       3. Cultural treatment of food began to select for smaller dentition.
       4. Cultural manipulation of the environment allowed *erectus* to exploit a wider array of environments.

III. Out of Africa

    A. Paleolithic Tools
       1. Three Paleolithic Divisions
          a. Lower Paleolithic (*Homo erectus*).
          b. Middle Paleolithic (archaic *Homo sapiens*, including Neandertals).
          c. Upper Paleolithic (*Homo sapiens sapiens*, up to 15,000 years ago).
       2. Technique Differentiation
          a. Paleolithic stone tool-making was marked by advancing refinement of technique, recognizable groupings of which are called tool-making traditions.
          b. A basic distinction is between *core* and *flake* tools.
          c. The primary tradition of the Lower Paleolithic is the Acheulian.

B. Adaptive Strategies of *Homo erectus*
  1. Culture/Biology Synergy
     a. Acheulian tools and essentially modern bipedalism aided hunting.
     b. *H. erectus'* average brain size (1000 cc) is double that of the australopithecines.
     c. Larger skulls select for neotony, because of the constraints bipedalism puts on the size of the birth canal.
     d. Neotony causes a long dependency period, which allows for the emphasis on cultural transmission of information.
     e. Dependent children create an environment which increasingly selects for interdependent social groups.
  2 Hunting and Gathering
     a. *H. erectus'* bipedalism, the--relative to the australopithecines--de-emphasis on chewing (smaller molars), and the emphasis on the front teeth (possibly for eating flesh) all suggest hunting and gathering as its primary adaptive strategy.
     b. The skeletal evidence for hunting and gathering is supported by site remains, such as those found at Terra Amata (approximately 300,000 years ago).
  3. Language
     a. No evidence clearly supporting *H. erectus'* use of language exists.
     b. Kottak argues that Acheulian tools and apparent, complex hunting techniques, which *do* exist in the fossil record, support the possibility of rudimentary speech.

C. The Evolution and Expansion of *Homo erectus*
  1. Major *H. erectus* Sites
     a. East, West Turkana, Kenya, dated 1.6 m.y.a. (Leakey).
     b. Upper Bed II, Olduvai, dated 1 m.y.a.
     c. Trinil, Java, Indonesia, dated approximately 700,000 years ago (Dubois).
     d. Zhoukoudian, China (a.k.a. "Peking Man") is a massive site, dated 500,000-350,000 years ago.
     e. Europe has non-skeletal remains dating 700,000 years ago, and skeletal remains dated at 500,000.
  2. The vast environmental differences encompassed by the *H. erectus* sites, and the associated lack of physical variation attest to the success of culture as an adaptive strategy.

IV. Archaic *Homo sapiens*

  A. It is likely that the Archaic *Homo sapiens* population was most concentrated in tropical regions, but thus far more work has been done in Europe.

  B. Archaic *Homo sapiens* (300,000-35,000 B.P.) includes *Homo sapiens neandertalensis* (Neandertals, 130,000-35,000 years ago).

  C. The range of *Homo sapiens* was even more extensive than that of *Homo erectus*.

V. The Neandertals

  A. Cold-Adapted Neandertals
     1. The combination of relatively large torso and short limbs, along with large, broad nasal passages are evidence of adaptation to a cold climate.
     2. Neandertal front teeth were extremely large and the remains of these show evidence of wear.
     3. The face, particularly the large brow ridge, was designed to support considerable stress on the front teeth (possibly the result of chewing animal hides).
     4. Neandertal cranial capacity was well within (possibly exceeding) the average for *H. sapiens* (1350 cc.).

B. Later Neandertal remains show a decrease in the robustness of the front teeth and face, suggesting the use of tools (Mousterian) replaced teeth, and suggesting selection against the larger teeth (possibly due to infections in crowded jaws).

C. Neandertals in Relation to Anatomically Modern Humans
   1. Two basic models attempt to answer the Debate about Neandertals' Place in *Homo sapiens sapiens* Ancestry.
      a. Neandertals were fully *Homo sapiens*, their differences constituting a minor sub-specific variation that disappeared as Neandertals were assimilated into the broader *H. sapiens* population.
      b. "Replacement Hypothesis": Neandertals were the product of a split within the *H. erectus* population, wherein one side moved into northern Europe and became Neandertals, and the other side evolved into *Homo sapiens sapiens* (**Anatomically Modern Humans--or AMHs**) in the Middle East, Africa, or Asia, and then drove Neandertals to extinction upon moving into their territories.
   2. Neandertals differed from AMHs in their comparatively rugged skeletons and faces, huge front teeth, larger cranial capacity, and greater sexual dimorphism.
   3. However, these differences were exaggerated on the basis of a misinterpretation of the La Chapelle-aux-Saints find, which turned out to be the skeleton of an old Neandertal man who had suffered from osteoarthritis.
   4. Current interpretations of the fossil evidence and dating seem to support the replacement hypothesis.

D. About Eve
   1. Mitochondrial DNA (mtDNA)
      a. Only the mother contributes mtDNA to an offspring, and this occurs through cloning, thus only mutation may change the pattern of mtDNA from one generation to the next.
      b. Researchers from Berkeley generated a computerized model of *Homo* evolution, based upon the average rate of mutation in known samples of mtDNA.
      c. The model describes an evolutionary tree, at the base of which is a single female, called "Eve," in sub-Saharan Africa 200,000 B.P., from whom all modern humans have descended.
   2. Evidence Contradicting the "Eve" Hypothesis
      a. Other researchers have identified traits associated with particular geographic ranges that begin before "Eve" and occur continuously in those places across the change from *H. erectus* to *H. sapiens*.
      b. The continuity of these traits contradicts the notion that "Eve-based" populations could have moved in and replaced the *H. erectus* populations in which the traits originated.
      c. This counter-evidence suggests a model wherein many different *H. erectus* populations evolved into *H. sapiens* simultaneously, while gene flow ensured that the populations remained conspecific.

E. Recent DNA Evidence
   1. Recently, researchers have been able to extract Neandertal DNA and compare it to DNA from modern humans.
   2. The research suggests that Neandertals and AMHs were distinct groups that split apart around 600,000 years ago.
   3. This research also indicates that Neandertals died out without leaving a genetic legacy with the AMH populations that eventually displaced them in western Europe.

VI. Advances in Technology

A. Tool-making technology shifted from flaking (Mousterian) to the making of blades, which is much more efficient and allows for greater specialization and diversity.

B. An increase the distribution and number of technological remains is evidence of an overall increase in *Homo*'s population.

C. Tool Diversity
   1. Different tool shapes, in connection with other site remains, can be associated with specific tasks, thus giving evidence as to how ancient human populations fit in their ecological niches.
   2. Some features of tools are not so much related to function as they are to traditions specific to a population.

VII. Glacial Retreat

A. During the glacial period, large game hunting constituted a major feature in the adaptive strategies of most *Homo* populations.

B. Changes Due to Glacial Retreat.
   1. The continental shelf was covered with water, creating a zone for new marine life that was accessible to humans.
   2. Particularly in northern regions, biodiversity increased overall, as the plains of southwestern Europe were replaced by forests.
   3. Broad-spectrum revolution: as a result of the post-glacial changes, human populations' means of exploiting their environments became correspondingly more diverse, setting the stage for food production.

VIII. Cave Art.

A. Most cave paintings are concentrated in southwestern France and northern Spain.

B. Various magical or ritual functions have been proposed as the reason for the cave paintings: ceremonies of increase, improved hunting, rites of passage.

C. In the News: Prehistoric Art Treasure is Found in French Cave.
   1. In December, 1994, near the French village of Vallon-Pont-d'Arc, more than 300 images of animals and human hands painted during the Upper Paleolithic (about 20,000 years ago) were discovered.
   2. The scale of the site is on par with other major examples of Paleolithic art, such as Lascaux (France) and Altamira (Spain).
   3. Researchers are hopeful that the new discovery will provide insight into the evolution of human symbolism.
   4. Of particular interest is the fact that the depictions included non-game animals (e.g., bears, rhinos, an owl, a hyena, and a panther), unlike the massive Lascaux site.
   5. One prevailing hypothesis is that such caves served not as habitats, being too dark, but as ritual sites.

IX. The Mesolithic.

A. The Mesolithic followed the Upper Paleolithic, and is also marked by the trends of diversification called the broad-spectrum revolution.

B. Physical Evidence.
   1. Most known Mesolithic remains are the result of archaeological research done in Europe.
   2. Microliths are small stone tools that are typical of Mesolithic technology: fishhooks, harpoon tips, and dart tips.
   3. The technology reflects the shift from a focus on herd game hunting (since these animals had moved north with glacial retreat) to more varied and specialized activities.

C. Mesolithic saw the domestication of the dog, the development of food preservation techniques, the spread of the bow and arrow, the development of wood and leather working, and actual carpentry.

D. Gathering.
1. "Broad-spectrum" changes caused gathering, rather than hunting, to become the mainstay of human economies.
2. Based on what we know from comparisons of modern hunting-based societies with hunter-gatherer societies, the role of women in Mesolithic subsistence economies probably increased as gathering became more important.

X. Beyond the Classroom: Meat and Marrow: Paleolithic Butchering at Verberie

A. Kelsey Foster studied the faunal assemblage from the site of Verberie to better understand the butchering patterns used by the Paleolithic hunters at the site.

B. His analysis suggests that the butchering that was done at the site was primarily directed at extracting marrow and that the meat was extracted later, at a different site.

LECTURE TOPICS

1. This chapter provides a good opportunity to discuss "what is culture". Different definitions of culture can be evaluated based on their relevance to the rise of culture. What aspect of cultural behavior develop first? When do we have clear evidence for fully developed culture?

2. The debate about the origins of *Homo sapiens* from *Homo erectus* is still quite active. In outlining the basic positions, (Out of Africa/Mitochondrial Eve *vs.* Multiregional Evolution) you can not only clarify the debate for the students, but also give them a case study on how explanatory models progress with the arrival of new evidence.

3. Discuss the role that the environment plays in the spread of *Homo*. Discuss both biological and cultural forms of adaptation. To what degree can the environment be used to explain patterns of behavior? Is this possible without invoking environmental determinism? What biological changes were necessary to allow for the cultural adaptations?

SUGGESTED FILMS

In Search of Human Origins: 3--The Creative Revolution

video 1994 60 min color
Originally part of the series produced for *Nova* on PBS. Paleoanthropologist and narrator Donald Johanson examines evidence and theories pertaining to the archaeology of early humans. He discusses art, mortuary remains, evidence of trade and travel, and the transition to anatomically modern humans. Boston: WGBH Educational Foundation.

Sons of the Moon

video 25 min 1984 color
Traces evidence on several continents that many ancient civilizations were ardent sky watchers, with the lunar month as a basic time unit. Examines how this finds expression today among the Ngas of central Nigeria. A chanted version of their history and rituals examines the metaphors they act out in their ceremonies. An accompanying handbook explains the symbolism.

The Caves of Altamira

26 min color
The 20,000-year-old caves of Altamira are among the greatest and the least known of the monuments of man's pre-history. Closed to visitors to prevent disintegration through pollution, the caves are known only through a replica located in the Archaeological Museum in Madrid. This tour of Altamira shows the cave paintings in their extraordinary power as they depict the daily life of Magdalenian man seeking to bend animal life to his will while himself at the mercy of magical powers he sought to placate. The camera is able to clarify what the naked eye cannot--the artistic relationship between the caves themselves and the art with which these proto-Spaniards decorated them. From Films for the Humanities & Sciences

The Pre-History of Spain

23 min color
The Hall of Prehistory at Madrid's National Archaeological Museum is the site for this voyage to Spain before recorded history. The program sets the natural scene in which Stone Age man lived, it shows us the fossil remains of the animals represented on the walls of the Altamira Caves and the tools with which they were hunted. It documents the development of agriculture in the Iberian peninsula; shows the fascinating Albunol Bat Cave in Granada and its trove of artifacts--tools, ceramics, skeletal remains; and traces the various cultural stages of Spain through metallurgical and ceramic finds of increasing complexity and sophistication. The program concludes with the arrival of a new Indo-European people, with different customs and styles; together with the cultures of Southwestern Spain, they would provide the framework for the development of historic Spain. From Films for the Humanities & Sciences

Prehistoric Monuments of Europe

43 min color
This program documents some of the most imposing testimonials to human history in Europe: the avenues of megaliths at Carnac in Brittany, which are presumed to have been a celestial observatory; nearby, the mysterious royal tomb at Gavrinis with its giant fingerprints, and the temple beneath the sea on the isle of Er-Lanic; in Corsica, the oldest sculptures in Europe; the nuraghens in Sardinia, once thought to be giant fortifications but now believed to be shrines of sun worshippers and an ingenious system of communication; and the oldest European temples as well as underground labyrinths for the dead, located on the islands of Malta and Gozo. From Films for the Humanities & Sciences

The Making of Mankind: 4--Beyond Africa

video 1981 55 min color
At the famous site of Zhoukoudian in China, Richard Leakey tells the story of Peking man, who used fire for heat and light and possibly for cooking. He also discusses the increasing intelligence of early humans and explains how and why humans began to speak.

The Making of Mankind: 5-A New Era

video 1981 52 min color
Richard Leakey details the emergence of *Homo sapiens*, and explains that although Neandertal man is usually thought of as brutish and of low intelligence, the cave art at Lascaux suggests otherwise.

MULTIPLE-CHOICE QUESTIONS

1. What is punctuated equilibrium?

   a. The ecological conditions which selected for bipedalism among hominids.
   b. A variant of catastrophism, related to scientific creationism.
   c. The theory upon which evolutionism is historically based.
   d. The idea that evolution occurs mainly through short periods of quick change interspersed by longer periods of relative stability.
   e. The idea, as conceived by Darwin, that evolution proceeds in a gradual, orderly fashion.

2. Which of the following factors led to an environment that selected for higher intelligence among *Homo erectus* populations?

   a. neotony (immature birth)
   d. bipedalism
   b. greater reliance on hunting
   c. more complex social environment
   e. all of the above

3. What is the name of the time period that begins with the appearance of Oldowan pebble tools and lasted until about 15,000 years ago?

   a. Oldowan
   b. Acheulian
   c. Chalcolithic
   d. Paleolithic
   e. Neolithic

4. What model of evolutionary change does the sharp contrast between *Homo habilis* and *Homo erectus* support?

   a. gradualism
   b. creationism
   c. uniformitarianism
   d. punctuated equilibrium
   e. broad-spectrum revolution

5. The spread of *Homo erectus* from tropical and subtropical climates into temperate zones (such as Beijing, China) was probably facilitated by which of the following?

   a. The harnessing of fire.
   b. Living in rock shelters and caves.
   c. The use of animal skins as clothing.
   d. Increasingly efficient hunting methods.
   e. all of the above

6. What kind of change does the hominid fossil record exemplify?

   a. gradualism
   b. punctuated equilibrium
   c. creationism
   d. both a and b
   e. all of the above

7. What does the campsite excavated at Terra Amata indicate?

   a. Neandertals were not fully human.
   b. *Homo habilis* had language.
   c. early hominids cultivated plants.
   d. *Homo erectus* led an essentially human lifestyle.
   e. Cro Magnons and *Homo erectus* engaged in warfare.

8. Which of the following is *not* associated with *Homo erectus*?

   a. more sophisticated tool making
   b. massive ridge over the eyebrows
   c. massive molars
   d. use of fire
   e. all of the above are associated with *Homo erectus*

9. Which of the following statements describes a difference between Oldowan and Acheulian tools?

   a. Oldowan tools show an increase in size and a focus on hunting.
   b. Acheulian tools constitute a move away from wood toward more plastic media, such as clay.
   c. Acheulian tools are made from more elaborately worked cores and refined flakes.
   d. Acheulian tools show increasingly elaborate representations of the human form on the non-functional surfaces.
   e. all of the above

10. What species is associated with the site of Zhoukoudian?

   a. *Homo habilis*
   b. *Homo erectus*
   c. archaic *Homo sapiens*
   d. Neandertals
   e. *Homo sapiens sapiens*

11. Which of the following sites is *not* included in the probable *Homo erectus* range?

   a. Java
   b. China
   c. South Africa
   d. Alaska
   e. Palestine

12. Which of the following is a trend in hominid evolution since the australopithecines?

   a. Sexual dimorphism has disappeared.
   b. Molar size has decreased.
   c. Population numbers have remained stable.
   d. Bipedalism has appeared.
   e. The geographic range of the hominids has decreased.

13.   Which of the following traits contributed to the increasing adaptability of *Homo erectus*?

    a.   A varied tool kit that facilitated cooperative hunting.
    b.   An essentially modern postcranial skeleton, permitting long-distance stalking and endurance during a hunt.
    c.   An average brain size that was double that of the australopithecines.
    d.   A period of childhood dependency that exceeded that of australopithecines.
    e.   all of the above

14.   Why is there such a high number of European archaic *Homo sapiens* finds?

    a.   *Homo sapiens* evolved in France.
    b.   The long history of Paleolithic archaeology in Europe.
    c.   Archaic *Homo sapiens* were driven there by the more aggressive Cro Magnons.
    d.   The stratigraphic disturbances by caused glaciers.
    e.   all of the above

15.   The conclusion that *Homo erectus* relied on hunting for subsistence was suggested by which of the following lines of evidence?

    a.   Fossil evidence showing reduction of cheek and jaw size.
    b.   Animal bones found in H. erectus.
    c.   The presence of hearths, indicating that H. erectus used fire to cook meat and trap game.
    d.   The presence of increasingly complex stone tool kits campsites.
    e.   all of the above

16.   How does Kottak classify Neandertals?

    a.   He places them in the Qafzeh/Skhul mosaic.
    b.   He groups them with the hyperrobust australopithecines.
    c.   He classifies them as Archaic *Homo sapiens*.
    d.   He groups them with Anatomically Modern Humans.
    e.   He places them in the group of fossils known as "Peking Man".

17.   Where have *Homo erectus* fossils *never* been found?

    a.   China.
    b.   Brazil.
    c.   France.
    d.   Indonesia.
    e.   Hungary.

18.   What species is associated with the cave paintings in western Europe?

    a.   *Homo habilis*
    b.   *Homo erectus*
    c.   archaic *Homo sapiens*
    d.   Neandertals
    e.   *Homo sapiens sapiens*

19.   The recent discovery in France of a very large collection of cave paintings has led researchers to hypothesize that

   a.   such paintings were used in mate selection, as suggested by the high number of "Venus figurines".
   b.   such a high concentration of paintings clearly suggests the caves were used as year-round living sites.
   c.   such paintings were used in rites of passage as a test of courage (fire-eating).
   d.   the paintings were forged by French intellectuals to lure business away from EuroDisney.
   e.   such sites were not homes, but probably had a specific religious function.

20.   *Homo erectus* is generally associated with which of the following technologies?

   a.   Neolithic
   b.   Oldowan
   c.   Mousterian
   d.   Acheulian
   e.   Upper Paleolithic

21.   Which of the following theories argues that the entire *Homo erectus* population gradually evolved into *Homo sapiens*?

   a.   Mousterian conversion
   b.   "out of Africa"
   c.   mitochondrial "Eve"
   d.   multiregional evolution
   e.   the Piltdown hoax

22.   Taken together, Neandertal traits exhibit a trend toward adaptation to

   a.   vegetarianism.
   b.   lack of *full* human speech.
   c.   extreme, dry heat.
   d.   cold.
   e.   the interglacial environment.

23.   What is the name of the stone tool tradition associated with Neandertals?

   a.   Oldowan
   b.   Acheulian
   c.   Mousterian
   d.   blades
   e.   microliths

24.   Which of the following traits does *not* characterize a Neandertal skull?

   a.   a broad face
   b.   a large brow ridge
   c.   huge front teeth
   d.   huge molars
   e.   An average cranial capacity larger than that of modern humans.

25. Which of the following is *not* associated with Neandertals?

    a. **cave paintings**
    b. Mousterian tools
    c. stocky physique
    d. hunting
    e. all of the above are associated with Neandertals

26. Which of the following traits aided Neandertals in adapting to bitterly cold environments?

    a. a stocky anatomy
    b. facial projection
    c. wearing clothes probably made from animal skins
    d. massive nasal cavities and brow ridges
    e. **all of the above**

27. What does the modern debate about Neandertals' relation to anatomically modern humans focus on?

    a. Whether Neandertals were human or a *H. erectus* hybrid.
    b. **Whether Neandertals are directly in anatomically modern humans evolutionary line, or constitute an extinct offshoot.**
    c. Whether Neandertals are the isolated ancestors of the Caucasian race, or more general ancestors.
    d. Whether Neandertals are the founders of the Native American population.
    e. none of the above

28. Which of the following models suggests that European Neandertals were replaced by a wave of Anatomically Modern Humans?

    a. broad-spectrum revolution
    b. phyletic transformation
    c. Mousterian conversion
    d. multiregional evolution
    e. **out of Africa**

29. What does the *gradual transition* from Mousterian to Upper Paleolithic tools suggest?

    a. **The transition from Neandertals to modern humans may also have been gradual.**
    b. Neandertals were gradually replaced by *Homo erectus* in Europe.
    c. there really is no difference between Mousterian and Upper Paleolithic tools.
    d. Neandertals were quickly wiped out by modern humans as they radiated into Europe.
    e. Neandertals gradually adapted to invasions of modern humans by developing a new technology.

30. According the mtDNA analyses, when did the first modern humans leave Africa?

    a. 2 m.y.a.
    b. 1 m.y.a.
    c. 735,000 years ago
    d. 535,000 years ago
    e. **135,000 years ago**

31. What species is associated with the broad-spectrum revolution?

    a. robust *australopithecines*
    b. Neandertals
    c. *Homo sapiens sapiens*
    d. archaic *Homo sapiens*
    e. *Homo erectus*

32. Which of the following characterizes the Upper Paleolithic?

    a. hand axes
    b. pebble tools
    c. metallurgy
    d. plant domestication
    e. blade tools

33. What kind of stone tool tradition is the Mousterian?

    a. river cobbles
    b. hand-axes
    c. flakes
    d. blades
    e. microliths

34. The geographic expansion of the hominid range

    a. reflects the evolutionary success of increasing reliance on tools, language, and culture.
    b. is limited to Europe and Africa prior to the *Homo sapiens* stage of human evolution.
    c. was nearly completed when Neandertal foragers entered the New World.
    d. usually involved large migrations over long distances, triggered by natural disasters like flood and drought.
    e. all of the above

35. What was the broad-spectrum revolution?

    a. The time when the greatest diversity of hominids lived in Africa.
    b. The period when glacial retreats led to the exploitation of a greater variety of food sources and hunting-gathering techniques.
    c. The period when *Homo sapiens sapiens* populations overtook Neandertal caves and began to draw animal figures.
    d. When primates developed the ability to see more than just the primary colors and could therefore distinguish different types of leaves.
    e. none of the above

36. Why was broad-spectrum revolution was a significant event in human evolution?

    a. It led to the extinction of the Neandertals, who had survived by eating big game animals.
    b. It provided new environmental circumstances that made important socio-cultural adaptations like the development plant cultivation more likely.
    c. It provided the environmental circumstances that selected for the evolution of "Mitochondrial Eve".
    d. It consists of a massive fluorescence of colored cave paintings beginning 70,000 B.P., which suggests the evolution of color vision and a truly human-style brain organization.
    e. all of the above

37. Which of the following is a general trend in hominid evolution?

    a. an increase in cranial capacity
    b. an increase in the quantity and quality of tools
    c. population growth
    d. both a and b
    e. all of the above

38. Analysis of large samples of human mitochondrial DNA has led some researchers to hypothesize that

    a. all modern humans are descended from Neandertals from Western Europe.
    b. all current human mitochondrial DNA comes from one woman who lived in Africa 200,000 years ago.
    c. all modern humans are descended directly from chimpanzees and gorillas, but not orangutans.
    d. all modern humans are not descended from robust australopithecines.
    e. all *Homo erectus* populations around the world eventually evolved into populations of *Homo sapiens*.

39. What researcher developed the idea of the broad-spectrum revolution?

    a. Meave Leakey
    b. Jane Goodall
    c. Milford Wolpoff
    d. Kent Flannery
    e. Timothy White

40. What kinds of tools characterize the Mesolithic?

    a. core choppers
    b. hand-axes
    c. large flaked tools
    d. microliths
    e. early pottery

41. Which of the following has been suggested as an explanation for why ancient humans made cave paintings?

    a. The paintings were fertility magic, intended to increase the number of game animals.
    b. The paintings were magical representations of successful hunts.
    c. The paintings were historical representations.
    d. The paintings were associated with rites of passage.
    e. all of the above

42. Which was the *first* hominid to have a range that extended beyond Africa?

    a. *Homo erectus*
    b. *Australopithecus afarensis*
    c. *Homo sapiens*
    d. *Australopithecus africanus*
    e. *Homo sapiens neandertalensis*

88

ESSAY QUESTIONS

43. Summarize the fossil evidence for the evolution of *Homo erectus* out of australopithecine ancestors.

44. Discuss the major anatomical differences between the australopithecines and *Homo erectus*.

45. Drawing on biological and cultural evidence, discuss the major similarities and differences in the sociocultural adaptive means employed by *Australopithecus* and *Homo erectus*.

46. Discuss the Neandertals-their form, dating, and geographic distributions. Review and evaluate the various positions that have been taken in interpreting the relationship between Neandertals and *Homo sapiens sapiens*.

47. Evaluate different explanations that have been offered for Upper Paleolithic cave paintings. What evidence prompts you to accept one explanation or type of explanation over another? Discuss.

48. Identify and discuss the significance-in terms of environmental, economic, and social changes of the broad-spectrum revolution in southwestern Europe.

49. Outline the relationship between tool types and the major stages of human evolution: *Australopithecus, Homo erectus, Homo sapiens neandertalensis,* and *Homo sapiens sapiens* (through the Mesolithic).

50. How do biological changes in *Homo erectus* reflect new cultural adaptive strategies?

51. What are the main morphological differences between Neandertals and moderns? How have these differences been interpreted?

52. What is the evidence for increasing dependence on culture during hominid evolution?

53. What is meant by "the Eve Hypothesis?" What is the evidence supporting this hypothesis? What is the evidence contradicting this hypothesis? Is there an alternative hypothesis that takes both sides into account?

54. Are Neandertals in anatomically modern humans' direct line of descent? What evidence points to a "yes" answer (and why)? What evidence points to a "no" answer (and why)?

55. Any of the above multiple choice questions may be converted to an essay question by requiring students to choose the correct answer and justify their selection in essay form. Such justifications should include explanations as to why the chosen answer is correct and why those responses not chosen are incorrect.

56. Consider the two leading hypotheses concerning the evolutionary course from *Homo erectus* to *Homo sapiens* (i.e., Out of Africa vs. Multiregional Evolution) and answer the following question. How does either of these hypotheses support or refute the concept of "biological race" as this is described in Chapter 4 of this book?

57. What does ancient art, such as the cave paintings at Vallon-Pont d'Arc, tell us about the nature of the hominids that produced it? Does this sort of evidence support the notion that the brains of the painters were more primitive than ours, or that they were essentially the same? Is this evidence for presence of a human-style language, or does such evidence not speak to this issue at all?

TRUE OR FALSE QUESTIONS

58. True or **False**   The fossil record documenting the emergence of *Homo erectus* supports gradualist theories of evolution.

59. True or False   The punctuated equilibrium model of evolution asserts that long periods of stability are interrupted abruptly by rapid periods of change.

60. True or False   A greater reliance on cultural means of adaptation (e.g. tools) may explain the rapid emergence of *Homo erectus*.

61. True or **False**   With the movement of *Homo erectus* out of Africa, *Homo erectus* eventually colonized Australia.

62. True or **False**   The Acheulian tradition is characterized by cobble choppers that were made by removing flakes from one end of a cobble.

63. True or False   Due to its enlarged brain. *Homo erectus* infants were born immature and required extended periods of childhood dependency.

64. True or **False**   Terra Amata was a campsite that was occupied by Neandertals during the Upper Paleolithic.

65. True or False   Both "Peking man" and "Java man" are *Homo erectus* specimens.

66. True or False   Most of what is known today about archaic *Homo sapiens* comes from Europe.

67. True or False   In addition to their stocky bodies that conserved heat, Neandertals made clothes, developed elaborate tools, and hunted reindeer, mammoths, and woolly rhinos in order to adapt to the cold climate in Europe during the Würm glaciation.

68. True or **False**   The stone tool tradition associated with Neandertals is called the Acheulian.

69. True or **False**   Compared to anatomically modern humans (AMHs), Neandertals exhibit a much less pronounced degree of sexual dimorphism.

70. True or False   The evidence from the Mount Carmel caves in Israel indicate the AMHs were evolving directing out of the archaic *Homo sapiens* populations in the region long before the Neandertals in Europe died out.

71. True or **False**   Recent genetic research comparing Neandertal DNA and modern human DNA supports the theory Neandertals evolved into the European populations of AMHs.

72. True or False   The stone tool traditions of the Upper Paleolithic were based primarily on blade tools which compared to the Mousterian are faster to make and are better at maximizing the amount of cutting edge from the same amount of stone.

73. True or **False**   Unlike the Mousterian which had many different kinds of stone tools, the tool traditions of the Upper Paleolithic included only a few different kinds of implements.

74. **True** or False   With the end of the Würm glaciation, human groups shifted their subsistence strategies to a more broad-spectrum of species that they exploited.

75. True or **False**   The oldest cave paintings date to 15,000 years ago.

76. True or **False**   Most researchers today no longer believe that the Upper Paleolithic cave paintings were ritual, rather they argue that these paintings were used to decorate domestic residences.

77. **True** or False   The Mesolithic is characterized by microlithic tool industries being used by AMHs to exploit a wide range of wild plants and animals.

CHAPTER 8

HUMAN DIVERSITY AND "RACE"

CHAPTER OUTLINE

I. Race: A Discredited Concept in Biology

    A. In biological terms, a race is a geographically isolated subdivision of a species that can reproduce with individuals from other subspecies of the same species, but does not because of its geographic isolation.
        1. Human populations vary biologically, but there are no sharp breaks between populations.
        2. Human biological variation is distributed gradually between populations along clines.

    B. Ethnicity and race are not synonymous, although American culture does not discriminate between the two terms.

    C. Races Are Not Biologically Distinct
        1. Race is supposed to describe genetic variation but racial categories (particularly early on) are based on phenotypes.
            a. Phenotypes are the product of genetic, developmental, and environmental factors.
            b. There is no clear logical hierarchy to phenotypic traits, thus it is difficult to demonstrate which should be a definitive racial feature.
        2. The so-called "three great races" (white, black, and yellow) are more a reflection of European colonialist politics than an accurate representation of human biological diversity.
        3. Even skin color-based race models that include more than three categories do not accurately represent the wide range of skin color diversity among human populations.
        4. Fundamental Problems with Phenotype-based Race.
            a. Populations grouped into one race based upon phenotypic similarity may be genetically distinct; such similarities may be the result of parallel evolution or other factors.
            b. Genetic traits occur simultaneously due to selective forces of the environments in which they evolved, and therefore do not constitute an internally coherent "type."

    D. Interesting Issues: American Anthropological Association (AAA) Statement on "Race"
        1. Human populations are not unambiguous, clearly demarcated, biologically distinct groups.
        2. There is greater genetic variation within racial groups than between them.
        3. Physical variations are distributed gradually rather than abruptly through space.
        4. Physical variations in human populations have no meaning other than the social ones societies attribute to them.
        5. Historically, racial categories have been used to divide, rank, and control populations ethnically separate from Western Europe.
            a. Some populations have been assigned to a perpetual low status (e.g. African-Americans).
            b. Other populations have been assigned to a perpetual high status with access to privilege, power, and wealth.

    E. Explaining Skin Color
        1. Natural selection "is the process by which nature selects the forms most fit to survive and reproduce in a given environment."
        2. Variation in skin color is determined by the amount of melanin in the skin cells, which is in turn genetically determined.

3. Prior to the sixteenth century, darker skinned populations were closest to the equator, while lighter skinned populations were closer to the poles.
4. Selective Advantages and Disadvantages
   a. Light skin in the tropics is selected against because it burns more easily, thus subjecting light-skinned individuals to a greater likelihood of infection and disease.
   b. Sunburn impairs the body's ability to withstand heat by reducing the skin's ability to sweat.
   c. Light skin is more susceptible to skin cancer.
   d. The effect of sunlight on vitamin D formation indicates how dark skin might have been selected *for* in tropical environments (protection against hypervitaminosis D), and *against* in lower-sunlight environments (protection against rickets); and it further indicates how light skin might have been selected *for* in low-sunlight environments, and *against* in the tropics.

II. Social Race

A. "Race," as it is used in everyday discourse, refers to a social category, rather than a biological category.

B. Hypodescent: Race in the United States
1. In the United States, race is most commonly ascribed to people without reference to genotype.
2. In extreme cases, offspring of "genetically mixed" unions are ascribed entirely to the lower status race of one parent, an example of the process called hypodescent.
3. The arbitrary lumping of bisexuals with homosexuals and the controversy surrounding the casting of Eurasian roles in the play, Miss Saigon, are suggested as examples of hypodescent.
4. In the U.S., there are a growing number of interracial, biracial, or multiracial individuals who do not identify themselves with one "racial" identity.

C. Not Us: Race in Japan
1. Despite the presence of a substantial (10%), various minority population, the dominant racial ideology of Japan describes the country as racially and ethnically homogeneous.
2. Dominant Japanese uses a clear "us-not us" dichotomy as the basis for their construction of race.
3. While dominant Japanese perceive their construction of race to be based upon biology, the *burakumin* construct provides evidence to the contrary.
   a. *Burakumin* are descendants of a low-status social class.
   b. Despite the fact that *burakumin* are genetically indistinguishable from the dominant population, they are treated as a different race.
4. The mixed Japanese-Koreans are treated as wholly foreign, despite otherwise complete cultural and linguistic assimilation.

D. Phenotype and Fluidity: Race in Brazil
1. While it has some historical and social similarities with the United States, race in Brazil is very different from race in the United States and Japan.
2. The Brazilian construction of race is attuned to relatively slight phenotypic differences.
   a. More than 500 distinct racial labels have been reported.
   b. Brazilian "race" is far more flexible than the two other examples cited, in that an individual's racial classification may change due to achieved status, developmental biological changes, and other irregular factors.
   c. The multiplicity and overlap of Brazilian race labels allows one individual to "be" more than one race.
3. The complex flexibility of Brazilian race categories has made racial discrimination less likely to occur on the same scale as in the United States and Japan.

E. Beyond the Classroom: Skin Pigmentation in Papua New Guinea
   1. Heather Norton examined variation in mitochondrial DNA sequences in order to identify patterns of migration in Melanesia.
   2. She is trying to determine if skin pigmentation data supports the theory that non-Austronesian speakers migrated to New Guinea first, followed by a second wave of Austronesian speaking groups.

LECTURE TOPICS

1. Read questions from intelligence and aptitude tests and discuss how the knowledge tested by the questions might be culture-dependent. Some alternative tests have been developed, written explicitly from the perspective of a minority culture. It might be informative to read from these tests, and tests composed at different times, for the purpose of comparison.

2. Discuss racial categorizations in other societies and cultures, or other state societies. Show how such categories are related to class and wealth. Ancient Greece and modern Japan are good examples, as are areas like the Near East, Southeast Asia, and Africa, where many ethnic groups are in close proximity and are engaged in economic competition.

3. Discuss the implications of the fact that race is a cultural construct, not a biological reality. Why is it crucial to understand the arbitrary nature on racial systems of classification?

4. If you had the class prepare a description of race earlier in the course, use that description now as a basis for discussion. How does their description of race differ from those given in the text for the United States and other countries?

5. Some students feel confusion and even anger if they perceive the arguments posed in the text as de-legitimizing the political solidarity of some minority groups. Stress that the deconstruction of the concept of biological race does not preclude existence of a basis for the political unity of groups of people who are oppressed *as* races. Give an example of the political consciousness of race in support of this.

6. Use yourself as an example. Ask the students to classify you racially, then probe them on their reasons for making this classification. Ask them what their response would be if you self-identified as a member of a race other than the one they have assigned you to (*e.g.*, you are "White" and self-identify as African American). Use their responses to lead them to the realization that one's race is not the simple product of biology, but the result of a negotiation in which phenotypic features act as signs, carrying culturally constructed meanings.

SUGGESTED FILMS

Intelligence: A Complex Concept

16mm 1978 21 min
Because there are hundreds of different ideas about the nature of intelligence, the question is raised: If so many types of intelligence exist, how can we test for intelligence with any confidence? The problems inherent in testing are examined and a variety of test types, including individual versus group testing and the Leiter International Performance Test are shown. From the Developmental Psychology: Infancy to Adolescence series. From The University of Illinois Film and Video Center.

A Class Divided

video 1985 58min color/b&w
Originally broadcasted as an episode of the PBS series, Frontline (Judy Woodruff, host), this film updates the earlier documentary, *Eye of the Storm*. The program documents a reunion of Iowa teacher Jane Elliot's third-grade class of 1970 (the subjects of the earlier documentary), and discusses the impact of her experimental teaching on the evils of racial discrimination. The excerpts from early grade-school class sessions and more recent sessions with adults helps demonstrate the deleterious effects discrimination has on performance, and suggests that such experiences have a long term impact. Published in Washington, D.C.: PBS Video (distributors).

Black Is, Black Ain't

88 min 1995 color video
Marlon Riggs meets a cross-section of African Americans grappling with the paradox of numerous, often contradictory definitions of "Blackness," including many who have felt uncomfortable, even silenced within this identity because of their complexion, class, sexuality, gender, or speech has rendered them "not Black enough," or, conversely, "too Black." Independent Television Service, California Newsreel.

Franz Boas (1858-1942)

The Shackles of Tradition

52 min color
In 1883, a young German scientist, Franz Boas, arrived in the Canadian Arctic to map the coastline and indulge in his new interest: the study of other cultures. As he charted Baffin Island, he recorded the lives and ideas of the Eskimos who helped him with his work. A year of living as an Eskimo among Eskimos caused him to turn from his former interests and devote himself to learning to understand the determinants of human behavior. He became so absorbed by the common features that unite humans everywhere that he made the study of culture his life's work, doing field work in both the Arctic and on the northwest coast of America among the Indian tribes. Boas was the first distinguished social scientist in the United States to challenge the prevailing concept of racial inferiority, and actively campaigned on behalf of black people in America in the early part of the twentieth century. He wrote: "There is no reason to believe that one race is in nature so much more intelligent and endowed with greater willpower nor emotionally more stable than another." Considered the founding father of American anthropology, Boas taught at Columbia University for fifty years, encouraging his students to follow his example by actually working in the field. Among those of his students who did so was Margaret Mead. From Films for the Humanities & Sciences.

MULTIPLE-CHOICE QUESTIONS

1. Which of the following statements about the concept of race in the United States is true?

    a. **The American concept of race is inconsistent, referring to groups defined by phenotypic and cultural similarities and differences.**
    b. The American concept of race is based on the western science of genetics.
    c. The American concept of race is determined by the juxtaposition of alleles.
    d. The American concept of race does not include what used to be called "subraces," since these are now called "ethnic groups."
    e. The American concept of race occurs only in Southern regional dialect.

2.   Why is it important to understand that racial categories are based upon *perceptions* of phenotypic features, and not on genotypes?
   a.   This means that racial categories are internationally standardized.
   b.   This means that race should be determined by skeletal measurements, especially cranial capacity (skull size).
   c.   This means that race is socially constructed, not biologically based.
   d.   This means that you are in a place that does not use genealogy.
   e.   This means that racial genotypes are more accurate.

3.   Which of the following statements about American racial categories is true?

   a.   They are applied to endogamous breeding populations.
   b.   They are juridically valid, as demonstrated by the Phipps case.
   c.   They are culturally arbitrary, even though most people assume them to be based in biology.
   d.   They are based on genetics, while Japan's are based upon undemonstrated descent.
   e.   all of the above

4.   What is the term for a gradual shift in gene frequencies between neighboring populations?

   a.   cline
   b.   genotype
   c.   phenotype
   d.   cluster
   e.   allele

5.   Which of the following is the most likely reason for the dark skin color shared by tropical Africans and southern Indians?

   a.   dietary adaptation
   b.   malarial resistance
   c.   prevention of hypervitaminosis D
   d.   recent common ancestry
   e.   all of the above

6.   Which of the following factors prevents the accurate classification of an individual according to biological race?

   a.   There are no pure races
   b.   There has been continual genetic drift throughout the human range
   c.   Racial classifications reflect social, not biological, categories
   d.   Some diagnostic traits are due to nutrition, not heredity
   e.   All of the above

7.   Rather than attempting to classify humans into racial categories, biologists and anthropologists are _____.

   a.   denying the existence of any biological variation among humankind
   b.   attempting to create new categories based on blood type only
   c.   increasingly focusing their attention on explaining why specific biological variations occur
   d.   trying to verify the anthropometric data from the turn of the century
   e.   doing none of the above

8.   Which of the following is a reason that "race" is not a good explanation of human variation?

   a.   Racial categories were often based on a limited number of arbitrarily selected phenotypic traits.
   b.   Genetic and phenotypic traits do not vary together over time.
   c.   Racial categories have not explained phenotypic variation between populations; they have merely oversimplified it.
   d.   Scientists trying to prove race used data that reflected their prejudices on the subject.
   e.   **All of the above are true**

9.   Some populations like the Polynesians, the San, or the people of northern India have phenotypes that do not fit neatly into the "standard" race categories. This is evidence suggesting that

   a.   It is best to classify humans into a large number of racial categories.
   b.   There has been a lot of allele flow in the time since the origin of the three major human races.
   c.   These populations must have originated sometime before the major racial groups originated.
   d.   **The natural distribution of human phenotypes exhibits gradual trends of difference across geographic zones, not the categorical differences of race.**
   e.   None of the above is true

10. Which of the following facts refutes the idea that race is a biological reality?

   a.   Traits such as skin color, hair type, and facial features evolve independently of one another.
   b.   Most of the phenotypes used in racial classifications are distributed along clines.
   c.   The way in which races are classified varies from culture to culture.
   d.   Phenotypical similarities and differences do not necessarily have a genetic basis.
   e.   **all of the above**

11. An examination of racial taxonomies from around the world indicates that
   _____.

   a.   all cultures classify races similarly
   b.   **the classification of racial types is an arbitrary and culturally specific process**
   c.   classifying racial types can best be done by considering only phenotypic traits
   d.   classifying racial types can best be done by considering only genotype
   e.   the best classification of racial types considers genotype as well as phenotype

12. Which of the following is a major difference between Brazilian and American racial taxonomies?

   a.   Brazilians do not recognize racial differences.
   b.   American categories are "purer" than Brazilian categories.
   c.   There are no important differences between the two taxonomies.
   d.   **In the United States, social race is determined at birth and does not change, but in Brazil, race can change from day to day.**
   e.   Brazilian racial categories are based on genotype, whereas American categories are based on phenotype.

13. What is the term for the rule that automatically places the children of a union between members of different socioeconomic groups in the less-privileged group?

    a. hypervitaminosis
    b. polygyny
    c. polyandry
    d. hypodescent
    e. hypogamy

14. Which of the following statements about the concept of race in Brazil is true?

    a. A person's race can change from day to day.
    b. There are over 500 different terms that are used to describe phenotypes.
    c. The large number of racial categories does not easily lend itself to socioeconomic discrimination based on race.
    d. Siblings can belong to different races.
    e. all of the above are true

15. In Japan, *Burakumin* _____.

    a. are perceived as "pure" Japanese even though one of their parents is not Japanese
    b. are Japanese citizens of mixed ancestry who face discrimination
    c. are the "cream" of Japan's racial categories, having the purest blood
    d. no longer face any discrimination
    e. constitute a numerical majority in Japan

16. Which of the following statements about human skin color is *not* true?

    a. The amount of melanin in the skin affects the bodies ability to process lactose.
    b. The amount of melanin in the skin affects the body's production of vitamin D.
    c. Light skin is at a selective disadvantage in the tropics because it is more susceptible to sunburn.
    d. Light skin is at a selective disadvantage in the tropics because it is more susceptible to infectious disease and less efficient at sweating.
    e. none of the above are true

17. In prehistoric times, why was lighter skin color in humans found most commonly in temperate climates?

    a. It protected against hypervitaminosis D.
    b. It existed in a balanced polymorphism.
    c. It helped prevent rickets.
    d. It helped protect against skin cancer.
    e. All of the above are true.

18. Which of the following plays a role in determining skin color?

    a. Hb^S allele
    b. ultraviolet radiation
    c. Allen's rule
    d. Bergmann's rule
    e. Thompson's rule

19. The Kottak text argues that hypervitaminosis D and rickets have selected for dark and light skin colors, respectively. Why is this *not* seen as evidence supporting the biological nature of race?

    a.   It shows how traits such as skin color and intelligence are racially connected.
    b.   It explains how identical twins can come have different skin colors.
    c.   It shows that specific traits are selected for separately, rather than as part of a "racial" set.
    d.   It demonstrates that such differences as skin color are very ancient, in genetic terms.
    e.   Hypervitaminosis D and rickets also affect intelligence and this explains why skin color and intelligence co-vary better than a racial model does.

20. What are the three basic groups in the traditional European tripartite racial classification?

    a.   white, black, red
    b.   white, black, Caucasoid
    c.   Polynesian, Anglican, African
    d.   white, yellow, black
    e.   white, black, café

21. Which of the following causes hypervitaminosis D?

    a.   blocking out most of the ultraviolet radiation
    b.   an underproduction of vitamin D
    c.   absorbing too little ultraviolet radiation
    d.   an overproduction of vitamin D
    e.   none of the above

22. What is the term Appiah (1990) uses for the belief that a perceived racial difference is a sufficient reason to value one person less than another?

    a.   intrinsic racism
    b.   extrinsic racism
    c.   hypodescent
    d.   hyperdescent
    e.   de jure discrimination

23. What happens to a person's racial classification, as they become wealthier?

    a.   money has no impact on a person's race in Brazil
    b.   they become darker
    c.   they become lighter
    d.   they lose their racial identity and are classified are "wealthy"
    e.   they get to chose their own race

24. Which of the following helps explain the differences between American and Brazilian constructions of race?

    a.   Their different colonial histories.
    b.   The lack of large native populations in Brazil.
    c.   The Portuguese language has a greater number of intermediate color terms than the English language.
    d.   English concepts of race were very different from those of the Portuguese.
    e.   English settlers in America came over as families, while the Portuguese settlers in Brazil were mostly male.

25. Which of the following groups opposed the addition of a "multiracial" category to the 2000 census?

    a. AAA
    b. NAACP
    c. ICAC
    d. SAA
    e. NCAA

ESSAY QUESTIONS

26. Any of the above multiple choice questions may be converted to an essay question by requiring students to choose the correct answer and justify their selection in essay form. Such justifications should include explanations as to why the chosen answer is correct and why those responses not chosen are incorrect.

27. Support or refute this statement: By rejecting the race concept, anthropologists are ignoring obvious human biological variation.

28. What is folk taxonomy? What are the major differences between Brazilian and American systems of racial classification? Now compare American with Japanese racial classification.

29. What is meant by the term "social race?" How does this concept differ from race as perceived by the average Middle Class American (use the description given in the text)?

30. How was the concept of race used by early biologists?

31. Populations in equatorial Africa and Papua New Guinea are quite similar, phenotypically. They are both dark-skinned, with similar hair and facial features. How would a typical racial model explain these similarities? How would evolutionary biology's explanation differ? Which model does a better job of explaining this data?

32. Describe the theories which best explain the evolutionary reasons for differential distribution of skin color throughout the world?

TRUE OR FALSE QUESTIONS

33. True or **False**   There is no difference between the biological and cultural definitions of race.

34. **True** or False   In cultural terms, a race is an ethnic group that is assumed to have a biological basis.

35. True or **False**   Most Americans are very precise in distinguishing between the terms "race" and "ethnicity."

36. True or **False**   Hypodescent refers to individuals who are racially pure.

37. **True** or False   Hypodescent does not characterize Brazilian notions of race.

38. True or **False**   The Phipps case demonstrates the fluidity of racial classifications in the U.S.

39. **True** or False   Interracial, biracial, and multiracial identities are becoming more and more common in the U.S.

40. **True** or False Racial categories in Japan are used to distinguish between pure Japanese and others.

41. True or **False** In Japan, the *burakumin* represent an isolated breeding population that is genetically distinct from the rest of the country.

42. **True** or False Racial categories in Brazil are not rigid, rather they often change depending on the social setting.

43. True or **False** Brazilian racial classification is based exclusively on an individual's phenotype.

44. **True** or False Hypodescent in the U.S. has enabled minority racial groups like Native Americans to grow while similar groups are shrinking in number in Brazil.

45. True or **False** Biologists have rejected the idea of three great races (white, black, and yellow) largely because it fails to account for Native Americans.

46. **True** or False Physical features do not cluster into discrete genetic units.

47. True or **False** Higher amounts of melanin in the skin enhances the body's ability to manufacture vitamin D.

48. **True** or False Rickets is caused by a shortage of vitamin D in the body.

49. True or **False** The indigenous communities in the tropical regions of the New World are not as dark skinned as populations living in other tropical regions because the dense vegetation in the New World blocks out much of the sunlight.

50. **True** or False Hypervitaminosis D is caused by an overproduction of vitamin D.

51. True or **False** Dark skinned individuals living in northern climates are high-risk candidates for hypervitaminosis D.

52. True or **False** Of the major physical traits used to racially classify people in the U.S., skin color is the most reliable.

CHAPTER 9
THE FIRST FARMERS

CHAPTER OUTLINE

I. Introduction

    A. Change in human subsistence systems over time is a type of social evolution.

    B. Basic foraging was the primary subsistence mode for *Homo*, from *erectus* to well beyond the appearance of anatomically modern humans.

    C. Changes in human subsistence techniques resulted from a combination of human invention (e.g., the Neolithic revolution) and changes in environmental pressures (such as post-glacial warming).

    D. "Neolithic period" originally referred only to the presence of advanced stone tool-making techniques, but now refers to that period in a given region wherein the first signs of domestication are present, with which Neolithic tools are commonly associated.

    E. The earliest Neolithic period occurred in the Middle East, around 10,000 B.P.

II. The First Farmers and Herders in the Middle East

    A. The Fertile Crescent's Environmental Zones
        1. The four main environmental zones involved in the origin of cultivation were the high plateau, the hilly flanks, the steppe, and the alluvial plain.
        2. While deliberate cultivation eventually became most intensely practiced on the alluvial plain, it did not start there because the climate was too dry, requiring irrigation.
        3. In the hilly flanks, habitual harvesting of wild grains did occur, and it is suggested that this abundance led to the first sedentary villages (the Natufians) dependent on harvesting *wild* grains.
        4. Deliberate cultivation most likely came in response to documented climatic changes (a drying trend, 11,000 B.P., shrinking the zone of abundant wild grain), which led inhabitants on the fringe of the hilly flanks to artificially duplicate the dense stands of wheat and barley that grew in the hilly flanks.

    B. Other Sequences
        1. The term vertical economy refers to the patterned adaptation that occurs in areas where several different ecological zones in hilly or mountainous terrain occur close to one another.
        2. The adjacent ecological zones invite modification of local varieties to preserve in one zone what is available in another.
        3. Many of the places where food production evolved (Middle East, Peru, Mesoamerica) were areas of vertical economy.

    C. Trade
        1. The different ecological zones all had resources peculiar to them: the hilly flanks had grains, the steppe had asphalt, and the high plateau had copper and turquoise.
        2. These resources gained in value through interregional trade, which in turn resulted in intensified exploitation of the resources.

3. Another result was the movement of the grains outside their indigenous zone, where they were subjected to different selective pressures, resulting in different strains of wheat and barley.

D. Genetic Changes and Domestication
   1. In wild grains, the axis (the stem connecting the seed to the stalk) is brittle, which allows the grain to reseed itself easily.
   2. First as an accidental by-product of harvesting, later intentionally, humans selected grains, in which the axis was tougher, allowing less grain to fall to the ground, thus raising yields.
   3. Humans also selected plants, which were more easily husked.
   4. Humans selected woolly animals from among wild sheep (who are not normally woolly); thus acquiring livestock better suited to lowland heat and from which could also obtain wool.
   5. Fossil remains indicate that domestication of sheep and goats was accompanied by a decrease in the size of the animal.

E. Food Production and the State
   1. The early stages of food production in the Middle East were marked by gradual transition from foraging to producing economies.
   2. Changes caused by food production, such as population increase and the resulting migration, forced other areas to respond (e.g., in the hilly flanks, people had to begin cultivating grains, wild yields were no longer sufficient).
   3. There had also been a gradual, general population increase (based on the native richness of the environment), that spurred the spread of food production.
   4. In the Tigris-Euphrates alluvial plain (Mesopotamia), cultivation required irrigation, which began around 7000 B.P.
   5. By 6000 B.P., irrigation systems had become far larger and more complex, and were associated with a new political system, "based on central government, extreme contrasts of wealth, and social classes."
   6. The written and archaeological record indicates that the early Mesopotamian states were city-states (Sumer and Elam), ruled by a literate theocracy that managed virtually all major aspects of the economy (which was overwhelmingly agrarian).
   7. By 4,500 B.P., the theocracy had been replaced by a secular, military monarchy, based upon an elaborate class system.

III. Other Old World Farmers

A. Cultivation evolved independently in areas other than Mesopotamia, based upon crops other than barley and wheat.
   1. A list of the other areas and their chief crops.
      a. Sub-Saharan Africa: millets and plantains.
      b. Southeast Asia: rice.
      c. China: millet and rice.
      d. Mesoamerica: maize (corn).
      e. South America: potatoes.

B. In some areas, domestication may have occurred as early as it did in the Middle East.
   1. Millet was widely cultivated in northern China as early as 7500 B.P.
   2. Rice was domesticated southern China also around 7500 B.P.

IV. In the News: The Iceman

A. The article documents the discovery of the remains of a Neolithic man (dated at 5300 B.P.), that were found remarkably well preserved in a glacier in the Italian Alps in 1991.

B. Among the more archaeologically significant aspects of the find are the artifacts and perishable objects (such as fur, cloth, and leather clothing) that were preserved by the ice.

C. The man's copper axe and other artifacts indicate that he lived during the transition from stone to metal tools.

V. The First American Farmers

    A. America's First Immigrants
1. America was first settled by immigrant *H. sapiens* from Asia, who followed big game (mammoth) herds across Beringia, perhaps 25,000 years ago.
2. Descendants of these Paleoindians gradually moved throughout the continent, hunting big game and reaching a florescence marked by the sophisticated stone technology called the Clovis Tradition.

    B. The Foundations of Food Production
1. Big-game-focused foraging was a widely successful strategy in North America later than in Europe, because of the lasting abundance of game.
2. This caused the independent development of food production in the New World to occur 3000-4000 years after it occurred in Europe and Africa.
3. In contrast to the Old World, large game animals were not domesticated in the New World, and domesticated animals were never important to the economy.
4. Staple crops in the New World were maize, potatoes, and manioc.

    C. Early Farming in the Mexican Highlands
1. The Valley of Oaxaca
    a. Inhabitants first practiced broad spectrum foraging, but Oaxaca became the original center of maize domestication.
    b. The foragers practiced a seasonal economy, making societal and geographical adjustments as they moved among the different ecological zones (micro bands during the dry season, macro bands during the abundant season).
    c. The apparent ancestor of maize was a wild grass, teocentli, which (similar to wheat and barley in Mesopotamia) experienced combination of incidental and intentional selective pressures due to gathering and cultivation (a large cob, seeds that cling to the cob, tough axes, etc.).
2. As in the Old World, several millennia passed after the origin of cultivation before the first states arose.

    D. From Early Farming to the State
1. Unlike in the Old World, the development of food production preceded the existence of sedentary village life in Mesoamerica.
2. Around 3500 B.P., sedentary life developed separately in two parts of Mexico: the Gulf Coast and the Pacific.
3. Early village farming communities also developed in a few highland valleys (such as Oaxaca) with conditions uniquely (for the mountains) favorable to cultivation, such as constant water sources (for pot irrigation) and a later frost.
4. Maize reached the lowlands by 3500 B.P. where, in combination with the easy water, longer growing season, rich adjacent microenvironments, maize cultivation quickly gave rise to sedentary village farming communities.
5. Maize change (through selection), along with methods of cultivating it, which allowed for food production to become more widespread.
6. Archaeological evidence of an elite level (a sub-societal group with differential access to resources and goods, the presence of which is diagnostic for chiefdoms and states) has been dated as early as 3500 B.P.
7. The Olmecs were a chiefly society flourishing between 3200 and 2500 B.P., who built ritual centers of a scale associated with elites who could marshal mass labor.

8. The Olmecs were followed by the city-state of Teotihuacan (1900-1300 B.P.), and the Aztec state (A.D. 1325 -- conquest).

E. Interesting Issues: Pseudo-Archaeology
   1. The *Indiana Jones* series and other popular works like it suggest, erroneously, that archaeologists focus on great artifacts and, moreover, treat these artifacts like art objects, rather than part of an archaeological sequence.
   2. Contrary to claims by Heyerdahl, even if contact between ancient civilizations did occur, there is no evidence that suggests that civilization originated only once and then diffused globally.
   3. Rather, evidence clearly shows that, when civilizations arose, it did so because indigenous conditions supported such a transition.
   4. Evidence of gradual transitions, existing in many different archaeological sequences, refute claims like those of van Daniken, which argue that civilization was seeded through interstellar contact.

F. State Formation in the Valley of Mexico
   1. In 2500 B.P., changes in maize cultivation (such as the development of a strain with a shorter growing season) allowed small-scale cultivation to take place in the relatively northern Valley of Mexico.
   2. By A.D. 1, a settlement hierarchy, with communities of different size, function, and types of structures, had emerged, with the religious center, Teotihuacan, at the top of the hierarchy, smaller cities between, and rural farming outposts at the bottom.
   3. Such a three-tiered settlement hierarchy (capital city, smaller intermediate cities, and rural villages) is considered evidence of state organization.
   4. In the case of Teotihuacan, this pattern was associated with intensive, irrigation-based agriculture.
   5. After its peak (A.D. 100-700), Teotihuacan experienced a rapid decline in size and power, its population dispersed, and it was succeeded by the lesser Toltec state (900-1200 A.D.), and then the Aztecs.
   6. As agriculture intensified and immigration brought greater population growth to the valley, the basis for the Aztec state developed.

VI. Costs and Benefits

A. Food production generated enough surpluses for economic diversification and specialized trades to develop, providing the basis for the many benefits seen to come from advanced civilization.

B. However, foraging subsistence economies are less time consuming, and are typically associated with a healthier human diet (more variety, less emphasis on carbohydrates and fats).

C. States are also associated with greater social inequality, intensified warfare, and crime, and uniquely associated with slavery.

VII. Beyond the Classroom: Late Postclassic Economy in Northern Belize

A. Maxine Oland looked at trade and exchange networks of raw stone tool materials in northern Belize between A.D. 900 – 1500.

B. By locating the local sources for stone tools and identifying which tools came from which sources, Oland was able to conclude that formal stone tools were being made exclusively at specialized tool production site, while more expedient tools were being made with materials from more readily available sources.

LECTURE TOPICS

1. Discuss domestication as a process of unintended selection that resulted from humans trying to reduce risk and increase yields.

2. Discuss the development of food production as a process of growing mutual interdependence between humans and the plants and animals they domesticated. In that light, discuss the changes in human anatomy since domestication as consequences of our own domestication.

3. Discuss the growth of nucleated settlement during the process of the development of food production. Discuss the reasons for such settlements, the consequences, and how such settlements became the adaptive base for the later development of states.

SUGGESTED FILMS

Myths and the Moundbuilders

60 min 1981 video
A general look at archaeological exploration of the Hopewell culture, with a critical assessment of earlier theories on the origins of the moundbuilders, and a presentation of more recent findings. This film not only provides excellent explanatory footage on the nature of archaeological inquiry; it presents a sensitive, sensible critique of archaeological theorizing about Native American cultures. From the *Odyssey* series. Written, produced, and directed by Graham Chedd. Published by PBS Video, Washington, D.C.

Maya, Lords of the Jungle

60 min 1981 video
A critical assessment of earlier theories about the origins and evolution of the Mayan sequence and great architecture. Researchers present their findings, with their own theories. From the *Odyssey* series. Published by PBS Video, Washington, D.C.

Reliving the Past: Alonzo Pond and The 1930 Logan African Expedition

45 min 1986 color
Documents the 1930 archaeological expedition to Algeria headed by Alonzo Pond. In 1985, surviving members of the expedition, including 92-year-old Pond, had a reunion at Beloit College. Original footage from the expedition is interspersed with interviews of the members.

The Making of Mankind: 6--Settling Down

video 1981 55 min color
Richard Leakey explains why people living in the Fertile Crescent more than 12,000 years ago began to plant and harvest cereal grains and traces the most fundamental shift from a nomadic hunter-gatherer way of life to the settled villager and farmer.

Exploring Japanese Archaeology: Life in the Jomon Period

16mm 46 min
Looks at the village of Miyada, a Jomon site in the Ina Valley of Nagano Prefecture, Japan, discovered and excavated in the course of developing rice fields. Demonstrates techniques used to uncover new sites. From the Japan Foundation.

Prehistoric Monuments of Europe

video 43 min color
This program documents some of the most imposing testimonials to human history in Europe: the avenues of megaliths at Carnac in Brittany, which are presumed to have been a celestial observatory; nearby, the mysterious royal tomb at Cavrinis with its giant fingerprints, and the temple beneath the sea on the isle of Er-Lanic; in Corsica, the oldest sculptures in Europe; the nuraghens in Sardinia, once thought to be giant fortifications but now believed to be shrines of sun worshippers and an ingenious system of communications, and the oldest European temples as well as underground labyrinths for the dead, located on the islands of Malta and Cozo. From Prehistoric Man: The Artifacts series. From Films for the Humanities & Sciences

Sahara: Before the Desert

video 43 min color
Although its very name is now synonymous with "desert," 10,000-year-old cave paintings in southern Algeria depict a green and fruitful Sahara. The descendants of the people depicted here can be found among the nomadic tribesmen of the Niger region. But when and how did the Sahara become desert? In examining these questions, the program also shows the steps being taken by the Saharan countries to keep the desert from growing and, if possible, to turn it back. From Prehistoric Man: The Artifacts series. From Films for the Humanities & Sciences

MULTIPLE CHOICE QUESTIONS

1. Which of the following is *not* one of the areas where food production was independently invented?

   a. Eastern United States
   b. Central Mexico
   c. Middle East
   d. Pacific Northwest
   e. South China

2. What is the name given to the first cultural period in which the first signs of domestication are present?

   a. Upper Paleolithic
   b. Mesolithic
   c. Neolithic
   d. Chalcolithic
   e. Microlithic

3. What was the first hominid found to arrive in the New World?

   a. *Homo erectus*
   b. *Australopithecus boisei*
   c. Neandertal
   d. *Homo sapiens sapiens*
   e. *Homo habilis*

4. The Neolithic began around 10,000 B.P. in the Middle East, 8000 B.P. in South and Southeast Asia, 7000 B.P. in Africa and Eastern Europe, and 5000 B.P. in Western Europe and Mexico. The Neolithic is marked as beginning at different times in different areas because

    a. It was not until the times given above that *Homo sapiens* groups made their way into each of these areas.
    b. The Neolithic was mistakenly tied to the "agricultural revolution," instead of the "broad-spectrum revolution," which happen several thousand years earlier.
    c. These times are when the first signs of domestication show up in each of these areas.
    d. The times given above mark when the necessary climatic conditions took place for the Neolithic to begin in the respective areas.
    e. all of the above

5. Which of the following was a consequence of domestication?

    a. Humans had to work less than previously to acquire food.
    b. There was a decline in disease.
    c. Sedentary life became more widespread.
    d. There was an increase in the diversity of the diet.
    e. There was a gradual decrease in population size.

6. What is the term that refers to life in permanent villages?

    a. transhumant
    b. levallois
    c. nomadism
    d. sedentism
    e. mercantilism

7. Where do scholars believe that food production first began in the Middle East?

    a. alluvial desert
    b. marginal zones
    c. hilly flanks
    d. desert oases
    e. high plateau

8. Why is agricultural intensification associated with the development of the state in Mesopotamia?

    a. Agricultural intensification made it possible for the number of people supported by a given area of land to increase.
    b. Creating and maintaining canals required a more centralized and hierarchical decision making body.
    c. Agriculture created a surplus, which allowed for economic specialization.
    d. Irrigation of larger areas required increasingly complex and centralized political organization.
    e. All of the above are reasons.

9. When did sedentary life develop in the Middle East?

    a. before farming and herding
    b. after farming, but before herding
    c. after herding, but before farming
    d. after farming and herding
    e. at the same time that farming and herding developed

10. With domestication, what happened to the husk of wild cereals?

   a. It became tougher.
   b. It became thicker.
   c. It became darker.
   d. It became more brittle.
   e. Wild cereal do no have husks.

11. What is the name of a system that exploits environmental zones that although close together in space, contrast with one another in altitude, rainfall, overall climate, and vegetation?

   a. a hydraulic economy
   b. a Classic Neolithic Society
   c. an evanescent economy
   d. a vertical economy
   e. a subsistence economy

12. Which of the following statements about sheep is *not* true?

   a. Woolly sheep are the product of domestication.
   b. Wool from sheep can be used to make clothing.
   c. The wool of domesticated sheep offers protection against extreme heat.
   d. Wild sheep produces purer wool, as compared to domesticated sheep.
   e. all of the above are true

13. Why do most domesticated grains (such as wheat and barley) have a tougher axis and husk than wild grains?

   a. Grains with a tough axis and husk could not survive in the wild.
   b. The process of harvesting and storing grain by early humans gradually selected for these features.
   c. They get better nutrients through being domesticated.
   d. The first domesticated grains were from the alluvial plains, where caprine influences strengthened the axis and husk.
   e. c and d only

14. What happened around 10,000 B.P in the Near East?

   a. Foraging became the characteristic human subsistence strategy.
   b. The first states arose.
   c. Modern humans began colonizing the New World and Australia.
   d. A major economic shift from food producing to big-game hunting occurred.
   e. The domestication of plants and animals began to replace foraging as the basis of subsistence.

15. Which of the following was *not* domesticated in China?

   a. rice
   b. millet
   c. chickens
   d. water buffalo
   e. quinoa

16. Which of the following was *not* domesticated in the Eastern United States?

    a. goosefoot
    b. marsh elder
    c. beans
    d. squash
    e. sunflower

17. Which of the following conditions did *not* contribute to the development of food production in the Middle East?

    a. The shift to a broad-spectrum subsistence pattern at the end of the Upper Paleolithic.
    b. The availability of annual grasses with edible grains.
    c. The diffusion of domesticated animal species from southern Europe.
    d. Population increase, leading people to try planting grasses in new ecological niches.
    e. Favorable changes in cultivated grains through artificial selection.

18. Why did the first *Homo sapiens* come to the New World?

    a. They were fleeing from warlike Cro Magnon groups.
    b. They crossed Beringia in order to take advantage of large flint deposits in South America.
    c. They followed herds of big game animals (woolly mammoths, especially).
    d. The first *Homo sapiens* in the New World were foragers who were gradually forced into new territories by the expansion of more advanced agricultural groups.
    e. The first *Homo sapiens* in the New World were European colonists--Native Americans are descended from Neandertals.

19. What is the name of the tool tradition associated with the first humans to arrive in North America?

    a. Mousterian
    b. Acheulian
    c. Neolithic
    d. La Chapelle
    e. Clovis

20. Which of the following supported the rapid expansion of human populations throughout North America?

    a. the invention of the wheel
    b. abundant big game animals
    c. the domestication of primitive horses
    d. widespread slash-and-burn horticulture
    e. a combination of all of the above

21. Where did food production begin in the New World?

    a. Mexico
    b. New England
    c. Patagonia
    d. Beringia
    e. It did not originate in the New World; it was diffused from Mesopotamia

22. What is the name of the land bridge that linked the eastern tip of Siberia to Alaska 12,000 years ago?

   a. Tehuantepec
   b. Beringia
   c. Clovis
   d. Pont-Terre
   e. Monte Verde

23. Where did the earliest domestication of animals and plants in the Middle East occur?

   a. In an oasis, in the desert
   b. In the area where wild forms of wheat and barley grew
   c. Along the banks of the Nile
   d. In the marginal zone next to the Hilly Flanks
   e. In the Fertile Crescent, where the world's first civilization emerged

24. Which of the following statements about life in the Valley of Oaxaca prior to cultivation is true?

   a. People ate maguey, cactus, tree pods, deer, and rabbit
   b. The inhabitants were foragers
   c. The populations shifted seasonally between bands and microbands
   d. The people periodically harvested the wild grass, teocentli
   e. all of the above

25. Which of the following species was *not* domesticated in South America?

   a. llamas
   b. manioc
   c. potatoes
   d. quinoa
   e. all of the above were domesticated in South America

26. The first human populations in the Americas _____.

   a. were big-game hunters who came across Beringia
   b. evolved from a native Neandertal population in glacial North America
   c. became extinct by the end of the Pleistocene and were replaced by more advanced human populations
   d. came from Africa in boats, probably made from animal skins or bark, and definitely did not come from outer space in flying saucers
   e. brought their herds of domesticated sheep with them

27. Which of the following was domesticated in the New World?

   a. maize
   b. potatoes
   c. cassava
   d. dogs
   e. all of the above

28. What were the three caloric staples domesticated in the New World?

    a. maize, beans, and squash
    b. maize, goosefoot, and marsh elder
    c. potatoes, sunflower, and beans
    d. manioc, squash, and goosefoot
    e. manioc, potatoes, and maize

29. What is the name of the wild ancestor of maize?

    a. corn
    b. guajalote
    c. cavia
    d. teocintli
    e. elote

30. When did the first permanent villages develop in Mesoamerica?

    a. When more than one crop of maize was grown each year
    c. When frost-resistant (short-season) strains of maize were developed
    b. When cultivated crops and a broad spectrum of natural resources were both
        exploited
    d. When pot irrigation became a viable method for increasing the amount of arable
        land on a regular basis in areas of micro-environmental diversity
    e. all of the above occurred

31. Which of the following is a difference between the food-producing traditions of
    Mesopotamia and Mesoamerica?

    a. Food production occurred as a gradual process in Mesoamerica but was
        revolutionary in Mesopotamia.
    b. In Mesoamerica, goats, sheep, and pigs were domesticated, while in
        Mesopotamia, only dogs were domesticated.
    c. Food production emerged in Mesoamerica thousands of years prior to
        Mesopotamia.
    **d. Domesticated animals played an important role in Mesopotamia, but were
        absent from Mesoamerica.**
    e. Maize was the staple grain in Mesopotamia grain, while the primary grain in
        Mesoamerica was wheat.

32. Unlike the Old World, plant domestication in the New World _____.

    a. occurred after the first sedentary communities
    b. occurred before the first sedentary communities
    c. was apparently not necessary for the development of states, such as Teotihuacan
    d. involved no food plants, but instead was used to increase the production of
        utilitarian plants such as bottle gourds and hemp
    e. began and abandoned before there was a chance for societies to develop into
        states

34. Which of the following statements about the Olmec is *not* true?

    a. They were the first Mesoamerican state
    b. They lived in the lowlands of Mexico's Gulf Coast
    c. They built large earthen mounds
    d. They sculpted massive stone heads
    e. They were one of the early Mesoamerican chiefdoms

35. Which of the following is *not* a benefit of farming?

   a. broader diet breadth
   b. better health
   c. less work
   d. fewer diseases
   e. none of the above is a benefit of farming

36. Which of the following is true?

   a. Food production allowed most people to work less
   b. Food production reduced warfare
   c. Food production yielded more nutritious diets
   d. Food producers worked harder than foragers
   e. Food producing societies are more egalitarian than foraging societies

37. Which of the following is true?

   a. Food production allowed most people to work less
   b. Food production reduced warfare
   c. Food production yielded more nutritious diets
   d. Food production led to an increase in social inequality
   e. Food producing societies are more egalitarian than foraging societies

ESSAY QUESTIONS

38. Discuss the appropriateness of the term Neolithic Revolution, citing specific evidence from two parts of the world.

39. Discuss parallels in the transition from foraging to food production in the Middle East and Mesoamerica.

40. Using specific evidence, support or refute the statement that food production is a more specialized economy than is foraging.

41. Discuss genetic changes in the domestication of plants in the New World and the Old World, and compare the selective factors for these changes in the two areas. How do these facts and their role in the history of domestication help explain the differences between natural selection and artificial selection?

42. What is a vertical economy? Why is this concept significant in the history of domestication and food production?

43. What is the nature of the archaeological evidence that casts doubt on the neocreationist positions of Heyerdahl and von Daniken?

44. What archaeological evidence can be used to support interpretations of either a food-producing "revolution," or a gradual transition from foraging to strategies that relied more heavily on domesticated plants and animals?

45. Review two theories for the origin of food production that have been rejected in the text. Why were they rejected?

46. What were the major plant and animal domesticates in the Old World and the New World? What was the main contrast in the food-producing economies of the Old World and New World?

47. Any of the above multiple choice questions may be converted to an essay question by requiring students to choose the correct answer and justify their selection in essay form. Such justifications should include explanations as to why the chosen answer is correct and why those responses not chosen are incorrect.

TRUE OR FALSE QUESTIONS

48. True or False — The broad-spectrum revolution was a critical step towards the transition to food production.

49. True or **False** — Most researchers today argue that the domestication of plants in the Middle East took place in the Hilly Flanks region where the wild ancestors naturally grew.

50. True or **False** — In the Middle East, sedentism developed only after plants and animals were domesticated.

51. True or False — A vertical economy exploits environmental zones that are close together in space, but separated by altitude, rainfall, overall climate, and vegetation.

52. True or False — Compared to wild plants, the seeds of domesticated plants are larger and less likely to shatter and disperse.

53. True or **False** — Animals, like plants, became larger with domestication.

54. True or False — As subsistence economies became more specialized and more dependent of domesticated species, population centers began to emerge that had canals for irrigating fields, temples, and writing.

55. True or **False** — Agricultural intensification enabled people to farm for only part of the year, and then leave the cities to live away from the problems endemic to urban populations for the rest of the year.

56. True or **False** — Rice was domesticated on northern China around 7500 B.P.

57. True or False — China was host to two different centers of domestication, one in the north and one in the south.

58. True or **False** — The domesticated millet that appears in China around 7500 B.P. was first domesticated in sub-Saharan Africa around 8000 B.P., it then diffused to China through long-distance trade networks.

59. True or False — One of the earliest stone tool technologies in North America is called the Clovis tradition.

60. True or False — Unlike the centers of domestication in the Old World, very few animals were ever domesticated in the New World.

61. True or **False** — Manioc, beans, and squash were the major crops to be domesticated in Mexico.

62. True or False — There were three independent centers of domestication in the New World.

63. True or False — In the New World, sedentism occurred only after domestication.

64. True or **False**   The subsistence base of the Olmec culture was based primarily on manioc and guinea pigs.

65. True or False   The Valley of Mexico has witnessed a series of civilizations rise and fall from Teotihuacan, to the Toltecs, to the Aztecs.

66. True or **False**   One of the benefits of food production is that it frees up a lot of time that would have otherwise been spent collecting food.

67. True or **False**   With a more reliable food source, the early food producers were considerably more healthy than hunter-gatherers.

CHAPTER 10
THE FIRST CITIES AND STATES

CHAPTER OUTLINE

I. Attributes of the State

    A. A state is a society with a formal, central government and a division of society into classes.

    B. A state controls s specific regional territory.

    C. Early states had productive farming economies, supporting dense populations.
      1. Often these populations were nucleated in cities.
      2. The agricultural economies usually involved some form of water control or irrigation.

    D. Early states used tribute and taxation to accumulate, at a central place, resources needed to support hundreds, or thousands, of specialists

    E. States are stratified into social classes (e.g. elites, commoners, and slaves).

    F. Early states had imposing public buildings and architecture, including temples, palaces, and storehouses.

    G. Early states developed some form of record-keeping system, usually in a written script.

II. State Formation in the Middle East

    A. Urban Life
      1. The first towns arose around 10,000 years ago in the Middle East.
      2. Jericho
        a. Located in modern Israel.
        b. It was settled by the Natufians around 11,000 B.P.
        c. Around 9,000 B.P., the town was destroyed and rebuilt with square houses with plaster floors and burials beneath the floors.
        d. Pottery first appears at Jericho around 8000 B.P.
      3. Çatal Hüyük
        a. Located in the central part of modern Turkey.
        b. It was possibly the largest settlement of the Neolithic.
        c. It flourished between 8000 and 7000 B.P. with up to 10,000 people living at the site.
        d. People lived in square mud-brick dwellings that had separate areas for secular and ritual activities.
        e. Ritual spaces were decorated with ox images and motifs.
        f. Burials were placed beneath the house floors.
        g. Çatal Hüyük shows no signs or state-level sociopolitical organization.

    B. The Elite Level
      1. Halafian pottery (7500-6500 B.P.)
        a. Delicate pottery associated with elites.
        b. Used as evidence, for one of the first chiefdoms in the northern part of the Middle East.

2. Ubaid pottery (7000-6000 B.P.)
   a. First found and identified at the site of Tell el-Ubaid located in the southern part of modern Iraq.
   b. Is associated with advanced chiefdoms and perhaps the first states in southern Mesopotamia.

C. Social Ranking and Chiefdoms
   1. Egalitarian society
      a. Most typically found among foragers and tribes.
      b. These societies lack status distinctions except for those based on age, gender, and individual qualities, talents, and achievements.
      c. Everybody is born equal, but during the course of his or her life, will achieve different statuses.
   2. Ranked society
      a. These societies have hereditary inequality, but lack social stratification.
      b. There is a continuum of status as individuals are ranked in terms of their genealogical distance from the chief.
      c. Not all ranked societies are chiefdoms, only those in which there is a loss of village autonomy are called chiefdoms.
   3. Chiefdoms
      a. Chiefdom is a ranked society in which relations among villages as well as individuals are unequal.
      b. Primary states emerge from competition among chiefdoms, as one chiefdom managed to conquer its neighbors and integrate them into a larger political unit.
      c. Chiefdoms first appear in the Middle East around 7300 B.P. and in Mesoamerica around 3000 B.P.
      d. One of the archaeological markers of chiefdoms is the presence of wealthy burials of children too young to have achieved or earned prestige of their own, but were born into elite families.

D. Advanced Chiefdoms
   1. Excavations at Tell Hamoukar suggest that advanced chiefdoms arose in northern areas of the Middle East independently of the developments in southern Mesopotamia.
   2. The site covers 32 acres and was surrounded by a defensive wall.
   3. There is evidence of large-scale food storage and preparation, which indicates that the elites were hosting and entertaining in a chiefly manner.
   4. The excavators have also recovered seals used too mark storage containers.

E. Interesting Issues: How Ethnography Helps in Interpreting the Archaeological Record
   1. Archaeologists use ethnographic case studies to help interpret the archaeological record.
   2. Through ethnographic analogy, archaeologists generate hypotheses that can be tested through archaeological fieldwork.
   3. Archaeology is to ethnography as paleontology is to zoology.

F. The Rise of the State
   1. Uruk Period (6700-5200 B.P.)
      a. first cities appear
      b. centralized leadership
      c. settlements spread north into modern Syria and Turkey
   2. Writing
      a. First developed in southern Mesopotamia.
      b. Was used to keep accounts, reflecting the needs of trade.
      c. The first kind of writing in Mesopotamia is called cuneiform.
   3. Temples and Writing
      a. Temples managed herding, farming, manufacture, and trade.
      b. Priests used cuneiform to keep track of the temples' economic activities.

4. Metallurgy is the knowledge of the properties of metals.
   a. Smelting is the process of using high temperatures to extract pure metal from an ore.
   b. After 5000 B.P., metallurgy evolved rapidly.
   c. The Iron Age began around 3200 B.P.
5. Bronze Age Mesopotamian States
   a. Large populations were densely concentrated in walled cities.
   b. Secular authority replaced temple rule around 4600 B.P.
   c. A well-defined class structure, with a complex stratification into nobles, commoners, and slaves was present by 4600 B.P.

III. Other Early States

A. Indus Civilization
   1. The Indus state flourished between 4600 and 3900 B.P.
   2. The major cities were Harappa and Mohenjo Daro exhibited urban planning with carefully laid out wastewater systems and residential sectors.
   3. The Indus civilization developed its own writing system.

B. China
   1. The first Chinese state belongs to the Shang Dynasty (3750 B.P.).
   2. The Shang state was characterized by urbanism, palaces, human sacrifice, and distinct social classes.
   3. The Shang state developed its own writing system.
   4. The Shang state is well known for its bronze metallurgy.

IV. State Formation in Mesoamerica

A. Early Chiefdoms and Elites
   1. Three centers of early chiefdom development in Mesoamerica.
      a. Valley of Oaxaca
      b. Valley of Mexico
      c. Olmec lowlands
   2. The Olmec chiefdoms flourished between 3200 and 2500 B.P.
      a. The chiefly centers consisted of large earthen mounds arranged around a central plaza.
      b. They also have large carved stone heads.
   3. Long-distance exchange networks linked these three regions of early chiefdom development.
   4. By 2500 B.P., the city of Monte Albán in the Valley of Oaxaca was founded.
   5. The city of Teotihuacan flourished between 1900 and 1300 B.P. (A.D. 100-700).

B. States in the Valley of Mexico
   1. In 2500 B.P., changes in maize cultivation (such as the development of a strain with a shorter growing season) allowed small-scale cultivation to take place in the relatively northern Valley of Mexico.
   2. By A.D. 1, a settlement hierarchy, with communities of different size, function, and types of structures, had emerged, with the religious center, Teotihuacan, at the top of the hierarchy, smaller cities between, and rural farming outposts at the bottom.
   3. Such a three-tiered settlement hierarchy (capital city, smaller intermediate cities, and rural villages) is considered evidence of state organization.
   4. In the case of Teotihuacan, this pattern was associated with intensive, irrigation-based agriculture.
   5. After its peak (A.D. 100-700), Teotihuacan experienced a rapid decline in size and power, its population dispersed, and it was succeeded by the lesser Toltec state (A.D. 900-1200), and then the Aztecs.
   6. As agriculture intensified and immigration brought greater population growth to the valley, the basis for the Aztec state developed.

V. The Origin of the State

    A. Hydraulic Systems (Wittfogel)
        1. In certain arid areas, states have emerged to manage systems of irrigation, drainage, and flood control.
        2. However, hydraulic agriculture is neither a sufficient nor a necessary condition for the rise of states.
            a. There are many societies with hydraulic agriculture that are not states.
            b. There are many states that developed without hydraulic agriculture.
        3. Water control increases agricultural production, which increases population growth, which requires a political system that can regulate interpersonal relations and the means of production.

    B. Long-Distance Trade Routes
        1. Some researchers believe that states emerged at strategic locations in regional trade networks.
        2. Like hydraulic agriculture, long-distance trade is neither a sufficient nor a necessary condition for the rise of states.

    C. Population, War, and Circumscription (Carneiro)
        1. This is a multivariate theory for state formation in that it incorporates three factors working together instead of a single cause.
        2. According to Carneiro, wherever and whenever environmental circumscription (or resource concentration), increasing population, and warfare exist, state formation will begin.
        3. Circumscription
            a. Physically circumscribed environments include small islands, river plains, oases, and valleys.
            b. Social circumscription exists when neighboring societies block expansion, emigration, or access to resources.
        4. This theory explains many, but not all cases of state formation.
        5. Highland New Guinea has environmental circumscription, warfare, and increasing population, but the region has never been host to a state.

VI. Why States Collapse

    A. Causes
        1. Invasion
        2. Disease
        3. Environmental degradation
            a. Canals in Mesopotamia feed the cities but also poisoned the land.
            b. As the water evaporated from the canals, the water-borne salts became concentrated in the fields.
            c. Mashkan-shapir
        4. States collapse when they fail to do what they are supposed to do, such as maintain social order, protect themselves against outsiders, and allow their people to feed themselves.

    B. The Mayan Decline
        1. The Maya state of the Classic Period flourished between A.D. 300 and 900 (1700-1100 B.P.) in what is now southern Mexico, Guatemala, western Honduras, Belize, and El Salvador.
        2. Copán was the largest site in the southeastern region of the Maya area.
            a. Last inscribed monument has the date of A.D. 822.
            b. Copán's collapse was linked to erosion, soil exhaustion, and overpopulation.

C. Beyond the Classroom: The Akhenaten Temple Project
1. Jerusha Achterberg spent a field season excavating at the site of Mendes in Egypt.
2. Achterberg learned that in addition to digging, archaeological excavation requires a lot of note taking and drawing.

LECTURE TOPICS

1. Discuss how states differ from other forms of sociopolitical organization and how those differences are manifested in the archaeological record.

2. Discuss the differences between egalitarian, ranked, and stratified societies. How are the differences between these kinds of societies manifested in the archaeological record?

3. Compare and contrast cultural and biological evolution. How useful is an evolutionary framework to the study of sociopolitical change through time and space?

4. Discuss why states collapse. Be sure to point out that just as no single variable can explain the rise of states, one variable cannot completely explain their collapse.

SUGGESTED FILMS

The Valley of the Kings

29 min   color
The tombs of Ipi the workman and Kha the architect, which illustrate the daily round of ancient Egyptian life. From Films for the Humanities and Sciences. Contents: Art as a communal activity; the tools, furniture, clothes, kitchen utensils, and foods (if Ipi and Kha, and the money with which they were paid; how the Egyptians divided the person into body, soul, and image; the Colossi of Memnon and King Amen Hotep's deed giving the temple to the god; the tomb of Tutmose III. From Films for the Humanities and Sciences.

America's First City: Teotihuacan

16mm   18 min   1975   color
The world-famous pyramids of Teotihuacan are the remains of a great city founded 2000 years ago--the first metropolis in America. Presents the story of this city through scenes of its ruins. Dominating the site is the Pyramid of the Sun, as tall as a 20-story building, now worn and weathered but originally plastered and brilliantly painted. The lavishly decorated Pyramid of Quetzelcoatl is the outstanding example of the architectural and engineering genius of those early builders. The legend of the Fifth Sun, the Aztec tale of the birth of Teotihuacan, is reenacted. Teotihuacan was abandoned around A.D. 800, but it is still revered by Mexicans as an example of the skills and artistry of their ancestors. From the Mexico Heritage series. From The University of Illinois Film and Video Center.

The Story of the Aztecs

20 min   1975   color
Traces the history and past glories of the Aztec Empire. In 1125 the Aztecs entered the Valley of Mexico, and there they founded their shimmering capital city, Tenochtitlan. A huge complex of ceremonial buildings, marketplaces and palaces, it was a fitting center for a tribe who ruled over an empire that included all of Mexico as far south as Guatemala. The Aztecs were fierce

and cruel, taking slaves to build their temples and captives to use as human sacrifices to their gods. In 1519 the fabled Aztec Empire was destroyed by the Spaniards, and the ruins of Tenochtitlan lie beneath modern Mexico City. From the *Mexico Heritage* series. From The University of Illinois Film and Video Center.

These Were the Maya!

19 min   1975   color
Achievements of the Mayan civilization in architecture, mathematics, astrology, and art were very advanced for their time, and make a fascinating visual and historical study. Reviews the evidences remaining of these cultural monuments, including their calendar, codices, and system of counting. In Spanish of intermediate difficulty. An English version is entitled *These Were the Maya!* From the Mexico Heritage series. From The University of Illinois Film and Video Center.

Viva Mexico! A Cultural Portrait

28 min   1971   color
Mexico's combined heritage of Indian and Spanish civilizations are visible in the costumes, architecture, food, folk art, and traditional celebrations depicted in the film. Scenes from the Mayan and Aztec ruins are skillfully blended with scenes of contemporary Indian society and views of pre-Columbian artifacts housed in the National Museum of Anthropology. Other highlights include colorful fiestas, a rodeo, and a visit with some famous Mexican potters at work. Features accompanying folk music score and appropriate sounds recorded on-site. From The University of Illinois Film and Video Center.

Chinese History: 1--The Beginnings

16mm   1976   19 min
Depicts the search for the origins of Chinese civilization (to 1100 B.C.). The earliest inhabitants-Lan-t'ien Man, Peking Man, and Upper Cave Man were followed about 6,000 years ago by Neolithic cultures, one of which, Lung-Shan, developed into the first Chinese historical dynasty, Shang. When China entered the Bronze Age, advances were made in technology, art, and architecture. From The University of Illinois Film and Video Center.

Chinese History: 2--The Making of a Civilization

16mm   1976   18 min
Describes the conquest of Shang and the rule of Chou (c. 1100 to 475 B.C.). The Chou dynasty established a type of feudal system with a king as absolute ruler. In 770 B.C., the capital was moved eastward to protect it from invasion, dividing the dynasty into Western and Eastern Chou periods. This latter period witnessed the replacement of serfdom with land ownership, the advent of the Iron Age, and the search by Confucius for the deeper meaning of man and nature. From The University of Illinois Film and Video Center.

MULTIPLE-CHOICE QUESTIONS

1. What kind of society has a formal, central government and a division of society into classes?

   a. a chiefdom
   b.   a state
   c. a tribe
   d. a band
   e. a cohort

2. Which of the following is *not* a characteristic of states?

   a. They control specific regional territories
   b. They have productive farming economies
   c.   They have low levels of specialization
   d. They are stratified into social classes
   e. They have record keeping systems

3. Where is Mesopotamia?

   a.   The area between the Tigris and Euphrates rivers is what is today Iraq and southwestern Iran.
   b. The area between Mexico City and Nicaragua.
   c. The area between Quito, Ecuador and Lima, Peru.
   d. The area along the Indus river in Pakistan.
   e. The area between the Yellow and Yangtze rivers in modern China.

4. Which of the following statements about Jericho is *not* true?

   a. It is located in the Levant.
   b. It has a large tower and a city wall.
   c. It was first settled by the Natufians.
   d. After 9000 B.P., the inhabitants buried their dead below their house floors.
   e.   It has a series of shrines decorated with bull motifs.

5. Which of the following statements about Çatal Hüyük is *not* true?

   a. The dwellings at the site were entered through the roof.
   b.   It was first settled by Natufians.
   c. The ritual life was centered on animals, danger, and death.
   d. The dead were buried beneath the house floors.
   e. Food was stored and processed collectively.

6. When did pottery become widespread in the Middle East?

   a. 15,000 B.P.
   b. 12,000 B.P.
   c. 10,000 B.P.
   d.   7000 B.P.
   e. 4000 B.P.

7. What is the name of the cultural period during which the first chiefdoms emerged in northern Syria?

   a. Natufian
   b. P.P.N.A.
   c. Halafian
   d. Ubaid
   e. Uruk

8. What is the name of the cultural period during which the first chiefdoms emerged in southern Mesopotamia?

   a. Natufian
   b. P.P.N.A.
   c. Halafian
   d. Ubaid
   e. Uruk

9. What term refers to a society that lacks status distinctions except those based on age, gender, and individual qualities, talents, and achievements?

   a. gendered society
   b. communism
   c. socialism
   d. fascism
   e. egalitarian society

10. Which of the following statements about egalitarian society is *not* true?

    a. everybody is of equal status
    b. everybody is born equal
    c. there are no social classes
    d. there is no hereditary inequality
    e. a person's status is based on their age, gender, and individual qualities, talents, and achievements

11. How are ranked societies different from states?

    a. states lack hereditary inequality
    b. ranked societies lack hereditary inequality
    c. states have chiefs
    d. states have social classes
    e. ranked societies have social classes

12. In what kind of society is a person's status based on their genealogical distance from the chief?

    a. egalitarian
    b. state
    c. stratified
    d. communal
    e. ranked

13. Which of the following statements about ranked societies is *not* true?

   a.   all ranked societies are chiefdoms
   b.   there is a continuum of status
   c.   all chiefdoms are ranked societies
   d.   they lack social strata
   e.   they have hereditary inequality

14. What term refers to a ranked society that has lost village autonomy?

   a.   a primary state
   b.   a chiefdom
   c.   an archaic state
   d.   a tribe
   e.   a band

15. What were the precursors to primary states?

   a.   archaic states
   b.   tribes
   c.   city-states
   d.   bands
   e.   chiefdoms

16. Which of the following conditions was not present during the time of primary state formation in southern Mesopotamia?

   a.   an expanding population
   b.   increasing specialization
   c.   increasing isolation of communities
   d.   a growing central leadership
   e.   increasing trade

17. Where did writing first develop in the Middle East?

   a.   Çatal Hüyük
   b.   the Levant
   c.   northern Mesopotamia
   d.   southern Mesopotamia
   e.   central Iran

18. What is the name of the earliest writing in Mesopotamia?

   a.   cuneiform
   b.   hieroglyphics
   c.   sanskrit
   d.   linear B
   e.   kanji

19. Which of the following statements about the earliest writing is *not* true?

   a.   It was developed as a form of record keeping.
   b.   It spread from Mesopotamia to Egypt.
   c.   It had no role in the development of Mesoamerican writing systems.
   d.   It was syllabic.
   e.   It was scrawled on wet clay with a stylus.

20. Who dominated the economies of the first Mesopotamian states?

   a.　the military
   b.　the merchants
   c.　the temple
   d.　the artists
   e.　the curers

21. When did metallurgy begin to develop rapidly in Mesopotamia?

   a.　around 10,000 B.P.
   b.　around 7000 B.P.
   c.　around 5000 B.P.
   d.　around 3000 B.P.
   e.　around 1000 B.P.

22. What is the name of the first state in Pakistan and western India?

   a.　Shang
   b.　Zapotec
   c.　Uruk
   d.　Moche
   e.　Indus

23. Which of the following is *not* a characteristic of the first state in Pakistan and western India?

   a.　a writing system
   b.　a standard system of weights
   c.　wealthy tombs of nobles
   d.　sophisticated craft industries
   e.　careful city planning

24. What is the name of the first Chinese state?

   a.　Shang
   b.　Taipei
   c.　Chin
   d.　Dim sum
   e.　Nok Nok

25. What kind of society where the Olmec?

   a.　a state
   b.　a empire
   c.　a tribe
   d.　a chiefdom
   e.　a band

26. Which of the following statements about the Olmec is *not* true?

   a.　They lived along the Gulf Coast of modern Mexico.
   b.　They were the first Mesoamerican empire.
   c.　They lived between 3,200 and 2,500 years ago.
   d.　They carved massive stone heads.
   e.　They built earthen mounds grouped around a plaza.

27. What prestige item was crafted by inhabitants of the Valley of Oaxaca and traded with other Mesoamerican chiefdoms?

   a. **mirrors**
   b. colossal heads
   c. standard weights
   d. stoneware bangles
   e. iron axes

28. What was the capital of the first state to develop in the Valley of Mexico?

   a. Tehuantepec
   b. La Venta
   c. Tenochtitlan
   d. Monte Albán
   e. **Teotihuacan**

29. Which of the following is *not* a characteristic of the Teotihuacan state?

   a. large-scale irrigation
   b. complex architecture
   c. careful city planning
   d. large population
   e. **all of the above are characteristics**

30. What do proponents of the hydraulic theory for the origin of the state argue?

   a. Irrigation began in China and spread along ancient trade routes.
   b. **States were the by-products of the organizational requirements of large irrigation systems.**
   c. Irrigation systems favored democracy.
   d. Irrigation provided the advantage that allowed *Homo sapiens sapiens* to displace the Neandertals.
   e. Mesolithic states developed so that they could build irrigation systems.

31. Which variable does not enter into Carneiro's theory of state formation?

   a. warfare
   b. population growth
   c. environmental circumscription
   d. resource concentration
   e. **long-distance trade**

32. According to Kottak, what is the most complete explanation of primary state formation?

   a. a prime-mover explanation based on irrigation
   b. **a multivariate approach**
   c. a set of nine ecological and social factors determining the evolution of social stratification
   d. the development of a four-level hierarchy composed of peasant villages, subchiefdoms, chiefdoms, and capital cities
   e. a great increase in the incidence of sexuality

33. Why do states collapse?

    a.   when they fail to maintain social order
    b.   when they fail to protect themselves against outsiders
    c.   when they fail to allow people to feed themselves
    d.   when they fail to do what they are supposed to do
    e.   **all of the above**

34. What caused the collapse at Mashkan-shapir?

    a.   external conquest
    b.   **destruction of the fields by mineral salts**
    c.   earthquake
    d.   erosion
    e.   landslide due to heavy mountain rains

35. Which of the following statements about the collapse of Copán is true?

    a.   It took place around A.D. 830.
    b.   It was linked to erosion.
    c.   It was linked to soil exhaustion.
    d.   There were about 25,000 people living at Copán at the time of collapse.
    e.   **all of the above**

ESSAY QUESTIONS

36. Summarize evidence against any two of the following prime-mover theories of state formation:
    a.   hydraulic management
    b.   regulation of ecological diversity
    c.   long-distance trade
    d.   population pressure

37. Why do states collapse? Is there a single model that can explain every case in which states have collapsed?

38. Summarize Carneiro's multivariate approach to state formation. What variables are involved?

39. How are chiefdoms different from states? How do archaeologists distinguish between the two?

40. Compare and contrast egalitarian, ranked, and stratified societies.

TRUE OR FALSE QUESTIONS

41. True or **False**   States are complex systems of sociopolitical organizations that aim to control and administer everything from conflict resolution, to fiscal systems, to population movements.

42. **True** or False   Early states had productive farming economies.

43. True or **False**   Early states lack social classes.

44. True or **False**   All early states developed a form of syllabic writing.

45. **True** or False   The earliest states emerged in Mesopotamia.

46. True or **False**   Mesoamerica refers to the land between the Tigris and Euphrates rivers.

47. **True** or False   Jericho and Çatal Hüyük are two of the earliest towns in the Middle East.

48. **True** or False   Çatal Hüyük is located in central Turkey.

49. True or **False**   The inhabitants of both Jericho and Çatal Hüyük lived in round houses.

50. **True** or False   The Halaf and Ubaid periods are when the first chiefdoms appeared in the Middle East.

51. True or **False**   In an egalitarian society, everybody is of equal status.

52. **True** or False   All bands are egalitarian.

53. True or **False**   Tribes were the precursors to primary states.

54. **True** or False   Ranked societies lack social classes.

55. True or **False**   Most researchers today believe that states emerged in response to the growing administrative requirements for building, maintaining, and administering public hydraulic works.

56. **True** or False   Carneiro's circumscription model argues that states emerged only in areas where societies were physically circumscribed.

57. True or **False**   A key feature of Carneiro's model for the origin of states is that it includes a series of variables.

58. **True** or False   The Shang dynasty had bronze metallurgy and writing.

59. **True** or False   Environmental degradation often contributes to the collapse of states.

60. True or **False**   The Olmec was the first state in Mesoamerica.

CHAPTER 11
CULTURE

CHAPTER OUTLINE

I. Introduction

    A. Kottak uses Tylor's definition of "culture," which can be defined as, "that complex whole which includes, knowledge, belief, arts, morals, law, custom, and any other capabilities and habits acquired by man as a member of society."

    B. Enculturation is the process by which a child learns his or her culture.

II. What is Culture?

    A. Culture is Learned
        1. Cultural learning is unique to humans.
        2. Cultural learning is the accumulation of knowledge about experiences and information not perceived directly by the organism, but transmitted through symbols.
          a. Symbols are signs that have no necessary or natural connection with the things for which they stand.
          b. Geertz defines culture as ideas based on cultural learning and symbols.
        3. Culture is learned through both direct instruction and through observation (both conscious and unconscious).
        4. Anthropologists in the 19th century argued for the "psychic unity of man."
          a. This doctrine acknowledges that individuals vary in their emotional and intellectual tendencies and capacities.
          b. However, this doctrine asserted that all human populations share the same capacity for culture.

    B. Culture is Shared
        1. Culture is located and transmitted in groups.
        2. The social transmission of culture tends to unify people by providing us with a common experience.
        3. The commonalty of experience in turn tends to generate a common understanding of future events.

    C. Interesting Issues: Touching, Affection, Love, and Sex
        1. Even such things as apparently "natural" as emotions and sex can be culturally constructed.
        2. Americans do not clearly differentiate among physical expressions of affection as opposed to sex, while Brazilians do.
        3. Consequently, unspoken dynamics of interactions from representatives of these to cultures might lead to one constructing the other as either "cold" or overbearing.
        4. Kottak treats the clearer Brazilian distinction between affection and sex as more realistic.

    D. Culture is Symbolic
        1. The human ability to use symbols is the basis of culture (a symbol is something verbal or nonverbal within a particular language or culture that comes to stand for something else).
        2. While human symbol use is overwhelmingly linguistic, a symbol is anything that is used to represent any other thing, when the relationship between the two is arbitrary (e.g. a flag).

3. Other primates have demonstrated rudimentary ability to use symbols, but only humans have elaborated cultural abilities – to learn, to communicate, to store, to process, and to use symbols.

E. Culture and Nature
   1. Humans interact with cultural constructions of nature, rather than directly with nature itself.
   2. Culture converts natural urges and acts into cultural customs.

F. Culture is All-Encompassing
   1. The anthropological concept of culture is a model that includes all aspects of human group behavior.
   2. Everyone is cultured, not just wealthy people with an elite education.

G. Culture is Integrated
   1. A culture is a system: changes in one aspect will likely generate changes in other aspects.
   2. Core values are sets of ideas, attitudes, and beliefs, which are basic in that they provide an organizational logic for the rest of the culture.

H. People Use Culture Creatively
   1. Humans have the ability to avoid, manipulate, subvert and change the "rules" and patterns of their own cultures.
   2. "Ideal culture" refers to normative descriptions of a culture given by its natives.
   3. "Real culture" refers to "actual behavior as observed by an anthropologist."
   4. Culture is both public and individual because individuals internalize the meanings of public (cultural) messages.

I. Culture is Adaptive and Maladaptive
   1. Culture is an adaptive strategy employed by hominids.
   2. Because cultural behavior is motivated by cultural factors, and not by environmental constraints, cultural behavior can be maladaptive.
   3. Determining whether a cultural practice is adaptive or maladaptive frequently requires viewing the results of that practice from several perspectives (from the point of view of a different culture, species, or time frame, for example).

J. Levels of Culture
   1. National culture refers to the experiences, beliefs, "learned behavior" patterns, and values shared by citizens of the same nation.
   2. International culture refers to cultural practices, which are common to an identifiable group, extending beyond the boundaries of one culture.
   3. Subcultures are identifiable cultural patterns existing within a larger culture.
   4. Cultural practices and artifacts are transmitted through diffusion.
      a. Direct diffusion occurs when members of two or more previously distinct cultures interact with each other.
      b. Indirect diffusion occurs when cultural artifacts or practices are transmitted from one culture to another through an intermediate third (or more) culture.

K. Ethnocentrism, Cultural Relativism, and Human Rights
   1. Ethnocentrism is the use of values, ideals, and mores from one's own culture to judge the behavior of someone from another culture.
      a. Ethnocentrism is a cultural universal.
      b. Ethnocentrism contributes to social solidarity.
   2. Cultural Relativism asserts that cultural values are arbitrary, and therefore the values of one culture should not be used as standards to evaluate the behavior of persons from outside that culture.

3. The idea of universal, unalienable, individual human rights challenges cultural relativism by invoking a moral and ethical code that is superior to any country, culture, or religion.
4. Cultural rights are vested in groups and include a group's ability to preserve its cultural tradition.
5. Kottak argues that cultural relativism does not preclude an anthropologist from respecting "international standards of justice and morality."

III. Universality, Particularity, and Generality

A. Introduction
1. Cultural universals are features that are found in every culture.
2. Cultural generalities include features that are common to several, but not all human groups.
3. Cultural particularities are features that are unique to certain cultural traditions.

B. Universality
1. Cultural universals are those traits that distinguish *Homo sapiens* from other species.
2. Some biological universals include a long period of infant dependency, year-round sexuality, and a complex brain that enables us to use symbols, languages, and tools.
3. Some psychological universals include the common ways in which humans think, feel, and process information.
4. Some social universals include: incest taboos, life in groups, families (of some kind), and food sharing.

C. Generality
1. Certain practices, beliefs, and the like may be held commonly by more than one culture, but not be universal; these are called "generalities."
2. Diffusion and independent invention are two main sources of cultural generalities.
3. The nuclear family is a cultural generality since it is present in most, but not all societies.

D. Particularity
1. Cultural practices that are unique to any one culture are "cultural particulars."
2. That these particulars may be of fundamental importance to the population is indicative of the need to study the sources of cultural diversity.

IV. Beyond the Classroom: Folklore Reveals the Ethos of Heating Plant Workers

A. Mark Dennis investigated the social and cultural manifestations of folklore among the workers of the University of Calgary's heating and cooling plant.

B. He found that the folklore functioned to create and maintain social cohesion among the plant workers in addition to helping alleviate job-related stress.

V. Mechanisms of Cultural Change

A. Diffusion
1. Diffusion is defined as the spread of culture traits through borrowing from one culture to another; it has been a source of culture change throughout human history.
2. Diffusion can be direct (between two adjacent cultures) or indirect (across one or more intervening cultures or through some long distance medium).
3. Diffusion can be forced (through warfare, colonization, or some other kind of domination) or unforced (*e.g.,* intermarriage, trade, and the like).

B. Acculturation
1. Acculturation is the exchange of features that results when groups come into continuous firsthand contact.

2. Acculturation may occur in any or all groups engaged in such contact.
3. A pidgin is an example of acculturation, because it is a language form that develops by borrowing language elements from two linguistically different populations in order to facilitate communication between the two.

C. Independent Invention
1. Independent invention is defined as the creative innovation of new solutions to old and new problems.
2. Cultural generalities are partly explained by the independent invention of similar responses to similar cultural and environmental circumstances.
3. The independent invention of agriculture in both the Middle East and Mexico is cited as an example.

D. Cultural Convergence or Convergent Cultural Evolution
1. Cultural convergence is the development of similar traits, institutions, and behavior patterns by separate groups as a result of adaptation to similar environments.
2. Julian Steward pointed to instances of cultural convergence to support the hypothesis that scientific laws govern cultural change.

VI. Globalization

A. Globalization encompasses a series of processes that work to make modern nations and people increasingly interlinked and mutually dependent.

B. Economic and political forces take advantage of modern systems of communication and transportation to promote globalization.

C. Globalization allows for the domination of local peoples by larger (these may be based regionally, nationally, and worldwide) economic and political systems.

D. Recognizing the breadth and nature of changes wrought through globalization carries the concomitant need to recognize practices of resistance, accommodation, and survival that occur in response.

LECTURE TOPICS

1. Discuss the history of how people defined culture. Be sure to set the definitions in the context within which they were produced.

2. Emphasize the distinction between the biological basis for culture and particular human cultures. Note the non-heritability of cultures (what languages do second generation immigrants speak, for example). Discuss the debate focusing on the claims of sociobiology.

3. Discuss the deep tenacity of values, illustrating it by citing cases in which people have gone to great sacrifices to maintain the value systems of their cultures.

4. Describe the process of enculturation to any common subculture with which you are familiar, such as the academic professional subculture.

5. American undergraduate students like any natives who have little experience of other cultures, usually do not recognize their values as culturally relative. Pick common American values, such as freedom, autonomy, individuality, cleanliness, innocence, and fairness, and show how they are not shared by other cultures. To emphasize the point, pick values common to undergraduate subculture and show how limited they are.

SUGGESTED FILMS

Perception

16mm   1979   29 min
Uses film clips, visual experiments, and works of art to identify the various factors, such as social upbringing, culture, and media, that affect the way people develop personal and subjective awareness of objects and events around them. Shows that no two people "see" the same thing in precisely the same way and depicts, in several business and social vignettes, the consequences of individuals perceiving situations differently. Distributed by the University of Illinois Film and Video Center.

The Path

16mm   1972   34 min
Documents a traditional early autumn Japanese thin-tea ceremony. The film style and tea ritual provides insight into the underlying currents of structure, psychology, and esthetic feelings that characterize traditional Japanese culture. Distributed by the University of Illinois Film and Video Center.

Trobriand Cricket: An Ingenious Response to Colonialism

16mm   1976   55 min
An ethnographic documentary about cultural creativity among the Trobriand Islanders of Papua-New Guinea. Shows how the Trobrianders have taken the very controlled game of British cricket, first introduced by missionaries, and changed it into an outlet for mock warfare and intervillage competition, political reputation building among leaders, erotic dancing and chanting, and riotous fun. The game is a gigantic message about people's attitudes, responses, and experiences under colonialism. Distributed by the University of Illinois Film and Video Center.

MULTIPLE-CHOICE QUESTIONS

1. Culture _____.

    a.   **is acquired by humans as members of society**
    b.   is more developed in the United States than among hunters and gatherers
    c.   is being destroyed by popular culture
    d.   developed around 10,000 years ago
    e.   is acquired through biological heredity

2. How is culture acquired?

    a.   consciously
    b.   unconsciously
    c.   through observation
    d.   through direct instruction
    e.   **all of the above**

133

3. Which of the following statements about enculturation is *not* true?

    a.   It occurs through a process of conscious and unconscious learning.
    b.   It requires interaction with others.
    c.   It results in internalization of a cultural tradition.
    d.   It may involve direct teaching.
    e.   all of the above are true statements

4. According to Leslie White, when did culture, and therefore humanity, come into existence?

    a.   when our ancestors began to walk erect
    b.   when our ancestors began to think rationally
    c.   when our ancestors began to use symbols
    d.   when our ancestors began to make fire
    e.   when our ancestors began to make tools

5. The fact that Americans and Brazilians, in general, have profoundly different ideas about appropriate social touching, sex, and even emotions is evidence that

    a.   Brazilians and Americans have been genetically distinct populations for many generations.
    b.   instinctive behavior may vary even among human populations.
    c.   even apparently natural behaviors may be fundamentally shaped by culture.
    d.   warm environments select for one kind of psychological pattern, while temperate and cold climates select for another.
    e.   all of the above

6. What do anthropologists mean when they say culture is shared?

    a.   Culture is an attribute of particular individuals.
    b.   Culture is an attribute of individuals as members of groups.
    c.   Culture is what ensures that all people raised in the same society have the same opinions.
    d.   Culture is universally regarded as more important than the concept of the individual.
    e.   Enculturation is accomplished by more than one person.

7. What is the term for a sign that has no necessary or natural connection to the thing for which it stands?

    a.   morpheme
    b.   lexicon
    c.   phoneme
    d.   symbol
    e.   collateral

8. What process is most responsible for the existence of international culture?

    a.   ethnocentrism
    b.   cultural relativism
    c.   dendritic acculturation
    d.   gene flow
    e.   diffusion

9. What is cultural relativism?

    a. It is a cultural universal, based upon the human capacity to use symbols.
    b. It is the argument that behavior in a particular culture should not be judged by the standards of another culture.
    c. It is a cultural particular, based upon the interrelatedness of humans.
    d. It is the opposite of participant observation.
    e. It is the same thing as ethnocentrism, but it applies only to family structures.

10. What are exogamy and the incest taboo examples of?

    a. cultural particulars
    b. cultural relativisms
    c. cultural universals
    d. primitive superstitions
    e. modern superstitions

11. What is the opposite of ethnocentrism?

    a. secular humanism
    d. psychological anthropology
    b. universalism
    e. diffusion
    c. cultural relativism

12. What are cultural particulars?

    a. Traits isolated from other traits in the same culture
    b. Traits unique to given culture, not shared with any others
    c. Different levels of culture
    d. The most general aspect of culture patterns
    e. Cultural traits of individuals, rather than groups

13. Which of the following statements about culture is *not* true?

    a. Cultural learning is uniquely elaborated among humans.
    b. Culture is the major reason for human adaptability.
    c. All humans share the capacity for culture.
    d. Human groups differ in their capacities for culture.
    e. all of the above are true

14. The incest taboo is a cultural universal, but _____.

    a. the definition of what constitutes incest varies widely across cultures
    b. it does not count as such, since higher primates do it, too
    c. it has disappeared among modern societies
    d. it has only recently appeared among tribal societies
    e. none of the above

15. Which of the following statements about culture is *not* true?

    a. It is a distinctive possession of humanity.
    b. It is acquired by all humans as members of society through enculturation.
    c. It encompasses rule-governed, shared, symbol-based, learned behavior and beliefs transmitted across the generations.
    d. Everyone is cultured.
    e. It is transmitted genetically.

16. Which of the following statements about culture is *not* true?

    a. Cultural practices are always learned.
    b. Cultural practices are always adaptive.
    c. Cultural practices are always shared.
    d. Cultures are all encompassing.
    e. Cultures can be national, international, or regional.

17. Which of the following statements about cultural relativism is *not* true?

    a. Cultural relativism argues that some cultures are relatively better than others.
    b. Cultural relativism argues that each culture is a uniquely different integrated whole.
    c. Cultural relativism argues that we shouldn't use our own standards to judge conduct in other cultures.
    d. Cultural relativism argues that no one culture is better than any other
    e. none of the above

18. How are cultural rights different from human rights?

    a. Human rights are real, while cultural rights are just perceived.
    b. The United Nations protects human rights, but not cultural rights.
    c. Cultural rights are vested in groups, not in individuals.
    d. Cultural rights are more clear-cut than human rights.
    e. Cultural rights are politically correct synonyms for human rights.

19. Which of the following is a cultural generality?

    a. nuclear family
    b. the use of fire
    c. incest taboo
    d. use of symbols
    e. none of the above is a cultural generality

20. Which statement about subcultures is *not* true?

    a. Subcultures exemplify "levels of culture"
    b. Subcultures have different learning experiences
    c. Subcultures have shared learning experiences
    d. Subcultures may originate in ethnicity, class, region, or religion
    e. Subcultures are mutually exclusive; individuals may not participate in more than one subculture

21. What kind of diffusion takes place when two cultures trade, inter-marry, or wage war on one another?

    a. forced diffusion
    b. direct diffusion
    c. indirect diffusion
    d. enculturated diffusion
    e. bilateral diffusion

22. What is the term for cultural change that results when two or more cultures have continuous firsthand contact?

   a. **acculturation**
   b. enculturation
   c. independent invention
   d. colonization
   e. imperialism

23. What is the term for the processes that are making nations and people increasingly interlinked and mutually dependent?

   a. acculturation
   b. diffusion
   c. **globalization**
   d. enculturation
   e. independent invention

24. Jazz music is popular all over the world, but it was started in the United States. Which of the following mechanisms of cultural change is responsible for this?

   a. acculturation
   b. enculturation
   c. independent invention
   d. colonization
   e. **diffusion**

25. There were at least seven different regions where agriculture developed. Therefore, agriculture is an example of which of the following mechanisms of cultural change?

   a. acculturation
   b. enculturation
   c. **independent invention**
   d. colonization
   e. diffusion

ESSAY QUESTIONS

26. What does it mean to say that culture is all encompassing?

27. Explain the difference between culture in the general sense and culture in the specific sense.

28. What are the different kinds of learning? On which is culture based?

29. What does it mean to say that culture is symbolic?

30. What does it mean to say that culture is shared?

31. What does it mean to say that culture is patterned or integrated? How is culture patterned?

32. How is culture adaptive? Can culture be maladaptive? How so?

33. How are human adaptability and culture related?

34. What does it mean to say that there are levels of culture? What are they?

35. What are ethnocentrism and cultural relativism and what are their problems?

36. Explain the distinctions among cultural universals, generalities, and particularities and give examples of each.

37. How is the concept of cultural particularity related to the notion of cultural patterning or integration?

38. Compare and contrast the various types of cultural change listed at the end of this chapter. In particular, to what extent does each model for change suggest that culture shapes human behavior or is shaped by human behavior?

39. Kottak mentions that cultural generalities may occur as different cultures innovate similarly to similar circumstances, suggesting thereby that environmental circumstances might limit the reasonable options for innovation. To what extent are cultural members free or constrained in their ability to change their culture through innovation?

40. Any of the multiple-choice questions listed above may be converted to an essay question by requiring the students to justify their answers. To accomplish this, the student should explain why and how the correct response answers the question (providing examples where necessary and feasible) and also explaining why the incorrect responses are incorrect.

TRUE OR FALSE QUESTIONS

41. True or False   One's culture helps you to define the world in which you live, express feelings and ideas, and helps guide your behavior and perceptions.

42. True or **False**   Cultural is transmitted by formal instruction, not by observation.

43. True or False   Culture is transmitted in society.

44. True or False   According to Leslie White, culture is dependent on the ability to create and use symbols.

45. True or **False**   Brazil and the U.S. have similar nations regarding touching, affection, love, and sex.

46. True or **False**   Cultural habits, perceptions, and inventions are genetically determined.

47. True or False   Cultures are integrated, patterned systems in which change in one part often leads to changes in other parts.

48. True or **False**   Once an individual has been enculturated, that person must adhere to the cultural rules that governs that culture.

49. True or False   Although culture is one of the principle means that humans adapt to their environment, some cultural traits can be harmful to a groups' survival.

50. True or **False**   Although there are many different levels of culture, an individual can participate in only one level at a time.

51. True or **False**   Only people living in the industrialized, capitalist countries of Western Europe and the U.S. are ethnocentric.

52. True or False   Cultural relativists believe that a culture should be judged only according to the standards and traditions of that culture and not according to standards of other cultural traditions.

53. True or False   The idea of universal and unalienable human rights that are superior to the laws and ethics of any culture can conflict with some of the ideas central to cultural relativism.

54. True or **False**   Food sharing is found only in cultures whose subsistence is based on hunting and gathering.

55. True or **False**   The nuclear family is a feature of all known cultures.

56. True or False   Diffusion plays an important role in spreading cultural traits around the world.

57. True or False   Independent invention is when two or more cultures independently come up with similar solutions to a common problem.

58. True or **False**   Acculturation is the process by which people lose the culture that they learned as children.

59. True or **False**   Indigenous cultures are at the mercy of the forces of globalization as they can do nothing to stop the threats to their cultural identity, autonomy, and livelihood.

60. True or False   Modern means of transportation and communication have facilitated the process of globalization.

CHAPTER 12
ETHNICITY

CHAPTER OUTLINE

I. Ethnic Groups and Ethnicity

    A. Ethnicity and Race
       1. An ethnic group may define themselves as different because of their language, religion, geography, history, ancestry, or physical traits.
       2. When an ethnic group is assumed to have a biological basis, it is called a race.
       3. Most Americans fail to distinguish between ethnicity and race.
       a. Many people think that ethnicity is just the politically correct term for race.
       b. Ethnicity is based on cultural traditions, while races are based mainly on biological traits.

    B. Ethnic Markers, Identities, and Statuses
       1. Ethnic groups are formed around the same features as cultures: common beliefs, values, customs, history, and the like.
       2. Ethnicity entails identification with a given ethnic group, but it also involves the maintenance of a distinction from other groups.
       3. Status refers to any position in a society, which can be filled by an individual.
       a. Ascribed status is status into which people enter automatically without choice, usually at birth or through some other universal event in the life cycle.
       b. Achieved status is status that people acquire through their own actions.
       4. Within complex societies, ascribed status can describe large sub-groups: minority groups, majority groups, and races are all examples of *ascribed* statuses.
       5. Differences in ascribed status are commonly associated with differences in social-political power.
       6. The definitive feature of a minority group is that its members systematically experience lesser income, authority, and power that other members of their society; a minority group is not necessarily a smaller population than other groups.

    C. In The News: Sosa vs. McGwire: It's a Race, but Is It Also About Race?
       1. The 1998 home run race between Sammy Sosa and Mark McGwire highlighted some of the problems with American notions of race.
       2. Both Latino and Black communities claimed Sosa, as one of their own, while McGwire was the darling for most of the white community.

    D. Status Shifting
       1. Most status is susceptible to change, particular through the influence of social contexts.
       2. Adjusting or switching one's status in reaction to different social contexts is called the *situational negotiation of social identity.*
       3. The application of a social category label, such as an ethnic label, to a particular individual depends on perception by others of that person's status, as well as that person's own assertions of status.

II. Ethnic Groups, Nations, and Nationalities

    A. Nation-States Defined
       1. Nation and nation-state now refer to an autonomous, centrally organized political entity.
       2. Ethnic groups are not necessarily so formally politically organized.

3. The majority of all nation-states have more than one ethnic group in their constituent populations, and the multiethnicity of all countries is increasing.

B. Nationalities and Imagined Communities
1. Nationalities are ethnic groups that aspire to autonomous statehood (regardless of their political history).
2. The term "imagined communities," coined by Benedict Anderson, has been used to describe nationalities, since most of their member population feel a bond with each other in the absence of any "real" acquaintance.
3. Mass media and the language arts have helped to form such imagined communities by becoming the means of establishing a commonalty of values, motivations, language, and the like.
4. Colonialism refers to the political, social, economic, and cultural domination of a territory and its people by a foreign power for an extended period of time.
5. Colonialism helped create imagined communities as different ethnic groups under the control of the same colonial administration often pooled resources in opposition to the colonial power.
   a. *Négritude* ("African identity") developed out of the common experience of French colonial rule in a variety of African countries.
   b. The fact that negritude crosses several present-day national boundaries makes it no more or less an imagined community than any nation-state.

C. Interesting Issues: Ethnic Nationalism Run Wild
1. The breakup of Yugoslavia along ethnic lines in the early 1990s is outlined to provide an example of the interplay between history, ethnic identity, and nationalism.
2. Serbs, Croats, and Muslim Slavs are divided into various groups based on religion, culture, and political and military history (particularly, Serb retaliation for actions taken against them by Croats during the Second World War).
3. The (largely) Serbian practice of "ethnic cleansing," the policy of killing or driving out non-Serbs is described.
4. Kottak suggests, following Barth, that the highly blended nature of former Yugoslav society reduced the possibility for ecological specialization and the concomitant economic interdependence that (according to Barth) supports peaceful pluralism.

III. Peaceful Coexistence

A. Assimilation
1. Assimilation occurs when a minority group adopts the patterns and norms of a more powerful culture, as when a migrant ethnic group conforms itself to its host culture.
2. Assimilation is not uniform, it may be forced or relatively benign depending on historical particularities.
3. Brazil (as opposed to the United States and Canada) is cited as a highly assimilative society wherein ethnic neighborhoods are virtually unknown.

B. The Plural Society
1. Plural society refers to a multiethnic nation-state wherein the sub-groups do not assimilate but remain essentially distinct, in (relatively) stable coexistence.
2. Barth defines plural society as a society combining ethnic contrasts and the economic interdependence of the ethnic groups.
3. Such interdependence tends to be structured by ecological specialization (use of different environment resources).
4. Barth argued that cultural differences were part of the "natural" environment of ethnic groups, and thus peaceful, egalitarian coexistence was a possibility, particularly when there was no competition for resources.

C. Multiculturalism
1. Multiculturalism is "the view of cultural diversity in a country as something good and desirable."

2. This is opposed to assimilationism, which expects subordinate groups to take on the culture of the dominant group while abandoning their own.
3. Basic aspects of multiculturalism at the government level are the official espousal of some degree of cultural relativism along with the promotion of distinct ethnic practices.
4. A number of factors have caused the United States to move away from an assimilationist and toward a multicultural model.
    a. Large-scale migration has brought in substantial minorities in a time span too short for assimilation to take place.
    b. An ethnic consciousness may take root in reaction to consistent discrimination.
    c. Studies have demonstrated that closely maintained ethnic ties have been a successful strategy for recent immigrants.

IV. Roots of Ethnic Conflict

A. Prejudice and Discrimination
1. Prejudice is the devaluation of a given group based upon the assumed characteristics of that group (see the description of the first King beating trial).
2. Discrimination is disproportionately harmful treatment of a group: it may be *de jure* or *de facto*.
3. Attitudinal discrimination is discrimination against a group based only upon its existence as a group.
4. Genocide, "the deliberate elimination of a group through mass murder", is the most extreme form of discrimination.
5. Institutional discrimination is the formalized pursuance of discriminatory practices by a government or similar institution.

B. Chips in the Multicultural Mosaic
1. Despite the fact that the 1992 Los Angeles riot began as a reaction to the first Rodney King verdict, much of the violence played out along ethnic lines: prosperous, culturally isolated Korean merchants were targeted for looting and violence.
2. Subsequent public discussion indicated that much of the enmity was due to culturally based miscommunication.
3. There is some suggestion that miscommunication and noncommunication between successful Korean store owners and the surrounding African American population made it more likely that the Koreans would be subjected to such leveling mechanisms as looting and boycotts.

C. The Aftermaths of Oppression
1. The Politics of Cultural Oppression
    a. Ethnic differentiation sometimes interferes with the dominant group's consolidation of power.
    b. Such conditions perceived or real have resulted in brutal discrimination: forced assimilation, ethnocide, ethnic expulsion, and cultural colonialism.
    c. A discussion of the political, historical, and cultural motivations behind the Bosnia-Herzegovina civil war is used as an example.
2. Colonialism
    a. Colonialism "refers to the political, social, and cultural domination of a territory and its people by a foreign power for an extended time."
    b. Colonialism perpetrated by both western and soviet block nations not only created a worldwide economic hierarchy, but also caused long-term ethnic oppression in the colonized countries.

LECTURE TOPICS

1. It is important to make sure that your students can distinguish between an ethnic group and race. There are many examples of ethnicities that were once considered races. For example, the British used to believe that the Irish were of inferior genetic stock, which prevented them from reaching the level of civilized culture of the British. However, the Irish are no longer considered a race.

2. Discuss the nature of multiculturalism and assimilation throughout the history of the United States. In the textbook, Kottak talks about chips in the multicultural mosaic of the United States. What are the origins of these chips? Also, discuss what the future trends will be for multiculturalism in the U.S. What role will NAFTA play in the future? Use the U.S. census as a proxy for national attitudes about multiculturalism in the U.S.

3. Discuss the differences between genocide and ethnocide. Which of the two tends to get more attention by the media? Is it possible to completely reverse the effects of ethnocide?

MULTIPLE-CHOICE QUESTIONS

1. What is the term for the identification with, and feeling part of, a cultural tradition, and exclusion from other cultural traditions?

    a. culture shock
    b. ethnicity
    c. cultural relativism
    d. assimilation
    e. ethnocentrism

2. What is an *ascribed* status?

    a. A status that people have little or no choice about occupying.
    b. A status that you choose for yourself.
    c. A status that you earn, as when a successful law student becomes a lawyer.
    d. A status that has a position of dominance in society, for example that of a king.
    e. A status that is based on standardized test scores.

3. What is the term for any position that determines where someone fits in society?

    a. role
    b. genealogy
    c. status
    d. network
    e. identity

4. What is the term for a social status based on talents, actions, efforts, activities, and accomplishments?

    a. ascribed status
    b. achieved status
    c. situational status
    d. negotiated status
    e. ethnicity

5. Which of the following is *not* an example of an ascribed status?

  a. age
  b. race
  c. minority group member
  d. gender
  e. teacher

6. Which of the following statements about ethnicity is *not* true?

  a. Ethnicity and race are synonyms.
  b. Ethnicity is based on common biological features.
  c. Americans maintain a clear distinction between ethnicity and race.
  d. Ethnicity is the politically correct term for race.
  e. none of the above are true

7. What term refers to a culture that shares a single language, religion, history, territory, ancestry, and kinship?

  a. monoculture
  b. country
  c. nation
  d. state
  e. homeland

8. What is the term for ethnic groups that once had, or wish to have or regain, autonomous political status?

  a. ethnicities
  b. captive nations
  c. nations
  d. nationalities
  e. ethnic avengers

9. Which of the following statements about ethnic groups that once had, or wish to regain, autonomous political status is *not* true?

  a. They are called nationalities
  b. They have been called "imagined communities"
  c. Their members usually meet regularly
  d. They include the Kurds, Germans, and Koreans
  e. all of the above statements are true

10. What term refers to describe an independent centrally organized political unit, in a government?

  a. state
  b. nation
  c. nationality
  d. country
  e. culture

11. Which of the following statements about nation-states is true?

   a. Nation-states are ethnically homogeneous.
   b. Nation-states are defined by their lack of ethnic identity.
   c. **Nation-states sometimes encourage ethnic divisions for political and economic ends.**
   d. Nation-state is a synonym of tribe and ethnic group.
   e. Nation-states are parts of other states.

12. How did language and print spur national consciousness in Europe?

   a. The national print language carved a new level of culture.
   b. The national print language created a unified field of mass communication between Latin and regional dialects.
   c. Printing helped build an idea of permanent recorded history.
   d. Print established certain dialects as new languages of power.
   e. **all of the above**

13. What is the term for dispersed populations, which have spread out, voluntarily or not, from a common homeland?

   a. pidgin
   b. assimilation
   c. négritude
   d. **diaspora**
   e. colonialism

14. What is the term for the colonial practice of splitting up ethnic groups between colonies to dilute their strength in numbers?

   a. manifest destiny
   b. **divide and rule**
   c. mission civilisatrice
   d. white man's burden
   e. négritude

15. What is the term for the interdependence of nations in a world system linked economically and through mass media and modern transportation systems?

   a. cultural imperialism
   b. **globalization**
   c. international assimilation
   d. acculturation
   e. multiculturalism

16. "Ethnic cleansing" policies (the murder and forcible expulsion of non-Serbs living in areas designated by the Serbs as their homeland) practiced by Serbs of former Yugoslavia were _____.

   a. an attempt to dismantle interethnic coexistence established in socialist Yugoslavia
   b. an attempt to avenge historic affronts by Muslims and Croats
   c. suggested by Kottak as partly resulting from economic competition among the ethnic groups involved
   d. suggested by Kottak as partly resulting from the existence of separate imagined communities
   e. **all of the above**

17. The presence of ethnic neighborhoods indicates what kind of coexistence?

    a.   assimilation
    b.   acculturation
    c.   enculturation
    d.   colonialism
    e.   **multiculturalism**

18. What term does Barth use to refer to a society that combines ethnic contrasts, ecological specialization, and the economic interdependence of those groups?

    a.   pluralism
    b.   broad spectrum subsistence
    c.   **plural society**
    d.   multicultural
    e.   assimilation

19. According to Barth's theories about ethnic identity, when are ethnic boundaries most stable?

    a.   When ethnic groups are culturally very similar and tend to pursue the same goals
    b.   **When ethnic groups occupy different ecological niches**
    c.   When ethnic groups share the same nation-state
    d.   When the members of the ethnic groups are highly educated, as with post-colonial states
    e.   all of the above

20. Which of the following has propelled North America away from assimilation and toward multiculturalism?

    a.   rapid population growth in less-developed countries
    b.   modern means of transportation
    c.   insufficient jobs in less-developed countries
    d.   the decline of traditional rural economies in less-developed countries
    e.   **all of the above**

21. What is the term for policies and practices that harm a group and its members?

    a.   colonialism
    b.   racism
    c.   prejudice
    d.   ethnocentrism
    e.   **discrimination**

22. What term refers to the laws, policies, and arrangements that deny equal rights to members of particular groups?

    a.   attitudinal discrimination
    b.   intervention discrimination
    c.   establishment discrimination
    d.   **institutional discrimination**
    e.   environmental discrimination

23. What is the term for the political, social, economic, and cultural domination of a territory and its people by a foreign power?

   a.   colonialism
   b.   racism
   c.   prejudice
   d.   ethnocentrism
   e.   discrimination

24. What is the term for the systematic use of institutionally based power by a majority group to make policy decisions that create disproportionate hazards in minority communities?

   a.   dumping
   b.   genocide
   c.   institutional discrimination
   d.   environmental racism
   e.   apartheid

25. What is the term for the use of force by a dominant group to compel a minority to adopt the dominant culture?

   a.   attitudinal discrimination
   b.   genocide
   c.   forced assimilation
   d.   ethnocentrism
   e.   environmental racism

26. What is the term for the deliberate elimination of a group through mass murder?

   a.   ethnic expulsion
   b.   genocide
   c.   forced assimilation
   d.   ethnocentrism
   e.   racist expulsion

27. What is the term for programs, policies, and arrangements that intentionally or unintentionally deny equal rights and opportunities to, or differentially harm members of particular groups?

   a.   institutional discrimination
   b.   cultural imperialism
   c.   colonialism
   d.   acculturation
   e.   attitudinal discrimination

28. People may engage in a variety of different social statuses during their lives, or even during the course of a day. What term refers to a person's ability to emphasize one's identity in a particular setting and another in a different setting?

   a.   ethnic identity
   b.   racial substitution
   c.   situational negotiation of identity
   d.   discourse analysis
   e.   rotating core personality traits

29. In Benedict Anderson's term "imagined communities," what does the word "imagined" refer to?

   a. Only post-colonial states are imagined, because these did not exist until they were thought up by the colonial governments.
   b. Identity in such communities is not established by direct social interaction with other members, but through interactions with the public media, like a national print media.
   c. These communities do not exist in real terms; they are the fictional and temporary products of the ruling intelligentsia.
   d. Such communities are comprised of many different ethnic groups and subcultures, and therefore will fall apart at any moment.
   e. The members of such a community self-consciously compare it to an idealized past, such as life on the farm or in a quasi-historical "homeland".

30. Which of the following statements about cultural colonialism is true?

   a. The internal domination by one group and its culture/ideology over others.
   b. It is exemplified by the domination of the former Soviet empire by Russian people, language, and culture.
   c. It is reflected in schools, the media, and public interaction.
   d. It may entail flooding ethnic areas with members of the dominant ethnic group.
   e. all of the above

31. What term refers to the devaluing of a group because of its assumed behavior, values, abilities, or attributes?

   a. discrimination
   b. apartheid
   c. assimilation
   d. diaspora
   e. prejudice

32. What term refers to the destruction of the culture of an ethnic group?

   a. genocide
   b. prejudice
   c. ethnocide
   d. discrimination
   e. diaspora

ESSAY QUESTIONS

33. Any of the above multiple choice questions may be converted to an essay question by requiring students to choose the correct answer and justify their selection in essay form. Such justifications should include explanations as to why the chosen answer is correct and why those responses not chosen are incorrect.

34. Use the example of *negritude*, as described in the chapter on ethnicity, to discuss the effect colonialism has had on the condition of present-day ethnic groups.

35. Describe the political aspect of ethnicity. Give examples. How is multiculturalism an attempt to "depoliticize" ethnicity? (Hint: start out with a careful definition of what you mean by "political.")

36. What is an imagined community? Social roles such as ethnicity and nationality are important to this concept--explain how.

37.   Is it contradictory to say that membership in an ethnic group is an ascribed status, while arguing that "we negotiate our social identities?" Why or why not?

38.   The second half of the Twentieth Century has seen a great increase in the significance of ethnicity as a factor in regional and world identity politics. What are the historical, social, and cultural reasons for this?

39.   Why are such forms of mass media such as print and television important to the existence of what Anderson calls an imagined community?

TRUE OR FALSE QUESTIONS

40. True or **False**   Ascribed status is based on an individual's talents, abilities, and actions.

41. True or **False**   Status shifting is possible only for people who are bilingual.

42. **True** or False   The term nation refers to an ethnic group that share a single religion, language, history, territory, ancestry, and kinship.

43. **True** or False   A state is a centrally organized political unit.

44. True or **False**   A nation-state refers to an ethnic group that is not politically autonomous.

45. **True** or False   "Imagined communities" is a common byproduct of colonialism.

46. **True** or False   Colonialism often involves dividing up ethnic groups to weaken their authority.

47. True or **False**   Host countries that emphasize assimilation tend to encourage minority ethnic groups to retain their identities.

48. **True** or False   A plural society is the opposite of a society that forces groups to assimilate.

49. True or **False**   Multiculturalism emphasizes the need for a series of cultures to abandon their old ethnic identities and join together to forge a new and unique cultural identity.

50. **True** or False   A key element of multiculturalism is a respect for ethnic diversity.

51. **True** or False   Migration and rapid population growth are fueling multiculturalism in countries like the U.S. and Canada.

52. True or **False**   Only dominant or majority groups can have prejudiced views; minority groups are not capable of being prejudiced.

53. True or **False**   *De facto* discrimination is when laws exist that harm a specific group and its members.

54. **True** or False   Genocide refers to deliberate elimination of a group through mass murder.

55. True or **False**   Institutional discrimination is when institutions rather than individuals are the targets of discrimination.

56. **True** or False   Ethnocide refers to the deliberate elimination of a cultural tradition through aggressive policies forcing assimilation.

57. True or **False**   As the Second World (the former Soviet Union and the Socialist and non-Socialist countries of Eastern Europe and Asia) disintegrates, multiculturalism based on the American and Canadian examples is becoming increasingly popular.

58. True or **False**   Cultural colonialism is an external process of assimilation that occurs when a developing nation-state request financial support from a First World nation-state.

59. **True** or False   One of the most striking examples of cultural colonialism involves the policies of forced assimilation by the former Soviet Union in Tajikistan.

CHAPTER 13
LANGUAGE AND COMMUNICATION

CHAPTER OUTLINE

I. Introduction

    A. Language is our primary means of communication.
       1. Language is transmitted through learning, as part of enculturation.
       2. Language is based on arbitrary, learned associations between words and the things they represent.
       3. Only humans have the linguistic capacity to discuss the past and future in addition to the present. *as far as we know*

    B. Anthropologists study language in its social and cultural context.

II. Animal Communication

    A. Call Systems
       1. Call systems consist of a limited number of sounds that are produced in response to specific stimuli (e.g. food or danger).
         a. Calls cannot be combined to produce new calls.
         b. Calls are reflexive in that they are automatic responses to specific stimuli.
       2. Although primates use call systems, their vocal tract is not suitable for speech.

    B. Sign Language
       1. A few nonhuman primates have been able to learn to use American Sign Language (ASL).
         a. Washoe, a chimpanzee, eventually acquired a vocabulary of over 100 ASL signs.
         b. Lucy, another chimpanzee, lived in a foster family until she was introduced to the "wild" where she was killed by poachers.
         c. Koko, a gorilla, regularly uses 400 ASL signs and has used 700 at least once.
       2. These nonhuman primates have displayed some "human-like" capacities with ASL.
         a. Joking and lying.
         b. Cultural transmission: they have tried to teach ASL to other animals.
         c. Productivity: they have combined two or more signs to create new expressions.
         d. Displacement: the ability to talk about things that are not present.
       3. The experiments with ASL demonstrate that chimps and gorillas have a rudimentary capacity for language.
         a. It is important to remember that humans taught these animals ASL.
         b. There are no known instances where chimps or gorillas in the wild have developed a comparable system of signs on their own.

    C. The Origin of Language
       1. The human capacity for language developed over hundreds of thousands of years, as call systems were transformed into language.
       2. Language is a uniquely effective vehicle for learning that enables humans to adapt more rapidly to new stimuli than other primates.

III. Nonverbal Communication

    A. Kinesics is the study of communication through body movements, stances, gestures and facial expressions.

151

B. Odors also play an important role in nonverbal communication.

IV. The Structure of Language

    A. The scientific study of spoken language involves several levels of organization: phonology, morphology, lexicon, and syntax.
        1. Phonology is the study of the sound use in speech.
        2. Morphology studies the forms in which sounds are grouped in speech.
        3. A language's lexicon is a dictionary containing all of the smallest units of speech that have a meaning (morpheme).
        4. Syntax refers to the rules that order words and phrases into sentences.

    B. Speech Sounds
        1. In any given language, phonemes are the smallest sound contrasts that distinguish meaning (they carry no meaning themselves).
        2. Phones are the sounds made by humans that might act as phonemes in any given language.
        3. Phonetics is the study of human speech sounds; phonemics is the study of phones as they act in a particular language.
        4. Phonemics studies only the significant sound contrasts of a given language.

V. Language, Thought, and Culture

    A. Chomsky argues that the universal grammar is finite, and the fact that any language is translatable to any other language is taken to be evidence supporting this claim.

    B. The Sapir-Whorf Hypothesis: Sapir and Whorf are described as early advocates of the view that different languages imply different ways of thinking (e.g., Palaung vs. English, Hopi speculative tense).

    C. Focal Vocabulary
        1. Lexical elaboration that corresponds to an activity or item that is culturally central is called a focal vocabulary.
        2. It is argued that, while language, thought, and culture are interrelated, change is more likely to move from culture to language, rather than the reverse.

    D. Meaning
        1. Semantics "refers to a language's meaning system."
        2. Ethnoscience, or ethnosemantics, is the study of linguistic categorization of difference, such as in classification systems, taxonomies, and specialized terminologies (such as astronomy and medicine).

VI. Interesting Issues: Do Midwesterners Have Accents?

    A. Every region has its own dialect based on regional patterns of speech, pronunciation, and word choice.

    B. Some dialects, like that of Midwestern Americans, have few stigmatized variants that people readily notice.

VII. Sociolinguistics

    A. Introduction
        1. Sociolinguistics is the study of the relation between linguistic performance and the social context of that performance.
        2. The notion that linguistic variation is a product of constantly ongoing general forces for change is called linguistic uniformitarianism.

B. Linguistic Diversity
   1. The ethnic and class diversity of nation-states is mirrored by linguistic diversity.
   2. Single individuals may change the way they talk depending upon the social requirements of a given setting--this is called style shifting.
   3. Diglossia is the regular shifting from one dialect to another (e.g., high and low variants of a language) by members of a single linguistic population.
   4. Linguistic relativity says that no language is superior to any other as a means of communication.

C. Gender Speech Contrasts
   1. In America and England, there are regular differences between men's speech and women's speech that cut across sub-cultural boundaries.
   2. The fact that women in these populations tend to speak a more "standard" dialect and use fewer "power" words is attributed to women's lack of socioeconomic power.

D. Stratification and Symbolic Domination
   1. In situations where social stratification exists, the dialect of the dominant strata is considered "standard" and valued more than the dialects of the lower strata.
   2. Sociolinguistic studies have indicated that status-linked dialects affect the economic and social prospects of the people who speak them, a situation to which Bourdieu applies the term, *symbolic capital*.
   3. According to Bourdieu, overall societal consensus that one dialect is more prestigious results in "symbolic domination."

E. In the News: Japan's Feminine Falsetto
   1. Most languages are expressive of and also create gendered differences through grammatical, phonological, or performance patterns.
   2. One such gendered style occurs in Japan, wherein the tradition was for women to adopt a stylized, high-pitched voice when speaking in public.
   3. This style has begun to disappear as a result of having been challenged through increased awareness of alternatives, some presented directly via feminism, others coming as a more incidental by-product of intercultural contact (e.g., women announcers in the television news).

F. Black English Vernacular (BEV), a.k.a. "Ebonics"
   1. Most linguists view BEV as a dialect of American English, with roots in southern English.
   2. William Labov writes that BEV is the "relatively uniform dialect spoken by the majority of black youth in most parts of the U.S. today..."
   3. BEV has its own complex system of linguistic rules; it is not an unstructured selection of words and phrases.
      a. BEV speakers do not pronounce intervocalic *r*'s.
      b. BEV speakers use *copula deletion* to eliminate the verb *to be* from their speech.
   4. Standard English is not superior in terms of ability to communicate ideas, but it is the prestige dialect.

VIII. Historical Linguistics

   A. Historical linguistics studies the long-term variation of speech by studying protolanguages and daughter languages.

   B. Anthropologists are interested in historical linguistics because cultural features sometimes correlate with the distribution of language families.

IX. Cyberspace: A New Realm of Communication.

  A. Terms
    1. Cyberspace: that part of the world that is navigable by computer.
    2. AIT: (Advanced Information Technology) is the high technology communications environment that has given rise to cyberspace.

  B. AIT as a medium has allowed for the creation of transnational affinity groups and also created means by which populations have begun to resist the pressure of authoritarian governments.
    1. These groups and others that are formed around different sorts of interest, as well as the nature of relations among these groups and with the rest of the world, are rapidly becoming the subjects of anthropological inquiry.
    2. Transecting groups create direct communication channels between groups that previously had, or otherwise have trouble communicating--e.g. physicians and patients.

  C. Access to cyberspace is not equal.
    1. Poverty and underdevelopment limit access to cyberspace for some populations.
    2. Some governments use artificially high costs to limit the connectivity of ordinary people.
    3. Class also affects access in the United States, although this is mitigated somewhat by the existence of public access computers.
    4. While class has not been eliminated entirely from cyberspace, some of the markers of class are not as functional--for example, language/writing style in cyberspace is marked by informality.
    5. Recent studies have shown that the marking of class and gender still exists, and that some of the gendered dynamics born outside of cyberspace are carried on within it.
    6. One area wherein inequality has persisted is in the delivery of the latest high technology equipment to schools, which consistently reflects class and race bias, as well as socioeconomic inequality.
    7. "Netiquette" is the term applied to uses and styles deemed appropriate and polite in cyberspace communication (such as the avoidance of using all capital letters, which connotes strong emotion or "shouting").

  D. Elitism and Gate-keeping Cyberspace
    1. As access and interest have increased the numbers of people using the Internet, "Old Guard" vs. "New Guard" elitism has developed.
    2. As use has broadened, problematic and criminal practices on the Internet have also increased, generating a corresponding interest in the regulation of such communication (e.g., laws against pornography on the Internet).
    3. There are also techniques employed by ordinary users and sysops ("systems operators") to prevent and punish transgression of various ilk.
    4. Kottak applies the term "gatekeepers" to people who enforce the various regulations and norms of Internet communication.

  E. The fluidity of social reality in cyberspace
    1. The various uses of cyberspace and computer technology have generated a whole new realm of ways to manipulate one's identity (e.g., role-playing games, presenting various selves in course of cyberspace conversations, etc.).
    2. The relationship between cyberspace behavior and behavior in "face-to-face" communities is under investigation.

X. Beyond the Classroom: Cybercommunication in Collegespace

    A. Robert Herbert studied how the Internet has affected the sense of community at the State University of New York in Binghamton.

    B. Based on his ethnographic research, Herbert argues that cyberspace does not detract from face-to-face interaction between students.
        1. People who are social offline, tend to be social online.
        2. People use the Internet to supplement rather than replace their face-to-face interactions.

LECTURE TOPICS

1.   Almost all students are puzzled by the concepts of deep structure, surface structure, and transformations. Present them with several examples, some from different languages. You may relate ape language experiments to your discussion of human neurologically based language capacities.

2.   Students often find it difficult to believe that they filter out some sounds, that they are not sensitive to all the differences to which other language speakers are sensitive, or that other speakers cannot hear differences that are important to them. Illustrate the principles with clear examples of at least two languages.

3.   As with many monolingual people, most American students believe that their words are a simple reflection of the natural world. They find it hard to recognize the conventionality or the semantic "bundling" that occurs in their words. They have a tendency to believe that other languages are essentially a word-for-word replacement of their own. Accordingly, present to words from languages related to English, such as French and German, that are similar, but have a quite different connotation or range of meaning. Give them words or phrases from another language that can be translated only clumsily into English.

4.   Many students have hard time understanding the debate over B.E.V. Discuss what B.E.V. is and clarify what the debate is over. Many students think that proponents of B.E.V. are demanding that it be taught in schools just like Spanish, German, or French.

5.   Some comparisons have been made between early users of cyberspace and the "pioneers" of the American western frontier, including motivations of quests for freedom, and scathing contempt for "greenhorns." The cultural types and images developed on the western frontier have played a substantial role in subsequent shaping of American society. Can cyberspace be envisaged as doing the same? What effect has the transnational quality of cyberspace communication made with regard to the construction of imagined cyberspace communities?

SUGGESTED FILMS

The Human Language Series:

Part One: Discovering the Human Language: Colorless Green Ideas

video 55 min 1995 color
The first of three films on human language. The perspective is largely Chomskian (Noam Chomsky is the presenter) and this film explores notions of universal grammar and the powers and limitations granted by this structure. New York: Ways of Knowing, Inc.

Part Two: Acquiring the Human Language: Playing the Language Game

video 55 min. 1995 color
The second of three films on human language. This program looks at language acquisition in children as evidence of Chomskian universal grammar (Noam Chomsky is the host). New York: Ways of Knowing, Inc.

Part Three: The Human Language Evolves: With and Without Words

video 55 min 1995 color
The third film in the series. This program explores how and why human language may have evolved and its possible biological basis. Linguists and educators discuss universal facial expressions, differences in communication styles between men and women, body language and gesture. New York: Ways of Knowing, Inc.

In Search of the First Language

video 54 min 1994 color
From the PBS series, *Nova*. The program presents a glottochronological investigation of the origins of identified language families and in the process looks at evidence looks at the history of languages, generally. Boston, Mass., WGBH Educational Foundation.

The First Signs of Washoe

16mm or video 1976 59 min
The film documents the early stages of the chimpanzee, Washoe, as she learns to use sign language. It also compares Washoe to another chimpanzee who is learning to communicate through a computer. Distributed by Time-Life Multimedia.

Signs of the Apes, Songs of the Whales

video 57 min 1984 color
A relatively recent look at the research done on the ability of other species to use symbols. Narrated by Maureen Stapleton. Distributed by Ambrose Video Publications, New York, New York.

Gullah Tales

video 30 min 1987 color
Gullah tales is set in 1930 in southern Georgia and South Carolina and is based on folklore of peoples of African descent. The Gullah dialect is fairly well know as striking admixture of African and English influences. Produced by the Office of Educational Media, director: Gary Moss. Published by Los Angeles, CA: Direct Cinema, 1987.

The Performed Word

video 59 min 1989 color
The power of the African American performed word, particularly that of Black preachers, is examined. Includes excerpts from services and interviews with Bishop E.E. Cleveland of Berkeley, California (Church of God in Christ), and his daughter, past Ernestine Cleveland Reems. Produced at the Anthropology Film Center Foundation (Red Taurus Films Production) by Gerald L. Davis, Directors: Ernest Shinagawa and Carlos de Jesus. Published by Santa Fe: The Foundation; Memphis, Tenn.: Center for Southern Folklore.

Larynx and Voice (Functions of the Normal Larynx)

16mm 1958 20 min
Ultrahighspeed photography of a normally functioning larynx shows the workings of the whole larynx during normal phonation. From the University of Illinois Film and Video Center.

Language Development

16mm 1973 19 min
Demonstrates how children process language differently from adults. Explores the influence of semantic information on sentence comprehension. Comprehension processes are revealed by children at various phases of development as they act out the meaning of sentences with toys. From the University of Illinois Film and Video Center.

Communications: The Printed Word

16mm 1973 18 min
A comprehensive history of printing that describes printing's effect on civilization in general and on communication in particular, showing how technology and art are often mutually influential. From the University of Illinois Film and Video Center.

MULTIPLE-CHOICE QUESTIONS

1. What are phonemes?

    a. The rules by which deep structure is translated into surface structure
    b. Regional differences in dialect
    c. Syntactical structures that distinguish passive constructions from active ones
    d. **The minimal sound contrasts that distinguish meaning in a language**
    e. Electromagnetic signals that carry messages between speakers in a telephone conversation

2. Which of the following is a minimal pair?

    a. cat/dog
    b. fat/get
    c. **of/off**
    d. leg/legal
    e. /r/ and /b/

3. When Washoe and Lucy tried to teach sign language to other chimpanzees, this was an example of

    a. **cultural transmission**
    b. displacement
    c. call systems
    d. productivity
    e. estrus

4. What is the term for the ability to refer to things not physically present?

   a. productivity
   b. cultural transmission
   c. extrasomatism
   d. displacement
   e. portability

5. What does the Sapir-Whorf hypothesis state?

   a. The degree of cultural complexity is associated with the effectiveness of languages as systems of communication.
   b. The language people speak influences the way their culture is structured.
   c. The Hopi does not use three verb tenses; they have no concept of time.
   d. Our culture determines what our language is able to refer to.
   e. Dialect variation is the result of toilet-training practices.

6. Which of the following statements about animal call systems is true?

   a. They are stimuli-dependent
   b. They consist of a limited number of calls
   c. They tend to be species specific
   d. They lack the displacement
   e. all of the above

7. What is the term of the ability to create new expressions by combining other expressions?

   a. displacement
   b. diglossia
   c. productivity
   d. morphemic utility
   e. phonemic utility

8. What term refers to the existence of "high" and "low" dialects within a single language?

   a. displacement
   b. diglossia
   c. semantics
   d. kinesics
   e. lexicon

9. What is the study of communication through body movements, stances, gestures, and facial expressions?

   a. ethnosemantics
   b. biosemantics
   c. protolanguagistics
   d. diglossia
   e. kinesics

10. What term refers to the arrangement and order of words into sentences?

    a. syntax
    b. lexicon
    c. grammar
    d. phonology
    e. morphology

11. What is the study of the forms in which sounds combine to form words?

    a. phonology
    b. syntax
    c. morphology
    d. lexicon
    e. grammar

12. What are phonemes?

    a. The rules by which deep structure is translated into surface structure
    b. Regional differences in dialect
    c. Syntactic structures that distinguish passive constructions from active ones
    d. The minimal sound contrasts recognized by speakers of a language
    e. Shares of stock in AT&T

13. Which of the following was studied by Sapir and Whorf?

    a. The influence of culture on language
    b. The influence of language on thought
    c. The influence of deep structure on surface structure
    d. The influence of deep structure on semantic domains
    e. none of the above

14. According to the Kottak text, which of the following social qualities can be attributed to the Internet and related environments?

    a. They may encourage and maintain differences between groups of people
    b. They may promote transnational linkages
    c. They reflect and strengthen socioeconomic stratification
    d. They may equalize class distinctions
    e. all of the above

15. How has social classes been reinforced by the use of Advanced Information Technology (AIT)?

    a. Through the use of "markers" on the Internet, which inform other users as to what brand of computer the sender is using
    b. Internet users pay very close attention to language "errors" and people who employ lower-class dialects on line are shunned
    c. Sysops hack into the Social Security Administration and distribute stolen economic information about their system users
    d. Through differential access, for example when poor schools get less new technology than wealthy schools
    e. all of the above

16. What term refers to the specialized set of terms and distinctions that are particularly important to certain groups?

    a. syntactical vocabulary
    b. spatial vocabulary
    c. focal vocabulary
    d. vernacular vocabulary
    e. temporal vocabulary

17.   What is the term for the variations in speech due to different contexts or situations?

      a.   linguistic confusion
      b.   situational syntax
      c.   contextual phonetics
      d.   Chomskian verbosity
      e.   style shifting

18.   What does a sociolinguist study?

      a.   speech in its social context
      b.   cross-cultural comparison of phonemic distinctions
      c.   the universal grammar of language
      d.   linguistic competence
      e.   all of the above

19.   Which of the following statements about sociolinguists is true?

      a.   They focus on surface structure
      b.   They are concerned more with performance than with competence
      c.   They look at society and at language
      d.   They are concerned with linguistic change
      e.   all of the above are true

20.   Which of the following is an example of restricting access or behavior on the Internet?

      a.   The U.S. Senate bill promoting "communications decency"
      b.   Savvy net users lambasting novice AOL users
      c.   Individual Internet users "flaming" other users for what they perceive as inappropriate behavior
      d.   A government keeps its pricing of access to the Internet artificially high
      e.   all of the above

21.   In a stratified society, even people who do not speak the prestige dialect tend to accept it as "standard" or superior. This is an instance of

      a.   glossalalia
      b.   creolization
      c.   symbolic domination
      d.   hypercorrection
      e.   style shifting

22.   Which of the following statements about B.E.V. is true?

      a.   Linguists view B.E.V. as a dialect of S.E., not a different language.
      b.   B.E.V. is not an ungrammatical collection of S.E. expressions.
      c.   B.E.V. is not inferior to S.E.
      d.   Many aspects of B.E.V. are also present in southern white speech.
      e.   all of the above

23. The English language contains many words that were borrowed from the French language, but only a few words in it were borrowed from the Filipino language. What is the best explanation for this?

   a. **There has been more extensive cultural contact between French and English speakers than there has been between English speakers and speakers of Filipino languages.**
   b. English is more closely related to French than it is to Filipino languages.
   c. Filipino language uses a different set of deep structures, while French and English use the same set of deep structures.
   d. English is more closely related to Filipino languages than it is to French.
   e. There has been more extensive cultural contact between English speakers and speakers of Filipino languages than there has been between French and English speakers.

24. What is a grammar?

   a. Two deep structures and one surface structure
   b. The sum total of all morphemes in a given language
   c. **The set of abstract rules that link sound and meaning in a language**
   d. The dominant dialect in any given language
   e. A minimal dialectical difference within a language

25. What is the term for all of a language's morphemes and their meanings?

   a. syntax
   b. **lexicon**
   c. ethnosemantics
   d. ethnoscience
   e. phonology

26. When does copula deletion occur in B.E.V.?

   a. **It occurs where SE has contractions**
   b. It occurs randomly
   c. It occurs in the past tense
   d. It occurs in the future tense
   e. Copula deletion occurs in S.E., not B.E.V.

27. What are minimal pairs used to identify?

   a. **phonemes**
   b. phones
   c. aspiration
   d. allomorphs
   e. bound morphemes

28. What is the study of the sounds used in speech?

   a. phones
   b. phonemes
   c. **phonology**
   d. phonetics
   e. phonemics

29. What term refers to the languages that has descended from the same ancestral language?

    a.   F2 languages
    b.   sibling languages
    c.   daughter languages
    d.   brother languages
    e.   protolanguages

30. What is a pidgin?

    a.   A partial language that results from primitive tribes' attempts to learn the language of a modern industrialized state
    b.   A mixed language that develops to ease communication between members of different cultures in contact, usually in situations of trade or colonial domination
    c.   A rhythmic sub-language present in any human language that is believed to reveal the touch of the serpent on the mind of Eve
    d.   A set of languages believed to be most like the original human language, spoken by a small population of Indian Ocean islanders
    e.   A metalanguage developed by computer programmers that have yielded valuable insights into the workings of the human brain

ESSAY QUESTIONS

31. Contrast traditional descriptive linguistics, which studies a language in discrete levels, with the transformational-generative approach.

32. Is cyberspace a whole new arena for human social interaction, or is it just one more tool that humans put to a remarkable range of uses without really changing in any fundamental way? How does cyberspace compare to forms of sociopolitical organization? Cite examples to support your argument.

33. Discuss factors that increase linguistic diversity among speakers of the same language, and give a brief example of each factor.

34. What are significant differences and similarities between the evolution of language and biological evolution?

35. What are some ways in which linguistics can aid archeologists, biological anthropologists, and sociocultural anthropologists who are interested in history? Discuss.

36. Discuss some common interests of linguistics and ethnography. Of what use can knowledge of linguistic techniques and principles be to the ethnographer?

37. What is linguistic relativity? Illustrate how it applies to languages and to dialects of English.

38. Any of the above multiple choice questions may be converted to an essay question by requiring students to choose the correct answer and justify their selection in essay form. Such justifications should include explanations as to why the chosen answer is correct and why those responses not chosen are incorrect.

39. We know that chimpanzees and gorillas show considerable linguistic ability in laboratory settings. Does this mean that they use language in the wild? Why, or why not?

TRUE OR FALSE QUESTIONS

40. True or **False**   Animal call systems exhibit linguistic productivity.

41. True or **False**   All human nonverbal communication is instinctive, not influenced by cultural factors.

42. True or False   Phonology is the study of speech sounds.

43. True or False   Syntax refers to the rules that dictate the order of words in a language.

44. True or False   Creole languages are commonly found in regions where different linguistic groups come into contact with one another.

45. True or **False**   Sapir and Whorf argued that all humans share a single set of universal grammatical categories.

46. True or **False**   Focal vocabularies are found only in non-Western societies like the Eskimo and the Nuer.

47. True or False   In the text, Kottak argues against the Sapir-Whorf hypothesis states that a cultural change leads to change in language.

48. True or False   Ethnosemantics is concerned with studying how different members of different linguistic groups organize, categorize, and classify their experiences and perceptions.

49. True or **False**   Sociolinguists study linguistic performance by categorizing speakers as inadequate, competent, or highly proficient.

50. True or **False**   Diglossia refers to linguistic groups, like those is Papua New Guinea and Australia, that distinguish between only two colors: black and white or dark and light.

51. True or False   All languages and dialects are equally effective as systems of communication.

52. True or **False**   Bourdieu argues that languages with the highest *symbolic capital* are better systems of communication.

53. True or **False**   Sociolinguistics has demonstrated that men lack the linguistic capacity to distinguish between slight changes in color.

54. True or False   Studies investigating differences in the way men and women talk are examples of sociolinguistics.

55. True or **False**   Black English Vernacular is an incomplete linguistic system that is only able to express thoughts and ideas related to life in inner-city communities.

56. True or **False**   The origins of Black English Vernacular are found mostly in West Africa, not to the dialects of the southern part of the United States.

57. True or False   Historical linguists use linguistic similarities and differences in the world today to study long term changes in language.

58. True or False   AIT has led to the formation of transecting groups that greatly improve the flow of information between groups that otherwise would have trouble communicating.

59. True or **False**   The most amazing aspect of AIT is that access to it is not restricted by class, race, ethnicity, gender, education, profession, age, or family background.

CHAPTER 14
MAKING A LIVING

CHAPTER OUTLINE

I. Adaptive Strategies

    A. Yehudi Cohen used the term *adaptive strategy* to describe a group's system of economic production.

    B. Cohen has developed a typology of cultures using this distinction, referring to a relationship between economies and social features, arguing that the most important reason for similarities between unrelated cultures is their possession of a similar adaptive strategy.

II. Foraging

    A. Human groups with foraging economies are not ecologically dominant.

    B. The primary reason for the continuing survival of foraging economies is the inapplicability of their environmental settings to food production.

    C. Correlates of Foraging
        1. Band-organization is typical of foraging societies, because its flexibility allows for seasonal adjustments.
        2. Members of foraging societies typically are socially mobile, having the ability to affiliate with more than one group during their lifetimes (e.g., through fictive kinship).
        3. The typical foraging society gender-based division of labor has women gathering and men hunting and fishing, with gathering contributing more to the group diet.
        4. All foraging societies distinguish among their members according to age and gender, but are relatively *egalitarian* (making only minor distinctions in status) compared to other societal types.

III. Cultivation

    A. Horticulture
        1. Horticulture is non-intensive plant cultivation, based on the use of simple tools and cyclical, non-continuous use croplands.
        2. Slash-and-burn cultivation and *shifting* cultivation are alternative labels for horticulture.

    B. Agriculture
        1. Agriculture is cultivation involving the continuous use of cropland, and is more labor-intensive (due to the ancillary needs generated by farm animals and cropland formation) than horticulture.
        2. Domesticated animals are commonly used in agriculture, mainly to ease labor and provide manure.
        3. Irrigation is one of the agricultural techniques that free cultivation from seasonal domination.
        4. Terracing is an agricultural technique which renders land otherwise too steep for most forms of cultivation (particularly irrigated cultivation) susceptible to agriculture (e.g., the Ifugao of Central Luzon, in the Philippines).

5. The Costs and Benefits of Agriculture
    a. Agriculture is far more labor-intensive and capital-intensive than horticulture, but does not necessarily yield more than horticulture (under ideal conditions) does.
    b. Agriculture's long-term production (per area) is far more stable than horticulture's.

C. The Cultivation Continuum
    1. In reality, non-industrial economies do not always fit cleanly into the distinct categories given above, thus it is useful to think in terms of a cultivation continuum.
    2. Sectorial fallowing: a plot of land may be planted two-to-three years before shifting (as with the Kuikuru, South American manioc horticulturalists) then allowed to lie fallow for a period of years.
    3. A baseline distinction between agriculture and horticulture is that horticulture requires regular fallowing (the length of which varies), whereas agriculture does not.

D. Intensification: People and the Environment
    1. Agriculture, by turning humans into ecological dominants, allows human populations to move into (and transform) a much wider range of environments than was possible prior to the development of cultivation.
    2. Intensified food production is associated with sedentism and rapid population increases.
    3. Most agriculturalists live in states because agricultural economies require regulatory mechanisms.

IV. Pastoralism

A. Pastoral economies are based upon domesticated herd animals, but members of such economies may get agricultural produce through trade or their own subsidiary cultivation.

B. Patterns of Pastoralism
    1. Pastoral Nomadism: all members of the pastoral society follow the herd throughout the year.
    2. Transhumance or Agro-pastoralism: part of the society follows the herd, while the other part maintains a home village (this is usually associated with some cultivation by the pastoralists).

V. Modes of Production

A. Economic anthropology studies economics in a comparative perspective.
    1. An economy is a study of production, distribution, and consumption of resources.
    2. Mode of production is defined as a way of organizing production--a set of social relations through which labor is deployed to wrest energy from nature using tools, skills, organization, and knowledge.
    3. Similarity of adaptive strategies between societies tends to correspond with similarity of mode of production: variations occur according to environmental particularities.

B. Production in Nonindustrial Populations
    1. All societies divide labor according to gender and age, but the nature of these divisions varies greatly from society to society.
    2. Valuation of the kinds of work ascribed to different groups varies, as well.
    3. Examples are taken from the Betsileo, of Madagascar.

C. Means of Production
    1. Means of production include land, labor, technology, and capital.
    2. Land: the importance of land varies according to method of production — land is less important to a foraging economy than it is to a cultivating economy.

3. Labor, tools, and specialization: nonindustrial economies are usually but not always characterized by more cooperation and less specialized labor than is found in industrial societies.

D. Alienation in Industrial Economies
1. By definition, a worker is alienated from the product of her or his work when the product is sold, with the profit going to an employer, while the worker is paid a wage.
2. A consequence of alienation is that a worker has less personal investment in the product, in contrast to the more intimate relationship existing between worker and product in nonindustrial societies.
3. Alienation may generalize to encompass not only worker-product relations, but coworker relations, as well.

VI. Economizing and Maximization

A. Classical economic theory assumes that individuals universally acted rationally, by economizing to maximize profits, but comparative data shows that people frequently respond to other motivations than profit.

B. Alternative Ends
1. People devote their time, resources, and energy to five broad categories of ends: subsistence, replacement, social, ceremonial, and rent.
2. Subsistence fund: work is done to replace calories lost through life activities.
3. Replacement fund: work is expended maintaining the technology necessary for life (broadly defined).
4. Social fund: work is expended to establish and maintain social ties.
5. Ceremonial fund: work is expended to fulfill ritual obligations.
6. Rent fund: work is expended to satisfy the obligations owed (or inflicted by) political or economic superiors.
7. Peasants have rent fund obligations.

C. Interesting Issues: Scarcity and the Betsileo
1. Kottak describes some of his fieldwork experiences on Madagascar, particularly in the Betsileo village of Ivato, which was a principal research site and where he made many friends.
2. The process of interviewing and sharing wine and cigarettes with his friends generated comparative comments from them regarding their perceptions of American wealth and which also revealed the sense that Ivatans felt they had all they needed.
3. Kottak uses these experiences as evidence to support the argument that the profit motive is culturally specific, being attached to Western-style consumerism.

VII. Distribution, Exchange

A. The Market Principle
1. The market principle obtains when exchange rates and organization are governed by an arbitrary money standard.
2. Price is set by the law of supply and demand.
3. The market principle is common to industrial societies.

B. Redistribution
1. Redistribution is the typical mode of exchange in chiefdoms and some non-industrial states.
2. In a redistributive system, product moves from the local level to the hierarchical center, where it is reorganized, and a proportion is sent back down to the local level.

C. Reciprocity
   1. Reciprocity is exchange between social equals and occurs in three degrees: generalized, balanced, and negative.
   2. Generalized reciprocity is most common to closely related exchange partners and involves giving with no *specific* expectation of exchange, but with a reliance upon similar opportunities being available to the giver (prevalent among foragers).
   3. Balanced reciprocity involves more distantly related partners, and involves giving with the expectation of equivalent (but not necessarily immediate) exchange (common in tribal societies, and has serious ramifications for the relationship of trading partners).
   4. Negative reciprocity involves very distant trading partners and is characterized by each partner attempting to maximize profit and an expectation of immediate exchange (e.g., market economies, and silent barter between Mbuti foragers and horticulturalist neighbors).

D. Coexistence of Exchange Principles
   1. Most economies are not exclusively characterized by a single mode of reciprocity.
   2. The United States economy has all three types of reciprocity.

VIII. Potlatching

   A. Potlatches, as once practiced by Northwest Coast Native American groups, are a widely studied ritual in which sponsors (helped by their entourages) gave away resources and manufactured wealth while generating prestige for themselves.

   B. Potlatching tribes (such as Kwakiutl and Salish peoples) were foragers but lived in sedentary villages and had chiefs--this political complexity is attributed to the overall richness of their environment.

   C. Dramatic depopulation resulting from post-contact diseases and the influx of new trade goods dramatically affected the nature of potlatches, which began to extend to the entire population.

   D. The result of the new surplus, cultural trauma, and the competition caused by wider inclusion was that prestige was created by the destruction of wealth, rather than the redistribution of it.

   E. Potlatches were once interpreted as wasteful displays generated by culturally induced mania for prestige, but Kottak argues that customs like the potlatch are adaptive, allowing adjustment for alternating periods of local abundance and shortage.

   F. The Northwest Coast tribes were unusual in that they were foraging populations living in a rich, non-marginal environmental setting.

LECTURE TOPICS

1. Pick a case of maladaptation and discuss how it is maladaptive, for whom, in what situations, and how it came to be that way. Cases involving soil erosion or pollution are usually clear and are currently relevant.

2. For individuals, the question of "adaptation to what?" is rather straightforward. For groups, the question is not always so clear, especially if social evolution is to be understood as the outcome of adaptation. The pressures leading to social adaptation should be catalogued--both pressures of scarce resources and pressures resulting from social contact or social organization. Typical social adaptations in response to such pressures should be discussed.

3. Discuss the various funds as they occur in American lives. Discuss the rent fund in the lives of peasants and other members of the state in contrast to the rent fund as it more explicitly occurs in American lives.

4. Reiterate the important point that evolution is not equated with moral progress. Note that even sociocultural evolution is keyed by environmental (here "environment" is defined to include cultural factors) pressures. An interesting example that conveys the complexities lost in such ideas as "modern" and "primitive" is the history of the Western "discovery" of the Tasaday, in the Philippines. There has been substantial retrospective analysis on the treatment of this group, initially idealized as pristine, living relic of the Stone Age.

5. Contrast the idealized free market with a chiefly redistribution system. Speculate on why a free market might or might not work in a chiefdom. Discuss why the free market could not develop in a chiefdom, and why some sort of market (ideally free or not) is likely to develop in a state.

SUGGESTED FILMS

A Poor Man Shames Us All

video 1992 55 min color
From the series, *Millenium: Tribal Wisdom in the Modern World,* hosted by anthropologist David Maybury-Lewis. The film takes a cross-cultural perspective on economics by looking at various societies, but most particularly at the Weyewa of eastern Indonesia. In examining "economics," Maybury-Lewis also addresses the values associated with tribal life and contrasts those to the zero-sum ethic associated with world capitalism. Alexandria, VA: PBS Video.

Black Harvest

video 1988 90 min color
A sequel to *First Contact* and *Joe Leahy's Neighbors,* the film features a joint business venture between Joe Leahy, a wealthy mixed-race coffee plantation owner, and the Ganiga, a tribal community in Papua New Guinea. The venture is devastated by the worldwide collapse of coffee prices, and the ensuing results, including warfare, provide a basis for analyzing both tribal politics and economics, and the world system. Watertown, Mass.: Documentary Educational Services.

Three Horsemen

video 1982 55 min color and b&w
This documentary touches on the economic and social conditions of the Pootchemunka Family and life on the Titree settlement in Northern Queensland, Australia. The Pootchemunka are from the Arujun Area. Produced by David and Judith MacDougall (directors) and the Australian Institute of Aboriginal Studies. Published by the University of California (Berkeley) Extension Media Center.

Asante Market Women

video 1982 55 min color
Describes and shows examples of the social power structures in the Asante tribe of Ghana. Women are subordinate in domestic matters, but have evolved their own power structure with regard to the market, where they work. Filmed in the city of Kumasi, it introduces women leaders by their market section: the tomato Queenmother, the yam Queenmother (final arbiter and most powerful). Touches on the way the polygamous structure is managed, and how the women feel about it. They express their dissatisfaction, but feel helpless to change matters. A man comments that he has learned patience and compassion in working with women.

The Bajao: Seagoing Nomads

16mm 18 min 1981 color
Presents the unique life style of the Bajao of Southeast Asia's waters, whose families wander the sea alone, each in its own outrigger canoe. Introduces a single family consisting of grandparents, parents, and children, with the boat that is their home. Shows them gathering shells to trade for supplies, and visiting islands for coconuts and water.

The Blooms of Banjeli: Technology and Gender in African Ironmaking

video 29 min 1986 color
Focuses on a Central West African group, which had for centuries produced high-quality iron blooms--an industry now in decline. Two anthropologists visit the community and are allowed the privilege of witnessing the process and describing the rituals, beliefs, and sexual prohibitions involved. The process is seen as a metaphoric extension of the reproductive capacity.

Inventing Reality

video 1992 60 min color
Has our desire for certainty and objectivity closed off the "magical" influence of the natural world? We are shown how in Mexico and Canada the certainties of science can combine with natural conceptions of physical disease both in the tribal world of the shaman and in the thinking of modern medical science. Then travel to the Aboriginal culture of Australia to examine dreamtime. Produced by Biniman Prod. Ltd., Adrian Malone Prod., Ltd., Los Angeles and BBC-TV, et al. Published by PBS Video, Alexandria, VA.

The Tragedy of the Commons

16mm 1971 25 min
An historical example of farmers sharing the benefits, but not the responsibilities, of common pastureland. Surveys the distribution of resources and clash of personal values, as well as a variety of possible outcomes and solutions. Drawn from an article by biologist Garrett Hardin.

The Cave People of the Philippines

1972 39 min color
An early take on the Tasaday, of Mindanao in the Philippines, depicting them as primordially gentle (in keeping with a contemporary Western construction of the primitive). Reported by Jack Reynolds. Filmed with the aid of the Panamin Foundation and the people of Barrio T'Boli.

The Last Tasmanian: Ancestors

1980 17 min color
Summarizes what is known of the Tasmanian aborigines in the period prior to 1803 when the British colonized the area. Research of Dr. Rhys Jones began in 1963, and archeological investigation gradually revealed elements of the most complete genocide on record. Thought to have been marooned there by the thaw which ended the Ice Age, the Tasmanian aborigines gradually lost the arts even of the simplest tools and artifacts, although they appear in older digs of the area covering the period from 8,000 to 3,500 years ago.

MULTIPLE CHOICE QUESTIONS

1. Which of the following is *not* one of the basic economic types found in nonindustrial societies?

   a. foraging
   b. agriculture
   c. horticulture
   d. pastoralism
   e. **hydroponics**

2. Which of the following is a characteristic shared by most present-day foragers?

   a. They fish a great deal
   b. They rely on welfare supplied by state-level societies
   c. They speak simplified languages
   d. **They live in environments that are of little interest to food-producing societies**
   e. They have devolved to foraging from a more advanced level of subsistence

3. Which of the following is most characteristic of foragers?

   a. unilineal descent and ancestor worship
   b. territoriality and organized warfare
   c. **high mobility and small groups with flexible affiliation**
   d. a redistributive economy and specialized leadership roles
   e. permanent villages and full-time priests

4. What is the hypothesis that serves as the basis for Cohen's comparative taxonomy of adaptive strategies?

   a. Economies are dependent on cultures
   b. The whole notion of "economy" as something distinguishable on its own makes no sense except when we are speaking of states
   c. Any economy is best understood by looking first at such cultural basics as kinship and religion
   d. Economy and culture are independent of one another, therefore economies can be compared directly
   e. **Similar economic causes produce similar cultural effects**

5. Which of the following statements about foraging societies is true?

    a.   All modern foraging societies live in nation-states
    b.   All modern foraging societies depend to some extent on government assistance
    c.   All modern foraging societies have contact with other, non-foraging societies
    d.   Many foragers have easily incorporated modern technology, such as rifles and snowmobiles, into their subsistence activities
    e.   all of the above

6. Which of the following statements about shifting cultivation is true?

    a.   It is typically associated with the use of draft animals
    b.   It cannot support permanent villages
    c.   It requires irrigation
    d.   It requires cultivators to change plots of land every 2-3 years
    e.   It relies extensively on chemical fertilizers

7. Which of the following generalizations is correct?

    a.   Pastoralists farm terraced fields
    b.   Horticulturalists do not fallow their fields
    c.   Transhumants do not cultivate
    d.   Horticulturalists do not forage
    e.   None of the above is correct

8. Why do slash-and-burn cultivators stop using a plot of land every 2-3 years?

    a.   Slash-and-burn cultivation is associated with big-game hunting, which requires regular movement so as not to deplete the animal population.
    b.   Slash-and-burn cultivation is unique to segmentary-lineage organized societies, and crop rotation follows the cycle of inter-lineage exchange.
    c.   They do not use fertilizer, thus their crops exhaust the soil quickly.
    d.   Slash-and-burn cultivators use relatively primitive irrigation systems, which have to be repaired every 3-4 years.
    e.   all of the above

9. Which of the following occurs as you move toward the more intensive end of the cultivating continuum?

    a.   increasing economic specialization
    b.   increased leisure time
    c.   increased reliance on swidden cultivation
    d.   increased egalitarianism
    e.   longer fallow periods

10. Which of the following is unique to state-level societies?

    a.   agriculture
    b.   sodalities
    c.   religion
    d.   vertical economy
    e.   social stratification

11.   Which of the following agricultural techniques is associated with wet-rice farming?

      a.   keening
      b.   wailing
      c.   low-labor, shifting plot
      d.   terracing
      e.   swiddening

12.   Why do anthropologists question the idea that present-day foragers can be compared to Paleolithic foragers?

      a.   There are no present-day foragers
      b.   Types of foraging vary so widely that few generalizations can be drawn
      c.   Present-day foragers have been in contact with food producing and industrialized societies for long periods of time
      d.   Paleolithic foragers were pre-linguistic
      e.   Paleolithic foragers were not *Homo sapiens*

13.   Which of the following refers to an obligatory interaction between groups or organisms that is beneficial to each?

      a.   estrus
      b.   swiddening
      c.   fallowing
      d.   symbiosis
      e.   transhumance

14.   According to data gathered by Lee, the !Kung diet _____.

      a.   was only minimally nutritious
      b.   was as nutritious as the average middle-class American's
      c.   required the equivalent of five work-days
      d.   overly stressed their environment
      e.   was protein-deficient

15.   Which of the following is a characteristic of most foraging societies?

      a.   social stratification
      b.   sedentism
      c.   egalitarianism
      d.   irrigation
      e.   large populations

16.   Which of the following is *not* characteristic of band-level societies?

      a.   egalitarian social structure
      b.   nuclear families
      c.   sexual division of labor
      d.   permanent villages ~ sedentary living
      e.   mechanisms of social control

17.   Which of the following is associated with horticultural systems of cultivation?

      a.   intensive use of land and human labor
      b.   use of irrigation and terracing
      c.   use of draft animals
      d.   location in arid areas
      e.   periodic cycles of cultivation and fallowing

18.   Which of the following terms is synonymous with horticulture?

        a.   **slash and burn cultivation**
        b.   foraging
        c.   hydraulic cultivation
        d.   agriculture
        e.   pastoralism

19.   What kinds of societies are typically associated with slash-and-burn cultivation?

        a.   foragers
        b.   state-level societies
        c.   hydraulic societies
        d.   **nonindustrial societies**
        e.   nomads

20.   Which of the following statements about horticulture is true?

        a.   It is usually associated with state-level societies
        b.   It requires more labor than agriculture
        c.   It usually leads to the destruction of the soil through overuse
        d.   **It can support permanent villages**
        e.   none of the above

21.   Which of the following does *not* occur as you move along the plant-cultivating continuum?

        a.   population density increases
        b.   **societies become more egalitarian**
        c.   village size increases
        d.   villages are located closer together
        e.   land is used more intensively

22.   What happens as one moves along the plant cultivating continuum?

        a.   ceremonies and rituals become less formal
        b.   more time for leisurely pursuits becomes available
        c.   **the use of land and labor intensifies**
        d.   there is a heavier reliance on swidden cultivation occurs
        e.   the use of communal cooking-houses becomes more common

23.   Which of the following statements about irrigation is true?

        a.   Irrigated fields typically increase in value through time
        b.   They are labor intensive compared to swidden fields
        c.   It usually enriches the soil
        d.   The Betsileo of Madagascar use irrigation
        e.   **all of the above**

24.   Which of the following statements about agriculturalists is true?

        a.   They clear a tract of land they wish to use by cutting down trees and setting fire to the grass
        b.   They generally have much more leisure time at their disposal than do foragers
        c.   They must be nomadic to take full advantage of their land
        d.   **They use their land intensively and continuously**
        e.   They subsist on a more nutritious diet than do horticulturists

25. What is the term that refers to the type of pastoral economy, in which part of the population moves with the herds, while the rest stays in the village?

    a. transhumant nomadism
    b. discretionary pastoralism
    c. pastoral transhumance
    d. foraging
    e. none of the above

26. Which of the following is found in all adaptive strategies?

    a. a division of labor based on gender
    b. transhumance
    c. an emphasis on technology
    d. domestication of animals for food
    e. a strong positive correlation between the importance of kinship and complexity of subsistence technology

27. Which of the following statements about foragers is true?

    a. Virtually all foraging societies exhibit a slight degree of gender inequality
    b. All present-day foragers live on land that is of little or no value to plant cultivators
    c. Some foraging societies have maintained a foraging lifestyle while adopting such modern technology as snowmobiles and rifles
    d. Foraging societies are most commonly organized as bands
    e. all of the above

28. How does horticulture differ from agriculture?

    a. the former utilizes domesticated animals, while the latter does not
    b. no agriculturalists use any form of fallowing
    c. agriculturalists often employ irrigation, while horticulturalists do not
    d. the former is labor intensive, while the latter is land intensive
    e. the former is confined to chiefdoms, the latter to nation-states

29. What is a mode of production?

    a. A post-industrial adaptive strategy, such as commercial agriculture and international mercantilism
    b. The land, labor, technology, and capital of production
    c. The way a society's social relations are organized to produce the labor necessary for generating the society's subsistence and energy needs
    d. Whether a society is foraging, horticulturalist, or agriculturist
    e. The cultural aspect of any given economy, such as changing fashions in the textile and clothing industry

30. When a farmer gives twenty percent of his crop to a landlord, what is he contributing to?

    a. social fund
    b. subsistence fund
    c. ceremonial fund
    d. replacement fund
    e. rent fund

31. Which of the following statements about generalized reciprocity is true?

   a.   It is characterized by the immediate return of the object exchanged
   b.   It is the dominant form of exchange in egalitarian societies
   c.   It usually develops after redistribution but before the market principle
   d.   It disappears with the origin of the state
   e.   It is exemplified by silent trade

32. Which of the following is an example of a means of production?

   a.   A set of horticultural plots owned by a descent group
   b.   Villages that are geographically close but specialize as to which crafts they produce
   c.   Berry trees belonging to a specific foraging band
   d.   Labor forces organized by kinship ties
   e.   all of the above

33. How are nonindustrial economic systems "embedded?"

   a.   People are not aware that they are working toward a goal
   b.   The economic system has little to do with the everyday life of the people
   c.   The economic system cannot easily be separated from the other systems, such as kinship
   d.   Most nonindustrial economies are managed systems
   e.   Most economic activity takes place far from the home

34. Economic relationships are usually embedded in other relationships, such as kinship in all of the following kinds of societies, except which?

   a.   states
   b.   foragers
   c.   horticulturalists
   d.   pastoralists
   e.   chiefdoms

35. What is economic alienation in industrial societies the result of?

   a.   loss of land
   b.   subculture of poverty
   c.   negative reciprocity
   d.   separation from the product of one's labor
   e.   discontent due to low pay

36. Which of the following statements about systems of production in nonindustrial societies is true?

   a.   Relations of production are often aspects of social relationships
   b.   An individual has access to the factors of production through ties of kinship, marriage, and fictive kinship
   c.   A personal relationship exists between producer and product
   d.   The market principle plays little to no role
   e.   all of the above

37. Which of the following kinds of exchange is characteristic among members of the same family?

   a. **generalized reciprocity**
   b. balanced reciprocity
   c. negative reciprocity
   d. redistribution
   e. none of the above

38. What is the silent trade between groups of "pygmy" foragers of the African equatorial forest and their neighboring horticultural villages an example of?

   a. generalized reciprocity
   b. balanced reciprocity
   c. **negative reciprocity**
   d. redistribution
   e. none of the above

39. Which of the following is *not* associated with the market principle?

   a. profit motive
   b. the law of supply and demand
   c. impersonal economic relations
   d. industrialism
   e. **kin-based generalized reciprocity**

40. Which of the following economic principles is generally dominant in an industrial society?

   a. generalized exchange
   b. **market principle**
   c. redistribution
   d. negative reciprocity
   e. all of the above

41. Which of the following statements about potlatching is *not* true?

   a. It is an example of competitive feasting
   b. It is an example of conspicuous consumption
   c. **It is a form of exchange common among foragers**
   d. It is a way that elites create and maintain social stratification
   e. all of the above are true

42. Which of the following inhibits stratification?

   a. class endogamy
   b. caste notions of purity and pollution
   c. monopoly on the legitimate use of force
   d. control over ideology by elites
   e. **ceremonial redistribution of material goods**

43. Which of the following activities illustrates expenditures in what Eric Wolf calls a "rent fund?"

    a.   the distribution of goods at a potlatch
    b.   an American farmer purchasing fertilizer
    c.   paying one's income tax
    d.   Yanomami men exchanging sisters
    e.   Yanomami men growing extra plantains for an intervillage feast

44. Which of the following statements about peasants is *not* true?

    a.   They all live in state-organized societies
    b.   They owe rent to landlords
    c.   They practice agriculture without modern technology, such as chemical fertilizers and tractors
    d.   They owe rent to the government
    e.   They are not part of the world market

45. Which of the following is *not* associated with the market principle?

    a.   profit motive
    b.   the law of supply and demand
    c.   fixed values for products
    d.   bargaining
    e.   industrialism

46. In what kind of society does reciprocity operate?

    a.   modern industrial societies
    b.   hunting and gathering societies
    c.   tribal societies without the office of "chief"
    d.   egalitarian societies
    e.   all of the above

47. Who are peasants?

    a.   People who ignore social norms of behavior
    b.   Small farmers who own their own land and sell all their crops to buy necessities
    c.   Rural people who produce food for their own subsistence, but also sell their surpluses
    d.   Anyone who lives in the country
    e.   Anyone who falls below the poverty line

ESSAY QUESTIONS

48. Any of the above multiple choice questions may be converted to an essay question by requiring students to choose the correct answer and justify their selection in essay form. Such justifications should include explanations as to why the chosen answer is correct and why those responses not chosen are incorrect.

49. Discuss the major differences in production between industrial and nonindustrial societies.

50. Anthropologists often say that in nonindustrial societies economic relationships are embedded in social relationships. What does this mean? Evaluate the assertion.

51. Imagine a pristine foraging society that operates largely according to principles of generalized reciprocity, just prior to being colonized. Now defend the following statement: "Capitalism is not just an economic system, it is also a cultural system."

52. What are some of the differences and similarities in the principles that govern exchange in industrial and nonindustrial societies? How does specialization in industrial societies differ from specialization in tribal societies and chiefdoms?

53. How does economic anthropology differ from classical economics? In what ways can economic anthropology serve as a safeguard against ethnocentrism?

54. Do people in all societies maximize? What do they maximize? Do anthropologists believe that maximization is a universal? What do you think? Explain your answer.

55. Are reciprocity, redistribution, and the market principle mutually exclusive for a given society? Give examples and include the contemporary United States or Canada in your answer.

56. How is a "rent fund" different from a "subsistence fund," according to Wolf's model? Cite examples to clarify your argument.

57. What is alienation? What kinds of activities are most likely to be associated with alienation? What activities in our own society are most alienating? Which are least so?

58. Contrast generalized, balanced, and negative reciprocity. How does negative reciprocity differ from the market principle?

59. Explain why the terms *history*, *progress*, and *change* are not synonymous with *evolution*. What is meant by evolution?

60. What are basic differences and similarities between horticultural and foraging populations? Indicate reasons for contrasts.

61. Is the contrast between horticulture and agriculture one of degree or of kind? Cite ethnographic evidence in your answer.

62. Which adaptive strategy appears to be more similar to foraging-horticulture or pastoralism? Discuss.

63. What are the features of Wolf's alternative ends model and how does it differ from classical Western economic theory?

TRUE OR FALSE QUESTIONS

64. True or **False**   Most of the groups who continue to forage as their primary adaptive strategy, live today in marginal zones.

65. True or **False**   Most modern foragers live in remote areas, completely cut off from contact with other modern, agricultural, and industrial communities.

66. **True** or False   Most foragers live in mobile bands that disperse in the dry season and aggregate in the rainy season.

67. **True** or False   Horticulture refers to low intensity farming using slash and burn techniques to clear land.

68. True or **False**   Domesticated animals, more specifically their manure and pulling capabilities, are key components of horticulture.

69. True or False   In order to intensify production, agriculturalists frequently build irrigation canals and terraces.

70. True or **False**   Although agriculture is much more productive per acre than horticulture, horticulture is much more reliable and dependable in the long run.

71. True or False   Agriculturalists tend to live in permanent villages that are larger and closer to other settlements than the semi-permanent settlements of horticulturalists.

72. True or **False**   The high level of intensification and long-term dependability of horticulture paved the way for the emergence of large urban settlements and the first states.

73. True or False   Pastoralists are specialized herders whose subsistence strategies are focused on domesticated animals.

74. True or **False**   In transhumant societies, the entire group moves with the animals throughout the year.

75. True or False   A mode of production is a way of organizing production, whereas the means of production includes the factors of production like land, labor, and technology.

76. True or False   In most foraging societies, private ownership of land is almost nonexistent.

77. True or **False**   Band and tribal level societies actively promote craft and task specialization.

78. True or False   In nonindustrial societies, economic activities are embedded in the society.

79. True or **False**   The market principle dominates economic activities in band level foraging societies.

80. True or **False**   With generalized reciprocity, the individuals participating in the exchange usually do not know the other person prior to the exchange.

81. True or False   With balanced reciprocity the giver expects something in return equal to what was given.

82. True or False   Potlaching is a form of competitive feasting that enables individuals to redistribute surplus materials while simultaneously increasing one's prestige.

83. True or False   With the arrival of Europeans in the Pacific Northwest, potlaching became more destructive as material goods were burned and thrown into the sea.

CHAPTER 15
FAMILIES, KINSHIP, AND DESCENT

CHAPTER OUTLINE

I. Families

    A. Nuclear and Extended Families
1. The nuclear family consists of a married couple and their children.
2. The nuclear family is ego-centered, and impermanent, while descent groups are permanent (lasting beyond the life-spans of individual constituents) and reckoned according to a single ancestor.
3. One's family of orientation is the family in which one is born and grows up, while one's family of procreation is formed when one marries and has children.
4. Claims made for the universality of the nuclear family, based upon the universality of marriage, do not hold up--the nuclear family is widespread, but not universal.
5. In societies where the nuclear family is important, this structure acts as a primary arena for sexual, reproductive, economic, and enculturative functions, but it is not the only structure used by societies for these (e.g., the Etoro, Nayar, Betsileo, etc.).
6. In many societies, the extended families are the primary unit of social organization.
    a. Among the Muslims of western Bosnia, nuclear families are embedded within large extended families called *zadrugas* headed by a male household head and his wife.
    b. The Nayars are a matrilineal society in which extended families live in compounds called *tarawads* headed by a senior woman.

    B. Industrialism and Family Organization
1. The most prevalent residence pattern in the United States is families of procreation living neolocally.
2. In the U.S., as in other large, industrialized societies, patterns of residence and family types may change from class to class, in response to the conditions of these different contexts (e.g., extended families as a response to poverty).

    C. Changes in North American Kinship
1. In 1995, 25 percent of American households were inhabited by nuclear families.
2. Increasing representation of women in the work force is associated with a rise in marriage age.
3. The divorce rate rose steeply between 1970 and 1994.
4. The media is reflecting an intensifying change.
5. Comparatively, Americans (especially the middle class) identify a smaller range of kindred than members of nonindustrial societies.
6. A comparison between American and Brazilian kinship is made.

    D. The Family among Foragers
1. The two basic units of social organization among foragers are the nuclear family and the band.
2. Typically, the band exists only seasonally, breaking up into nuclear families when subsistence means require.

II. Descent

    A. Descent Groups
1. A descent group is a permanent social unit whose members claim common ancestry.
2. With matrilineal descent individuals automatically join the mother's descent group when they are born (see figure 15.1).
3. With patrilineal descent individuals automatically join the father's descent group when they are born (see figure 15.2).
4. Matrilineal and patrilineal descent are types of unilineal descent in which individuals only recognize one line of descent.
5. A lineage is a descent group who can demonstrate their common descent from an apical ancestor.
6. A clan is a descent group who claims common descent from an apical ancestor but cannot demonstrate it (stipulated descent).
7. When a clan's apical ancestor is nonhuman, it is called a totem.

    B. Interesting Issues: Brady Bunch Nirvana
1. The 1960's television program *The Brady Bunch* focused on a blended family.
2. The great familiarity introductory anthropology course students have with the characters of this program is contrasted with the lack of familiarity the same students have for the members of their own extended families.
3. Some reference to the role television plays in transmitting and shaping American culture is made.

    C. Lineages, Clans, and Residence Rules
1. In tribal societies, the descent group, not the nuclear family, is the fundamental unit.
2. In many societies, descent groups are corporate, sharing resources and property.
3. Unilocal Residence
    a. Patrilocality—married couple lives with husband's family; associated with patrilineal descent and is more common than matrilocality.
    b. Matrilocality—married couple lives with wife's family; associated with matrilineal descent and is less than patrilocaility.

    D. Ambilineal Descent
1. People can choose the descent group that they want to belong to.
2. Membership is fluid as people can change their descent group membership.
3. With unilineal descent, membership is ascribed, but for ambilineal descent, membership is achieved.

III. Kinship Calculation

    A. Kinship calculation is any systemic method for reckoning kin relations.

    B. Genealogical Kin Types and Kin Terms (see figure 15.3)
1. Kin terms are the labels given in a particular culture to different kinds of relatives.
2. Biological kin type refers to the degree of actual genealogical relatedness.

    C. Bilateral Kinship
1. Used by most Americans and Canadians
2. Kinship is traced through both male and female lines.
3. Kin links through males and females are perceived as being similar or equivalent.
4. In North American bilateral kinship there is often matrilineal skewing, a preference for relatives on the mother's side.

IV. Kinship Terminology

A. Kinship terminologies are native taxonomies (emic), not developed by anthropologists.

B. Lineal terminology: most Americans and Canadians use lineal terminology, which distinguishes lineal, collateral, and affinal relatives (figure 15.4 and figure 15.5).

C. Bifurcate merging terminology: this is the most common, associated with unilineal descent and unilocal residence (figure 15.6).

D. Generational terminology: typical of ambilineal societies, this calls ascending, same sex relatives by the same names (figure 15.7).

E. Bifurcate collateral terminology: common to North Africa and the Middle East, this is the most particular system (figure 15.8).

LECTURE TOPICS

1. Look at the different systems of land tenure, the need for land, and the various systems of kinship prevalent in the examples to show the relationship between resource size and kinship group size.

2. Discuss American kinship as a cultural system. Be sure to point out the ways in which American kinship differs from a purely genetic or biological analysis of relatedness.

3. Have the students interview a friend or relative in order to get a description of one informant's kinship terminology. Use their results as a supplement to your discussion of American kinship: what range of variation occurs, what are the reasons for it, etc.

4. If you use the multiple-choice questions, below, we suggest that you provide the students with a list of meanings associated with the biological kin type notations (M, MZ, S, Ego, and the like) while they are taking the test.

SUGGESTED FILMS

Strengths of Black Families

video 1984 43 min color
From the series *Working with Afro-American Families: A Cultural Approach*. Dr. J.E. Dodson lectures on the history of the Black family, from its West African origins to Black family life in America during and after slavery. Dodson concludes by highlighting six strengths of black families, including: strong kinship bonds, informal adoptions, adaptability of family roles, high achievement, strong religious orientation, and strong work orientation. Published Ann Arbor, MI: UMSSW, the University of Michigan Film and Video Library.

The Ax Fight

video 1975 30 min color
A four part analysis of a fight in a Yanomami Indian village between kin groups in 1971. It includes an unedited record of the event; a slow-motion replay of the fight; a discussion of the kinship structure of the fight; and an edited version. Published by Watertown, Mass.: Documentary Educational Resources.

Four Families

60 min   1959   b&w
In a comparison of family life in India, France, Japan, and Canada, Margaret Mead, author-anthropologist, discusses how the upbringing of a child contributes to a distinctive national character. Focuses, in each case, on a one-year-old baby in the family of a farmer of average means. Summarizes the typical national characteristics of the four countries. From The University of Illinois Film and Video Center.

I Want It All Now!

52 min   1978   color
An exploratory excursion into the life styles prevailing in Marin County, California, where a lot of people have leisure time and the money to enjoy it. Edwin Newman, serving as host, points out that since many of our national trends start in the San Francisco area, some observation on Marin County may be regarded as a forecast or warning of what is coming for the rest of the country. The first section, "The Me Business," notes that the pursuit of a raised consciousness has made therapy a big business. "A Search for It All" recounts a young divorcee's entry into the liberal realm where she hopes to find a better life. The last section, "What Happens to Children?" surveys how children fare in an environment with 75 percent of the parents divorced. Contains materials that may be considered unsuitable for classroom use. From The University of Illinois Film and Video Center.

William Rivers (1864-1922): Everything Is Relatives

video   1990(1985)   52 min   color
Originally produced by Central Independent Television in 1985. William Rivers was originally trained as a doctor. On a Cambridge University expedition to the Torres Straits north of Australia, his psychological tests on the islanders made him realize the importance of relatives in their society. His subsequent work as a pioneering psychologist in the First World War and his research into the workings of the nervous system and the action of drugs on the human body, enabled Rivers to bring something new to anthropology: a scientific approach. His field study with the hill tribe in southern India, the Todas, helped set the trend for anthropologists to go and visit the cultures in which they were interested, rather than staying at home and theorizing. From the *Strangers Abroad* series. From Films for the Humanities & Sciences.

MULTIPLE CHOICE QUESTIONS

1.   What does ego stand for in a depiction of a kinship system?

   a.   The sense of distinct individuality that is present in any society
   b.   The emotional attachment felt by the people who use the system
   c.   The point of reference used to determine which kin terms go where
   d.   The boundary between one's kin group and "outsiders"
   e.   A gender-free way of reckoning kinship

2.   What is the name of the post-marital residence pattern in which the married couple is expected to establish their own home?

   a.   neolocality
   b.   patrilocality
   c.   matrilocality
   d.   ambilocality
   e.   uxorilocality

3. What is the name of the extended family unit among Muslims of western Bosnia?

   a. tarawad
   b. zadruga
   c. lambic
   d. weiss
   e. urquell

4. In a matrilineal society, which relative would *not* be in the same lineage as a male ego?

   a. M
   b. Z
   c. S
   d. MZ
   e. MB

5. What kind of relative is your mother's brother?

   a. lineal relative
   b. affinal relative
   c. collateral relative
   d. nuclear family member
   e. member of the P2 generation

6. In a bifurcate merging kinship system, which of the following would be called by the same term?

   a. F and MB
   b. M and MZ
   c. MB and FB
   d. FZ and MZ
   e. JR and BJ

7. What makes up ego's nuclear family of orientation?

   a. ego's parents and siblings
   b. ego's spouse and offspring
   c. ego's extended family
   d. ego's lineal kin
   e. ego's collateral kin

8. Which of the following is one of the main differences between descent groups and nuclear families?

   a. Descent groups are typically not involved with politics, while nuclear families are
   b. Nuclear families are always exogamous, while descent groups are always endogamous
   c. Descent groups are permanent, nuclear families are not
   d. Members of descent groups are called "affines" while members of nuclear families are called "consanguines"
   e. all of the above

9. Why is the nuclear family a cultural universal?

   a. It regulates sexual reproduction
   b. It represents the most efficient use of the sexual division of labor
   c. It represents the basic unit of social organization
   d. It provides a support network for offspring
   e. The nuclear family is not a cultural universal

10. What kind of kinship is most common to the modern United States?

    a. matrilateral kinship
    b. bilateral kinship
    c. patrilateral kinship
    d. collateral kinship
    e. generational kinship

11. What term refers to a unilineal descent group whose members demonstrate their common descent from an apical ancestor?

    a. clan
    b. lineage
    c. extended family
    d. family of procreation
    e. family of orientation

12. In what kind of unilineal descent group is the apical ancestor often *not* human?

    a. lineage
    b. extended family
    c. family of procreation
    d. clan
    e. family of orientation

13. Which of the following statements about the nuclear family is *not* true?

    a. In America, non-nuclear family arrangements now outnumber nuclear family households by almost four to one
    b. A family of orientation may be a nuclear family
    c. A family of procreation may be a nuclear family
    d. The nuclear family is a cultural universal
    e. Most people belong to at least two nuclear families during their lives

14. Which of the following statements about corporate groups is true?

    a. Membership is always ascribed
    b. They continue to exist despite changes in personnel
    c. Land is never part of their estate
    d. They are confined to nonindustrial societies
    e. Membership is always dependent upon kinship

15. What term refers to the kind of descent in which people choose the descent group that they join?

    a. neolineal
    b. patrilineal
    c. ambilineal
    d. matrilineal
    e. bilineal

16. What are the two basic social units of foraging societies?

    a. the band and the clan
    b. the lineage and the nuclear family
    c. the extended family and the clan
    d. the nuclear family and the band
    e. the band and the extended family

17. Kottak argues that the relatively high incidence of expanded family household in the lower class is _____.

    a. the reason the families of lower class urbanites are dysfunctional
    b. an important strategy the urban poor use to adapt to poverty
    c. maladaptive, since poor families should be smaller in order to cut down on expenses
    d. caused by bifurcate merging, a practice that was brought to the United States by Scotch-Irish immigrants during the early part of this century
    e. all of the above

18. Which of the following belongs to ego's patrilineage?

    a. MB
    b. MF
    c. BD
    d. ZS
    e. M

19. Which of the following does *not* belong to ego's matrilineage?

    a. FM
    b. B
    c. ZS
    d. MB
    e. M

20. What is the system of kinship classification used in the United States?

    a. bifurcate merging
    b. lineal
    c. bifurcate collateral
    d. generational
    e. patrilineal

21. In a lineal system of kinship terminology, which of the following pairs would be called by the same term?

    a. M and FZ
    b. M and MZ
    c. FB and MB
    d. FB and FZ
    e. F and FB

22. A lineal kinship terminology_____.

   a. is generally found in societies with patrilineal descent rules
   b. uses two terms to identify ego's parents' siblings: one term for both FZ and MZ and one term for both FB and MB
   c. is often found in association with the distinction between parallel and cross-cousins
   d. stresses relationships with collaterals
   e. is all of the above

23. In a bifurcate merging kinship terminology, what is merged?

   a. lineal relatives with collateral relatives
   b. members of family of orientation and family of procreation
   c. affinal relatives and collateral relatives
   d. affinal relatives and lineal relatives
   e. none of the above

24. The nuclear family is the most important kin group in what kinds of societies?

   a. segmentary lineage organization/chiefdoms
   b. industrial middle class/foraging bands
   c. ambilineal/collateral
   d. lineages/clans
   e. patrilocal/matrilocal

25. Which of the following statements about bifurcate merging kinship terminologies is true?

   a. They are generally found in societies with unilineal descent
   b. They use the same term to describe F and FB and the same term for M and MZ.
   c. is generally found in societies with unilocal residence patterns
   d. They are often found in association with the kinship distinction between parallel and cross-cousins
   e. all of the above

26. Why are kinship terminologies important to anthropologists?

   a. They make their discipline seem as abstruse (intellectually complex) as the physical sciences
   b. They represent the rights and obligations important in social groups
   c. They are one of the fastest-changing aspects of culture
   d. They show whether other societies can think in logical Western ways
   e. They are one of the few areas of culture in which comparison is impossible

27. In what kind of kinship calculation are kin ties traced equally through males and females?

   a. bilineal
   b. bifurcate merging
   c. bifurcate collateral
   d. bilateral
   e. biluminous

28. What postmarital residence rule is most often found in societies with lineal kinship terminologies?

    a. ambilocal
    b. neolocal
    c. patrilocal
    d. matrilocal
    e. bilocal

29. Which of the following kin types is not ego's lineal relative?

    a. M
    b. B
    c. MM
    d. F
    e. S

30. What kind of relative is your mother's sister?

    a. lineal relative
    b. collateral relative
    c. affinal relative
    d. nuclear family member
    e. member of your family of procreation

31. Which of the following statements about nuclear families is true?

    a. They are everywhere recognized as the most significant kinship unit
    b. They are permanent units that continue to exist despite changes in personnel
    c. They are a cultural universal
    d. They are strongly associated with both social and geographic mobility
    e. They are dependent upon bilateral kinship calculation

32. In a bifurcate merging kinship terminology, which of the following pairs would be called by the same term?

    a. MB and FB
    b. MZ and MB
    c. MF and FF
    d. M and F
    e. none of the above

33. What is the name of the family in which a child is raised?

    a. family of procreation
    b. family of orientation
    c. family of nucleation
    d. family of exasperation
    e. family of perspiration

34. What kind of relative is your father's father?

    a. lineal
    b. collateral
    c. affinal
    d. uterine
    e. matrilineal

35. What is another name for a person's "in-laws?"

   a. family of orientation
   b. affinal relatives
   c. consanguinal relatives
   d. collateral relatives
   e. lineal relatives

36. What is the most stable social group among band societies with a seasonal dispersion of population?

   a. the lineage
   b. the band
   c. the nuclear family
   d. the clan
   e. the expanded family household

37. In which of the following societies would you expect to find a generational kinship terminology?

   a. A society where there has been a long history of nuclear families living by themselves, isolated from other kin
   b. A society where the mother's side of the family is seen as opposed to the father's side of the family
   c. a patrilineal society
   d. a matrilineal society
   e. A society where a child's aunts and uncles are among his/her most important teachers

ESSAY QUESTIONS

38. Cite evidence confirming or denying the universality of the nuclear family.

39. Is our kinship system more logical than the others we have studied? Why, or why not?

40. Discuss variation in kinship patterns from class to class in stratified societies.

41. Discuss ways in which kinship and descent help human populations adapt to their environments.

42. Discuss major similarities and differences among nuclear families, lineages, and industrial corporations.

43. "Anthropologists spend much of their time studying trivia like kinship." Do you agree with this statement? If so, why? If not, why not? Discuss.

44. In some systems of kinship terminology, lineal and collateral relatives are grouped together under the same kinship terms, and in others they are not. In terms of the sociocultural setting in which these terminologies exist, discuss reasons for the differences. Address yourself to lineal, bifurcate merging, and generational terminologies.

45. Why do anthropologists spend so much time studying systems of kinship terminology? Discuss.

46.   Any of the above multiple choice questions may be converted to an essay question by requiring students to choose the correct answer and justify their selection in essay form. Such justifications should include explanations as to why the chosen answer is correct and why those responses not chosen are incorrect.

47.   In what kinds of situations would you expect to find ambilineal descent? Unilineal descent? Why?

TRUE OR FALSE QUESTIONS

48. True or **False**   A descent group consists of only a married couple and their children.

49. True or **False**   With patrilineal descent you take your father's last name, but you recognize descent through both of your parents.

50. **True** or False   In unilineal descent, one ancestry is traced through only one line of descent.

51. **True** or False   Members of a clan stipulate descent from a common apical ancestor.

52. True or **False**   A nuclear family includes you, your parents, and your grandparents.

53. True or **False**   Your family of procreation is the one in which you were born.

54. **True** or False   Although nuclear families are found in many societies around the world, it is not a cultural universal.

55. True or **False**   *Tarawad* is the Nayar word for the nuclear family.

56. **True** or False   Neolocal postmarital residence rules require newly married couples to establish their own residence.

57. **True** or False   In Industrialized nations, extended families are more common in the lower class than in the upper class.

58. True or **False**   After reaching an all time low for the 20th century in the 1970s, the nuclear family is making a rebound accounting for a greater number of American households each year.

59. **True** or False   Industrialization increases mobility which plays a major role in the disappearance of extended families in the U.S.

60. True or **False**   Over the last thirty years, American notions regarding kinship and descent have been determined by the mass media, most notably television sitcoms.

61. **True** or False   Comparing notions of family between the U.S. and Brazil, the extended still plays a central role for most Brazilians.

62. **True** or False   Industrial and foraging societies differ from agricultural societies in that the nuclear family is both mobile and economically self-sufficient.

63. True or **False**   The most common postmarital residence rule is matrilocality in which the married couple moves in with the husband's family.

64. True or False   With unilineal descent one's lineage affiliation is ascribed at birth, but with ambilineal descent lineage affiliation is more fluid as each member chooses their descent group.

65. True or False   Kinship is a cultural construction.

66. True or **False**   A bifurcate merging kinship terminology distinguishes between collateral and lineal relatives.

67. True or **False**   A generational kinship terminology uses separate terms for each of the six kin types on the parental generation.

CHAPTER 16

MARRIAGE

CHAPTER OUTLINE

I. Introduction

    A. There is no single definition of marriage that is adequate to account for all of the diversity found in marriages cross-culturally.

    B. Edmund Leach argued that there are several different kinds of rights allocated by marriage.
        1. Marriage can establish the legal father of a woman's children and the legal mother of a man's.
        2. Marriage can give either or both spouses a monopoly in the sexuality of the other.
        3. Marriage can give either of both spouses rights to the labor of the other.
        4. Marriage can give either of both spouses rights over the other's property.
        5. Marriage can establish a joint fund of property—a partnership—for the benefit of the children.
        6. Marriage can establish a socially significant relationship of affinity between spouses and their relatives.

II. Same-Sex Marriage

    A. In the section Kottak argues that same-sex marriages are legitimate unions between two individuals because like other kinds of marriage, same-sex marriage can allocate all of the rights discussed by Leach.
        1. In the U.S., since same-sex marriage is illegal, same-sex couples are denied many of these rights (e.g. rights to the labor of the other, over the other's property, relationships of affinity with the other's relatives).
        2. This does not mean that same-sex marriages like any other cultural construction is not capable of meeting these needs; only that in the U.S. laws prevent it from doing so.

    B. There are many examples in which same-sex marriages are culturally sanctioned (e.g. the Nuer, the Azande, the Igbo, and the Lovedu).

III. Incest and Exogamy

    A. Exogamy is the practice of seeking a spouse outside one's own group.
        1. This practice forces people to create and maintain a wide social network.
        2. This wider social network nurtures, helps, and protects one's group during times of need.

    B. Incest refers to sexual relations with a close relative.
        1. The incest taboo is a cultural universal.
        2. What constitutes incest varies widely from culture to culture.

    C. In societies with unilineal descent systems (patrilineal or matrilineal), the incest taboo is often defined based on the distinction between two kinds of first cousins: parallel cousins and cross cousins.
        1. A sexual relation with a parallel cousin is incestuous, because they belong to the same generation and the same descent group (see figures 16.1 and 16.2).
        2. Sexual relations with a cross cousin is not incestuous because they belong to the opposite group or moiety (see figures 16.1 and 16.2).

D. Specific cultural examples are taken from the Yanomami, the Lakher, and middle class America.

IV. Explaining the Taboo

    A. Instinctive Horror
        1. This theory argues that *Homo sapiens* are genetically programmed to avoid incest.
        2. This theory has been refuted.
            a. However, cultural universality does not necessarily entail a genetic basis (e.g. fire making).
            b. If people really were genetically programmed to avoid incest, a formal incest taboo would be unnecessary.
            c. This theory cannot explain why in some societies people can marry their cross cousins but not their parallel cousins.

    B. Biological Degeneration
        1. This theory argues that the incest taboo developed in response to abnormal offspring born from incestuous unions.
        2. A decline in fertility and survival does accompany brother-sister mating across several generations.
        3. However, human marriage patterns are based on specific cultural beliefs rather than universal concerns about biological degeneration several generations in the future.
            a. Neither instinctive horror nor biological degeneration can explain the very widespread custom of marrying cross cousins.
            b. Also, fears about degeneration cannot explain why sexual unions between parallel cousins but not cross cousins is so often tabooed.

    C. Attempt and Contempt
        1. Malinowski (and Freud) argued that the incest taboo originated to direct sexual feelings away from one's family to avoid disrupting the family structure and relations (familiarity increases the chances for attempt).
        2. The opposite theory argues that people are less likely to be sexually attracted to those with whom they have grown up (familiarity breeds contempt).

    D. Marry Out or Die Out
        1. A more accepted argument is that the taboo originated to ensure exogamy.
            a. Incest taboos forces people to create and maintain wide social networks by extending peaceful relations beyond one's immediate group.
            b. With this theory, incest taboos are seen as an adaptively advantageous cultural construct.
        2. This argument focuses on the adaptive *social* results of exogamy, such as alliance formation, not simply on the idea of biological degeneration.
        3. Incest taboos also function to increase a group's genetic diversity.

V. Endogamy

    A. Endogamy and exogamy may operate in a single society, but do not apply to the same social unit.
        1. Endogamy can be seen as functioning to express and maintain social difference, particularly in stratified societies.
        2. Homogamy is the practice of marrying someone similar to you in terms of background, social status, aspirations, and interests.

    B. Caste
        1. India's caste system is an extreme example of endogamy.
        2. It is argued that, although India's *varna* and America's "races" are historically distinct, they share a caste-like ideology of endogamy.

C. Royal Incest
1. Royal families in widely diverse cultures have engaged in what would be called incest, even in their own cultures.
2. Manifest function is the reason given for a custom by its natives.
3. Latent function is the effect a custom has, that is not explicitly recognized by the natives.
4. The manifest function of royal incest in Polynesia was the necessity of marriage partners having commensurate *mana* (see pp. 351-2).
5. The latent function of Polynesian royal incest was that it maintained the ruling ideology.
6. The royal incest, generally, had a latent economic function: it consolidated royal wealth.

VI. Marriage as Group Alliance

A. Bridewealth
1. Particularly in descent-based societies, marriage partners represent an alliance of larger social units.
2. Bridewealth is a gift from the husband's kin to the wife's, which stabilizes the marriage by acting as an insurance against divorce.
3. Brideprice is rejected as an appropriate label, because the connotations of a sale are imposed; but progeny price is considered an equivalent term.
4. Dowry, much less common than bridewealth, correlates with low status for women.
5. Fertility is often considered essential to the stability of a marriage.
6. Polygyny may be practiced to ensure fertility.

B. In the News: Love and Marriage
1. Typically, anthropologists have overlooked romantic love as a factor in the interpersonal relationships of the people they study, but this has begun to change.
2. As motifs of romantic love have become more widespread, globally, it has come to play an increasingly important role in the selection of marriage partners, even to the extent of being a basis for resistance against arranged marriages, for example.

C. Durable alliances
1. The existence of customs such as the sororate and the levirate indicate the importance of marriage as an alliance between groups (see figure 16.4).
2. Sororate marriages involve the widower marrying one of his deceased wife's sisters.
3. Levirate marriages involve the widow marrying one of her deceased husband's brothers.

VII. Divorce

A. Divorce is found in many different societies.
1. Marriages that are political alliances between groups are harder to break up than marriages that are more individual affairs.
2. Payments of bridewealth also discourage divorce.
3. Divorce is more common in matrilineal societies as well as societies in which postmarital residence is matrilocal.
4. Divorce is harder in patrilocal societies as the woman may be less inclined to leave her children who as members of their father's lineage would need to stay him.

B. In foraging societies forces act to both promote and discourage divorce.
1. Promote divorce:
   a. Since foragers lack descent groups, marriages tend to be individual affairs with little importance placed on the political alliances.
   b. Foragers also have very few material possessions.

2. Discourage divorce:
   a. The family unit is the basic unit of society and division of labor is based on gender.
   b. The sparse population means that there are few alternative spouses if you divorce.

C. Divorce in the U.S.
   1. The U.S. has one of the world's highest divorce rates.
   2. The U.S. has a very large percentage of gainfully employed women.
   3. Americans value independence.

VIII. Plural Marriages

A. Polygamy is illegal in North America, but North Americans do practice serial monogamy, through multiple marriages and divorces.

B. Polygyny
   1. Even in cultures that approve of polygamy, monogamy still tends to be the norm, largely because most populations tend to have equal sex ratios.
   2. Polygyny is more common than polyandry because, where sex ratios are not equal, there tend to be more women than men.
   3. Multiple wives tend also to be associated with wealth and prestige (the Kanuri of Nigeria and the Betsileo are used as examples).

C. Polyandry
   1. Polyandry is quite rare, being practiced almost exclusively in South Asia.
   2. Among the Paharis of India, polyandry was associated with a relatively low female population, which was itself due to covert female infanticide.
   3. Polyandry is usually practiced in response to specific circumstances, and in conjunction with other marriage formats.
   4. In other cultures, polyandry resulted from the fact that men traveled a great deal, thus multiple husbands ensured the presence of a man in the home.

LECTURE TOPICS

1. Describe the pattern of mating that has recently developed in America, including early sex, "relationships," trial marriages, short early marriages followed by divorce, and more permanent subsequent marriages. Discuss that pattern in terms of adaptation to the current economic situation and in terms of American ideals about gender and marriage.

2. Discuss the various payments and exchanges that go along with marriages-their direction, their amounts, and their functions. Point out the vestiges of such exchanges in our own ideas about who pays for a marriage, who provides for household furnishings, and so on.

3. Discuss manifest and latent functions in practices such as the sororate, levirate, and the rules of endogamy or exogamy.

4. As gay marriages have become an issue in American political discourse, many writers (columnists, political commentators, social activists, etc.) have presented their arguments regarding the "true nature" of marriage. It is interesting to present several of the arguments and place them according to their cultural-political-historical context.

SUGGESTED FILMS

Strange Relations

video 60 min 1992 color
Part of the series *Millennium: Tribal Wisdom and the Modern World*, narrated by David Maybury-Lewis. The film uses cross-cultural comparison to examine various ways of constructing individual and social motivations for marriage. Examples are taken from a Nyinba couple in Nepal, the Wodaabe of Niger, and a couple in Canada. Alexandria: PBS Video.

Masai Women

video 1990 (1974) 52 min color
An ethnographic view of Masai culture and society, focusing on the preparation of young Masai girls for marriage and life in their society. The film uses candid interviews with an older woman to probe the feelings of Masai women about polygamy and women being denied the right to own property. Chicago: Films Incorporated Video.

The Kwegu

video 55 min 1982 color
A study of two southeast Ethiopian tribes, one of whom is totally subservient to the other. The Kwegu, who know the river better, put this and other skills at the service of the dominant Mursi. The Mursi, in turn, pay the dowry for Kwegu marriages, since Kwegu are not allowed property. From the Disappearing World series. From The University of Illinois Film and Video Center.

MULTIPLE CHOICE QUESTIONS

1. Who are your cross cousins?

    a. The children of your mother's sister or your father's brother
    b. The children of your mother's brother or your father's sister
    c. Your father's cousins' children
    d. Your mother's cousins' children
    e. Your cousins of the opposite sex

2. The incest taboo is a cultural universal, but _____.

    a. not all cultures have one
    b. not all cultures define incest the same way
    c. not all cultures know about incest
    d. some cultures have replaced it with the levirate
    e. some cultures practice gerontology anyway

3. Which of the following statements about societies with unilineal descent is true?

   a. Marriage between parallel cousins is preferred, while marriage between cross cousins is considered incest.
   b. Marriage between cross cousins is preferred, while marriage between parallel cousins is considered incest.
   c. Marriage between first cousins is preferred, while marriage between second cousins is considered incest.
   d. Marriage between sororal cousins is preferred, while marriage between levirate cousins is considered incest.
   e. Marriage between Crow cousins is preferred, while marriage between Omaha cousins is considered incest.

4. What term refers to a gift made by the husband and his kin to the kin of the bride?

   a. bride theft
   b. elopement
   c. dowry
   d. bridewealth
   e. cross-cousin marriage

5. What term is synonymous with bridewealth?

   a. dowry
   b. prestation
   c. tribute
   d. bride bribe
   e. progeny price

6. What is the name of the custom by which a widower marries the sister of his deceased wife?

   a. sororate marriage
   b. serial polyandry
   c. filial marriage
   d. levirate marriage
   e. fraternal marriage

7. Who is your socially recognized father?

   a. pater
   b. genitor
   c. creator
   d. father
   e. all of the above

8. What term refers to the biological father of a child?

   a. pater
   b. creator
   c. father
   d. genitor
   e. provider

9. In a society with two exogamous lineages (moieties), who is the preferred bride for a male ego?

   a. **MBD**
   b. MZD
   c. FBD
   d. FZS
   e. none of the above

10. Which of the following is ego's cross-cousin?

    a. **MBS**
    b. FBS
    c. MZD
    d. FBD
    e. MZS

11. What term refers to sexual relations with someone considered to be a close relative?

    a. levirate
    b. sororate
    c. fraternal
    d. **incest**
    e. exogamy

12. Which of the following is an example of a rule of endogamy?

    a. A taboo on marrying members of the same totemic group
    b. **The Nazi law forbidding "Aryans" from marrying anyone but other "Aryans"**
    c. A taboo against marrying within the same village
    d. A taboo on mating with members of one's extended family
    e. all of the above

13. How do rules of endogamy function in society?

    a. They prove that the incest taboo is not the cultural universal it was once thought to be
    b. They encourage the extension of affinal bonds to an ever-widening circle of people
    c. **They tend to maintain social distinctions between groups**
    d. They expand the gene pool
    e. none of the above

14. What term refers to the practice of marrying someone within a group to which one belongs?

    a. incest
    b. exogamy
    c. hyppgamy
    d. **endogamy**
    e. endosperm

15. How do the caste system in India and rules of hypodescent in the United States function in society?

   a. They differentiate individuals on the basis of achievement
   b. They maintain social, economic, and political distinctions
   c. They place people in positions according to their abilities
   d. They maintain the hierarchical control that is necessary for all organisms and all societies to survive
   e. none of the above

16. Which of the following statements about marriage is true?

   a. It is a cultural universal
   b. It must involve at least one biological male and at least one biological female
   c. It involves a woman and the genitor of her children
   d. It always involves a priest
   e. all of the above

17. What is term for the gift that the wife's group gives to the husband's family?

   a. polygamy
   b. bridewealth
   c. dowry
   d. progeny price
   e. brideservice

18. What is the practice through which widows are burned alive on their husband's funeral pyre?

   a. zadgruga
   b. fraternal
   c. tarawad
   d. sororate
   e. sati

19. Which of the following is not a form of polygamy?

   a. A man who marries, then divorces, then marries again, then divorces again, then marries again, each time to a different woman
   b. A man who has three wives
   c. A woman who has three husbands, all of whom are brothers
   d. A man who has three wives, all of whom are sisters
   e. A man who has two wives, one of whom is biologically female, while the other is biologically male, but is regarded has having the spirit of a woman

20. Which of the following customs does *not* help to maintain bonds between descent groups?

   a. bridewealth
   b. levirate
   c. sororate
   d. exogamy
   e. endogamy

21. In general, what happens as the value of bridewealth increases?

    a. marriages become more volatile
    b. marriages become more frequent
    c. **marriages become more stable**
    d. marriages become less frequent
    e. marriages become more symbolic

22. Which of the following statements about divorce is *not* true?

    a. Divorce is more common now than it was a century ago.
    b. The more substantial the joint property, the more complicated the divorce.
    c. Divorce is harder in a patrilineal society.
    d. **Divorce is unique to industrialized nation-states.**
    e. Substantial bridewealth may decrease the divorce rate.

23. Which of the following marital customs functions to maintain distinctions between groups?

    a. progeny price
    b. levirate
    c. sororate
    d. sororal polygyny
    e. **endogamy**

24. Which of the following best defines polygyny?

    a. The type of marriage in which there is more than one husband
    b. The custom whereby a wife marries the brother of her dead husband
    c. The type of marriage involving only two spouses
    d. The custom whereby a widower marries the sister of his dead wife
    e. **The type of marriage in which there is more than one wife**

25. Which of the following statements about romantic love is *not* true?

    a. **Romantic love is a cultural trait found only in the cultures of Western Europe and North America.**
    b. Romantic love is not the primary motivation for marriage in many societies around the world.
    c. Some form of romantic love seems to exist in a majority of the world's cultures.
    d. There is evidence that romantic love exists among foraging cultures, such as the !Kung San.
    e. The idea of romantic love as a reason for marriage is gaining popularity, partly as result of the spread of such Western cultural material as movies and pop music.

26. What are agnates?

    a. male members of the same society
    b. **members patrilineal descent group**
    c. members of the same matrilineal descent group
    d. members of the same ambilineal descent group
    e. male members of a patriline, female members of a matriline

27.   What term refers to one of two descent groups in a given population?

        a.   a levirate
        b.   a sororate
        c.   a moiety
        d.   a patriline
        e.   a matriline

28.   Which of the following statements about polygynous marriages is true?

        a.   They are characteristic of high social instability, as with serial monogamy in
                Southern California and Washington, D.C.
        b.   They frequently involve a hierarchical arrangement among the wives
        c.   They are associated with male infanticide
        d.   They are characterized by more than one husband in a single household
        e.   They occur in societies with more men than women

29.   How is exogamy adaptive?

        a.   It increases the number of individuals on whom one can rely in time of need
        b.   It increases the likelihood that disadvantageous alleles will find phenotypic
                expression and thus be eliminated from the population
        c.   It impedes peaceful relations among social groups and therefore promotes
                population expansion
        d.   It was an important causal factor in the origin of the state
        e.   all of the above

30.   In societies with a moiety organization, why can't you marry your parallel cousins?

        a.   They are considered "too close" for sexual partners
        b.   They belong to the same descent group as you do
        c.   They lie within the incest taboo
        d.   They are considered "siblings"
        e.   all of the above

31.   Which of the following statements about polyandry is true?

        a.   It is found only among fishing communities in Madagascar.
        b.   It is a cultural adaptation to the high labor demands of rice cultivation.
        **c.   It is a cultural adaptation to mobility associated with male travel for trade,
                commerce, and warfare.**
        d.   Polyandry is almost always sororate.
        e.   all of the above

ESSAY QUESTIONS

32.   Using what you know about cross-cultural comparisons of marital practices, discuss
        (criticize *and/or* defend) the following statement. "Serial monogamy is the result of a
        cultural emphasis on individualism, while polygamy is the result of a cultural emphasis
        on social responsibility."

33.   Does the practice of bridewealth necessarily imply gender inequality?

34.   How would you explain the universality of the incest taboo? You may draw on one or
        more of the explanations that have been offered previously.

35. Discuss some of the social functions of levirate, sororate, and bridewealth, and identify the sociocultural context of these customs.

36. What are some of the differences between endogamy and exogamy, and how absolute is the distinction implied by these terms? Use examples to illustrate your argument.

37. Discuss functional similarities between polyandry and endogamy.

38. Almost all cases of bridewealth are associated with patrilineal, patrilocal systems. Why? If there were such a thing as "groom price," where would you expect to find it? Why? Why do we not find groom service ethnographically?

39. Why does progeny price stabilize marriages?

40. What are postmarital residence rules? What varieties of such rules are there? How do they correlate with rules of descent?

41. Any of the above multiple choice questions may be converted to an essay question by requiring students to choose the correct answer and justify their selection in essay form. Such justifications should include explanations as to why the chosen answer is correct and why those responses not chosen are incorrect.

TRUE OR FALSE QUESTIONS

42. True or **False**   Kottak argues that same-sex marriages are not culturally viable institutions.

43. True or **False**   Exogamy is the practice of seeking out a mate within one's own group.

44. True or **False**   Incest is a cultural universal that is defined the same way by all cultures.

45. **True** or False   The children of your father's sister are called your cross cousins.

46. **True** or False   The instinctive horror explanation for the incest taboo has been rejected in part because if it were instinctive, a formal incest taboo would be unnecessary.

47. True or **False**   The biological degeneration explanation for the incest taboo has won over supporters because of universal concerns about biology.

48. **True** or False   One theory regarding the universality of the incest taboo argues that by forcing people to marrying outside their immediate kin group, peaceful alliances between people would extend to include a greater number of individuals.

49. True or **False**   Homogamy is the practice of marrying within a culturally prescribed group to which one belongs.

50. **True** or False   In the caste system of India, failure to adhere to class endogamy rules resulted in a ritually impure marriage.

51. **True** or False   Royal incest among Hawaiians functioned to limit the number of conflicts about royal succession.

52. **True** or False   A progeny price is paid to the bride's family so that her children permanently belong to the husband's group.

53. True or **False**   Dowries are most common in societies in which women occupy an elevated status position.

54. True or **False**   In tribal societies, unlike industrial ones, marriage entails only an agreement between the people getting married; descent groups play only a minor role.

55. True or False   With polyandry, a woman takes more than one husband.

56. True or False   If Hank marries his deceased brother's widow, this is called a levirate marriage.

57. True or **False**   Cross-culturally, divorce is known only in industrialized societies where a high percentage of women are gainfully employed.

58. True or **False**   Serial polygamy is the practice of having more than one wife, but never more than one at the same time.

59. True or False   Polygynous marriages often serve important economic and political functions with the number of wives a man has as an indicator of his wealth, prestige, and status.

60. True or False   Among the Pahari who were polyandrous, covert female infanticide helped to sustain the practice of polyandry.

61. True or **False**   Plural marriages are commonly found in societies where economic activities have become disembedded from kin ties.

CHAPTER 17
POLITICAL SYSTEMS

CHAPTER OUTLINE

I. Introduction

    A. Politics
1. *Power* is the ability to exercise one's will over others.
2. Authority is the socially approved use of power.
3. In 1962, Elman Service developed a typology of political organizations.
    a. *Bands* are small kin-based groups found among foragers.
    b. *Tribes* are associated with non-intensive food production and have villages and/or descent groups, but lack formal government and social classes.
    c. The chiefdom is a form of sociopolitical organization that is intermediate between the tribe and the state, still kin-based, but characterized by a permanent political structure with some degree of differential access to resources and a political structure.
    d. Formal government and social classes characterize the state.
4. In bands and tribes, the political order (polity) is not a distinct institution, but is embedded in the overall social order.
5. Because of this embeddedness, Kottak prefers to speak of *socio*political (rather than simply political) organization in discussing cross-cultural similarities and differences in the regulation or management of interrelations among groups and their representatives.

    B. Types and Trends
1. There are many correlations between economy and sociopolitical organization (see figure 17.2).
    a. Foragers tend to have band organization.
    b. Horticulturalists and pastoralists tend to have tribal organization.
    c. Agriculturalists tend to have either chiefdom-level or state-level organization.
2. In general, as the economy becomes more productive, population size increases leading to greater regulatory problems, which give rise to more complex social relations and linkages (greater social and political complexity).

II. Bands and Tribes

    A. Foraging Bands
1. In foraging societies the only two social groups that are significant are the nuclear family and the band.
    a. Membership in these groups is fluid and can change from year to year.
    b. Kin networks, both real and fictive, are created and maintained through marriage, trade, and visiting.
2. Foraging bands are egalitarian, in that all differences in status are achieved.
3. Foragers lack formal law, as conflict resolution is embedded in kinship and social ties (e.g. blood feuds).
4. Prestige refers to esteem, respect, or approval for culturally valued acts or qualities.

B. Tribal Cultivators
  1. Tribes usually have a horticultural or pastoral economy and are organized by village life and/or descent-group membership.
  2. Social classes and formal government are not found in tribes.
  3. Small-scale warfare or intervillage raiding is commonly found in tribes.
  4. The main regulatory officials are village heads, "big men", descent-group leaders, village councils, and leaders of pantribal associations.
    a. The officials have limited authority.
    b. They lead through persuasion and by example, not through coercion.
  5. Like foragers, tribes are egalitarian.
    a. Tribes often have marked gender stratification.
    b. Status in tribes is based on age, gender, and personal traits and abilities.
  6. Horticulturalists are egalitarian and tend to live in with small villages with low population density.

C. Interesting Issues: The Great Forager Debate
  1. In anthropology there is a debate between traditionalists and revisionists over the nature and state of foragers in the modern world.
    a. Traditionalists, including Richard Lee argue that foragers like the San of the Kalahari are autonomous foragers with a unique cultural identity.
    b. Revisionists, including Edwin Wilmsen argue that the San are not isolated foragers but are deeply integrated into the food producing communities in the area and as a result tell us very little about the foraging societies before the emergence of agriculture.
  2. Both sides are correct in that modern foragers are not living relic of the Stone Age, but to the extent that they base their subsistence strategies on foraging, they do provide important data regarding that way of life.

D. The Village Head
  1. The Yanomami are used as an example of a society with a village head.
  2. The position of village head is achieved and comes with very limited authority.
    a. He cannot force or coerce people to do things.
    b. He can only persuade, harangue, and try to influence people to do things.
  3. The Village head acts as a mediator in disputes, but he has no authority to back his decision or impose punishments.
  4. The village head must lead in generosity.
    a. He must be more generous, which means he must cultivate more land.
    b. He hosts feasts for other villages.
  5. In the last decade, particularly, the Yanomami have suffered greatly from violence and disease, both of which have come from the encroaching mining and ranching industries of Brazil.

E. The "Big Man"
  1. A big man is like a village head, except that his authority is regional, in that may have influence over more than one village.
  2. The big man is common to the South Pacific.
  3. Among the Kapauku, the big man is the only political figure beyond the household.
    a. The position is achieved through generosity, eloquence, bravery, physical fitness, and supernatural powers.
    b. His decisions are binding among his followers.
    c. He is an important regulator of regional events (e.g. feasts and markets).
  4. In order to be a tribal leader, a big man or village head, a person must be generous.
    a. They must work hard to create a surplus to give away.
    b. This surplus is converted into prestige.
  5. The big man is a temporary regional regulator who can mobilize supporters from several villages for produce and labor on specific occasions.

F. Segmentary Lineage Organization
1. Segmentary lineage organization (SLO) is based upon descent-group structure (typically patrilineal).
2. Segmentary lineages are composed hierarchically, with smaller units (potentially) combining into larger ones.
   a. Maximal lineages share a common ancestor who lived long ago and whose membership is spread over a large area (inclusive).
   b. Minimal lineages are the smallest unit in which members live in the same village and share a common ancestor who lived no more than four generations ago (exclusive).
3. Nilotic peoples, such as the Nuer, are exemplary of segmentary lineage organization.
4. With SLO, the closer the relationship in terms of descent, the greater the mutual support and the more distant the common ancestor, the greater the potential for hostility.
5. Conflict resolution
   a. When a dispute develops between people who share a common living ancestor, he intervenes to settle it.
   b. When the combatants do not share a common living ancestor, a blood feud may develop.

G. Pantribal Sodalities and Age Grades
1. Sodalities are non-kin based organizations, which may generate cross-societal linkages.
   a. They are often based on common age or gender.
   b. Some sodalities are confined to a single village.
   c. Some sodalities span several villages; these are called pantribal sodalities.
2. Pantribal sodalities tend to be found in areas where two or more different cultures come into regular contact.
   a. Especially in situations where warfare is frequent.
   b. Since pantribal sodalities draw their members from several villages, they can mobilize a large number of men for raids.
3. Pressure from European contact created conditions which promoted pan-tribal sodalities (age sets are one example) among the groups of the North American Great Plains of the eighteenth and nineteenth centuries.
4. Age sets are sodalities that include all of the men born during a certain time span.
   a. Similar to a cohort of class of students, like class of 2004.
   b. Members of an age set progress through a series of age grades together (e.g. initiated youth, warrior, adult, elder or in American universities: freshmen, sophomore, junior, senior, graduate).
5. Secret societies are sodalities with secret initiation ceremonies.
6. Sodalities create non-kin linkages between people based on age, gender, and ritual and create a sense of ethnic identity and belonging to the same cultural tradition.

H. Nomadic Politics
1. Nomads must interact with a variety of groups, unlike most sedentary societies.
2. Powerful chiefs are commonly found in nomadic groups that have large populations (e.g. the Basseri and the Qashqai of southern Iran).
3. The Basseri have a smaller population and their chief, *khan*, is similar to a village head or big man.
   a. The position is achieved.
   b. Allegiances are with the person, not the office.
4. The larger Qashqai have multiple levels of authority and more powerful chiefs.
   a. Their authority can be more coercive.
   b. Allegiances are with the office, not the person.

III. Chiefdoms

  A. Chiefdoms and States
    1. Chiefdoms are a transitional form of sociopolitical organization between tribes and states.
    2. Carneiro (1970) defines the state as "an autonomous political unit encompassing many communities within its territory, having a centralized government with the power to collect taxes, draft men for work or war, and decree and enforce laws."
      a. Archaic or nonindustrial states
      b. Industrial or modern states

  B. Political and Economic Systems in Chiefdoms
    1. Unlike band and tribal political systems, chiefdoms and states are permanent: their offices outlast the individuals who occupy them.
    2. An office is a permanent position of authority that exists independently of the person who occupies it.
      a. It must be refilled when it is vacated
      b. Offices ensure that the sociopolitical organization endures across generations.
    3. Chiefs play an important role in the production, distribution, and consumption of resources.
      a. Chiefs collect foodstuffs as tribute (upward movement).
      b. Chiefs later redistribute these collect foodstuffs at feasts (downward movement).

  C. Social Status in Chiefdoms
    1. In chiefdoms, social status is based on seniority of descent.
    2. All of the people in a chiefdom are believed to have descended from a group of common ancestors.
      a. The closer you and your lineage are related to those founding ancestors, the greater your prestige.
      b. In chiefdoms, there is a continuum of prestige with the chief at one end and the lowest ranking individuals at the other.
      c. The chief must demonstrate his seniority of descent.
    3. Chiefdoms lack social classes.

  D. Status Systems in Chiefdoms and States
    1. Unlike tribal and band organizations, there are systemic status distinctions in chiefly and state societies.
    2. State and chiefdom status systems are based upon differential access to wealth and resources, and differential allocation of rights and duties.
      a. States are characterized by much clearer class divisions than chiefdoms, typically associated with *stratum endogamy.*
      b. The result of stratum endogamy is social stratification, the hierarchical arrangement of unrelated classes.
      c. Social stratification, social classes, is one of the key distinguishing features of states.
    3. Weber's Dimensions of Social Stratification
      a. Wealth, or economic status.
      b. Political status is based upon power.
      c. Social status is based upon prestige.
      d. In chiefdoms, all three dimensions are tied to kinship and descent.
      e. In the early states, distinctions in all three dimensions appeared between endogamous groups for the first time.
    4. In archaic states there were two basic class distinctions.
      a. The superordinate stratum was the elite or higher class that had privileged access to wealth, power, and other valued resources.
      b. The subordinate stratum was the lower or underprivileged class.

IV. States

    A. States have specialized units that perform specific tasks.
       1. Population control: fixing boundaries, establishing citizenship, and the taking of a census.
       2. Judiciary: laws, legal procedure, and judges.
       3. Enforcement: permanent military and police forces.
       4. Fiscal: taxation.
       5. These subsystems were more or less embedded into the overall ruling systems of archaic states.

    B. Population Control
       1. States use administrative divisions to control their populations.
         a. Provinces, districts, counties, townships
         b. Each administrative division is managed by state officials.
       2. States displace the role and importance that kinship has in bands, tribes, and chiefdoms.
       3. States foster geographic mobility and resettlement.
       4. States assign differential rights to different status distinctions.
         a. citizens vs. non-citizens
         b. elites vs. commoners vs. slaves
         c. soldiers vs. civilians

    C. Judiciary
       1. Laws are explicit codes for behavior, issued by the state, and are distinct from the consensual mores and expectations that exist in non-state societies.
       2. The state is unique as a political system in that it governs family affairs.
       3. The presence of laws has not reduced violence--indeed, states are responsible for some of the most violent episodes in human history.

    D. Enforcement
       1. A judiciary obligates the existence of a system of enforcement.
       2. The judiciary and enforcement typically work not only to control internal and external conflict, but also to preserve the existing state hierarchy.

    E. Fiscal Systems
       1. State rulers typically perform no subsistence activities.
       2. The fiscal system serves to support the rulers and ruling structure by collecting a portion of that produced by other members of the state.
       3. Fiscal systems of archaic states also worked to maintain and elaborate class distinctions, as in the support of sumptuary goods for the elites.

V. Beyond the Classroom: Perspectives on Group Membership

    A. Abigail Dreibelbis researched the needs and desires for belonging and affiliation on her college campus.

    B. Using survey information collected from sorority and non-sorority members, Dreibelbis found that certain behaviors correlated with membership and nonmembership in sororities.
       1. Individuals who belonged to sororities tended to have a history of belong to formal organizations (student government) and generally placed a higher value on social involvement and acceptance for security and identity.
       2. Nonmembers or Independents tended to have emphasize more aesthetic, personal activities.

LECTURE TOPICS

1.   Discuss band-level notions of personality and privacy in contrast to American notions. The adaptive and cultural roots of the differences should be made explicit.

2.   The romanticization of band and tribal life in Western culture, in media and in the social sciences should be made clear and discussed, with examples from recent movies or television programs. The roots of that attitude in the social sciences, and its persistence, should also be made clear.

3.   The centrality of kinship relations in tribal life cannot be overemphasized. The key role of kinship can be illustrated by cataloging cases in which kinship determines political office, religious specialization, access to resources, and so on.

4.   It is important to note that the "egalitarian" does not mean that everybody is of equal status. Rather, egalitarian means that everybody is born equal, but that there are differences in status based on age, gender, personal attitudes and abilities.

5.   A stereotyped notion of nonindustrial groups is that they all have a chief. Explain why not all such groups have a chief as a prelude to discussing the characteristic of chiefs.

6.   A comparison of big men and chiefs with televangelists, movie stars, politicians, rock stars, and other powerful and morally charged figures helps to sort out the differences and similarities, and to prepare the way for a discussion of class relations.

7.   The notions of embeddedness and social roles are critical to understanding the differences between the different levels of social organization. Find ways to get the students to think about the various roles they fill, and how they are connected to other people (for example, what sort of activities do they do with their siblings: play, subsistence, warfare, anything?). Then compare their suggestions to a concrete example from a tribal society. This should help provide a basis for understanding the multiplex relationships between leaders and the led in non-industrialized societies.

SUGGESTED FILMS

Australia's Twilight of the Dreamtime

video   1988   60 min
Documentary about the environment and customs of a Northern Australian Aboriginal tribe. Produced by the National Geographic Society and WQED. Published by the National Geographic Society, Washington, D.C.

The Hunters

16mm   1958   73 min
A classic ethnographic film by John Marshall, centering on natives of the Kalahari Desert in southwest Africa as they organize a giraffe hunt. From the !Kung and G/wi Bushmen series. Distributed by the University of Illinois Film and Video Center.

Desert People

16mm   1966   about 53 min   b&w
A classic, faithful reconstruction of small band life among the Australian aborigines. Depicts gathering, grinding, and cooking of grains, and hunting of small game. Distributed by the University of Illinois Film and Video Center.

Dead Birds

16mm 1963 87 min
Robert Gardner's classic ethnographic study of the Dani people of West New Guinea, a tribe for whom warfare is a daily activity. Blue Ribbon winner of the American Film Festival. Distributed by the University of Illinois Film and Video Center.

The Nuer

75 min 1970 color
An anthropological documentary showing the practices of this southwest Ethiopian tribe: their daily life, the ceremonies of courtship, exorcism, animal sacrifice, and the custom of marking the skin of the body with patterned scars. Distributed by the University of Illinois Film and Video Center.

N!ai: the Story of a !Kung Woman

16mm 1980 59 min color
From the *Odyssey* series, this award-winning film provides an historical overview of the daily life of the !Kung San, a foraging people living in South Africa. The film covers N!ai's life from childhood to her mid thirties--a period of time which encompasses great change in the lifestyle of the !Kung San, including a move to a government camp in Namibia. Includes footage shot by John Marshall from the 1950's and 1978. Watertown, MA: Documentary Educational Resources/Public Broadcasting Association.

The Tightrope of Power

video 60 min 1992 color
From the *Millennium: Tribal Wisdom and the Modern World* Series. David Maybury-Lewis narrates a film that depicts the conflict among the interests of the indigenous First Nations, the government of Canada, and the secessionist-minded Quebecois. In particular, the film shows the leaders of the First Nations (especially Elijah Harper) attempting to prevent the passage of the Meech Lake Accord, a constitutional amendment that would have granted special status to Quebec, but overlooked the First Nations entirely. The film also provides a means for comparing chiefly politics (both as a practice and as a resistance ideology) with those of the nation-state. Alexandria, VA: PBS Video.

America's First City: Teotihuacan

16mm 18 min 1975 color
The world-famous pyramids of Teotihuacan are the remains of a great city founded 2000 years ago--the first metropolis in America. Presents the story of this city through scenes of its ruins. Dominating the site is the Pyramid of the Sun, as tall as a 20-story building, now worn and weathered but originally plastered and brilliantly painted. The lavishly decorated Pyramid of Quetzelcoatl is the outstanding example of the architectural and engineering genius of those early builders. The legend of the Fifth Sun, the Aztec tale of the birth of Teotihuacan, is reenacted. Teotihuacan was abandoned around A.D. 800, but it is still revered by Mexicans as an example of the skills and artistry of their ancestors. From the Mexico Heritage series. From The University of Illinois Film and Video Center.

Estos Fueron Los Mayas!

19 min   1975   color

Achievements of the Mayan civilization in architecture, mathematics, astrology, and art were very advanced for their time, and make a fascinating visual and historical study. Reviews the evidences remaining of these cultural monuments, including their calendar, codices, and system of counting. In Spanish of intermediate difficulty. An English version is entitled *These Were the Maya!* From the Mexico Heritage series. From The University of Illinois Film and Video Center.

The Story of the Aztecs

20 min   1975   color

Traces the history and past glories of the Aztec Empire. In 1125 the Aztecs entered the Valley of Mexico, and there they founded their shimmering capital city, Tenochtitlan. A huge complex of ceremonial buildings, marketplaces and palaces, it was a fitting center for a tribe who ruled over an empire that included all of Mexico as far south as Guatemala. The Aztecs were fierce and cruel, taking slaves to build their temples and captives to use as human sacrifices to their gods. In 1519 the Spaniards destroyed the fabled Aztec Empire, and the ruins of Tenochtitlan lie beneath modern Mexico City. From the *Mexico Heritage* series. From The University of Illinois Film and Video Center.

Viva Mexico! A Cultural Portrait

28 min   1971   color

Mexico's combined heritage of Indian and Spanish civilizations are visible in the costumes, architecture, food, folk art, and traditional celebrations depicted in the film. Scenes from the Mayan and Aztec ruins are skillfully blended with scenes of contemporary Indian society and views of pre-Columbian artifacts housed in the National Museum of Anthropology. Other highlights include colorful fiestas, a rodeo, and a visit with some famous Mexican potters at work. Features accompanying folk music score and appropriate sounds recorded on-site. From The University of Illinois Film and Video Center.

Chinese History: 1--The Beginnings

16mm   1976   19 min

Depicts the search for the origins of Chinese civilization (to 1100 B.C.). The earliest inhabitants-Lan-t'ien Man, Peking Man, and Upper Cave Man were followed about 6,000 years ago by Neolithic cultures, one of which, Lung-Shan, developed into the first Chinese historical dynasty, Shang. When China entered the Bronze Age, advances were made in technology, art, and architecture. From The University of Illinois Film and Video Center.

Chinese History: 2--The Making of a Civilization

16mm   1976   18 min

Describes the conquest of Shang and the rule of Chou (c. 1100 to 475 B.C.). The Chou dynasty established a type of feudal system with a king as absolute ruler. In 770 B.C. the capital was moved eastward to protect it from invasion, dividing the dynasty into Western and Eastern Chou periods. This latter period witnessed the replacement of serfdom with land ownership, the advent of the Iron Age, and the search by Confucius for the deeper meaning of man and nature. From The University of Illinois Film and Video Center.

23 min   color
An introduction to the land of Egypt at the height of its power, and its people--the pharaohs who inhabited the great tombs and the craftsmen who built those tombs. Contents: The contrast between the lush greenness near the Nile and the aridity of the desert, between the land of the living and that of the dead; Tutankhamen's tomb and its discovery by Howard Carter; our own discovery that we know a great deal about the people who built Tut's tomb. From Films for the Humanities and Sciences.

MULTIPLE CHOICE QUESTIONS

1.   What is the name of the anthropologist credited with originating the typology of political organization ("bands," "tribes," "chiefdoms," and "states")?

     a.   Leslie White
     b.   Elman Service
     c.   Bronislaw Malinowski
     d.   Clifford Geertz
     e.   Margaret Mead

2.   In which of the following forms of political organization is it *most* likely that the most important leaders will acquire their position based upon personal background or ability, rather than heredity?

     a.   tribal societies
     b.   feudal states
     c.   imagined communities
     d.   chiefdoms
     e.   agrarian, pre-industrial states

3.   Most of human history has been characterized by which level of political organization?

     a.   band
     b.   tribe
     c.   chiefdom
     d.   state
     e.   foraging

4.   What is a "big man?"

     a.   a person who holds a permanent political office
     b.   he is a hereditary ruler
     c.   he is a man of influence and prestige
     d.   he avoids excessive displays of generosity
     e.   he has tremendous power because he is regarded as divine

5.   Which of the following statements about non-state societies is true?

     a.   all political power is based on religion
     b.   political institutions are maintained totally separate from economic institutions
     c.   social control is maintained mostly through physical coercion
     d.   economic, political, and religious activities are often embedded in one another
     e.   all of the above

6. In band-level societies, what does the amount of respect or status attached to an individual depend on?

   a. rank ascribed at birth
   b. **culturally valued personal attributes**
   c. the number of possessions and their monetary value
   d. the amount of labor one can extract from spouse and children
   e. genealogical closeness to apical ancestors

7. Which of the following statements about tribes with patrilineal segmentary lineage organizations is true?

   a. Larger units called maximal lineages are subdivided into major, minor, and minimal lineages
   b. Individuals most closely related by descent will exhibit the greatest social solidarity
   c. One's allies can vary from one dispute to another depending on the genealogical distance of the parties in the dispute
   d. Common patrilineal elders help settle disputes between closely related individuals
   e. **all of the above are true**

8. What term refers to a descent group that determines membership through demonstrated descent?

   a. clan
   b. band
   c. bias group
   d. cognate
   e. **lineage**

9. Which of the following would *not* be considered a band society?

   a. !Kung San
   b. Eskimos
   c. **Betsileo**
   d. Australian aborigines
   e. Mbuti "pygmies"

10. Foraging economies are usually associated with which type of sociopolitical organization?

    a. **band**
    b. tribal
    c. state
    d. chiefdom
    e. primate

11. According to Kottak's discussion of the correlation between political forms and other sociocultural phenomena, what do many of the sociopolitical trends reflect?

    a. An instinctive human need for order based on binary logic
    b. The sum total of all-inclusive fitness maximizing behaviors practiced by humans over time
    c. **The increased regulatory demands associated with food reproduction**
    d. The logical results of human biological tendencies, most especially sexual dimorphism
    e. all of the above

12. Which of the following is *not* used by the traditional Eskimos to handle disputes?

    a.   blood feuds
    b.   song contests
    c.   killing of the offender
    d.   **courts of law**
    e.   all of the above are used

13. Which of the following statements about political leaders in foraging bands is true?

    a.   They maintain power by maintaining strong ties with the commoner class
    b.   They have inherited special access to strategic resources
    c.   They maintain control by conquering foreign territories
    d.   **They have no means of forcing people to follow their decisions**
    e.   They are the most dominant males in the largest, most powerful descent group

14. Which of the following statements about the Eskimo song contest is true?

    a.   **It is an institutionalized means of resolving social tension so as to forestall open conflict**
    b.   It is sometimes the occasion for a "treacherous feast"
    c.   It is a widespread feature of tribal society
    d.   It is a ritualized means of designating hunting lands
    e.   none of the above

15. Which of the following statements about foraging societies is *false*?

    a.   Recent studies indicate that modern foraging societies are experiencing wholesale change resulting from the world system.
    b.   All known modern foraging societies have links with external systems, including food-producers and nation-states.
    c.   There is a mistaken tendency to see all foraging societies as basically alike, as stereotypical primitive survivors of the Stone Age.
    d.   **The Tasaday of the Philippines are the only completely isolated, pristine foragers in the world today.**
    e.   The San of Southern Africa, have been looked upon as the quintessential hunter-gatherers, despite the fact that some San engage in other adaptive strategies.

16. Based upon Kottak's discussion of tribal political organization, which of the following pairs of terms is mismatched?

    a.   Eskimos/bands
    b.   tribal cultivators/descent groups
    c.   **tribal cultivators/socioeconomic stratification**
    d.   lineages/apical ancestors
    e.   Yanomami/village head

17. Which of the following does *not* accompany a shift toward the high-intensity end of the plant cultivation continuum?

    a.   increasing population density
    b.   increasing need for sociopolitical regulation
    c.   increasing labor input into food production
    d.   increasingly continuous land use
    e.   **decreasing political stratification**

18. In foraging and tribal societies, what is the basis for the amount of respect or status attached to an individual?

    a. rank ascribed at birth wives and children
    b. personal attributes, such as wisdom, leadership skills, and generosity
    c. the amount of possessions one owns and the ability to convert them into cash
    d. the amount of territory a person owns
    e. none of the above

19. What is the term for a social organization composed of patrilineal descent groups that are arranged as components of larger patrilineal descent groups, and which may break off and form subgroups relatively easily?

    a. a macroband-microband society
    b. classic band organization
    c. supremacist organization
    d. segmentary lineage organization
    e. graded sodalities

20. Which of the following is a political correlate of increasing intensity of land use?

    a. an increasing need to regulate the economy
    b. increasingly specialized leadership roles
    c. more frequent warfare
    d. a decrease in egalitarianism
    e. all of the above

21. Why does a big man accumulate wealth?

    a. Big men are village heads who are trying to turn their achieved status into something more permanent--the standard way of doing this is through conspicuous symbolic displays of wealth.
    b. The term "big man" refers to the liminal state a Kapauku youth enters before marriage: he accumulates wealth as a way of funding the wedding and paying bride price.
    c. Big men are typically war leaders and as such they must have a standing supply of "grievance gifts" to compensate the families of warriors who die under their command.
    d. The primary means of becoming a big man is the wearing of a *tonowi* shell necklace, which is imported from the coast and is therefore quite expensive by Kapauku standards.
    e. Big men do not keep the wealth they accumulate, instead they redistribute it to create and maintain alliances with political supporters.

22. Which of the following factors is responsible for the recent changes in Yanomami tribal society?

    a. They are being overrun by the more expansion-minded Nilotic peoples
    b. Modern-minded big men have amassed so much wealth that people have begun to regard them as chiefs
    c. The encroachment by gold miners and cattle ranchers
    d. Village raiding among tribal groups
    e. Sexual dimorphism

23. Of the following, which political leader is most likely to depend upon alliances formed by redistributing wealth he/she has accumulated outside his/her home village?

   a.   **the Kapauku tonowi**
   b.   the Queen of England
   c.   an apical ancestor in a segmentary lineage organization
   d.   a village head
   e.   a leopard-skin man among the Nuer

24. What is the basic principle of solidarity in segmentary lineage organization?

   a.   close, informal personal relationships are the key building blocks
   b.   clans are more coherent than lineages
   c.   **the closer the descent-group relationship, the greater the mutual support**
   d.   loyalty to a temporary leader, such as a "bigman"
   e.   the nuclear family

25. What does the Kapauku big man's position depend on?

   a.   hard work
   b.   creation of wealth superior to that of others
   c.   generosity
   d.   personal charisma
   e.   **all of the above**

26. If you are a member of a segmentary lineage organization and you have become involved in a dispute, who among the following is *most* likely to be your ally in this dispute?

   a.   **those people most closely related to you by descent**
   b.   those people whom you have recruited by sharing your wealth
   c.   the leopard skin man
   d.   the *tonowi*
   e.   the members of your age set

27. Which of the following statements about segmentary lineage organization is *not* true?

   a.   It can be adaptively advantageous in enabling populations to expand against their neighbors
   b.   **It is usually found in foraging societies**
   c.   It is associated with strong agnatic ties
   d.   Its segmentary structure becomes obvious only during disputes
   e.   It does not typically exist within states

28. With which kind of society is segmentary lineage organization is associated?

   a.   bands
   b.   **tribes**
   c.   chiefdoms
   d.   chiefdoms and states
   e.   states

29. According to Kottak, which of the following is an advantage that a Kapauku big man might have in comparison with a Yanomami village head?

   a. The big man's wealth exceeds that of his fellows
   b. The big man's followers recognize him as a leader and accept his decisions as binding
   c. The big man may help to determine the dates for feasts and markets
   d. He has influence that extends beyond the boundaries of his own village
   e. All of the above are listed as advantages for the big man

30. What is an age set?

   a. the same thing as a village council
   b. a pantribal sodality that represents a certain level of achievement in the society, much like the stages of an undergraduate's progress through college
   c. all men and women related by virtue of patrilineal descent from a human apical ancestor
   d. all men and women related by virtue of matrilineal descent from an a nonhuman apical ancestor
   e. a group uniting all men or women born during a certain certain span of time

31. Which of the following is the most important factor in determining an individual's power and prestige in a chiefdom?

   a. personality
   b. ancestry
   c. speaking ability
   d. anthropomorphism
   e. physical size

32. What is the political organization of states based on?

   a. kinship and marriage
   b. a segmentary lineage organization
   c. influence
   d. monopoly of force by a central authority
   e. egalitarian social organization

33. Which of the following is typical of state-level societies?

   a. a specialized decision-making system
   b. class stratification
   c. boundary maintenance systems
   d. intensive, managed agriculture
   e. all of the above

34. Which of the following is most likely to have stratum endogamy?

   a. a band
   b. a state
   c. a chiefdom
   d. a society with segmentary lineage organization
   e. a tribe

35. In what way are chiefdoms different from states?

    a.   chiefdoms are based on differential access
    b.   **chiefdoms lack socioeconomic stratification and stratum endogamy**
    c.   chiefdoms lack ascribed statuses
    d.   chiefdoms have permanent political regulation
    e.   chiefdoms have full-time religious specialists

36. According to Max Weber, what is prestige?

    a.   the basis of economic status
    b.   the basis of political status
    c.   **the basis of social status**
    d.   the basis of power
    e.   the basis of political capital

37. How do states differ from chiefdoms?

    a.   States are governed by a big man, whereas chiefdoms are ruled by a chief
    b.   States are egalitarian, whereas chiefdoms are socially stratified
    c.   Redistribution is characteristic of states, but is absent in chiefdoms
    d.   Status positions are usually ascribed in states, whereas they are almost always achieved in chiefdoms
    e.   **States are not normally organized on the basis of kinship, whereas chiefdoms are**

38. In what kind of society does differential access to strategic resources based on social stratification occur?

    a.   chiefdoms
    b.   bands
    c.   clans
    d.   tribes
    e.   **none of the above**

39. What does the success and spread of state organization reflect?

    a.   The state's ability to maintain order through legal and judicial subsystems
    b.   The state's strong, military organization
    c.   The state's higher levels of production
    d.   The state's regulation of occupational specialization
    e.   **all of the above**

40. Which of the following is *not* a subsystem specialization of archaic states?

    a.   **NGOs**
    b.   population control
    c.   judiciary
    d.   enforcement
    e.   fiscal

ESSAY QUESTIONS

41. What are the major results and implications of food production? How does reliance on food production affect the social, economic, and political organization of societies that practice it?

42. Anthropologists claim that in nonstate-organized societies, the political structure is embedded in relationships based on kinship, descent, and marriage. Use two ethnographic cases to illustrate this claim.

43. Discuss ways in which order is maintained in societies that lack chiefs and rulers.

44. Contrast two of the following as political regulators:
    a. sodalities based on age and gender
    b. village headmen
    c. village councils
    d. big men
    e. segmentary lineage organization
    f. pantribal sodalities

45. Contrast Eskimo and Yanomami with respect to reasons for disputes, effectiveness of means of resolving disputes, and enforcement of decisions about resolving disputes.

46. What factors are responsible for the variable development of political regulation and authority structures among pastoralists?

47. How did the advent of food production interact with population growth and distribution? How is population growth related to the rise of the state?

48. What is the difference between authority and power? How do the examples of tribal leaders such as the big man and the village head help us understand this difference?

49. How does one distinguish between a chiefdom and state? Is this a useful distinction? Is it always easy to make such a distinction?

50. What are the major political changes that occur along points of the plant-cultivating continuum?

51. Any of the above multiple choice questions may be converted to an essay question by requiring students to choose the correct answer and justify their selection in essay form. Such justifications should include explanations as to why the chosen answer is correct and why those responses not chosen are incorrect.

TRUE OR FALSE QUESTIONS

52. **True** or False   The sociopolitical organization of foragers tends to be bands.

53. True or **False**   In bands, the leader occupies an official office with coercive control over the band.

54. True or **False**   Since bands lack formalized law, they have no way of settling disputes.

55. **True** or False   In tribal level societies the village head leads by example and through persuasion, he lacks the ability to force people to do things.

56. True or **False**   Most band and tribal level societies in the world today are completely cut off from the rest of the world.

57. **True** or False — The key difference between a village head and a big man is that the big man has supporters in many villages, while the supporters of the village head are restricted to his respective village.

58. True or **False** — Segmentary lineage organization is a form of social stratification in which class endogamy is the rule.

59. **True** or False — Pantribal sodalities function to integrate the community by providing a series of important non-kin relationships.

60. **True** or False — Age grades represent stages in ones life with specific tasks, obligations, and duties for those individuals in a given grade.

61. True or **False** — The Qashqai and Basseri are both examples of nomadic foragers who live in modern day Iran.

62. **True** or False — In chiefdoms, chiefs occupy formal offices and administer or regulate a series of villages.

63. **True** or False — In chiefdoms, individuals were ranked according to seniority, but everyone was believed to have descended from a common set of ancestors.

64. True or **False** — Stratum endogamy is restricted to chiefdoms, where chiefs occupied a formal elite stratum in society.

65. **True** or False — Status in chiefdoms and states is based primarily upon differential access to resources.

66. True or **False** — Of the specialized subsystems in states discussed in the textbook, the religious system is the most important.

67. True or **False** — With the rise of state level sociopolitical organization, kinship's role in society continued to grow and dominate daily activities.

68. **True** or False — States are complex systems of sociopolitical organization that aim to control and administer everything from conflict resolution, to fiscal systems, to population movements.

69. True or **False** — A fiscal system includes the judges, laws, and courts that resolve conflicts.

70. True or **False** — Population control in states refers to police and military.

71. **True** or False — The elites of archaic states restricts access to sumptuary goods.

CHAPTER 18
GENDER

CHAPTER OUTLINE

I. Introduction

    A. The investigation of cultural constructions of gender is frequently an arena for a version of the nature-nurture debate.

    B. *Sex* refers to biological differences, while *gender* refers to the cultural construction of male and female characteristics.

    C. Sexual dimorphism refers to marked differences in male and female biology *besides* the primary and secondary sexual features (for example, the average difference in height and weight between men and women is an aspect of sexual dimorphism, but *not* the differences in genitalia and breasts).

    D. Preliminary Definitions
        1. Gender roles are the tasks and activities that a culture assigns to the sexes.
        2. Gender stereotypes are oversimplified but strongly held ideas of the characteristics of men and women.
        3. Gender stratification describes an unequal distribution of rewards (socially valued resources, power, prestige, and personal freedom) between men and women, reflecting their different positions in social hierarchy.

II. Gender among Foragers

    A. Economic Roles and Gender Stratification
        1. Roughly equal contributions to subsistence by men and women correlates with decreased gender stratification.
        2. As women's contributions to subsistence becomes differentially high or low, gender stratification increases.
        3. Gender stratification is lower when domestic and public spheres are not clearly distinguished.

    B. The Public-Domestic Dichotomy
        1. Strong differentiation between the home and the outside world is called the domestic-public dichotomy, or the *private-public contrast.*
          a. The activities of the domestic sphere tend to be performed by women.
          b. The activities of the public sphere tend to be restricted to only to men.
        2. Public activities tend to have greater prestige then domestic ones, which promotes gender stratification.

    C. Sex-Linked Activities
        1. All cultures have a division of labor based on gender, but the particular tasks assigned to men and women vary from culture to culture.
        2. Almost universally, the greater size, strength and mobility of men have led to their exclusive service in the roles of hunters and warriors.
        3. Lactation and pregnancy also tend to preclude the possibility of women being the primary hunters in foraging societies.
        4. However, these distinctions are very general, and there is always overlap (!Kung San are used as an example).

D. Natural Form of Human Society
   1. Before 10,000 years ago, all human groups were foragers.
   2. In foraging societies, the public-domestic spheres are least separate, hierarchy is least marked, aggression and competition are most discouraged, and the rights, activities, and spheres of influence of men and women overlap the most.
   3. Relative gender equality is most likely the ancestral pattern of human society

III. Gender among Horticulturalists

   A. Martin and Voorhies (1975) studied of 515 horticultural societies to investigate how gender roles and stratification varied according to economy and social structure.
   1. Women were found to be the main producers in horticultural societies.
   2. In half of the societies, women did most of the cultivating.
   3. In a third of the societies, men and women made equal contributions to cultivation.
   4. In only 17% of the societies did men do most of the work.
   5. Women dominated horticulture in 64% of the matrilineal societies and in 50% of the patrilineal societies.

   B. Reduced Gender Stratification—Matrilineal, Matrilocal Societies
   1. Female status tends to be relatively high in matrilineal, matrilocal societies (e.g. Minangkabau).
   2. Reasons for high female status were that women had economic power due to inheritance, and the residence pattern lent itself to female solidarity.
   3. A matriarchy is a society ruled by women.
   4. Anthropologists have never discovered a matriarchy, but the Iroquois show that women's political and ritual influence can rival that of men.
      a. Warfare was external only, as is typical of matrilineal societies.
      b. Women controlled local economy; men hunted and fished.
      c. Matrons determined entry in longhouses and also had power of impeachment over chiefs.

   C. Reduced Gender Stratification—Matrifocal Societies
   1. A survey of matrifocal (mother-centered, often with no resident husband-father) societies indicates that male travel combined with a prominent female economic role reduced gender stratification.
   2. The example of the Igbo (Nigeria) demonstrated that members of either sex might fill gender roles.

   D. Increased Gender Stratification—Patrilineal-Patrilocal Societies
   1. The spread of patrilineal-patrilocal societies has been associated with pressure on resources and increased local warfare.
      a. As resources become scarcer, warfare often increases.
      b. The patrilineal-patrilocal complex concentrates related males in villages, which solidifies their alliances for warfare.
   2. This combination tends to enhance male prestige opportunities and result in relatively high gender stratification (e.g. highland Papua-New Guinea).
      a. Women do most of the cultivation, cooking, and raising children, but are isolated from the public domain.
      b. Males dominate the public domain (politics, feasts, and warfare).

   E. Homosexual Behavior among the Etoro
   1. Etoro culture is used as an example of extreme male-female sexual antagonism and the degree to which gender is culturally constructed.
   2. Etoro men believe that semen is necessary to give life force to a fetus
      a. Men have a limited supply of semen.
      b. Sexuality depletes this supply and saps male vitality.

3. Heterosexual intercourse is seen as a necessary to reproduce, but unpleasant because it will lead to a man's eventual death.
   a. Heterosexual sex is discouraged and limited to only about 100 days a year.
   b. Heterosexual sex is banned from community life and must take place in the woods far from the village.
4. Although heterosexual sex is discouraged, homosexual sex between males is viewed as essential.
   a. In order for boys to grow into men, they must orally receive semen from older men.
   b. Homosexual acts can take place in the village.
5. Etoro homosexuality is governed by a code of conduct.
   a. Homosexual sex between older men and younger boys is seen as essential.
   b. Homosexual sex between boys of the same age is discouraged.

IV. Sexualities and Gender

   A. Sexual Orientation
      1. All human activities, including sexual preferences are to some extent learned and malleable.
      2. Sexual orientation refers to a person's habitual sexual attractions and activities.
         a. Heterosexuality refers to the sexual preference for members of the opposite sex.
         b. Homosexuality refers to the sexual preference for members of the same sex.
         c. Bisexuality refers to the sexual preference for members of both sexes.
         d. Asexuality refers to indifference toward or lack of attraction to either sex.

   B. Sexual norms vary considerably cross-culturally and through time.
      1. There tends to be greater cross-cultural acceptance of homosexuality than of bestiality and masturbation.
      2. Flexibility in human sexual expression is part of our primate heritage.
         a. Masturbation exists among chimpanzee and other primates.
         b. Homosexual behavior exists among chimpanzee and other primates.
      3. Sexuality is a matter that culture and environment determines and limit.

V. Gender among Agriculturalists

   A. With agriculture, women become cut off from production.
      1. Martin and Voorhies (1975) found that women were the main workers in only 15% of the agricultural societies, down from 50% of the horticultural ones.
      2. Martin and Voorhies (1975) found that males dominated the cultivation in 81% of the agricultural societies, up from only 17% of the horticultural ones.
      3. This shift is due in part to the increase of heavier labor that characterizes agriculture and the increase in the number of children to raise.

   B. Social changes that accompany agriculture also functioned to reduce the status of women.
      1. Belief systems started to contrast men's valuable extra domestic labor with women's domestic role, now viewed as inferior.
      2. The decline of polygyny and the rise of the importance of the nuclear family isolated women from her kin and co-wives.
      3. Female sexuality is carefully supervised in agricultural societies, which results in men having greater access to divorce and extramarital sex.

   C. However, there are many exceptions to this, wherein women still do most of the cultivation work, and have a correspondingly high status (e.g. Betsileo).

D. Interesting Issues: Hidden Women, Public Men—Public Women, Hidden Men
  1. In Brazil, gender is constructed largely along an active-passive dichotomy that produces ideas of maleness and femaleness that differ greatly from those found in middle class America.
  2. One manifestation of this is the presence of transvestitism as a third alternative to male (active) and female (passive) constructions.

VI. Patriarchy and Violence

  A. Patriarchal Societies
   1. The male role in warfare is highly valued.
   2. Violent acts against women are common and include dowry murders, female infanticide, and clitoridectomies.

  B. Domestic Violence
   1. Family violence is a worldwide problem.
   2. Abuse of women is more common in societies where women are separated from their supportive kin ties (e.g. patrilineal, patrifocal, and patrilocal societies).

VII. Gender and Industrialism

  A. Early American Industrialism
   1. The public-domestic dichotomy as it is manifested in America ("a woman's place...") is a relatively recent development.
   2. Initially, women and children worked in factories, but were supplanted by immigrant men who were willing to work for low wages.
   3. This shift coincided with associated beliefs about the unfitness of women for labor.
   4. Since World War II, the number of women in the work force has increased dramatically, driven in large part by industry's search for cheap, educated labor, in combination with technology mitigating the effect of notions about appropriate work for women.

  B. The Feminization of Poverty
   1. The number of single-parent, female headed households has doubled since 1959, with the largest proportion of these being minorities.
   2. The combination of dual responsibilities (parenting and work) and poorer employment opportunities means that these households are increasingly poverty stricken.

VIII. What Determines Gender Variation?

  A. In economies where both sexes contribute more or less equally (foragers, matrilineal cultivators), there is relatively little gender stratification.

  B. Resource competition, warfare, patrilocality, patrilineality, and reduced female role in the public economy correlate with high gender stratification.

LECTURE TOPICS

1. Outline the relationship between the public prominence of men or women and their importance in gaining and controlling key resources. Stress that their role in production might not be the same as their role in control, give examples where the two differ, and explain the cases where they differ.

2. That sex and gender can differ is now an anthropological truism, but few systematic examples are ever given. Give systematic examples of the gender systems of several societies and indicate how they might not coincide with a naive notion of biological sex.

3. Discuss the sex and gender systems, the relationship to gaining and controlling key resources, and the roles and stereotypes among the various classes in a state society. Give a plausible explanation for the differences.

4. Sexual/gendered violence can be a productive topic when you are trying to get students to think rigorously about the sex/gender distinction. Is domestic violence culturally structured, or is it a "natural" by-product of human biology? You may wish to bring in data from non-human primates (e.g., compare the non-violent sexual practices among extremely dimorphic gorillas with the violent practices of extremely dimorphic orangutans...). You may even want to invite a representative from a local domestic abuse shelter to talk to students about gendered violence.

SUGGESTED FILMS

Secrets Underground
video 1995 60 min color
This film profiles the work of archaeologist Patty Jo Watson as she pursues her study of early humans and gender roles at cave sites in the Rocky Mountains, China, Kentucky, and Tennessee. Michelle Pfeiffer narrates. Boston: WGBH Educational Foundation; Princeton, NJ: Films for the Humanities and Sciences.

Mayordomia: Ritual, Gender, and Cultural Identity in a Zapotec Community

video 1991 20 min color
This film looks at the Mayordomia, an annual religious festival among the Zapotec of southern Mexico, to explore the Zapotec construction of gender and related issues. Austin: University of Texas Press.

Tongues Untied

video 1989 55 min color
Produced and directed by Marlon Riggs. Derogatory accusations, judgments, and jokes in our culture are met head-on in this video about black, male, and gay identity. Poetry, personal testimony, and drama oppose the homophobia and racism that call upon a person to split into opposing loyalties. San Francisco: Frameline.

The Sexual Brain

video 1991 28 min color
This film explores the some of the evidence supporting the gender/sex distinction by looking at the sexual differences in human brain and discussing what ramifications these might have. Princeton, NJ: Films for the Humanities and Sciences.

Masai Women

video 1990(1974) 52 min color
An ethnographic view of Masai culture and society, focusing on the preparation of young Masai girls for marriage and life in their society. The film uses candid interviews with an older woman to probe the feelings of Masai women about polygamy and women being denied the right to own property. Chicago: Films Incorporated Video.

Clotheslines

16mm   1981   30 min   color

Blends still shots, documentary footage, vintage film and voice-overs on the topic of laundry--its social, aesthetic, and cultural aspects. Reveals how the task of cleaning the family's clothes has fallen onto the shoulders of women and the deep feelings women have toward this responsibility. Shows how creative energies of women have often been sapped by mundane tasks and how such tasks reflect a ritualistic approach to life and survival. Produced and directed by Roberta Cantow. Published by New York: Buffalo Rose Productions.

An Initiation Kut for a Korean Shaman

video   1991   37 min   color

A thirty-two year old woman decides to become a shaman. Her explanation of why she has chosen this is also a commentary on the marginalized position of some women in Korean society. Finally, the film shows scenes from her two-day initiation ceremony under the guidance of an experienced shaman. Honolulu, HI: The University of Hawaii Press.

The Fight to Be Male

16mm   1979   50 min

Examines gender determination from biochemical, genetic, behavioral, and human developmental perspectives using a case history approach. Includes discussion about the physiological versus social determinants of homosexuality. Contains explicit scenes of surgical reconstruction of genitalia and breasts. Produced by the BBC for the Horizon series. From the University of Illinois Film and Video Center.

N!ai, the Story of a !Kung Woman

16mm   1978   59 min

Footage accumulated by John Marshall over a thirty-year period documents the life of a !Kung woman from childhood to middle age and shows how her life changed after the !Kung were removed from their nomadic life on the Kalahari Desert in southern Africa and relocated on a government settlement. Includes N!ai's commentary on the events of her life and her own evaluation of the changes wrought by government intervention. From the University of Illinois Film and Video Center.

Asante Market Women

55 min   1982   color

Describes and shows examples of the social power structures in the Asante tribe of Ghana. Women are subordinate in domestic matters, but have evolved their own power structure with regard to the market, where they work. Filmed in the city of Kumasi, it introduces women leaders by their market section: the tomato Queenmother, the yam Queenmother (final arbiter and most powerful.) Touches on the way the polygamous structure is managed, and how the women feel about it. They express their dissatisfaction, but feel helpless to change matters. A man comments that he has learned patience and compassion in working with women. From the University of Illinois Film and Video Center.

Love & Sex

52 min   color
Falling in love, having sex, making babies-these are easy; understanding human sexuality is not. Phil Donahue takes viewers on an odyssey showing women at a male strip club and a gay rights march, into a hospital room where an unwed teenage mother is giving birth, and into the classroom where teachers and parents are trying to help teenagers come to grips with their sexual selves. Love, monogamy, hetero- and homosexuality are among the topics covered by Donahue, consultants Dr. William Masters of the Masters & Johnson Institute and Dr. June Reinisch of the Kinsey Institute, and by Donahue's best resource, ordinary people. From Films for the Humanities & Sciences.

Woman & Man

52 min   color
Virginia Woolf said it: "Men and women are different. What needs to be made equal is the value placed on these differences." Phil Donahue looks at the differences. The brain, for instance-women generally have a greater response on the logical and analytical side, and men on the spatial side. Society has groomed men to be the astronauts, though women have more of the traits desirable in an astronaut; it has built the largest sports arenas to cheer the performances of men. Phil Donahue speaks with men and women in many walks of life and finds that the role differences between woman and man are beginning to fade. From Films for the Humanities & Sciences.

MULTIPLE CHOICE QUESTIONS

1.   Among foragers _____.

   a.   men excel in the harsh life, and therefore accrue vastly more prestige than women
   b.   warfare makes men dominant over women
   c.   the status of women falls when they provide most of the food
   d.   men and women are completely equal; there is no gender inequality
   e.   **the lack of a clear public-domestic dichotomy seems to be related to relatively mild gender inequality**

2.   Among patrilineal-patrilocal cultivators _____.

   a.   **women remain the primary producers of subsistence crops**
   b.   women govern the extra domestic distribution of prestige items
   c.   women fear contacts, including sexual intercourse, with men
   d.   polygyny decreases household productivity because a man must provide for more than one wife
   e.   population pressure on strategic resources is relaxed

3.   All of the following are associated with plow agriculture *except*

   a.   A decline in both polygyny and unilineal descent
   b.   Differential rights in divorce and sexuality for men and women
   c.   **An overall increase in the status of women as new production techniques called for female as well as male labor**
   d.   A sharp contrast between the domestic and extra domestic realms
   e.   Isolation of women in nuclear family households

4. In comparing gender roles in different societies, which of the following is true?

    a. Equality between the genders is common among horticulturalists.
    b. There are some societies in which women control all the strategic resources and carry out the most prestigious activities.
    c. Patriarchies are strongest in societies in which men control significant goods that are exchanged with people outside the family.
    d. The more women contribute to the domestic sphere, the more publicly recognized power they achieve.
    e. all of the above are true

5. Which of the following is *not* culturally constructed?

    a. race
    b. gender
    c. kinship
    d. sex
    e. sexual norms

6. What is largely responsible for developing the notion of gender as an analytical construct for understanding culture?

    a. social anthropology
    b. cultural anthropology
    c. the study of foraging societies
    d. psychological anthropology
    e. feminist anthropology

7. According to Kottak, which of the following plays a role in causing differences and similarities in gender in different cultures?

    a. specific environments
    b. adaptive strategies
    c. social and political complexity
    d. cultural traditions
    e. all of the above

8. In which type of society would you expect women's status to be highest?

    a. pastoralists
    b. agriculturalists
    c. societies where there is much population pressure
    d. tropical hunters and gatherers
    e. industrial states with high unemployment

9. In general, the status of women _____

    a. rises as dependence on food production intensifies
    b. is higher in those societies in which males do most of the work in food production
    c. is higher in agricultural than in foraging societies
    d. is higher in societies with matrilineal descent than in those with patrilineal descent
    e. is higher among the Yanomami than among the Iroquois

10. What term refers to the tasks and activities that a culture assigns to the sexes?

   a.   sex roles
   b.   sex stereotypes
   c.   gender stereotypes
   d.   gender roles
   e.   gender duties

11. What have recent cross-cultural studies of gender roles demonstrated?

   a.   The gender roles of men and women are largely determined by their biological capabilities-relative strength, endurance, intelligence, and so on.
   b.   Women are subservient in nearly all societies because their subsistence activities contribute much less to the total diet than do those of men.
   c.   The relative status of women is variable, depending on factors such as subsistence strategy, the importance of warfare, and the prevalence of a domestic-public dichotomy.
   d.   Foraging, horticultural, pastoral, and industrial societies all have similar attitudes toward gender roles.
   e.   Changes in the gender roles of men and women are usually associated with social decay and anarchy.

12. Which of the following statements about groups with the patrilineal, patrilocal complex is true?

   a.   They are often characterized by the view that women are polluting
   b.   They often have polygyny and patterns of inter-village raiding
   c.   They have strongly developed private-public dichotomies
   d.   They have their prestige goods under male control
   e.   all of the above

13. Why do the young Etoro men and boys engage in homosexual relationships?

   a.   They are too primitive to understand reproduction, which is why they don't exist.
   b.   The status of Etoro women is the highest in the world.
   c.   Genetic drift has created a population dominated by a homosexual gene.
   d.   They believe it is necessary for boys to ingest semen in order to mature in a healthy way.
   e.   A warrior cult of older adult men vigorously enforces a monopoly on access to women.

14. Of the following factors, which is historically associated with the lowering of women's status in the United States?

   a.   European immigration around 1900
   b.   World War II
   c.   voting rights for women
   d.   inflation
   e.   all of the above

15. Which of the following statements about gender differences among tropical and semitropical foragers is true?

   a. The status of women is much lower than it is among northern foragers like the Eskimo.
   b. **Women's work usually contributes more to the diet than does men's work, consequently there is less gender stratification.**
   c. The distinction between public and domestic spheres of activity is much sharper than it is in most horticultural societies.
   d. There is no sex-based division of labor.
   e. Women never take part in hunting.

16. Which of the following statements about patrilineal, patrilocal horticulturalists is true?

   a. **Men control the distribution of goods outside the domestic sphere.**
   b. Men work harder at food production and manufacturing than do women.
   c. Men are in short supply owing to the practice of male infanticide.
   d. Men are approximately equal in status to women.
   e. Men trade subsistence goods but not prestige items.

17. Which of the following statements about the domestic-public dichotomy is true?

   a. **It is stronger among peasants than among foragers**
   b. It is stronger among foragers than among peasants
   c. It is not significant in urban industrial societies
   d. It is reinforced in American society by women working both inside and outside the home
   e. none of the above

18. What does the domestic-public dichotomy refer to?

   a. the separation of spheres of exchange
   b. the separation of secular and sacred
   c. the separation of elite and commoners
   d. **the separation of domestic and extra domestic**
   e. none of the above

19. The idea, common in American Middle Class culture, that "a woman's place is in the home" _____.

   a. is actually a cultural universal
   b. **actually did not start to become prominent until 1900, when industrialism began to replace farming as the primary source of employment**
   c. accurately reflects the worldwide sexual division of labor
   d. is based in the pre-industrial era, and began to disappear as women moved into the factories in the 1900s
   e. was part of the Pledge of Allegiance until Bitsy Fromm blew herself up on the steps of the Capitol

20.   The percentage of women in the American workforce has risen since the 1950s.
        Researchers disagree on _____.

        a.   whether this is due to the increasing physical size of women (with better
                nutrition)
        b.   whether this is due to a higher birth rate for female infants since 1937
        c.   whether this is the result of the designated hitter rule being allowed in the
                American League
        d.   whether this is due to a sharp decline in the number of arranged marriages since
                the 1950s
        e.   **whether women are replacing men in the work force or simply entering new
                jobs**

21.   As of 1992, more than half of all American families with sub poverty-level incomes

        a.   were patrifocal
        b.   were blended
        c.   were headed by men
        d.   **were headed by women**
        e.   were dichotomized

22.   Regarding gender inequality in the United States _____
        _____.

        a.   it has been virtually eliminated by equal-opportunity legislation.
        b.   **since 1970, the rise in the number of people below the poverty line has been
                constituted almost entirely by women and families headed by single women.**
        c.   there has never been a clear public-private dichotomy
        d.   matrifocality (mom, apple pie, etc.) has accounted for the generally high status
                of women since the industrial revolution
        e.   all of the above

23.   Which of the following is *not* part of the patrilineal-patrilocal complex?

        a.   patrilineality
        b.   patrilocality
        c.   warfare
        d.   **reduced gender stratification**
        e.   male supremacy

24.   Which of the following statements about Etoro conceptions of heterosexual intercourse
        is *not* true?

        a.   It is thought to sap a man's vitality
        b.   Women who want too much heterosexual intercourse are viewed as witches
        c.   It is permitted only 100 days a year
        d.   **It is permitted to take place only in the couple's residence**
        e.   It is seen as a necessary sacrifice that will eventually lead to a man's death

25.   Which of the following is *not* a sexual orientation discussed in the textbook?

        a.   heterosexuality
        b.   asexuality
        c.   bisexuality
        d.   **unisexuality**
        e.   homosexuality

26. Based on a cross-cultural study, which of the activities has the greatest cross-cultural acceptance?

    a. human-animal sex
    b. masturbation
    c. homosexuality
    d. necrophilia
    e. pedophilia

27. In what kind of society do anthropologists most typically find forced female genital operations, inter-village raiding, preference for males, female infanticide, and dowry?

    a. matrilineal-patrilocal
    b. matrilineal-matrilocal
    c. patrilineal-matrilocal
    d. patrilineal-neolocal
    e. patrilineal-patrilocal

28. Which of the following statements is *not* true?

    a. The feminization of poverty is unique to the United States.
    b. Households headed by women tend to be poorer than those headed by men.
    c. Married couples are much more secure economically than single mothers.
    d. Women now head over half of the households in the United States.
    e. The feminization of poverty has serious consequences with regard to living standards and health.

ESSAY QUESTIONS

29. What position do most anthropologists take on the matter of whether male dominance is a cultural universal? What is your own view on the matter?

30. Contrast gender roles in two of the following:
    a. foraging societies
    b. matrilineal, matrilocal societies
    c. patrilineal, patrilocal societies
    d. pastoralists
    e. agriculturalists

31. What is the public-private dichotomy? In what kinds of societies does it occur, and in what kinds of societies is it absent? What factors contribute to its presence or absence, and what are its effects on gender roles?

32. Comment on the claim that recent American feminism is the major cause of increased female cash employment.

33. Are certain sexual preferences more natural than others? What factors compel some societies to deviate from the heterosexual norm found in most human societies?

34. How are sexuality, sex, and gender related to each other? What are the differences between these three analytical constructs?

35. Any of the above multiple choice questions may be converted to an essay question by requiring students to choose the correct answer and justify their selection in essay form. Such justifications should include explanations as to why the chosen answer is correct and why those responses not chosen are incorrect.

TRUE OR FALSE QUESTIONS

36. True or **False** Cultural determinists argue that cultural behaviors are determined by biology.

37. True or **False** Gender roles are the instinctual behaviors that are the exclusive domain of each sex.

38. **True** or False Gender stratification refers to an unequal distribution of socially valued resources, power, prestige, and personal freedom between men and women.

39. **True** or False Cross-culturally, women's roles tend to be focused on activities associated with the home, while men are more active in the public domain.

40. **True** or False The specific roles assigned to each gender varies from culture to culture.

41. True or **False** Kottak argues that the relative gender equality found in horticultural societies most likely characterizes the most "natural" state of gender differentiation.

42. **True** or False Women in matrilineal societies tend to occupy elevated status positions.

43. True or **False** The Negeri Sembilan are one of the few matriarchies known in the world.

44. True or **False** In addition to controlling alliances between descent groups, Iroquois men were responsible for managing production and distribution.

45. **True** or False Gender stratification tends to be extremely pronounced in patrilineal-patrilocal societies.

46. True or **False** Homosexuality among the Etoro demonstrates that homosexuality is more pronounced in matrifocal societies.

47. **True** or False The way that heterosexual sex has been stigmatized by the Etoro is similar in some ways to the notions in the U.S. regarding homosexuality.

48. True or **False** At the age of 12, Azande boys are taken to hunting lodges in the mountains where they ingest adult male semen.

49. True or **False** In agricultural societies, women generally dominate the subsistence labor.

50. **True** or False Domestic violence against women is a prevalent in patrilineal-patrilocal systems in which women are cutoff from their supportive kin ties.

51. **True** or False In the U.S., attitudes regarding the role of women in the work place have varied according to economic needs.

52. True or **False** With the baby boom and the increase in industrialization, women have contributed more and more to the workplace while receiving pay equal to their male coworkers.

53. True or **False** The reason the there are more modern day Rosie-the-Riveter's is because modern industry is even more physically demanding than it was during World War II.

54. **True** or False   Even though women represent more that half of the American workforce, single parent families headed by women represent more than half of the households below the poverty line.

55. **True** or False   Some of the reasons why there are so many single parent families headed by women includes male migration, divorce, abandonment, and the idea that women are responsible for the children.

CHAPTER 19
RELIGION

CHAPTER OUTLINE

I. Introduction

    A. Religion is defined, following Wallace, as belief and ritual concerned with supernatural beings, powers, and forces.

    B. So defined, religion is a cultural universal

II. Origins, Functions, and Expressions of Religion

    A. Neanderthal mortuary remains provide the earliest evidence of what probably was religious activity.

    B. Animism
        1. Tylor first studied religion anthropologically, and developed a taxonomy of religions.
        2. Animism was seen as the most primitive, and is defined as a belief in souls that derives from the first attempt to explain dreams and like phenomena.

    C. Mana and Taboo
        1. Mana is defined as belief in an immanent supernatural domain or life-force, potentially subject to human manipulation.
        2. The Polynesian and Melanesian concepts of mana are contrasted.
            a. Melanesian mana is defined as a sacred impersonal force that is much like the Western concept of luck.
            b. Polynesian mana and the related concept of taboo are related to the more hierarchical nature of Polynesian society.

    D. Magic and Religion
        1. Magic refers to supernatural techniques intended to accomplish specific aims.
        2. Magic may be *imitative* (as with voodoo dolls) or contagious (accomplished through contact).

    E. Anxiety, Control, Solace
        1. Magic is an instrument of control, but religion serves to provide stability when no control or understanding is possible.
        2. Malinowski saw tribal religions as being focused on life crises.

    F. Rituals
        1. Rituals are formal, performed in sacred contexts.
        2. Rituals convey information about the culture of the participants and, hence, the participants themselves.
        3. Rituals are inherently social, and participation in them necessarily implies social commitment.

    G. Rites of Passage
        1. Rites of passage are religious rituals which mark and facilitate a persons movement from one (social) state of being to another (e.g. Plains Indians' vision quests).

2. Rites of passage have three phases:
    a. Separation – the participant(s) withdraws from the group and begin moving from one place to another.
    b. Liminality – the period between states, during which the participant(s) has left one place but has not yet, entered the next.
    c. Incorporation – the participant(s) reenters society with a new status having completed the rite.
3. Liminality is part of every rite of passage, and involves the temporary suspension and even reversal of everyday social distinctions.
4. Communitas refers to collective liminality, characterized by enhanced feelings of social solidarity and minimized distinctions.

H. Totemism
    1. Rituals play an important role in creating and maintaining group solidarity.
    2. In totemic societies, each descent group has an animal, plant, of geographical feature from which they claim descent.
        a. Totems are the apical ancestors of clans.
        b. The members of a clan did not kill or eat their totem, except once a year when the members of the clan gathered for ceremonies dedicated to the totem.
        c. See discussion of clans and lineages in Chapter 15.
    Totemism is a religion in which elements of nature act as sacred templates for society by means of symbolic association.
    2. Totemism uses nature as a model for society.
        a. Each descent group has a totem, which occupies a specific niche in nature.
        b. Social differences mirror the natural order of the environment.
        c. The unity of the human social order is enhanced by symbolic association with and imitation of the natural order.

III. Religion and Cultural Ecology

A. Sacred Cattle in India
    1. *Ahimsa* is the Hindu doctrine of nonviolence that forbids the killing of animals.
    2. Western economic development experts often use this principle as an example of how religion can stand in the way of development.
        a. Hindus seem to irrationally ignore a valuable food source (beef).
        b. Hindus also raise scraggly and thin cows, unlike the bigger cattle of Europe and the U.S.
    3. These views are ethnocentric and wrong as cattle play an important adaptive role in an Indian ecosystem that has evolved over thousands of years
        a. Hindus use cattle for transportation, traction, and manure.
        b. Bigger cattle eat more, making them more expensive to keep.

IV. Social Control

A. The power of religion affects action.
    1. Religion can be used to mobilize large segments of society through systems of real and perceived rewards and punishments.
    2. Witch hunts play an important role in limiting social deviancy in addition to functioning as leveling mechanisms to reduce differences in wealth and status between members of society.
    3. Many religions have a formal code of ethics that prohibit certain behavior while promoting other kinds of behavior.
    4. Religions also maintain social control by stressing the fleeting nature of life.

B. In the News: Religion and Social Control in Afghanistan
  1. This article describes the social conditions in Afghanistan under Taliban rule.
  2. The Taliban are invoking a very strict interpretation of the Koran as the basis for social behavior.
    a. Women are required to wear veils, remain indoors and are not allowed to males that are not blood relatives.
    b. Men are required to grow bushy beards and are barred from playing cards, flying kites, and keeping pigeons.

V. Kinds of Religion

A. Religious forms vary from culture to culture but there are correlations between political organization and religious type.

B. Religious Practitioners and Types
  1. Wallace defined religion as consisting of all a society's cult institutions (rituals and associated beliefs), and developed four categories from this (see figure 19.2).
  2. Shamanic religions shamans are part-time religious intermediaries who may act as curers--these religions are most characteristic of foragers.
  3. Communal religions have shamans, community rituals, multiple nature gods, and are more characteristic of food producers than foragers.
  4. Olympian religions first appeared with states, have full-time religious specialists whose organization may mimic the states, have potent anthropomorphic gods who may exist as a pantheon.
  5. Monotheistic religions have all the attributes of Olympian religions, except that the pantheon of gods is subsumed under a single eternal, omniscient, omnipotent, and omnipresent being.

VI. Religion in States

A. Christian Values
  1. Max Weber linked the spread of Capitalism to the values central to the Protestant faith: independent, entrepreneurial, hard working, future-oriented, and free thinking.
  2. The emphasis Catholics placed on immediate happiness and security and the notion that salvation was attainable only when a priest mediate on one's behalf, did not fit well with capitalism.

B. Religion in North America Today
  1. In the U.S. Protestants outnumber Catholics, but in Canada the reverse is true.
  2. Religious affiliation in North America varies with ethnic background, age, and geography.

VII. Religion and Change

A. Revitalization Movements
  1. Religious movements that act as mediums for social change are called revitalization movements.
  2. The colonial-era Iroquois reformation led by Handsome Lake is an example of a revitalization movement.

B. Syncretisms
  1. A syncretism is a cultural mix, including religious blends that emerge when two or more cultural traditions come into contact.
    a. Examples include voodoo, santeria, and candomlé.
    b. The cargo cults of Melanesia and Papua New Guinea are syncretism of Christian doctrine with aboriginal beliefs.
  2. Syncretisms often emerge when traditional, non-Western societies have regular contact with industrialized societies.

3. Syncretisms attempt to explain European domination and wealth and to achieve similar success magically by mimicking European behavior and symbols.

C. A New Age
1. Since the 1960s, there has been a decline in formal organized religions.
2. New Age religions have appropriated ideas, themes, symbols, and ways of life from the religious practices of Native Americans, Australian Aborigines, east Asian religions.

VIII. Secular Rituals

A. A Pilgrimage to Walt Disney World
1. Walt Disney World functions much like a sacred shrine, which is a major pilgrimage destination
   a. It has an inner, sacred center surrounded by an outer more secular domain.
   b. Parking lot designations are distinguished with totemlike images of the Disney cast of characters.
2. The monorail provides travelers with a brief liminal period as they cross between the outer, secular world into the inner, sacred center of the Magic Kingdom.

B. Within the Magic Kingdom
1. Spending time in the Magic Kingdom reaffirms, maintains, and solidifies the world of Disney as all of the pilgrims share a common status as visitors while experience the same adventures.
2. Most of the structures and attractions at the Magic Kingdom are designed to reaffirm and recall a traditional set of American values.

C. Recognizing Religion
1. It is difficult to distinguish between sacred and secular rituals as behavior can simultaneously have sacred and secular aspects.
2. Americans try to maintain a strict division between the sacred and the profane, but many other societies like the Betsileo do not.

LECTURE TOPICS

1. Discuss initiation into sports teams, the military, social clubs, subcultures, and so on, in terms of the standard terminology for rites of passage.

2. Discuss the differences among intellectual explanations, emotional explanations, and social explanations of religions. Be sure to point out how they complement each other.

3. Point out various magical techniques or beliefs in our own society, particularly in advertising. Discuss what aspects of our behavior or beliefs most frequently lead us to invoke such techniques.

4. Point out the equivalent of mana in our own culture, and also give examples of its incidence among many other cultures.

5. Discuss the connection between religion and identity (as in ethnicity, for example). Point out that while taxonomies may highlight the historical connection between generalized political and religious types, it is also important to pay attention to the role religion plays in identity politics. Post-colonial states are frequently good sources of examples for this, although the United States offers many excellent examples, also (Nation of Islam, Pan-Indianism, the abortion debate, etc.).

SUGGESTED FILMS

Trobriand Cricket: An Ingenious Response to Colonialism

16mm/video 1976 55 min color
An ethnographic documentary about cultural creativity among the Trobriand Islanders of Papua-New Guinea. Shows how the Trobrianders have taken the very controlled game of British cricket, first introduced by missionaries, and changed it into an outlet for mock warfare and inter-village competition, political reputation building among leaders, erotic dancing and chanting, and riotous fun. The game is a gigantic message about people's attitudes, experiences, and responses under colonialism. It is also a political act, the repercussions of which extend to your classroom, when you show it.

Powwow Highway

VHS (commercial film) 91 min 1988 color
Based upon the novel by David Seals. Philbert, a Cheyenne Indian from Montana, goes on a vision quest to find enlightenment. After he meets Buddy Red Bow, a fiery Indian activist, things really start to happen. The film is set in the 1970's and deals with events at Pine Ridge Reservation, where the inhabitants were divided into pro-federal government and activist Native American rights factions. A Handmade Films production; director: Jonathan Stewart. Distributed by Cannon Video, 1989, c1988.

Learning to Dance in Bali

video 1991 13 min b&w
Originally produced as a motion picture, this film is part of series written, produced, and directed by Gregory Bateson and Margaret Mead. A father, then his dance teacher teach a child dance movement, first by physically guiding his body. The student stands behind the teacher and imitates his movements. I Mario, most famous of Balinese dancers, exchanges dance lessons with a visiting dancer from India to the accompaniment of a gamelan orchestra. Published by New York, NY: Institute for Intercultural Studies; distributed by Audio-Visual Services, Pennsylvania State University, [1991?] c1988.

An Initiation "Kut" for a Korean Shaman

37 min 1991 color video
A thirty-two-year-old woman tells of the events, which led her to decide to become a shaman. Includes scenes from her two-day initiation. Produced at the Center for Visual Anthropology, University of Southern California. Anthropologist: Laurel Kendall; filmmaker: Diana S. Lee. Published by Honolulu, HI: University of Hawaii Press, 1991.

The Performed Word

59 min 1982 color video
The power of the African American performed word, particularly that of Black preachers, is examined. Includes excerpts from services and interviews with Bishop E.E. Cleveland of Berkeley, California (Church of God in Christ), and his daughter, past Ernestine Cleveland Reems. Produced at the Anthropology Film Center Foundation (Red Taurus Films Production) by Gerald L. Davis; directors: Ernest Shinagawa and Carlos de Jesus. Published by Santa Fe: The Foundation; Memphis, Tenn.: Center for Southern Folklore [distributor], 1982.

Witchcraft Among the Azande

55 min   1982   video
Focuses on the practice of witchcraft among the African Azande people, who depend upon oracles to explain events and predict the future. Shows an adultery trial in which a ritually poisoned chicken decides the outcome. Highlights the tribe's conflict and compromise between modernity and tradition, and between Christianity and magic. From the Disappearing World Series.

The Blooms of Banjeli: Technology and Gender in African Ironmaking

29 min   1986   color
Focuses on a Central West African group, which had for centuries produced high-quality iron blooms: an industry now in decline. Two anthropologists visit the community and are allowed the privilege of witnessing the process and describing the rituals, beliefs, and sexual prohibitions involved. The process is seen as a metaphoric extension of the reproductive capacity.

Ethnic Dance around the World

video   24 min   1983   color
Illustrates, with footage from many cultures, various types of dance patterns: processional, line, round, and storytelling. Examines basic reasons for dance: religious, entertainment, celebration, the rhythmic lightening of monotonous tasks, the teaching of history or custom, the welcoming of visitors, and the expression of gratitude for a good harvest. Shows Maori, American Indian, Balinese, Japanese, African, Peruvian, Mexican, Soviet, and Romanian dances.

Holy Ghost People

16mm   53 min   1968   b&w
Documentary filmed in a West Virginia Pentecostal snake-handling church. Edited from a year's filming, the footage includes individual testimonies and various practices typical of their worship. Winner San Francisco International Film Festival.

Our Knowledge, Our Beauty: The Expressive Culture of the Canelos Quichua of Ecuador

video   29 min   1985   color
Records a Quichua song expressing their basic creation myth, and furnishes voice-over translation and comment. Shows how principal myths of the culture are expressed in ceramic and wood artifacts. Describes the Quichua people, who speak a dialect of Inca, and who believe that music originates in the spirit world and conveys messages from it. Comments on features of their daily life, and on the role of the shaman in their society. Social change, initiated by tourists, has led men to engage in the arts (sculpture and poetry) formerly reserved to women.

Spite (N'Kpiti)

video   55 min   1984   color
Films some of the ministrations of prophet-healer Sebim Odjo, who combines Moslem, Christian, and traditional African beliefs in his healing ceremonies. Disease is thought to be of human origin, caused by rancor jealousy, evil spirits, witchcraft, and the like. The water cure in *Spite* is based on the premise that if you have the burden of spite on your heart, you are any easy prey to illness, emotion, and "creatures that inhabit the bush." From The University of Illinois Film and Video Center.

Sir Edward Evans-Pritchard (1902-1973): Strange Beliefs

52 min   color
University professor Sir Edward Evans-Pritchard taught that Western ideas have many features in common with other cultures and are just as weird and wonderful. He was the first trained anthropologist to do work in Africa, where he lived among the Azande and studied their belief in witchcraft; later, he worked with the Nuer tribe in the Sudan. His work on witchcraft found philosophers asking what could be considered rational thinking in any society; his study of tribal organization was intriguing to political theorists; and his attention to the sophisticated religious sentiments of so-called primitive peoples has had a strong influence on theologians. From the Strangers Abroad series. From Films for the Humanities & Sciences.

MULTIPLE CHOICE QUESTIONS

1.   When studying religion, what do anthropologists investigate?

    a.   the social roles of religion
    b.   the content and nature of religious acts
    c.   the verbal manifestations of religion
    d.   the material manifestations of religion
    e.   all of the above

2.   Which of the following is *not* a cultural universal?

    a.   religion
    b.   incest taboo
    c.   food sharing
    d.   nuclear family
    e.   family living

3.   Which of the following statements about the supernatural is true?

    a.   It refers to the extraordinary world outside (but believed to touch on) the ordinary world.
    b.   It is non-empirical.
    c.   It is unverifiable.
    d.   It is both personified and not personified.
    e.   all of the above

4.   According to Tylor, what is the sequence through which religion evolved?

    a.   olympianism, polytheism, monotheism
    b.   animism, polytheism, monotheism
    c.   mana, polytheism, monotheism
    d.   animism, cargo cults, monotheism
    e.   polytheism, animism, monotheism

5.   Who is mentioned in the text as the founder of the anthropology of religion?

    a.   Stephane Grappelly
    b.   Django Reinhardt
    c.   Sir Edward Evan Evans-Pritchard
    d.   Sir Edward Burnett Tylor
    e.   Bronislaw Malinowski

6. Based on cross-cultural analysis, anthropologists have claimed which of the following as a function of religion?

   a. They create and maintain social solidarity.
   b. They create and maintain divisions within a society.
   c. They codify culturally appropriate behavior.
   d. They help people adapt to their social and natural environment.
   e. all of the above

7. Which of the following statements about state religions is true?

   a. They function to maintain socioeconomic stratification.
   b. They focus on the worship of natural phenomena.
   c. They are superfluous features of state-level organizations.
   d. They are characterized by rituals, such as the potlatch, which serve to level differences in wealth between people.
   e. They are based mainly on animistic belief systems.

8. Which of the following kinds of religions involves full-time religious specialists?

   a. communal religion
   b. shamanic religion
   c. Olympian religion
   d. individualistic cults
   e. none of the above

9. What does Marvin Harris' analysis of the Hindu practice of not eating cattle suggest?

   a. Religion is a realm of behavior wherein people do *not* try to behave rationally (i.e., maximize profit and minimize loss).
   b. They illustrate generalized reciprocity.
   c. Religious beliefs often impede evolutionary progress by encouraging wasteful energy expenditure.
   d. Antagonism between the sexes characterizes primitive religious practice.
   e. Beliefs about the supernatural can function as part of a group's adaptation to the environment.

10. What kind of magic is based on the belief that whatever is done to an object will affect a person who once had contact with it?

    a. contagious magic
    b. imitative magic
    c. serial magic
    d. sequential magic
    e. simultaneous magic

11. What kind of religion is based on the idea that each human has a double, who is active during sleep?

    a. animatism
    b. totemism
    c. animism
    d. mana
    e. polytheism

12. Which of the following describes the concept of mana as used in Polynesia and Melanesia?

   a. Mana is bread.
   b. The concept of mana is absent in societies with differential access to strategic resources.
   c. Most anthropologists agree that mana is the most primitive religious doctrine.
   d. Mana is concerned with supernatural beings rather than with powers or forces.
   e. In Melanesia, anyone can get mana, but in Polynesia mana is attached to political elites

13. What term refers to the manipulation of the supernatural to accomplish specific goals?

   a. animism
   b. magic
   c. religion
   d. a rite of passage
   e. pantheism

14. What distinguishes rituals from other kinds of behavior?

   a. they are formal—stylized, repetitive, and stereotyped
   b. they include liturgical orders
   c. they take place is special places
   d. they are social acts
   e. all of the above

15. Which of the following phases is *not* included in passage rites?

   a. aggregation
   b. authorization
   c. marginality
   d. separation
   e. all of the above are included

16. What is typically observed during the of liminal phase of a rite of passage?

   a. symbolic reversals of ordinary behavior
   b. intensification of social hierarchy
   c. a forming of an implicit ranking system
   d. use of secular language
   e. all of the above

17. What are the induction into the U.S. Marine Corps and the vision quest of certain North American Indian societies examples of?

   a. binary opposition
   b. generalized exchange
   c. applied anthropology
   d. rites of passage
   e. genetic programming

18. What is the term for the marginal or in-between phase of a rite of passage?

    a.   voodoo
    b.   mana
    c.   taboo
    d.   liminality
    e.   animism

19. Which of the following function to reduce differences in wealth between members of a society and tend to be directed at socially marginal individuals?

    a.   blood feuds
    b.   Olympian religions
    c.   rites of passage
    d.   cargo cults
    e.   witchcraft accusations

20. How can religion be a powerful means of controlling people's beliefs and behavior?

    a.   It can be used to mobilize segments of society.
    b.   It can act as a leveling mechanism.
    c.   It can be used to discourage deviant social behavior.
    d.   It can instill feelings of guilt, regret, and shame as codes or morality become internalized.
    e.   all of the above

21. What is *communitas*?

    a.   A social inequality that is accepted even by those who are less privileged
    b.   collective liminality
    c.   anxiety
    d.   the Latin word for mana
    e.   the supernatural

22. Which of the following statements about religion has *not* been argued by anthropologists?

    a.   Nativistic movements tend to occur when a society is undergoing rapid social change
    b.   Different religious forms correspond to different levels of social complexity
    c.   Religion may function to maintain social solidarity
    d.   The Hindu taboo that forbids the killing of cattle is maladaptive
    e.   Rituals may regulate local and regional ecosystems

23. What is ahimsa?

    a.   the belief in souls or spiritual doubles
    b.   the sacred force in Melanesian and Polynesian religions
    c.   a Hindu principle of nonviolence that forbids the killing of animals
    d.   the Yanomami word for communitas
    e.   the power that a Nuer shaman possesses

24. Which of the following is *not* a reason that the Indian sacred cow is adaptive?

    a. Zebu cattle require less food per animal than do beef cattle.
    b. Wandering cattle indirectly provide fertilizer for agricultural fields.
    c. Zebu cattle are frequently slaughtered and their meat distributed on ceremonial occasions.
    d. Cattle dung provides a cheap source of heating and cooking energy.
    e. all of the above are adaptive functions

25. What did Handsome Lake lead around A.D. 1800 among the Iroquois?

    a. a shamanistic cult
    b. a revitalization movement
    c. a animistic-residualist front
    d. a structuralist movement
    e. a cargo cult

26. What term refers to a custom or social action that operates to reduce differences in wealth and bring standouts in line with community norms?

    a. rite of passage
    b. revitalization movement
    c. syncretism
    d. taboo
    e. leveling mechanism

27. Which of the following statements concerning religion and states is true?

    a. state organization precludes folk religions
    b. all state religions are monotheistic
    c. state religions follow the introduction of writing systems
    d. state religions often serve to make social stratification more acceptable
    e. although industrial states do not always have state religions, they are invariant features of archaic states

28. Which of the following statements about religions is *not* true?

    a. The functions of religious beliefs and practices vary with the society.
    b. Religion is often an instrument of societal change, even revolution.
    c. Religion serves only to maintain social solidarity; it does not create or maintain societal divisions.
    d. State religions have often served as a means of supporting the state structure.
    e. none of the above

29. What kind of religion is most frequently found in foraging bands?

    a. communal
    b. shamanic
    c. cargo cult
    d. monotheistic
    e. polytheistic

30. Which of the following statements about religion is true?

    a.   It creates and maintains social solidarity.
    b.   It creates and maintains divisions within society.
    c.   It is sometimes a source of conflict.
    d.   It is, in some cases, ecologically adaptive.
    e.   **all of the above**

31. What religion is recognized as a Church in the United States but is not recognized in Germany where it is seen as a dangerous nonreligious political movement?

    a.   Catholicism
    b.   Hinduism
    c.   Judaism
    d.   **Scientology**
    e.   Sunnis

32. According to Kottak, what role does the ride on the monorail between the parking lot and the entrance to the Magic Kingdom play in a pilgrimage to Walt Disney World?

    a.   It represents a brief period during which the travelers experience temporary liminal status.
    b.   It bridges the opposition between the outer, secular realm to the inner, sacred center.
    c.   It serves as a rite of passage for the travelers.
    d.   It symbolizes rebirth as the monorail passes through the Contemporary Resort Hotel.
    e.   **all of the above**

33. For Kottak, what is the most important feature of Cinderella's castle at Walt Disney World?

    a.   its utilitarian value
    b.   its grand entrance
    c.   its moat
    d.   **its symbolism**
    e.   all of the above

ESSAY QUESTIONS

34. On the basis of theories about the origins and functions of religion, what are the functions that organized religion serves in United States' society? Can religion in the United States be said to be embedded in other sociocultural institutions, such as politics?

35. How do you explain the universality of religion?

36. Contrast ritual behavior with ordinary behavior. Give examples of religious and secular rituals. What are the main differences between such kinds of ritual?

37. Is religion declining or becoming increasingly important in contemporary society? Why? If you believe that religion is declining, what is replacing it?

38. Comment on the following statement: "Unlike other cultural institutions, religion has little relationship to material adaptation and must be analyzed in social, symbolic, and psychological terms alone."

39. Discuss two cases of religion's role in social change.

40.   What is a state religion? What are some of its attributes and functions? Give examples.

41.   What are the similarities and differences between shamanistic and communal religions? How do these compare with Olympian religions and monotheism? What kinds of general evolutionary trends are discernible in religious worship?

42.   What is the adaptive significance of sacred cattle in India?

43.   Much religious and ritual behavior is adaptive. Can you think of cases in which it is not? What does it mean for religion to be maladaptive?

44.   Any of the above multiple choice questions may be converted to an essay question by requiring students to choose the correct answer and justify their selection in essay form. Such justifications should include explanations as to why the chosen answer is correct and why those responses not chosen are incorrect.

TRUE OR FALSE QUESTIONS

45. True or **False**   According to Tylor, religion evolved from polytheism to animism to monotheism.

46. True or False   In Melanesia, mana is an essential sacred life force that resides in people, animals, plants, and objects.

47. True or **False**   Voodoo dolls are an used to perform contagious magic.

48. True or False   According to Malinowski, religion provides people with emotional comfort during problematic times.

49. True or False   A major difference between rituals and plays is that the participants in rituals are performing in earnest.

50. True or False   By participating in a ritual, performers signal that they accept the common social and ethical order prescribed by the religion.

51. True or **False**   Rites of passage involve three phases: separation, liminality, and totemism.

52. True or **False**   *Communitas* is the strong feeling of collective unity shared by individuals at the core of society who define themselves in opposition the society's liminal members.

53. True or **False**   The Hindu principle of *ahimsa* functions to ensure that cattle are maximized for milk production.

54. True or False   Religion is a powerful means of controlling society.

55. True or False   Witch hunts are an example of how religion can be used to limit deviant social behavior by instilling strong motivations to behave properly.

56. True or **False**   Shamans are full-time religious practitioners generally found in state-level societies.

57. True or **False**   Max Weber argued that the spread of capitalism was closely linked to the ethics and values of Catholicism.

58. True or **False**   The Handsome Lake revitalization movement urged its followers to reaffirm the traditions of the Iroquois.

59. True or False   A syncretism is a mixture of cultural influences from series of different cultural traditions.

60. True or False   The cargo cults of Melanesia functioned to integrate Melanesians and set the stage for the formation of political parties and economic interest groups.

61. True or **False**   Kottak argues that the Disney corporation is a cult modeled after Christianity with Walt Disney as the Christ-figure.

62. True or False   The monorail that links the outer, more secular domain surrounding Walt Disney World to the inner sanctum serves as a kind of rite of passage for pilgrims.

63. True or False   The experiences inside the Magic Kingdom including the rides, shops, buildings, and shared experiences draw upon and reaffirm a set of American values.

64. True or **False**   Ritual activities are either sacred or secular, they cannot be both at the same time.

CHAPTER 20
THE ARTS

CHAPTER OUTLINE

I. What is Art?

    A. Art is very difficult to define, but it generally refers to the manifestations of human creativity through which people express themselves in dance, music, song, painting, sculpture, pottery, cloth, story telling, verse, prose, drama, and comedy.

    B. Art and Religion
        1. Definitions of both art and religion focus on the more than ordinary aspects of each with regard to how they are different from the ordinary and profane/secular.
        2. A lot of Western and non-Western art has been done in association with religion, but it is important to remember that not all non-Western art has ritual or religious importance.
        3. Art and religion both have formal (museums and churches, temples) and informal (parks, homes, and regular gathering places) venues of expression.
          a. State-level societies have permanent structures for religion and art.
          b. Nonstate-level societies lack permanent structures for religion and art.

    C. Locating Art
        1. In states, art is housed in special buildings like museums, concert halls, and theaters.
        2. In non-states, artistic expression takes place in public spaces that have been set aside for art.
        3. In states, critics, judges, and experts determine what is art and what is not.
        4. The Kalabari example demonstrates that not all sculpture is art because wooden carvings are manufactured exclusively for religious reasons.

    D. Art and Individuality
        1. Some anthropologists have criticized that the study of non-Western art ignores the individual and focuses too much on the group.
        2. However, in many non-Western societies, there is more collective production of art than in Western cultures.
        3. Bohannan argued that among the Tiv, the emphasis should be on the critics rather than the artists because the Tiv do not recognize the same connection between artists and their art.
        4. The degree to which artists can be separated from their work varies cross-culturally.

    E. The Work of Art
        1. In all societies art is work.
          a. In nonstate societies, artists cannot work on their art all of the time as they still must hunt, gather, fish, herd, or farm to eat.
          b. In states, artists are full-time specialists whose career is their work.
        2. Artistic completeness or mastery is determined and maintained by both formal and informal standards.

II. Art, Society, and Culture

    A. Art is usually a public phenomenon that is exhibited, performed, evaluated, and appreciated in society.
        1. Ethnomusicology is the comparative study of the musics of the world and of music as an aspect of culture and society.

2. Folk art, music, and lore refer to the expressive culture of ordinary people.
3. Art is a form of social communication.

B. The Cultural Transmission of the Arts
1. Art is a part of culture and as a result appreciation for the arts are internalized during enculturation.
2. The appreciation of different art forms varies cross-culturally.
3. In nonindustrialized societies, artistic traditions are generally transmitted through families and kin groups.
4. The art of storytelling plays a critical role in the transmission, preservation, and expression of cultural traditions.

C. Interesting Issues: I'll Get You, My Pretty, and Your Little R2
1. Myths are hallowed stories that express fundamental cultural values.
2. Kottak argues that the *Wizard of Oz* and the original *Star Wars* are modern American cultural myths.
3. He performs a structural analysis of the two films to demonstrate that *Star Wars* is a systematic transformation of *Wizard of Oz*.

D. The Artistic Career
1. In many non-Western societies children born into certain lineages are destined for a particular artistic career (e.g. leather working, wood carving, and making pottery)
2. Full craft specialists find support through their kin ties in non-Western societies or through patrons in Western societies.
3. The arts rely on individual talent, which is shaped through socially approved directions.

E. Continuity and Change
1. The arts are always changing.
2. The arts incorporate a wide variety of media.

F. Beyond the Classroom: Copier: The Afro-Brazilian Art of Unity and Survival
1. Anne Haggerson studied how capoeira, an Afro-Brazilian martial art, helped people overcome the forces of poverty, unemployment, racism, and failing schools.
2. She argues that capoeira is more than a pastime, it is a survival strategy and educational tool for the urban poor in Salvador, Brazil.

LECTURE TOPICS

1. Discuss how the modern world system is influencing the arts in both core and peripheral nations.

2. Discuss the problems with displaying ethnographic and archaeological "works of art" in art museums. Collectors remove objects that have significance not only in being a work of art, but more importantly as a powerful cultural symbols and place them in sterile museums where the cultural context is lost.

3. Discuss how the arts are being debated in contemporary politics. What is the status of the National Endowment of the Arts? Who supports it and who opposes it? Why? What should be the role of the state in terms of funding and patronizing the arts?

SUGGESTED FILMS

Land where the Blues Began

59 min   1979   color
Attempts to capture the local color and flavor of the culture that produced the blues. Visits the Mississippi hill country, talking with performers and filming performances of this local style, which became a universal favorite. Points out ancient roles played by the blues as work songs or as appeals for feminine company. From the University of Illinois Film and Video Center.

Masks

16mm   1962   12 min
A presentation of one of the world's greatest collections of masks, both primitive and modern. The film discusses the masks' importance in the performance of rituals, in the perpetuation of myths, in the dramatization of legends, and in the cultural and artistic life of all people.

Perception

16mm   1979   29 min
Uses film clips, visual experiments, and works of art to identify the various factors, such as social upbringing, culture, and media, that affect the way people develop personal and subjective awareness of objects and events around them. Shows that no two people "see" the same thing in precisely the same way and depicts, in several business and social vignettes, the consequences of individuals perceiving situations differently. Distributed by the University of Illinois Film and Video Center.

Learning to Dance in Bali

video   1991   13 min   b&w
Originally produced as a motion picture, this film is part of series written, produced, and directed by Gregory Bateson and Margaret Mead. A father, then his dance teacher teach a child dance movement, first by physically guiding his body. The student stands behind the teacher and imitates his movements. I Mario, most famous of Balinese dancers, exchanges dance lessons with a visiting dancer from India to the accompaniment of a gamelan orchestra. Published by New York, NY: Institute for Intercultural Studies; distributed by Audio-Visual Services, Pennsylvania State University, [1991?] c1988.

Ethnic Dance around the World

video   24 min   1983   color
Illustrates, with footage from many cultures, various types of dance patterns: processional, line, round, and storytelling. Examines basic reasons for dance: religious, entertainment, celebration, the rhythmic lightening of monotonous tasks, the teaching of history or custom, the welcoming of visitors, and the expression of gratitude for a good harvest. Shows Maori, American Indian, Balinese, Japanese, African, Peruvian, Mexican, Soviet, and Romanian dances.

The Blooms of Banjeli: Technology and Gender in African Ironmaking

29 min 1986 color
Focuses on a Central West African group, which had for centuries produced high-quality iron blooms: an industry now in decline. Two anthropologists visit the community and are allowed the privilege of witnessing the process and describing the rituals, beliefs, and sexual prohibitions involved. The process is seen as a metaphoric extension of the reproductive capacity.

Gullah Tales

video 30 min 1987 color
Gullah Tales is set in 1930 in southern Georgia and South Carolina and is based on folklore of peoples of African descent. The Gullah dialect is fairly well know as striking admixture of African and English influences. Produced by the Office of Educational Media; director: Gary Moss. Published by Los Angeles, CA: Direct Cinema, 1987.

The Performed Word

video 59 min 1989 color
The power of the African American performed word, particularly that of Black preachers, is examined. Includes excerpts from services and interviews with Bishop E.E. Cleveland of Berkeley, California (Church of God in Christ), and his daughter, past Ernestine Cleveland Reems. Produced at the Anthropology Film Center Foundation (Red Taurus Films Production) by Gerald L. Davis; directors: Ernest Shinagawa and Carlos de Jesus. Published by Santa Fe: The Foundation; Memphis, Tenn.: Center for Southern Folklore.

Our Knowledge, Our Beauty: The Expressive Culture of the Canelos Quichua of Ecuador

29 min 1985 color
Records a Quichua song expressing their basic creation myth, and furnishes voice-over translation and comment. Shows how the principal myths of the culture are expressed in ceramic and wood artifacts. Describes the Quichua people, who speak a dialect of Inca, and who believe that music originates in the spirit world and conveys messages from it. Comments on features of their daily life, and on the role of the shaman in their society. Social change, initiated by tourists, has led men to engage in the arts (sculpture and poetry) formerly reserved to women. From the University of Illinois Film and Video Center.

Viva Mexico! A Cultural Portrait

28 min 1971 general color
Mexico's combined heritage of Indian and Spanish civilizations are visible in the costumes, architecture, food, folk art, and traditional celebrations depicted in the film. Scenes of the Mayan and Aztec ruins are skillfully blended with scenes of contemporary Indian society and views of pre-Columbian artifacts housed in the National Museum of Anthropology. Other highlights include colorful fiestas, a rodeo, and a visit with some famous Mexican potters at work. Features accompanying folk music score and appropriate sounds recorded on-site. From the University of Illinois Film and Video Center.

MULTIPLE CHOICE QUESTIONS

1. How as art has been defined?

    a. As something that attracts your attention, catches your eye, and directs your thoughts.
    b. As the quality, production, expression, or realm of what is beautiful or of more than ordinary significance.
    c. As the class of objects subject to aesthetic criteria.
    d. As the express culture through which a person or persons can express themselves creatively in the visual arts, literature, music, and theater arts.
    e. all of the above.

2. What do scholars of art distinguish between?

    a. The artistic and the profane.
    b. The artistic and the ordinary.
    c. The secular and the ordinary.
    d. The profane and the secular.
    e. The sacred and the religious.

3. Which of the following statements about the relationship between art and religion is true?

    a. All non-Western art is produced for religious purposes.
    b. All of the greatest accomplishments in Western art have all been commissioned by formal religions.
    c. Since non-state societies lack permanent buildings dedicated to art (museums) or religion (temples, churches), there is no link between art and religion in these societies.
    d. In all societies, art is produced for religious purposes as well as its aesthetic value.
    e. both a and d are correct

4. In states, how do people determine what is and is not art?

    a. If something is mass produced, it cannot be art.
    b. State societies rely heavily on critics, judges, and experts to make these decisions.
    c. Only things intentionally created as art can be called art.
    d. Art can be created only by artists.
    e. both a and b are correct

5. Why do the Kalabari carve wooden sculptures of spirits?

    a. Purely for aesthetic reasons.
    b. The Kalabari practice carving these sculptures is an artifact of colonialism as the carvings were a form of resistance to the colonial intrusion as they were used in voodoo rituals.
    c. To market and sell them on the world capitalist market.
    d. To manipulate spiritual forces.
    e. all of the above

6. What did Bohannan learn during his work among the Tiv of Nigeria?

    a.   Highly skilled artists worked in private settings.
    b.   The study of Tiv art should focus on art critics and the products of the expressive culture.
    c.   Tiv did not recognize the same kind of connection between artists and their work as Western societies do.
    d.   Mediocre artists worked in public in part so that onlookers could make suggestions.
    e.   **all of the above**

7. Which of the following statements about individual artists in non-Western societies is true?

    a.   They tend to be iconoclastic and antisocial.
    b.   **They are more likely to be part of the cultural mainstream than Western artists are because social approval and acceptance is more important in non-Western societies.**
    c.   They are all trained in formal state-controlled schools for the arts.
    d.   They are nonexistent.
    e.   all of the above

8. Which of the following statements about artists in state-level societies is true?

    a.   They are specialists who have chosen careers in the visual arts, literature, music, and theater arts.
    b.   They depend heavily on extensive kin ties as specialization is kin based.
    c.   They form guilds and unions to protect the interests of its artist members.
    d.   They are major contributors to the subsistence base of the community.
    e.   **both a and c are true**

9. French impressionism was initially

    a.   heralded as one of the great innovations of 19th century painting.
    b.   based on abstract sand paintings from French colonies in West Africa.
    c.   **criticized for being too sketchy and spontaneous to be considered art.**
    d.   a throwback to "old school" painting styles.
    e.   all of the above

10. For the Basongye, music is

    a.   **a distinctly human social activity.**
    b.   originates in nature, which humans try to emulate with instruments.
    c.   performed only by individuals who belong the elite stratum of society.
    d.   a chaotic collection of random sounds emanating from nonhuman creatures.
    e.   both a and d are correct

11. Folk art, music, and lore refer to the

    a.   unrefined manifestations of human creativity produced by illiterate societies.
    b.   **expressive culture of ordinary people.**
    c.   forms of artistic expression found in the New World prior to the arrival of Columbus.
    d.   forms of artistic expression that exists independently of any given cultural system.
    e.   manifestations of human creativity that siblings exchange with their progenitors.

12. Actors, musicians, and dancers

    a.   are not artists since they perform but do not create art.
    b.   function as parasitic consumers of the creative works of artists.
    c.   distort and dilute the artistic mastery of other artists.
    d.   **function as intermediaries who translate the works and ideas of other artists.**
    e.   are marginal members of artistic communities around the world.

13. As a form of communication, art

    a.   is a very limited media.
    b.   can convey moral lessons.
    c.   can lead to an intense emotional release in the audience.
    d.   operates independently of cultural biases.
    e.   **both b and c are correct**

14. In his study of Navajo music, McAllester found that it reflected the overall culture in all of the following ways except

    a.   a general Navajo conservatism extended to music.
    b.   a general Navajo stress on proper form applied to music.
    c.   a general Navajo stress on individualism extended to music.
    d.   **a general Navajo liberalism extended to music.**
    e.   both a and d are correct

15. In many non-Western societies, how are traditional manifestations of expressive culture transmitted?

    a.   through formal state run schools for the arts
    b.   by chance
    c.   **in families**
    d.   through the non-productive members of society
    e.   only by fully initiated adults

16. Forced enculturation refers to situations in which a child's participation in a certain aspect of enculturation is the result of

    a.   peer pressure
    b.   the siblings' decision, not the individual child's
    c.   the child's decision, not the parents'
    d.   **the parents' decision, not the child's**
    e.   liminal statuses

17. In nonindustrial societies artists

    a.   tend to be full-time specialists
    b.   tend to be part-time specialists
    c.   are often born into a family that specializes in a particular form of artistic expression
    d.   are relegated to the hidden transcript of the social contract
    e.   **both b and c are correct**

18. During their work among the Tiwi, Goodall and Koss found that burial pole artists were

    a.   patronized by other community members while they worked on making burial poles.
    b.   temporarily excused from other social obligations to allow them to make burial poles.
    c.   the only people allowed to work near graves.
    d.   ceremonially commissioned to make a burial pole after a death in the community.
    e.   **all of the above.**

19. Which of the following does not influence artistic expression?

    a.   patronage and sponsorship
    b.   advice and criticism from judges and experts.
    c.   **etic categories of utilitarian and nonutilitarian**
    d.   public opinion
    e.   the desire of artists to express themselves

20. As we enter the 21st century, artistic expression

    a.   within industrialized states is becoming increasingly more isolated and independent between states.
    b.   is intentionally avoiding the use of multiple expressive media in favor of using only one medium.
    c.   **is increasingly incorporating elements from many cultures and incorporating them into contemporary art and performance.**
    d.   is disappearing from our cultural repertoire.
    e.   has lost most of its effectiveness.

21. Which of the following statements about myths is false?

    a.   **Myths always involve the actions of unreal, superhuman, or immortal characters.**
    b.   Myths always are at least partly fictionalized.
    c.   Myths can be set in the past, present, or future.
    d.   Myths often carry encoded messages that express fundamental cultural values.
    e.   Myths are statements about how people fit into their cultural universes.

22. What does Kottak argue based on his comparison of *The Wizard of Oz* and *Star Wars*?

    a.   ***Star Wars* is a systematic structural transformation of *The Wizard of Oz*.**
    b.   George Lucas is not as creative as people think he is because Lucas borrowed most of his ideas directly from *The Wizard of Oz*.
    c.   Both films focus on the main character's relationship with the parent of the opposite sex of the main character.
    d.   Both films focus on the main character's relationship with their cross-cousins within an ambilineal descent system.
    e.   Both films are terribly ethnocentric and should not be part of the corpus of contemporary myths in the U.S.

23. What term is synonymous with the arts?

    a.   social creativity
    b.   aesthetics
    c.   myth
    d.   **expressive culture**
    e.   performance

24. What kind of society has buildings dedicated to the arts?

    a. band
    b. tribe
    c. chiefdom
    d. segmentary lineage
    e. state

25. How do most Western societies view non-Western art?

    a. as purely secular
    b. as purely profane
    c. as always linked to religion
    d. as the product of individuals
    e. all of the above

26. What does Haapala (1998) argue about art?

    a. The work of art is an autonomous entity, independent of the creator.
    b. The work of art is a microcosm of a cultures values.
    c. The work of art is culturally maladaptive.
    d. The work of art is a cultural universal.
    e. The work of art and the creator are inseparable.

27. What is the study of the musics of the world and of music as an aspect of culture?

    a. acoustic-anthropology
    b. harmonic-anthropology
    c. tonal-anthropology
    d. ethnomusicology
    e. sociomusicology

ESSAY QUESTIONS

28. Discuss why it is so difficult to come up with a universally applicable definition for art.

29. What is the relationship between art and religion? Is all art religious? Are all religious objects art?.

30. Where is art found? Is art found in the same contexts in all kinds of societies?

31. To what extent can art be isolated from the person who created it? Be sure to include cross-cultural examples to support your answer.

32. What factors influence the production and appreciation of art? Do artists work in a cultural vacuum of pure personal self-expression? What role does society play?

33. Discuss the differences in artistic expression between complex, Western, industrialized states, and less complex, non-Western societies.

34. What role do the arts play as collective expressions of cultural identities? Is art conservative or liberal? Does art promote change or inhibit it?

35. Any of the above multiple choice questions may be converted to an essay question by requiring students to choose the correct answer and justify their selection in essay form. Such justifications should include explanations as to why the chosen answer is correct and why those responses not chosen are incorrect.

TRUE OR FALSE QUESTIONS

36. True or **False**   All art is beautiful.

37. True or **False**   Expressive culture refers the components of a culture that are expressed publicly, as opposed to the private aspects of culture that are hidden from anthropologists.

38. **True** or False   Art and religion are similar because both refer to aspects of culture that are of more than ordinary significance.

39. **True** or False   Appreciating art involves an aesthetic appreciation of form as well as feeling.

40. True or **False**   Traditionally, art and religion occupy mutually exclusive realms in society.

41. **True** or False   Non-state level societies generally lack permanent, specialized venues for art and religion.

42. True or **False**   In the U.S., there is a sharp distinction between what is considered art and what is not.

43. True or **False**   In modern states, there tends to be much more uniformity in the artistic standards compared to less-stratified societies.

44. True or **False**   Among the Kalabari, wood sculptures represent the highest form of purely artistic representation of loved ones.

45. **True** or False   There is more collective production and performance of art in non-Western societies than in Western, industrialized states.

46. **True** or False   During his work among the Tiv, Bohannan found that critics played a key role in the creative process for the production of works of art.

47. True or **False**   In non-Western societies, artists tend to be iconoclastic and antisocial.

48. True or **False**   In states, all artwork can be clearly attributed to a specific artist.

49. **True** or False   When discussing art, it is important to remember that it is still work.

50. **True** or False   In Western societies, the standards for artistic completeness and mastery are maintained in large part by critics, specialists, and experts.

51. **True** or False   Music is one of the most social kinds of artistic expression.

52. True or **False**   In general, folk art is much less symbolic than the artistic expression of full-time artists.

53. **True** or False   Since appreciation of the arts is acquired through enculturation, what one finds aesthetically pleasing depends in part on one's cultural background.

54. True or **False**   In Western societies, artistic and craft specialization is based on kin groups.

55. **True** or False   Myths, legends, and tales play an important role in the transmission of cultural values.

CHAPTER 21

THE MODERN WORLD SYSTEM

CHAPTER OUTLINE

I. The Emergence of the World System

   A. The world system is the result of the increasing interdependence of cultures and ecosystems that were once relatively isolated by distance and boundaries.

   B. Of particular significance to the development of the world system was the European Age of Discovery, wherein the European sphere of influence began to be exported far beyond its physical boundaries by means of conquest and trade.

   C. Influence of the Capitalist World Economy
      1. The defining attribute of capitalism is *economic orientation to the world market for profit.*
      2. Colonial plantation systems, which led to monocrop production in areas that once had diverse subsistence bases (beginning in the seventeenth century).
      3. Colonial commodity production oriented toward the European market.

   D. Wallerstein's World System Theory
      1. Wallerstein has argued that international trade has led to the creation of a capitalist world economy in which a social system based on wealth and power differentials extends beyond individual states.
      2. The world system is arranged according to influence: core (most dominant), to semi-periphery, to periphery (least dominant).
         a. The core consists of the strongest and most powerful nations in which technologically advanced, capital-intensive products are produced and exported to the semiperiphery and the periphery.
         b. The semiperiphery consists of industrialized Third World nations that lack the power and economic dominance of the core nations (Brazil is a semiperiphery nation).
         c. The periphery consists of nations whose economic activities are less mechanized and are primarily concerned with exporting raw materials and agricultural goods to the core and semiperiphery.

II. Industrialization

   A. Causes of the Industrial Revolution.
      1. The Industrial Revolution transformed Europe from a domestic (home handicraft) system to a capitalist industrial system.
      2. Industrialization initially produced goods that were already widely used and in great demand (cotton products, iron, and pottery).
      3. Manufacturing shifted from homes to factories where production was large scale and cheap.
      4. Industrialization fueled a new kind of urban growth in which factories clustered together in regions where coal and labor was cheap.

   B. England and France
      1. The Industrial Revolution began in England but no France.
      2. The French did not have to transform their domestic manufacturing system in order to increase production because it could draw on a larger labor force.

3. England however was already operating at maximum production so that in order to increase yields, innovation was necessary.
4. Weber argued that the pervasiveness of Protestant beliefs in values contributed to the spread and success of industrialization in England, while Catholicism inhibited industrialization in France.

III. Stratification

A. Industrial Stratification
1. Although initially, industrialization in England raised the overall standard of living, factory owners soon began to recruit cheap labor from among the poorest populations.
2. Marx saw this trend as an expression of a fundamental capitalist opposition: the bourgeoisie (capitalists) versus the proletariat (property-less workers).
3. According to Marx, the bourgeoisie owned the means of production, and promoted industrialization to maintain their position, consequently intensifying the dispossession of the workers (a process called proletarianization).
4. Weber argued that Marx' model oversimplified, and developed a model with three main factors contributing to socioeconomic stratification: wealth, power, and prestige (see previous chapter).
5. Class-consciousness (Marx) is the recognition of a commonalty of interest and identification with the other members of one's economic stratum.
6. With considerable modification, it is recognized that a combination of the Marxian and Weberian models may be used to describe the modern capitalist world.
7. The distinction, core-semiperiphery-periphery, is used to describe a worldwide division of labor and capital ownership, but it is pointed out that the growing middle class and the existence of peripheries within core nations complicates the issue beyond the vision of Marx or Weber.

B. Poverty on the Periphery
1. With the expansion of capitalism into the periphery, most of the local landowners have been displaced from their land by large landowners who in turn hired the displaced people at low wages to work the land they once owned.
2. Bangladesh is a good example of this in which British colonialism increased stratification, as most of the land is owned by only a few landowners.

C. Malaysian Factory Women
1. To combat rural poverty, the Malaysian government has encouraged large international companies to set up labor intensive manufacturing operations in rural Malaysia.
2. Factory life contrasts sharply with the traditional customs of the rural Malaysians.
3. Aihwa Ong has studied the effect of work in Japanese electronics factories on Malaysian women employees.
4. Severe contrasts between the work conditions and the culture of the women generate alienation, which results in stress.
5. This stress has been manifested as possession by weretigers, which expresses the workers' resistance, but has as yet effected little change in the overall situation.
6. Ong argues that spirit possession is a form of rebellion and resistance that enable factory women to avoid direct confrontation with the source of their distress.
7. Spirit possessions were not very effective at bringing about improvements in the factory conditions and actually they may help maintain the current conditions by operating as a safety valve for stress.

D. Open and Closed Class Systems
1. Formalized inequalities have taken many forms, such as caste, slavery, and class systems.
2. Caste systems are closed, hereditary systems of stratification that are often dictated by religion (the Hindu caste systems of the Indian subcontinent are given as an example).

3. South African apartheid is given as comparable to a caste system, in that it was ascriptive and closed through law.
4. State sanctioned slavery, wherein humans are treated as property, is the most extreme form of legalized inequality.
5. Vertical mobility refers to the upward or downward change in a person's status.
   a. Vertical mobility exists only in open class systems,
   b. Open class systems are more commonly found in modern states than in archaic states.

E. Interesting Issues: Troubles in Swooshland
   1. Beginning with a segment on *48 Hours* in 1996, Nike came under attack for using sweatshop labor in Viet Nam to bolster their profits in the U.S.
   2. In response to the criticism, Nike adopted new labor policies with regard to wages, working conditions, maximum hours in a work week, and minimum age for employment.

IV. The World System Today

A. World-system theory argues that the present-day interconnectedness of the world has generated a global culture, wherein the trends of complementarity and specialization are being manifested at an international level.
   1. The modern world system is the product of European imperialism and colonialism.
      a. Imperialism refers to a policy of extending rule of a nation or empire over foreign nations and of taking and holding foreign colonies.
      b. Colonialism refers to the political, social, economic, and cultural domination of a territory and its people by a foreign power for an extended period of time.
   2. The spread of industrialization and over-consumption has taken place form the core to the periphery.

B. Interesting Issues: The American Periphery
   1. Thomas Collins compared two counties at opposite ends of Tennessee, both of which used to have economies dominated by agriculture and timber, but now have few employment opportunities.
   2. The population in Hill County in eastern Tennessee is mostly white and opposes labor unions, which has attracted some Japanese companies to the county.
   3. The population in Delta County in western Tennessee is mostly black and strongly supports labor unions, which has deterred companies from setting up factories in the county.

C. Industrial Degradation
   1. The Industrial Revolution greatly accelerated the encompassment of the world by states, all but eliminating all previous cultural adaptations.
   2. Expansion of the world system is often accompanied by genocide, ethnocide, and ecocide.

D. Beyond the Classroom: The Residue of Apartheid in Southern Africa.
   1. During six months of travel in southern Africa, Chanelle MacNab came to see that Afrikaners were not as bad as their stereotypes portray them.
   2. She found that even though Apartheid had been formally dissolved, its legacy was found throughout southern Africa.

LECTURE TOPICS

1. Until recently, the world system core has been occupied almost exclusively by Western nations. Explain why this is so, and that this fact does not imply the superiority of Western nations. Speculate on changes in the self-image of the West as nonwestern nations, such as Japan, are moving into the core.

2.   Discuss the cultural roots of science and the Industrial Revolution in the West.

3.   Discuss the economic basis for classes. Discuss class-consciousness as it does, and does not, appear in American social life. Why is it resisted here?

4.   Colonialism has played a major role in shaping the world system. Pick a particular country or region and use it as a case study illustrating the nature and effects long-term colonial contact had on the societies involved. Southeast Asia is particularly interesting because there are numerous countries there, each with significantly different colonial experiences (Vietnam-France, Indonesia-Holland, Malaysia-Britain, Thailand-never colonized).

5.   Multinational corporations are relatively new players in the world system. The debate as to whether they constitute a new form of colonialism is of interest, particularly since it suggests a new shape for the system.

6.   Discuss industrial degradation in the context of the high gasoline prices and the rolling blackouts in the United States. How are these issues that need to be dealt with at the global level?

SUGGESTED FILMS

Cannibal Tours

video   77 min   1987   color
This film by Dennis O'Rourke is a documentary that follows the exploits of a group of Western tourists as they go on a guided tour of remote villages in New Guinea. The film features extensive commentary by both the tourists and the Papuans and consequently provides much information about the different perceptions and perspectives each group has (some more consciously than others) about the world system. New York: O'Rourke and Assoc., Direct Cinema, Ltd.

Inventing Reality

video   60 min   1992   color
Has our desire for certainty and objectivity closed off the "magical" influence of the natural world? We are shown how in Mexico and Canada the certainties of science can combine with natural conceptions of physical disease, both in the tribal world of the shaman and in the thinking of modern medical science. Then travel to the Aboriginal culture of Australia to examine dreamtime. Produced by Biniman Prod. Ltd., Adrian Malone Prod., Ltd., Los Angeles and BBC-TV, et. al. Published by PBS Video, Alexandria, VA.

The Last Tasmanian: Extinction

63 min   1980   color
Research of Dr. Rhys Jones, filmed in the environs that concern the life and genocide of the Tasmanian aborigines, summarizes the grim evolution of Britain's choice of Tasmania as a penal colony. Reveals something of how the story was reconstructed from minimal information; personalizes it with the story of Truganini, last of her race. From The University of Illinois Film and Video Center.

Hunger in America

16mm 1968 52 min
A grim, factual story of millions of Americans who go hungry every day: black sharecroppers in Alabama, Navajo Indians in Arizona, starving tenant farmers just twenty-five miles from the nation's capital, and Mexican-Americans in Texas. Shows undernourished, dead, and dying children, and a federal program that provides lard and peanut butter to people who desperately seek milk and meat. From the CBS Reports series. From The University of Illinois Film and Video Center.

In Doig's People's Ears: Portrait of a Changing Native Community

video 30 min 1984 color
Utilizes audiotapes and slides combined in videotape format to document the changes experienced by Beaver Indians of the Peace river area of British Columbia during a 20 year period as they make the transition from hunting and trapping to an industrial way of life. Includes narrative accounts of Peace River history by both Beaver Indian people and non-native settlers who recall times when the Beaver People led a more nomadic way of life. Shows how the Alaska Highway and agricultural and petrochemical development in the area has affected their way of life. Includes recordings of Beaver ceremonial music and Peace River soundscapes. Vancouver, B.C.: Daboidesh Productions.

Black Harvest

video 90 min 1992 color
The third in a series of films directed by Bob Connolly and Robin Anderson that document some of the events stemming from the 1930s era prospecting by the Leahy brothers of Australia. In this film, Joe Leahy (the "mixed race" son of Leahy brother Mick) attempts to establish a joint coffee plantation with his neighbors, the Ganiga. This effort was destroyed by a worldwide collapse of coffee prices, which reduced workers' wages and led to tribal warfare. Santa Monica, CA: Direct Cinema.

Popular films of interest: *The Milagro Beanfield War, Max Havelaar.*

MULTIPLE CHOICE QUESTIONS

1. How does the modern world system affect ethnographers?

    a. There are almost no truly isolated cultures left making it difficult to do real ethnographic research.
    b. **They need to be aware of the fact that any culture they study is influenced by and has influence on other cultures.**
    c. They must be careful when comparing their findings to those who did work in the first half of the Twentieth Century, when there were many isolated cultures.
    d. There are no more indigenous peoples.
    e. It has brought about a blending of the races, which makes it harder to identify specific cultures.

2. What fueled the European Age of Discovery?

   a. A desire to save the souls of the natives.
   b. Pilgrims fleeing persecution in their European homelands.
   c. The feudal kingdoms of East Asia reaching out to establish trade links with Europe, mainly through such Middle Eastern countries as Arabia.
   d. A seven-year-long drought in Europe that forced governments to look outside their borders to support their populations.
   e. European commercial interest in exotic raw materials, such as spices and tropical hardwoods.

3. Which of the following resulted in the growth of a market for sugar in Europe?

   a. A tremendous expansion in the strength of independent indigenous nations of Mexico and South America.
   b. The movement of sugar-producing nations from the periphery to the core of the world system.
   c. Capitalism, once a cultural trait specific to New Guinea (where sugar was first domesticated) moved to the rest of the world.
   d. The development of a trans-Atlantic slave trade.
   e. A long-term improvement in the distribution of wealth among the rural peasantry of England.

4. Which of the following did *not* result from Christopher Columbus' voyages?

   a. The Old World and New World were forever linked.
   b. Europeans extracted silver and gold from the land.
   c. Europeans enslaved Native Americans.
   d. Europeans offered statehood to Peru, Mexico, and Cuba.
   e. Europeans colonized New World lands.

5. How does subsistence farming differ from cash-cropping?

   a. Subsistence farmers plant only indigenous crops while cash croppers may plant imported crops.
   b. Subsistence farmers require advanced technology and fertilizer to produce, while cash-croppers farm organically.
   c. Cash-croppers tend to produce only enough to satisfy their household and community needs while subsistence farmers produce a surplus to be sold for profit.
   d. Subsistence farmers tend to produce only enough to satisfy their household and community needs while cash-croppers produce a surplus to be sold for profit.
   e. Subsistence farmers may also work at another job to make ends meet, while cash croppers support themselves with their farming alone.

6. What term refers to wealth or resources invested in business with the intent of producing a profit?

   a. the modern world system
   b. industrialization
   c. an open class system
   d. socioeconomic stratification
   e. capital

7. Which of the following statements about capitalist world economy is true?

   a. It grew through international trade.
   b. It is the basis of the world system.
   c. It rests on production for sale or exchange.
   d. It aims at maximizing profits.
   e. all of the above

8. World system theory

   a. has been written about by Wallerstein.
   b. sees society as consisting of parts assembled into an interrelated system.
   c. claims that a set of economic and political interconnections has characterized much of the globe since the sixteenth century.
   d. is based on political and economic specialization and interdependence.
   e. all of the above

9. What are the three structural positions of the modern world system?

   a. core, periphery, and semiperiphery
   b. metropole, satellite, and semisatellite
   c. state, nation-state, and nation
   d. wealth, power, and prestige
   e. preliterate, nonliterate and literate

10. Which is *not* true of core nations?

    a. They represent the dominant structural position in the world system.
    b. They consist of the strongest and most powerful states.
    c. They have advanced systems of production.
    d. They have complex economies.
    e. They export their raw materials to other countries.

11. Peripheral nations

    a. export to the core but not the semiperiphery.
    b. lack industrialization.
    c. are isolated from the world economy.
    d. have economies shaped to serve the interests of the core.
    e. all of the above

12. Which of the following is *not* an aspect of contemporary, semiperiphery nations?

    a. They are industrialized.
    b. They export industrial goods and commodities.
    c. They lack the power and economic dominance of core nations.
    d. Brazil is one of them.
    e. They import raw materials from core nations.

13. According to Karl Marx, classes were

    a. complementary, in that they each did different tasks necessary to survival of the society.
    b. part of the original, pre-industrial social system of humans.
    c. opposed to one another on the basis of conflicting economic interests.
    d. based more on notions of prestige and morality than on actual economic differences.
    e. all of the above

14. According to Karl Marx, class consciousness comes about as a result of

   a.   the continuation of ethic identities even though ethnic "markers" (distinct clothing styles, etc.) have more-or-less disappeared.
   b.   an elaboration of differing religious beliefs in complex industrialized societies.
   c.   people extending notions of cognatic kinship beyond the boundaries of actual biological relatedness.
   d.   **when people recognize they have a common economic interest and identify themselves as part of the group that shares that interest.**
   e.   the gradual elaboration of gendered differences first established during the period of peasant subsistence farming.

15. According to Marx, who are the bourgeoisie and the proletariat?

   a.   The product of gender differentiation from Europe's tribal past.
   b.   Destined to reconcile through the post-capitalist process of alienation.
   c.   **Distinct and opposed classes produced by the world capitalist economy.**
   d.   Exogamous social groups.
   e.   all of the above

16. Which of the following accompanied early English industrialization?

   a.   urbanization
   b.   agrarian intensification
   c.   mechanization
   d.   a population increasing faster than its food supply
   e.   **all of the above**

17. Why was late eighteenth-century France able to maintain the form of its domestic manufacturing system?

   a.   France had a smaller population than Great Britain did.
   b.   France had more productive New World colonies than Great Britain did
   c.   **The French could increase production without innovating.**
   d.   King Romer I, who ruled France, was a strong supporter of industry.
   e.   of the French Revolution.

18. Why did England industrialized before France?

   a.   England had rich deposits of coal and iron ore.
   b.   England had navigable waterways.
   c.   England was a seafaring island nation located at the crossroads of international trade.
   d.   England had a favored position for importing raw materials and exporting manufactured goods.
   e.   **of all of the above**

19. Which of the following statements about Karl Marx is *not* true?

   a.   He analyzed nineteenth century industrial production capitalism.
   b.   **He viewed socioeconomic stratification in terms of several classes with different but complementary interests.**
   c.   He called the owners of the means of production the bourgeoisie.
   d.   He called the people who sold their labor the proletariat.
   e.   He emphasized class consciousness.

20. What is the source of the widespread poverty in Bangladesh?

    a. the caste system
    b. The British colonial system diverting local subsistence and industry to the world economy.
    c. The post-World War II breakdown of the British colonial system.
    d. A series of natural catastrophes.
    e. Pernicious malnutrition between 1850 and 1886.

21. According to Weber, what are the three dimensions of social stratification?

    a. means of production, mode of production, measure of production
    b. status, exchange, religion
    c. gender, ethnicity, race
    d. wealth, power, prestige
    e. age, gender, ethnicity

22. Which of the following is *not* true about the modern world system?

    a. The distinction between bourgeoisie and proletariat has disappeared.
    b. The contrast between capitalists and property-less workers is worldwide.
    c. Stratification systems are not simple and dichotomous.
    d. There is a growing middle class of skilled and professional workers.
    e. Intermediate occupations create opportunities for social mobility.

23. What is the modern world system divided by?

    a. class contrasts.
    b. status groups.
    c. ethnic and religious groups.
    d. nations.
    e. all of the above

24. In order for a class system to be open, it must have

    a. apartheid.
    b. *anomie*.
    c. alienation.
    d. petty capitalism.
    e. vertical mobility.

25. Which of the following statements about cotton production in Bangladesh is *not* true?

    a. During colonial times, contact with the world market caused the prices of commodities to drop.
    b. During colonial times, wealth became increasingly concentrated in the hands of a small elite class.
    c. During pre-colonial times, subsistence farming provided the peasantry with most of their needs.
    d. During colonial times, land was part of the market economy.
    e. During pre-colonial times, there was a prosperous local cotton industry.

26. Which of the following forms of social organization consists of stratified, ascribed, endogamous, closed groups?

    a.   segmentary lineage organization
    b.   class in the United States
    c.   caste systems
    d.   chiefdoms
    e.   all of the above

27. How are slaves are like the proletariat?

    a.   They both lack control over the means of production.
    b.   They both have some control over where they work.
    c.   They both have some control over how much they work.
    d.   They both have some control over for whom they work.
    e.   They both have some control over what they do with their wages.

28. Which of the following statements about a truly open class system is true?

    a.   Individual achievement and personal merit would determine rank.
    b.   Hierarchical social status would be ascribed.
    c.   Achieved statuses would be unimportant.
    d.   Class contrasts would be clear.
    e.   all of the above

29. Which of the following statements about the world system is *not* true?

    a.   It is based on economies oriented toward world market for profit.
    b.   It depends on each nation producing all that is needed by its own population.
    c.   It was established primarily through European colonialism.
    d.   The standard of living tends to be higher for populations living in the core nations.
    e.   There has been some evidence that nations may change their positions in the world system.

30. How do Malaysian factory workers respond to their difficult working conditions?

    a.   through spirit possessions
    b.   by forming labor unions
    c.   through lawsuits in the Malaysian legal system
    d.   through witchcraft accusations
    e.   with voodoo

31. Which of the following is *not* true of twentieth-century industrialization?

    a.   It brought new industries and new jobs.
    b.   Lands belonging to tribal nations have remained largely untouched by it since W.W.II.
    c.   It brought mass production and the assembly line.
    d.   Increased production spurred strategies to sell everything industry could churn out.
    e.   Mass production gave rise to a culture of overconsumption.

32. Bodley has argued that indigenous peoples have resisted integration within nation-states because

   a.   their brains have been too strongly shaped by their primitive social organization.
   b.   it is economically more profitable for them to establish their own nation-state.
   c.   bilingual education has made them less able to perform the tasks necessary for living in industrialized societies.
   d.   such integration usually leads to a decline in their quality of life.
   e.   their societies are too simple to fit.

33. What is the term for the physical destruction of ethnic groups (by murder, warfare, and introduced diseases)?

   a.   sociocide
   b.   ethnocide
   c.   biocide
   d.   genocide
   e.   patricide

34. The American economy

   a.   has shifted from heavy goods manufacture toward high-tech industries.
   b.   has shifted from manufacturing toward information processing and specialized services.
   c.   has been called "postindustrial".
   d.   is a full participant in the world economy.
   e.   all of the above

35. Who are indigenous peoples?

   a.   People who live in autonomous, independent nation-states.
   b.   Peasants who are of the same ethnicity as the ruling elite.
   c.   Descendants of tribespeople who live on as culturally distinct colonized peoples, many of whom aspire to autonomy.
   d.   Any population living in a nation state on the periphery of the world system.
   e.   all of the above

36. Which of the following statements about the spirit possessions of Malaysian factory women is *not* true?

   a.   They are a form of indirect confrontation.
   b.   They express repressed resentment.
   c.   They were effective at improving working conditions.
   d.   They are a form of unconscious protest.
   e.   They involve a person being possessed by a weretiger.

37. Which of the following is a result of industrialization?

   a.   A shift from renewable resources to fossil fuels.
   b.   The creation of new industries and jobs.
   c.   The rise of a culture of overconsumption.
   d.   The development of the United States into a core nation
   e.   all of the above

38. Which of the following is *not* one of the causes of genocide identified by Bodley (1988)?

    a.   foreign diseases
    b.   spectrum revolution
    c.   warfare
    d.   slavery
    e.   land grabbing

39. In what kind of manufacture system does an entrepreneur supply raw materials to workers in their homes and collect the finished products from them?

    a.   capitalism
    b.   industrialism
    c.   tribute exchange
    d.   reciprocity
    e.   domestic system

40. Who viewed the nation-state as an instrument of oppression and religion as a method of diverting and controlling the masses?

    a.   Weber
    b.   Freud
    c.   Tylor
    d.   Marx
    e.   Morgan

ESSAY QUESTIONS

41. What is the world system perspective, and why is it important in anthropology?

42. What is the capitalist world economy? When did it originate and what are its features?

43. What are core, semiperiphery, and periphery? What is their relationship to world capitalism?

44. How do the worldwide effects of industrialism illustrate the general evolutionary trends of proliferation, specialization, integration, and expansion?

45. What was the Industrial Revolution, and how did it differ from previous life in villages, towns, and cities?

46. Why did the Industrial Revolution begin in England rather than France?

47. How did proletarianization contrast with previous human work?

48. How did the views of Marx and Weber on stratification differ?

49. How is the world stratification system related to the structural positions within the world capitalist economy?

50. Any of the above multiple choice questions may be converted to an essay question by requiring students to choose the correct answer and justify their selection in essay form. Such justifications should include explanations as to why the chosen answer is correct and why those responses not chosen are incorrect.

TRUE OR FALSE QUESTIONS

51. **True** or False — Sugar and cotton helped fuel the development of a capitalist world economy.

52. True or **False** — According to Wallerstein, the nations in the world system can be classified into three types: core, periphery, and frontier.

53. **True** or False — The Industrial Revolution did not begin in France because the French domestic manufacturing system could production without innovating.

54. True or **False** — Marx argued that socioeconomic stratification was based on the sharp and simple division between the successful Protestant industrialists and the poor Catholic peasantry.

55. True or **False** — According to Marx, the bourgeoisie is made up of the people who must sell their labor to survive.

56. True or **False** — Weber argued that without Catholic ethic and values, capitalism and industrialism would have never spread beyond England.

57. True or **False** — Weber argued that the only true capitalists were Protestants and that people who believed in any other faith could never fully mature as capitalists.

58. **True** or False — Higher wages and improved benefits for workers in core nations is possible only because added surplus from the periphery enables companies to maintain high profit margins.

59. **True** or False — Life in nations on the periphery is characterized by high percentages of poverty and frequent food shortages brought on by the high level of stratification between the few large landowners and the landless workers.

60. True or **False** — For Malaysian factory women, spirit possessions are an effective means of modifying poor factory conditions and low wages.

61. True or **False** — Caste systems are open, achieved systems of stratification that are legitimized by religion.

62. True or **False** — Vertical mobility refers to a subsystem within the capitalist world economy that exploits environmental zones that are close together in space, but contrast one another in elevation, rainfall, and vegetation.

63. **True** or False — Compared to peripheral and semiperipheral state, core states are more likely to have open class systems.

64. **True** or False — One of the characteristic features of industrial economic systems is continual expansion.

65. **True** or False — The U.S. originally started out as peripheral nation but by 1900 it had asserted itself as member of the industrialized core.

66. True or **False** — In Tennessee, Japanese investors looking to establish factories in the U.S. favor regions were labor unions have a strong presence because the labor force can be easily mobilized.

67. True or False Mass production has led to critical consumption as people are forced to make careful decisions regarding what is needed and what is excess.

68. True or False With the spread of industrialization, the existence of indigenous economies, ecologies, and populations has become threatened all over the world.

69. True or False Ethnocide refers to the intentional destruction of an ethnic group's traditional customs, beliefs, and behaviors.

70. True or False When indigenous peoples are incorporated into modern nation-states they usually become part of the impoverished classes.

CHAPTER 22

COLONIALISM AND DEVELOPMENT

CHAPTER OUTLINE

I. Colonialism

   A. Imperialism
      1. Imperialism refers to a policy of extending rule of a nation or empire over foreign nations and of taking and holding foreign colonies.
      2. Colonialism refers to the political, social, economic, and cultural domination of a territory and its people by a foreign power for an extended period of time.
      3. Imperialism is as old as the state.
      4. Modern colonialism began with the Age of Discovery during which European nations founded colonies throughout the New World.

   B. British Colonialism
      1. The search for resources and new markets to increase profits fueled British colonialism.
      2. The first phase of British colonialism was concentrated in New World, West Africa, and India and came to close with the American Revolution.
      3. During the second period of colonialism, Britain eventually controlled most of India, Australia, New Zealand, Canada, and large portions of eastern and southern Africa.
      4. British colonial efforts were justified by what Kipling called "white man's burden" which asserted that native peoples were not capable of governing themselves and needed the white British colonialist provide and maintain order.

   C. French Colonialism
      1. French colonialism was driven more by the state, the church, and the military, rather than by business interests.
      2. The first phase of French colonial efforts were focused in Canada, the Louisiana Territory, the Caribbean, and West Africa.
      3. During the second phase of French colonialism (1870 to World War II), the empire grew to include most of North Africa and Indochina.
      4. The ideological legitimization for French colonialism was *mission civilisatrice* (similar to "white man's burden"); to spread French culture, language, and religion throughout the colonies.
      5. The French used two forms of colonial rule.
         a. Indirect rule refers to the French practice of governing through native political structures and leaders.
         b. Direct rule refers to the French practice of imposing new governments upon native populations.

   D. Colonialism and Identity
      1. Ethnic and political distinctions around the world were severely disrupted by colonialism.
      2. For example, many of the modern political boundaries in West Africa are based on linguistic, political, and economic contrasts that are the result of European colonial policies in the region.

E. Postcolonial Studies
   1. Postcolonial studies refers to research that targets the interactions between European nations and the societies they colonized.
      a. The term has also been used to refer to the second half of the 20th century.
      b. The term may also be used to signify a position against imperialism and Eurocentrism.
   2. The postcolonies can be divided into settler, nonsettler, and mixed.
      a. Settler postcolonies include countries that are dominated by European settlers with only sparse native populations (e.g. Australia)
      b. Nonsettler postcolonies are characterized by large native populations and only a small number of Europeans (e.g. India).
      c. Mixed postcolonies refer to countries with both sizable native and European populations (e.g. South Africa and Kenya)

II. Development

   A. An intervention philosophy is an ideological justification for interference in the lives of natives, based upon the assumption that one is in possession of a superior way of doing or thinking.
      1. British Empire – white man's burden.
      2. French empire – *mission civilisatrice*.
      3. Economic development plans – industrialization, modernization, westernization, and individualism are desirable evolutionary advances that will bring long-term benefits to natives.

   B. Problems Associated with Narrowly Focused Intervention and Development.
      1. Situations construed as problems resulting from an indigenous lifestyle may in fact be a result of the world system's impact on that lifestyle.
      2. The systemic effects of development projects may actually be harmful (e.g., tax and rent increases in response to raised income).
      3. Narrowly focused experts are not as likely to be aware of the broad spectrum implications of development schemes.

   C. The Brazilian Sisal Scheme
      1. In the 1950's, Brazil's government attempted to introduce *sisal* as a cash crop into the subsistence economy of the *sertão*.
      2. Development increased dependence on the world economy, ruined the local subsistence economy, and worsened local health and income distribution.

   D. The Greening of Java
      1. Worldwide, the green revolution has increased food supplies and reduced food prices.
      2. However, the emphasis on front capital and advanced technological and chemical farming allowed the bureaucratic and economic elites of Java to strengthen their positions at the expense of poorer farmers.
      3. Ann Stoler's analysis of the green revolution's impact on Java suggested that it differentially affected such things as gender stratification, depending on class.

   E. Equity
      1. A common stated goal of development projects is increased equity, which means a reduction in poverty and a more even distribution of wealth.
      2. This goal is frequently thwarted by local elites acting to preserve or enhance their positions.

F. The Third World Talks Back
   1. Applied anthropologists have been criticized for ethnocentrism in their own approaches to development (see the reference to Guillermo Batalla).
      a. Too much focus on multiple and micro- causes while ignoring major social inequalities.
      b. Early projects were too psychologically oriented.
      c. Too much focus on technological diffusion as the primary source of change.
   2. Other critics have pointed out associations between anthropologists and certain government agencies.

III. Strategies for Innovation

   A. Kottak describes his comparative analysis of sixty-eight development projects, wherein he determined that culturally compatible economic development projects were twice as successfully financially as the incompatible ones.

   B. Overinnovation refers to development projects the require major changes on behalf of the target community
      1. Projects that are guilty of overinnovation are generally not successful.
      2. To avoid overinnovation, development projects need to be sensitive to the traditional culture and concerns of daily life in the target community.

   C. Underdifferentiation is the tendency to overlook cultural diversity and view less-developed countries as alike.
      1. Many development projects incorrectly assume that the nuclear family is the basic unit of production and land ownership.
      2. Many development projects also incorrectly assume that cooperatives based on models from the former eastern bloc will be readily incorporated by rural communities.

   D. In the News: People Be Dammed
      1. This article discusses some of the many problems facing the Three Gorges Dam in China with regard to the massive resettlement program (1.2 million people).
      2. Many groups within and outside of China are opposed to the dam, but construction is still progressing.

   E. Third World Models
      1. The best models for economic development are to be found in the target communities.
      2. Realistic development promotes change, not over-innovation, by preserving local systems while making them work better.
      3. The Malagasy example shows attention paid to local social forms (descent organization) and environmental conditions (e.g., taking livestock from strains adapted to a similar environment).

LECTURE TOPICS

1.   Discuss some of the examples of "first contact" from around the world. Try to draw on both native and European accounts and what are some of the discrepancies between the two perspectives (e.g. Captain Cook in Hawaii).

2.   Discuss various notions of what constitutes development, including those of natives, of professional development workers, of anthropologists, and of the general public. Show why there are systematic differences. If you believe in particular goals discuss and support them.

3.   Discuss both the cooperative and "economic" man as fallacies guiding development work. Point out their roots in Western ideology, and how they continue to appear in the media and in current political campaigns, although in a more benign or palatable disguise.

4.   Discuss the means by which multinational corporations are beginning to operate in the Third World (working conditions in factories, dealings with select, elite indigenous groups). What impacts have these policies had? Address the current debate about multinationals and "neocolonialism".

5.   Discuss the sequence of events that led to the American Anthropological Association's adoption of a code of ethics (anthropological participation in the Vietnam War). You might also note the participation by earlier generations of anthropologists in the administrations of colonial governments. This would be a good place to address criticisms by Batalla, Said, and others.

6.   Discuss the history of the relationship between colonialism and anthropology. How has it changed over the last 150 years? Where should it go in the future?

SUGGESTED FILMS

First Contact

video 55 min 1984 color/b&w
A modern classic, this documentary mixes footage from two time periods. When the Leahy brothers left Australia to prospect for gold in the interior of New Guinea during the early 1930's, they were perhaps the first Europeans to make significant contact with the peoples living there. They brought a film camera with them to document their journey. Footage from their prospecting trips is interspersed with interviews of the two surviving Leahys and the Papuans they involved themselves with. The film is both a vivid example of the first inroads of the modern world system into an area (Papuans comment on the changes in their labor patterns wrought by the Leahy's gold camps, for example) and haunting presentation of remembered history. Directed by Bob Connolly and Robin Anderson in association with Institute of Papua-New Guinea Studies. New York, NY: Filmmakers Library.

Joe Leahy's Neighbors

video 90 min 1988 color
The sequel to *First Contact*, also directed by Bob Connolly and Robin Anderson. Follows events in the live of Mick Leahy's "mixed-race" son, Joe (who was never acknowledged by his father). Joe has become wealthy but is the object of envy by members of the Ganiga tribe, who resent his manipulation of social ties (made possible by his marginal status) to enhance his wealth through land acquisition and cash cropping on the world market. Watertown, Mass.: Documentary Educational Resources.

No Easy Walk

60 min 1988 color video
Chronicles the history of colonialism and the struggle for independence in Ethiopia, including the 1896 Battle of Adowa, Emperor Menelik's modernization program, Mussolini's invasion in 1935, and the postwar establishment of the Organization for African Unity in Addis Ababa in 1963. Produced by Acacia Productions for Channel Four Television (J. Edward Milner); director: Bernard Odjidja. Published by New York: Cinema Guild, 1988.

"Toast"

13 min   1974   16mm
Uses the concept of net energy profit, which is what remains after the energy costs of getting and concentrating that energy are subtracted, to demonstrate that our daily toast is hardly a bargain. Humorous animated sequences trace the production and distribution of a loaf of bread from oil wellhead to end use, making the point that fossil-fuel energy used in the preparation and market of food results in little or no net energy profit. From the University of Illinois Film and Video Center.

Ishi in Two World

19 min   1967   general color
Presents a portrait of Ishi, Yahi Indian, believed to be the last person in North America to have spent most of his life leading a totally aboriginal existence. Chronicles the Yahi's fight against the white men and the eventual extermination of the tribe, except for Ishi, who hid in the forest for twenty-five years. He suddenly appeared near the town of Orville, California, in 1911, sick, starved, and middle-aged, and spent his remaining years as a guest of the University of California Museum of Anthropology. Rare photographs depict Ishi demonstrating his Yahi skills. Based on the book by Theodora Kroeber. Winner of a CINE Golden Eagle, 1968. From the University of Illinois Film and Video Center.

Land Where the Blues Began

59 min   1979   color
Attempts to capture the local color and flavor of the culture that produced the blues. Visits the Mississippi hill country, talking with performers and filming performances of this local style, which became a universal favorite. Points out ancient roles played by the blues as work songs or as appeals for feminine company. From the University of Illinois Film and Video Center.

The Last Tasmanian: Extinction

63 min   1980   color
Research of Dr. Rhys Jones, filmed in the environs that concern the life and genocide of the Tasmanian aborigines, summarizes the grim evolution of Britain's choice of Tasmania as a penal colony. Reveals something of how the story was reconstructed from minimal information; personalizes it with the story of Truganini, last of her race. From the University of Illinois Film and Video Center.

Our Knowledge, Our Beauty: The Expressive Culture of the Canelos Quichua of Ecuador

29 min   1985   color
Records a Quichua song expressing their basic creation myth, and furnishes voice-over translation and comment. Shows how the principal myths of the culture are expressed in ceramic and wood artifacts. Describes the Quichua people, who speak a dialect of Inca, and who believe that music originates in the spirit world and conveys messages from it. Comments on features of their daily life, and on the role of the shaman in their society. Social change, initiated by tourists, has led men to engage in the arts (sculpture and poetry) formerly reserved to women. From the University of Illinois Film and Video Center.

Viva Mexico! A Cultural Portrait

28 min   1971   general color
Mexico's combined heritage of Indian and Spanish civilizations are visible in the costumes, architecture, food, folk art, and traditional celebrations depicted in the film. Scenes of the Mayan and Aztec ruins are skillfully blended with scenes of contemporary Indian society and views of pre-Columbian artifacts housed in the National Museum of Anthropology. Other highlights include colorful fiestas, a rodeo, and a visit with some famous Mexican potters at work. Features accompanying folk music score and appropriate sounds recorded on-site. From the University of Illinois Film and Video Center.

Witchcraft among the Azande

55 min   1984   color
Follows the trial of a couple accused of adultery, showing how the outcome depends on the belief in ritual divination. The Azande believe that all misfortune comes from witchcraft. The couple in question denies guilt, but their fate will be determined by whether a ritually poisoned chicken lives or dies. The tribe has had some Christian teaching and calls itself Christian, but the priest shares influence with the witch doctor. From the Disappearing World Series. From the University of Illinois Film and Video Center.

MULTIPLE CHOICE QUESTIONS

1.   Which of the following statements about British colonialism is true?

   a.   It was driven by the business interests.
   b.   It can be divided into two stages.
   c.   It was legitimized by the racist notion of "white man's burden"
   d.   It began to fall apart after World War II.
   e.   **all of the above**

2.   What term is used by Kottak to describe the relations between European countries and their former colonies in the second half of the 20th century?

   a.   "mission civilisatrice"
   b.   direct rule
   c.   **post-colonialism**
   d.   post-imperialism
   e.   post-hegemony

3.   According to Kottak, what is a common problem for international development?

   a.   They lack an intervention philosophy.
   b.   **The assumption that the best way to increase production and income is through industrialization.**
   c.   They tend to use local cultural models and processes rather than the more advanced Western models.
   d.   They frequently make unnecessary attempts to extend indigenous lifestyles that are already obsolete.
   e.   all of the above

4. What is the common goal for most development projects?

   a. greater socioeconomic stratification
   b. ethnocide
   c. cultural assimilation
   d. decreased local autonomy
   e. increased equity

5. What spurred French colonialism?

   a. the state
   b. the church
   c. armed forces
   d. explorers
   e. all of the above

6. The Brazilian sisal scheme shows that

   a. nutrition improved gradually after peasants began growing sisal and working for wages.
   b. the production of sisal acted as a leveling mechanism, tending to equalize wealth and, hence, nutrition among different classes and groups.
   c. an increase in peasants' cash income may not benefit them.
   d. malnourished is, unfortunately, a necessary concomitant of peasant life.
   e. none of the above is true

7. Which of the following was a major shortcoming of the Brazilian sisal scheme?

   a. Sisal was not adapted to arid regions.
   b. Peasants tended to eat the sisal rather than prepare it for export.
   c. Malnutrition increased after peasants converted their garden plots to sisal.
   d. The local elites refused to support the scheme after the peasants bought decorticating machines.
   e. all of the above

8. Which of the following is *not* true of the shift to sisal cultivation in Brazil?

   a. Most sisal growers have completely abandoned subsistence crops.
   b. Most cultivators now rely on technology owned by members of the local elite.
   c. It is virtually impossible for many peasants to return to subsistence cultivation.
   d. The local diet has improved because people can buy imported food.
   e. All of the above are not true.

9. Which of the following categories was *not* part of the Principles of Professional Responsibility adopted by the American Anthropological Association in 1971?

   a. Responsibility to Those Studied
   b. Responsibility to the Local Elite
   c. Responsibility to Sponsors
   d. Responsibility to the Discipline
   e. Responsibility to Students

10. What have we learned from the sisal scheme in Brazil and the "greening" of Java?

    a. Economic development depends on advanced technology.
    b. Only cash cropping can lead to economic development.
    c. A strong central government is necessary for economic development.
    d. Mechanization always leads to increased food production.
    e. Economic development depends on both technological change and political factors.

11. In Java, what was the model of economic development that proved beneficial for peasants?

    a. put multinational corporations in charge
    b. require complete isolation of peasants from outsiders
    c. send students to work with, teach, and learn from peasants
    d. utilize effective global inputs to combat adversity in situation planning
    e. spread information about the "green revolution" through elites

12. Which of the following is *not* a reason for the failure of Java's "green revolution"?

    a. Management of the program was taken away from students and peasants and given to multinational corporations.
    b. Certain pesticides killed fish in the fields, thus removing an important source of already scarce protein.
    c. Elites, with vested interests in land, debt bondage, and cheap labor preferred to block changes that would reduce their socioeconomic advantages.
    d. Peasants had no family planning counseling during the period when they were adopting new cultivation techniques.
    e. The project sought to improve equity without significantly changing the way the rice farmers cultivated their fields.

13. What term refers to an ideological justification for outsiders to guide native groups in specific directions?

    a. development ideology
    b. intervention philosophy
    c. coercive philosophy
    d. development philosophy
    e. intrusive ideology

14. In a comparative study of sixty-eight development projects, Kottak determined that

    a. over-innovation was the most productive development model.
    b. culturally compatible development projects were twice as successful as incompatible ones.
    c. the socialist bloc model was the most successful.
    d. the capitalist bloc model was the most financially successful.
    e. the underdifferentiated model led to the most equity.

15. Changes that lead to long-range benefits that cannot be immediately recognized

    a. have only limited chances of succeeding.
    b. are the most successful kind of development scheme.
    c. have never taken place.
    d. are known as utopian intervention.
    e. are known as research and development.

16.   What was the intervention philosophy of the French Empire?

   a.   carte blanche
   b.   savoir-faire
   c.   coup d'état
   d.   mission civilisatrice
   e.   nom de plume

17.   On what does economic development rest?

   a.   new agricultural techniques
   b.   overcoming resistance by vested interests
   c.   political clout by agents of change
   d.   government support of change programs
   e.   all of the above

18.   What was the intervention philosophy of the British Empire?

   a.   manifest destiny
   b.   white man's burden
   c.   this land is our land
   d.   fifty-four forty or fight
   e.   in his majesty's domain

19.   Which of the following is a reason that the Madagascar project to increase rice production was successful

   a.   Malagasy leaders were of the peasantry and therefore prepared to follow the descent-group ethic of pooling resources for the good of the group as a whole.
   b.   the elites and the lower class were of different origins and therefore had no strong connections through kinship, descent, or marriage.
   c.   there is a clear fit between capitalist development schemes and corporate descent-group social organization.
   d.   it took into account the inevitability of native forms of social organization breaking down into nuclear family organization, impersonality, and alienation.
   e.   the educated members of Malagasy society are those who have struggled to fend for themselves, and therefore brought an innovative kind of independence to the project.

20.   Which of the following is *not* a criticism of applied anthropology projects in Latin America?

   a.   They overlook the relationship between local problems and the international circumstances that perpetuate the problems.
   b.   They misapply the concept of cultural relativism.
   c.   They assume that change must be accomplished through the diffusion of skills introduced by more advanced countries, like the United States.
   d.   They overlook major social and economic inequities.
   e.   They have under-utilized the multiple causation theory.

21.   In what part of Brazil was the sisal scheme introduced?

   a.   the llanos
   b.   the sertão
   c.   the lomas
   d.   the altiplano
   e.   the coast

22. Which of the following is *not* a valid criticism of many economic development projects?

    a. They often pay more attention to physical than to social features of the project setting.
    b. Project planners have no real interest in helping peasants.
    c. Project personnel too rarely visit and talk with people affected by the project.
    d. They do not take into account the relationship between population density and economy.
    e. People who know nothing about the area affected by the project have often done most or all of its planning, execution, and evaluation.

23. The Malagasy development program illustrates the importance of

    a. the local government's commitment to improving the lives of its citizens.
    b. replacing subsistence farming with a viable cash crop.
    c. replacing outdated traditional techniques of irrigation.
    d. breaking down corporate descent groups, which are too independent and interfere with development.
    e. all of the above

24. What term refers to the tendency to view less-developed countries as more alike than they are?

    a. cultural relativism
    b. ethnobias
    c. over-innovation
    d. under-differentiation
    e. intervention philosophy

25. What should all development projects aim to accomplish?

    a. To promote change, but not over-innovation.
    b. To preserve local systems, while working to make them better.
    c. To respect local traditions.
    d. To draw models of development from indigenous practices.
    e. all of the above

ESSAY QUESTIONS

26. Any of the above multiple choice questions may be converted to an essay question by requiring students to choose the correct answer and justify their selection in essay form. Such justifications should include explanations as to why the chosen answer is correct and why those responses not chosen are incorrect.

27. What were some of the major differences between British and French colonial policies?

28. What are some the lasting of effects of colonialism in the world today? How have ethnic, political, and religious identities been altered by colonialism?

29. What does it mean to say that an economic development project is culturally compatible? What are the advantages of ensuring that projects are culturally compatible?

30. Is there such a thing as disinterested development? How does your answer inform the discussion of how and whether or not anthropologists should help development projects?

31. What is the fallacy of under-differentiation? What are some possible alternatives to it?

32.   What is your position about the appropriate relationship between anthropologists and clients, including government agencies? What is your opinion of the statement of ethics issued by the American Anthropological Association? Defend your answer.

33.   Using material in this and previous chapters, identify impediments to development in Third World nations, discussing at least two cases. Is it possible to generalize about the relationships among sociocultural, political, and economic forms and their potentiality for development? Discuss.

34.   Discussing either Brazil or Java, comment on the value of an independent anthropological study of economic development programs with unanticipated results.

35.   What is the difference between having an anthropologist consult on a development project and having someone who is native to the project area consult. After all, would not a native consultant be better able to culturally "fine tune" the project?

36.   What traditional anthropological research methodologies are best suited to contributing to development work? Why?

TRUE OR FALSE QUESTIONS

37. True or **False**   Colonialism refers to the solicitation by peripheral countries for political and financial assistance from core nations.

38. **True** or False   Business interests were the driving forces behind British colonialism.

39. True or **False**   The conference of Berlin divided South America among several European nations.

40. **True** or False   The British notion of "white man's burden" is similar to the French concept of "mission civilisatrice" in that both were racist ideologies that were used to justify the colonial efforts of their respective country.

41. **True** or False   French colonial strategies incorporated both direct and indirect rule.

42. **True** or False   Many of the political, linguistic, religious, and economic distinctions between the countries of West Africa today are artifacts of colonialism.

43. True or **False**   Belgian colonial administrators were careful to use culturally significant differences to distinguish between the Hutus and Tutsis.

44. True or **False**   Settler post-colonies are characterized by large native populations that have displaced the former European colonists forcing them to settle in their country of origin.

45. **True** or False   Central to most intervention philosophies is the idea that modern, western, industrialization represents the way of life that all groups are trying to reach.

46. **True** or False   Anthropologists researching the effects of development at the local level are able to identify inadequacies that are often not detectable to economists working at the national and global level.

47. True or **False**   Development anthropology refers to the branch of anthropology that uses data collected from the local level to develop theories about the development of culture through time.

48. True or **False**   In Brazil, the transition from subsistence farming to cash cropping sisal in the *sertão* led to clearing huge regions of the rainforest.

49. **True** or False   The green revolution in Java involved the introduction of high-yield varieties of wheat, maize, and rice to rural communities.

50. **True** or False   Stoler argues that the green revolution in Java helped raise the status of landholding women.

51. True or **False**   Although the green revolution has some problems, in the end it alleviate the poverty in Indonesia.

52. True or **False**   Most of the development projects profiled by Kottak increased equity within the target communities.

53. True or **False**   Culturally compatible economic development is just a politically correct term for colonialism.

54. **True** or False   Over-innovation refers to development strategies that require the target communities adopt major changes to the traditional way of life.

55. **True** or False   Development projects are much more likely to succeed if they are based on traditional social organizations and respond to locally perceived needs.

56. True or **False**   The example of postcolonial development in Madagascar demonstrates that descent group organization represents a considerable obstruction for economic development.

CHAPTER 23

CULTURAL EXCHANGE AND SURVIVAL

CHAPTER OUTLINE

I. Contact and Domination

    A. The increased contact among cultures has created increased possibilities for the domination of one group by another, through various means.

    B. Development and Environmentalism
        1. Currently, domination comes most frequently in the form of core-based multinational corporations causing economic change in Third World cultures.
        2. It is noted that even well intentioned interference (such as the environmentalist movement) may be treated as a form of cultural domination by subject populations.
        3. Two sources of culture clash:
            a. When *development threatens indigenous peoples and their environments* (e.g., Brazil and New Guinea).
            b. When *external relations threaten indigenous peoples* (e.g., Madagascar, where sweeping international environmental regulations affect traditional subsistence life-ways).

    C. Religious Change
        1. Indiana Jones is symbol of western domination of all cultural aspects based upon specialized technological efficiency.
        2. Religious homogenization is a technique frequently used by states trying to subdue groups encompassed by their borders.

    D. Interesting Issues: Voices of the Rainforest
        1. International development of oil resources in the rainforest of Papua-New Guinea threatens to destroy the ecosystem in which groups like the Kaluli have their cultural base.
        2. An international case is being made to preserve the music of the Kaluli (which is interactive with the natural environment), and, by extension, the environment by promoting that music as a form of world music that is endangered.

II. Resistance and Survival

    A. Variation within Systems of Domination
        1. Scott (1990) differentiates between public and hidden transcripts of culturally and politically oppressed peoples.
            a. Public transcript refers to the open, public interactions between dominators and the oppressed.
            b. Hidden transcript refers to the critique of power that goes on offstage, where the dominators cannot see it.
        2. Gramsci's (1971) notion of hegemony applies to a politically hierarchical system wherein in the dominant ideology of the elites has been internalized by members of the lower classes.
        3. Bourdieu (1977) and Foucault (1979) argue that it is much easier to control people's minds than try to control their bodies.

    B. Weapons of the Weak
        1. As James Scott's (1990) work on Malay peasants suggests, oppressed groups may use subtle, non-confrontational methods to resist various forms of domination.

2. Examples of antihegemonic discourse include rituals (e.g., Carnaval), and folk literature.
3. Resistance is more likely to be public when the oppressed come together in groups (hence the anti-assembly laws of the antebellum South).

C. Cultural Imperialism
  1. Cultural imperialism refers to the spread of one culture at the expense of others usually because of differential economic or political influence.
  2. While mass media and related technology have contributed to the erosion of local cultures, they are increasingly being used as media for the outward diffusion of local cultures (e.g., television in Brazil).

D. In the News: Using Modern Technology to Preserve Linguistic and Cultural Diversity.
  1. Global linguistic diversity seems to be falling at an increasing rate.
  2. Some anthropologists are teaching native speakers of endangered languages to document their languages by way of a computer program that encodes speech.

III. Making and Remaking Culture

A. A text is defined as something that is creatively read, interpreted, and assigned meaning by each person who receives it.
  1. Readers of a text all derive their own meanings and feelings, which may be different from what the creators of the text intended.
  2. The hegemonic reading refers to the reading or meaning that the creators of a text intended.

B. Popular Culture
  1. According to Fiske (1989), each individual's use of popular culture is a creative act.
  2. Popular culture can be used to express resistance.

C. Indigenizing Popular Culture
  1. Cultural forms exported from one culture to another do not necessarily carry the same meaning from the former context to the latter context.
  2. Aboriginal interpretations of the movie, *Rambo*, demonstrate that meaning can be produced *from* a text, not *by* a text.
  3. Appadurai's analysis of Philippine indigenization of some American music forms demonstrates the uniqueness of the indigenized form.

D. A World System of Images
  1. Mass media can spread and create national and ethnic identities.
  2. Cross-cultural studies show that locally produced television shows are preferred to foreign imports.
  3. Mass media plays an important role in maintaining ethnic and national identities among people who lead transnational lives.

E. Transnational Culture of Consumption
  1. As with mass media, the flow of capital has become decentralized, carrying with it the cultural influences of many different sources (e.g., the United States, Japan, Britain, Canada, Germany, the Netherlands).
  2. Migrant labor also contributes to cultural diffusion.

IV. Linkages

A. In People in Motion, Kottak discusses how the diaspora has become an increasingly important cultural identity base, as a result of population migration and displacement.

287

B. Postmodernism

　　1. Postmodernity describes our time and situation--today's world in flux, these people on the move who have learned to manage multiple identities depending on place and context.

　　2. Postmodern refers the collapsing of old distinctions, rules, canons, and the like.

　　3. Postmodernism (derived from the architectural style) refers the theoretical assertion and acceptance of multiple forms of rightness, in contradistinction to modernism, which was based on the assumed supremacy of Western technology and values.

　　4. *Globalization* refers to the increasing connectedness of the world and its peoples.

　　5. With this connectedness, however, come new bases for identities (e.g., the Panindian identity growing among formerly disparate tribes).

C. Postmodern Moments refers to a series of personal examples bearing out global linkages.

LECTURE TOPICS

1.　Concepts like hegemony, discourse, and resistance are founded in a sense of opposition that is likely to be overlooked by students brought up in America, where the prevailing ideology is one of value-free status positions. Moreover, this sense of opposition differentiates these concepts from other anthropological constructions of social stratification. Therefore, you might want to provide your students with a brief history of the development of these ideas and their incorporation into anthropology.

2.　The history of Native Americans is likely already somewhat familiar to your students. Some specific case studies (Ghost Dance, present-day causes such as land claim cases and the public representation of Indians) should be both well-documented and (from the students' perspective) approachable. Pertinent selections from Native American literature or even commercial films (e.g. *Powwow Highway, Thunderheart*) are a pleasant way to supplement this.

3.　Discuss the importance of representation (possibly in connection with Scott's notions of hidden and public texts). An interesting way to do this is to discuss current public perceptions of Martin Luther King (who has been turned into textbook fodder) as compared to Malcolm X (who is now perceived by many as the more dynamic of the two leaders). That much of what these two men said publicly was directed at each other, as well as at various other audiences has been overlooked in the standardized depictions of today.

SUGGESTED FILMS

Natives: Immigrant Bashing on the Border

video　1991　28 min　b&w

Documentary on the xenophobia of some Americans living on the U.S.-Mexican border. Reacting to the influx of undocumented aliens, whom they believe are draining community resources and committing crimes, they are forming nativistic organizations in an attempt to keep potential immigrants out. Produced at the Center for Visual Anthropology, by Jess Lerner, Scott Sterling, and The University of Southern California. Published by Filmmakers Library, New York, New York, 1991.

In Her Own Time

video 1986 color 59 min
Focuses on cultural anthropologist Barbara Meyerhoff's study of the community of Hasidic Jews in Los Angeles' Fairfax Neighborhood. Tells also how, after exhausting medical treatment for cancer, she found strength among the traditions, faith, and caring of these orthodox Jews. Produced at the Center for Visual Anthropology by Vikram Jayanti and Lynn Littman. Published by Direct Cinema, Los Angeles, California, 1986.

Trobriand Cricket: An Ingenious Response to Colonialism

16mm 1976 55 min
An ethnographic documentary about cultural creativity among the Trobriand Islanders of Papua-New Guinea. Shows how the Trobrianders have taken the very controlled game of British cricket, first introduced by missionaries, and changed it into an outlet for mock warfare and inter-village competition, political reputation building among leaders, erotic dancing and chanting, and riotous fun. The game is a gigantic message about people's attitudes, experiences, and responses under colonialism.

Powwow Highway

video (commercial film) 91 min 1988
Based upon the novel by David Seals. Philbert, a Cheyenne Indian from Montana, goes on a vision quest to find enlightenment. After he meets Buddy Red Bow, a fiery Indian activist, things really start to happen. The film is set in the 1970's and deals with events at Pine Ridge Reservation, where the inhabitants were divided into pro-federal government and activist Native American rights factions. A Handmade Films production; director: Jonathan Stewart. Distributed by Cannon Video, 1989, c1988.

O Povo Organizado [The People Organized]

16mm 1976 color 67 min
Surveys Mozambique's 10-year guerrilla war against Portuguese colonialism, the impact of the April 25, 1974 coup in Portugal, and the declaration of independence on June 25, 1975. Depicts the continuing nature of social revolution; the contradictions inherent in the assumption of power by the revolutionary organization, Frelimo; the difficulties encountered in reshaping the economic system; and how colonialism and imperialism have affected the lives of the people. Director: Robert Van Lierop. Published by Berkeley CA: Tricontinental Films, c1976. (Sequel to *A Luta Continua*--the struggle continues.)

First Contact

16mm 1983 color and b&w 54 min
This renowned film is an anthropological study of the relationships of whites and aborigines in Papua New Guinea. Includes original footage of the first encounter between the groups during the 1930s gold rush days and interviews with some of the same individuals fifty years later. Arundel Productions (Bob Connolly and Robin Anderson). Published by New York: Filmmakers Library, 1983.

MULTIPLE CHOICE QUESTIONS

1. What term refers to changes that result when groups come into continuous firsthand contact?

    a.   acculturation
    b.   hegemony
    c.   enculturation
    d.   diffusion
    e.   colonialism

2. Unlike acculturation, diffusion

    a.   does not include westernization
    b.   requires firsthand contact
    c.   can occur without firsthand contact
    d.   has ceased in the modern world
    e.   does not involve cultural borrowing

3. What term can be used to refer to members of a diaspora who consider themselves to be a recognizable social group?

    a.   a primordial horde
    b.   a clan
    c.   a moiety
    d.   a race
    e.   an imagined community

4. Westernization is a form of what kind of cultural change?

    a.   exodus
    b.   imperialism
    c.   acculturation
    d.   enculturation
    e.   migration

5. Which of the following is *not* true of postmodernism?

    a.   It originally described a style and movement in architecture
    b.   It rejects rules, geometric order, and austerity
    c.   It has a clear and functional design or structure
    d.   It draws on a diversity of styles from different times and places
    e.   It extends "value" well beyond classic, elite, and Western cultural forms

6. What is the term for our contemporary world in flux, with people on-the-move, in which established groups, boundaries, identities, contrasts, and standards are reaching out and breaking down?

    a.   postmodernity
    b.   postmodernism
    c.   diaspora
    d.   hegemony
    e.   globalization

7. Which of the following would be considered an agent of the world system?

    a.   an Indian cloth merchant in Kenya
    b.   a Chinese grocer in Tanzania
    c.   a Czech hockey player in the NHL
    d.   a Peace Corps volunteer in Ethiopia
    e.   **all of the above**

8. Which of the following statements about environmentalism is *not* true?

    a.   **It began in the Third World, in response to the destruction of tropical forests**
    b.   Brazilians complain that First World moralists preach about global needs and saving the Amazon after having destroyed their own forests for First World economic growth
    c.   Much of the non-Western world sees western ecological morality as yet another imperialist message
    d.   Often it is an intervention philosophy
    e.   Its advocates can be as ethnocentric as are advocates of development

9. What is one of the main reasons for deforestation?

    a.   global warming
    b.   globalization
    c.   **commercial expansion**
    d.   biodiversity
    e.   the ozone layer

10. Indigenous music from Papua-New Guinea

    a.   has been influenced by the music of the Grateful Dead
    b.   **incorporates the sounds of birds and frogs**
    c.   has been abandoned because of acculturation
    d.   has become more popular than American music in South America
    e.   uses melodies, but no rhythms

11. The Handsome Lake religion _____.

    a.   led the Iroquois Indians to reject European farming techniques
    b.   was compatible with the Iroquois' stress on female over male labor
    c.   led the Iroquois to adopt communal longhouses
    d.   **led the Iroquois to reject matrilineal descent groups for nuclear family organization**
    e.   involved no ethnocide

12. Which of the following statements about Sudan is true?

    a.   It has no more tribal religions, because every one has converted to either Christianity or Islam
    b.   It is the largest country in Papua-New Guinea
    c.   **It has adopted a policy of cultural imperialism**
    d.   It has little ethnic or religious diversity
    e.   It developed cargo cults based on jihads and sudan chairs

13. What term refers to the rapid spread or advance of one culture at the expense of others, or its imposition on other cultures?

   a. diasporation
   b. symbolic domination
   c. cultural imperialism
   d. conquest
   e. colonialism

14. What term refers to the public interactions between dominators and the oppressed?

   a. hegemony
   b. public transcript
   c. symbolic capital
   d. collegiality
   e. hidden transcripts

15. What term refers to the critique of power by the oppressed that goes on offstage where the power holders cannot see it?

   a. hegemony
   b. texts
   c. symbolic capital
   d. collegiality
   e. hidden transcripts

16. What is a stratified social order in which subordinates comply with domination by internalizing the dominators' values and accepting their domination as natural?

   a. colonialism
   b. imperialism
   c. ethnocide
   d. hegemony
   e. conquest

17. What term is used to refer to the reading or meaning of a "text" that the creators intended, or the one the elites consider to be the intended or correct meaning?

   a. correct reading
   b. transtextual reading
   c. postmodern meaning
   d. intertextual meaning
   e. hegemonic reading

18. Systems of domination

   a. are political rather than cultural or religious
   b. have both private and public dimensions
   c. are rarely questioned "offstage"
   d. require subordinates, but not dominants, to adopt certain habitual behavior patterns
   e. all of the above

19. Where do hidden transcripts tend to be publicly expressed?

    a. in chance meetings between subordinates and dominants
    b. at small family gatherings
    c. **at festivals and markets**
    d. in words rather than deeds
    e. in deeds rather than words

20. What term refers to the blurring and breakdown of established canons (rules, standards), categories, distinctions, and boundaries?

    a. chaos
    b. entropy
    c. **postmodern**
    d. agoraphobia
    e. diaspora

21. Which of the following was *not* a form of resistance used by slaves in the American South?

    a. They developed their own popular culture
    b. They developed their own linguistic codes
    c. sabotage
    d. They established free communities in isolated areas
    e. **They used of Carnaval as a social critique**

22. Which of the following is a way that dominators can discourage or curb resistance?

    a. Get subordinates to assemble
    b. Provide settings where subordinates can express their private transcript
    c. **Get subordinates to internalize a dominant ideology**
    d. Stress stories that celebrate freedom--thus providing an outlet for pent-up frustrations
    e. all of the above

23. Usual weapons of the weak, in resisting domination

    a. are major acts of full-scale resistance
    b. are direct
    c. include rioting, demonstrating, and protesting
    d. **tend to avoid direct confrontation**
    e. are never effective

24. Which of the following statements about television is true?

    a. Studies show that people reject its messages without much processing or reinterpretation
    b. **It plays a role in allowing social groups to express themselves and in disseminating local cultures**
    c. It is especially favored by the French because of its role in promoting the exposing the French to other cultures
    d. It is more popular in urban than in rural areas
    e. It plays no "top-down" role

25. What term refers to a cultural event, such as a ritual, or even a historical moment, such as the Rodney King beating, that becomes generally known and subject to various interpretations and understandings?

    a.   **a text**
    b.   a discourse
    c.   a theme
    d.   a subject
    e.   an object

26. Meaning is

    a.   imposed by a text
    b.   **locally manufactured**
    c.   inherent in a text
    d.   produced by a text, not from it
    e.   all of the above

27. How did the Native Australians "read" the movie *Rambo*

    a.   They saw Rambo as an imperialist agent.
    b.   They saw Rambo as a Communist spy.
    c.   They assigned Rambo to the kangaroo clan.
    d.   **They created tribal ties and kin links between Rambo and the prisoners he was rescuing.**
    e.   They "creatively opposed" the film as a form of resistance to the world system.

28. Who are responsible for the changing nature of Third World economies?

    a.   **multinational corporations**
    b.   the governments of core nations
    c.   television programs created in the core
    d.   the governments of nations on the periphery
    e.   indigenous movements

29. Which of the following is *not* an agent of the modern world system?

    a.   CEO of a multinational corporation
    b.   a rug merchant in Istanbul
    c.   an anthropologist
    d.   a Peace Corp volunteer in Mexico
    e.   **all of the above are agents**

30. How is Catholicism often seen in Latin America?

    a.   as the religion of men
    b.   as a public transcript
    c.   as a hidden transcript
    d.   **as the religion of women**
    e.   as a cargo cult

31.   According to Bourdieu and Foucault, what is the most effective way to dominate people?

        a.   by controlling their bodies
        b.   by controlling their government
        c.   by controlling their economy
        d.   **by controlling their minds**
        e.   by controlling their industry

32.   Which of the following is a way to curb resistance?

        a.   get subordinates to internalize the dominant ideology
        b.   let subordinates think they will eventually gain power
        c.   solitary confinement
        d.   isolate subordinates
        e.   **all of the above**

33.   In medieval Europe, what was the main public place where the dominant ideology was questioned?

        a.   the castle
        b.   **the market**
        c.   the home
        d.   the docks
        e.   the factories

34.   What role do modern technology and mass media play as agents of cultural imperialism?

        a.   They are erasing cultural differences
        b.   They allow local cultures to express themselves
        c.   They help stimulate local activities
        d.   They help spread "topdown" institutions
        e.   **all of the above**

35.   Which of the following can be viewed as a text?

        a.   Carnaval
        b.   the movie *Star Wars*
        c.   soap operas
        d.   the Bible
        e.   **all of the above**

ESSAY QUESTIONS

36.   Compare the theoretical constructs of "culture" and "hegemony." How do they differ? How are they similar? Are these constructs mutually exclusive?

37.   Explain the differences between acculturation and diffusion, citing examples of each.

38.   What is the difference between postmodernity and postmodernism? How has postmodernity affected the units of anthropological study?

39.   Discuss some of the main strategies that oppressed people use to resist domination. Provide examples indicating times and places in which resistance is expressed.

40.   Explain how cargo cults are related both to traditional social structure and to the expansion of the world capitalist economy.

41. What are some of the arguments for and against the interpretation of the mass media as forms of cultural imperialism?

42. What is a "text," and how does its reading relate to the role of the individual in popular culture?

43. Any of the above multiple choice questions may be converted to an essay question by requiring students to choose the correct answer and justify their selection in essay form. Such justifications should include explanations as to why the chosen answer is correct and why those responses not chosen are incorrect.

TRUE OR FALSE QUESTIONS

44. **True** or False   Acculturation is the forced or voluntary adoption of customs from another culture.

45. **True** or False   One of the problems in the world system today is that many peripheral nations support the predatory enterprises of core corporations that are seeking cheap labor and resources in the periphery.

46. True or **False**   Unlike economic development projects that need to be culturally compatible, external regulation does not need to consider the traditions indigenous communities because the regulations are intended to save the environment.

47. True or **False**   As a vehicle of change, religious proselytizing is a culturally neutral factor.

48. **True** or False   The public transcript refers to the open, public interactions between dominators and resistors.

49. True or **False**   The hidden transcript refers to the mode of armed, hidden resistance called guerilla warfare.

50. True or **False**   According to Gramsci, hegemony refers to the assertion of power that goes on offstage, where the resistors cannot see it.

51. **True** or False   With its costumed anonymity, *Carnaval* is a popular forum for the expression of resistance.

52. True or **False**   In medieval Europe, hegemonic control was most visible in the marketplace, pubs, taverns, and inns.

53. **True** or False   Modern technology play an important role in both facilitating cultural imperialism and resisting it.

54. True or **False**   For anthropologists, a text refers to anything that is codified, fixed, and permanent in a given culture.

55. True or **False**   Popular culture is the politically correct term for the hegemonic cultural standards imposed by the dominators over the resistors.

56. True or **False**   Cultural forces are indigenized when native traditions are presented to and appreciated by the former colonialists who acknowledge these forces as indigenous or native.

57. **True** or False   Mass media can play an important role is constructing and maintaining national and ethnic identities.

58. True or **False**   Programming that is culturally alien tends to out perform native programming when the alien programming comes from the U.S., Great Britain, and France.

59. **True** or False   Forces influencing production and consumption are no longer restricted by national boundaries.

60. **True** or False   Multilocal residence patterns are commonly found in many migrant communities in the U.S.

61. True or **False**   A diaspora refers to the hegemonic policy of dominators to isolate individuals who publicly resist from the rest of the population.

62. **True** or False   Postmodernism refers to the breakdown of traditional categories, standards, and boundaries in favor of a more fluid, context dependent set of identities.

63. **True** or False   Globalization promotes intercultural communication, migration, and commerce, thereby increasing the opportunities for what Kottak calls postmodern moments.

CHAPTER 24

APPLIED ANTHROPOLOGY

CHAPTER OUTLINE

I. Introduction

  A. Applied anthropology refers to the application of anthropological data, perspectives, theory, and methods to identify, assess, and solve social problems.

  B. Anthropologists have held three views about applying anthropology.
  1. The ivory tower view contends that anthropologists should avoid practical matters and focus on research, publication, and teaching.
  2. The schizoid view holds that anthropologists should carry out, but not make or criticize, policy.
  3. The advocacy view argues that since anthropologists are experts on human problems and social change, they should make policy affecting people.
     a. Identify locally perceived needs for change.
     b. Work with those people to design culturally appropriate and socially sensitive change.
     c. Protect local people from harmful development schemes.
  4. Kottak favors advocacy.

  C. Professional anthropologists work for a wide variety of employers: tribal and ethnic associations, governments, nongovernmental organizations (NGOs), etc.
  1. During World War II, anthropologists worked for the U.S. government to study Japanese and German culture "at a distance."
  2. Malinowski advocated working with the British Empire to study indigenous land tenure to determine how much land should be left to the natives and how much the empire could seize.

II. Academic and Applied Anthropology

  A. After World War II, the baby boom fueled the growth of the American educational system and anthropology along with it starting the era of academic anthropology.

  B. Applied anthropology began to grow in the 1970s as anthropologists found jobs with international organizations, governments, businesses, hospitals, and schools.

III. Theory and Practice

  A. Like other disciplines, anthropology boomed immediately after the second World War, and again in the sixties as the strengths of the discipline fit with prevailing social interests, which began a turn toward practical applications.

  B. Anthropology's ethnographic method, holism, and systemic perspective make it uniquely valuable in application to social problems.

  C. Applied anthropologists are more likely to focus on a local, grass roots perspective in approaching a problem than to consult with officials and experts.

D. Applied Anthropology and the Subdisciplines
  1. Cultural resource management refers to excavations done to gather as much data as possible from sites threatened by construction or other projects.
  2. Cultural anthropologists frequently consult with other professionals, to facilitate the extension of health, economic, and other services to various populations.

E. In the News: The Anthropology of a Massacre
  1. This article describes the work of forensic and archaeological anthropologists to document the massacre of 376 villagers in Guatemala, 17 years after it happened.
  2. The anthropologists excavated the village and the mass graves to collect evidence of the massacre.

IV. Anthropology and Education

  A. In particular, anthropology has helped facilitate the accommodation of cultural differences in classroom settings.

  B. Examples include: English as a second language taught to Spanish-speaking students; different, culturally based reactions to various pedagogical techniques, the application of linguistic relativism in the classroom to BEV.

V. Urban Anthropology

  A. Human populations are becoming increasingly urban.

  B. Urban versus Rural
  1. Robert Redfield was an early student of the differences between the rural and urban contexts.
  2. Various instances of urban social forms are given as examples, African urban (Kampala, Uganda) social networks in particular.

VI. Medical Anthropology

  A. Medical anthropology is both academic (theoretical) and applied (practical).
  1. Medical anthropology is the study of disease and illness in their sociocultural context.
  2. Disease is a scientifically defined ailment.
  3. Illness is an ailment, as experienced and perceived by the sufferer.

  B. The spread of certain diseases, like malaria and schistosomiasis have been associated with population growth and economic development.

  C. There are three basic theories about the causes of illnesses.
  1. Personalistic disease theories blame illness on agents such as sorcerers, witches, ghosts, or ancestral spirits.
  2. Naturalistic disease theories explain illness in impersonal terms (e.g. Western biomedicine).
  3. Emotionalistic disease theories assume emotional experiences cause illness (e.g., *susto* among Latino populations).

  E. Health-care Systems
  1. All societies have health-care systems.
  2. Health-care systems consist of beliefs, customs, specialists, and techniques aimed at ensuring health and preventing, diagnosing, and treating illness.

F. Health-care Specialists
   1. All cultures have health-care specialists (e.g. curers, shaman, and doctors).
   2. Health-care specialists emerge through a culturally defined process of selection and training.

G. Lessons from Non-Western Medicine
   1. Non-western systems of medicine are often more successful at treating mental illness than Western medicine.
   2. Non-western systems of medicine often explain mental illnesses by causes that are easier to identify and combat.
   3. Non-western systems of medicine diagnose and treat the mentally ill in cohesive groups with full support of their kin.

H. Western Medicine
   1. Despite its advances, Western medicine is not without its problems.
      a. Over prescription of drugs and tranquilizers
      b. Unnecessary surgery
      c. Impersonality and inequality of the patient-physician relationship
      d. Overuse of antibiotics
   2. Biomedicine surpasses non-Western medicine in many ways.
      a. Thousands of effective drugs
      b. Preventive health care
      c. Surgery

I. Medical Development
   1. Like economic development, medical development must fit into local systems of heath care.
   2. Medical anthropologists can serve as cultural interpreters between local systems and Western medicine.

VII. Anthropology and Business

   A. Through studying institutions such as businesses, anthropologists have identified the process of microenculturation, through which people in finite systems learn their specific roles.

   B. More recently, cross-cultural studies of business practices has become more important (e.g. the study of Japanese business techniques).

VIII. Careers in Anthropology

   A. Because of its breadth, a degree in anthropology may provide a flexible basis for many different careers (with appropriate planning).

   B. In the News
   Hot Asset in Corporate: Anthropology Degrees
   1. This article discusses how people with anthropology degrees are finding employment in business due to the importance of observing how consumers choose and use products.
   2. Companies are turning more frequently to anthropologists and ethnographers to gather data about the preferences of consumers.

   C. Other fields, such as business, have begun to recognize the worth of such anthropological concepts as microcultures.

   D. Anthropologists work professionally as consultants to indigenous groups at risk from external systems.

E. Other employers of anthropologists include: USAID, USDA, the World Bank, private voluntary organizations, etc.

F. Beyond the Classroom: A Forensic Anthropology Analysis of Human Skeletal Remains
   1. Beau Goldstein conducted forensic anthropologic analyses on skeletons from the University of South Florida's Department of Anatomy to test certain techniques and to demonstrate the amount of variation that exists in skeletal remains.
   2. Using a computer program to analyze the data he collected from the skeletons, he was able to determine that the skeletons all came from the same population that he believes originated in India.

IX. The Continuance of Diversity

A. Anthropology has a crucial role to play in promoting a more humanistic vision of social change, one that respects the value of cultural diversity.

B. The existence of anthropology is itself a tribute to the continuing need to understand social and cultural similarities and differences.

LECTURE TOPICS

1.   List the many ways in which anthropologists are personally involved in practical matters. Give examples of how they have made a difference.

2.   Discuss attitudes toward the Third World, both popular attitudes and those of social scientists. The work of Batalla can be used as the basis for this discussion.

3.   Describe the sequence of ethnic assimilation in the United States and its relationship to crime. Discuss the case of African-Americans and how they fit, or do not fit, into the typical sequence.

4.   An interventionist way of thinking is still relatively strong among Americans, and there is a tendency to view foreign aid and development projects without criticism (aside from objections over money not spent at home). Conversely, there is also an opposing-but-also-prevalent mindset that condemns development of any kind. Compare two development projects (a "good" one and a "bad" one) in order to carry the point that objections and admiration are best directed at actual practice, and to show the practical value of an anthropological perspective.

SUGGESTED FILMS

Land Where the Blues Began

59 min   1979   color
Attempts to capture the local color and flavor of the culture that produced the blues. Visits the Mississippi hill country, talking with performers and filming performances of this local style that became a universal favorite. Points out ancient roles played by the blues as work songs or as appeals for feminine company. From the University of Illinois Film and Video Center.

Spite (N'Kpiti)

55 min   1984   color
Films some of the ministrations of prophet-healer Sebim Odjo, who combines Moslem, Christian and traditional African beliefs in his healing ceremonies. Disease is thought to be of human origin, caused by rancor, jealousy, evil spirits, witchcraft, and lies. The water cure in Spite is based on the premise that if you have the burden of spite on your heart, you are an easy prey to illness, emotion, and "creatures that inhabit the bush!" From the University of Illinois Film and Video Center.

MULTIPLE CHOICE QUESTIONS

1.   Outside of colleges and universities, where are most anthropologists employed?

      a.   the United States government
      b.   the commercial sector
      c.   the armed forces
      d.   the European Economic Community
      e.   nongovernmental organizations

2.   According to Kottak, anthropological theory _____.

      a.   is generally considered a drawback to practice because it is mainly based on work among tribal societies
      b.   until 1978, formally forbade anthropologists from doing applied work
      c.   is now read widely throughout the commercial sector of Western economies
      d.   promotes a systemic perspective that aids the successful implementation of development projects
      e.   all of the above

3.   What is the most valuable and distinctive tool of the applied anthropologist?

      a.   the ethnographic research method
      b.   knowledge of genetics
      c.   familiarity with farming techniques
      d.   statistical expertise
      e.   teaching ability

4.   Which of the following is an example of cultural resource management?

      a.   Any archaeological work done in a core nation-state
      b.   The emergency excavation and cataloging of a site that is about to be destroyed by a new highway
      c.   Any archaeology done in a periphery nation-state
      d.   Archaeology sponsored by indigenous peoples
      e.   A museum returning archaeological finds to the indigenous peoples whose ancestors produced the artifacts

5.   What term is synonymous with applied anthropologists?

      a.   working anthropologists
      b.   active anthropologists
      c.   functioning anthropologists
      d.   practicing anthropologists
      e.   performing anthropologists

6.   Which of the following is a procedure unique to the applied anthropologist?

    a.   They enter the affected communities and talk with villagers
    b.   They gather government statistics
    c.   They consult project managers
    d.   They consult government officials and other experts
    e.   They promote social change

7.   According to the systemic perspective on change _____.

    a.   social changes can be forced to occur in predictable ways
    b.   change programs have multiple consequences, some unintended
    c.   harmful effects of planned change can be prevented in most cases
    d.   computers are essential to planning of projects
    e.   all of the above

8.   Education-school programs designed to enhance teachers' understanding of cultural differences _____.

    a.   have usually made Indian children feel better, since teachers mention their cultural heritage
    b.   were the first test cases of applied anthropology
    c.   have sometimes led to ethnic stereotyping
    d.   have made Indians feel closer to their classmates
    e.   all of the above

9.   The systemic perspective promoted by anthropological theory and practice helps avoid

    a.   savage archaeology
    b.   unintended consequences
    c.   naturalistic theories of disease causation
    d.   ethnic perspectives
    e.   inappropriate eruptions of tribal sentiment, such as Samoan *matai*

10.   What did Malinowski include in his definition of applied anthropology?

    a.   Anthropologists should actively participate in the politics of colonialism
    b.   Anthropologists should work actively to oppose colonialism
    c.   Anthropologists should just ignore colonial projects
    d.   Anthropologists should avoid politics by concentrating on facts and processes
    e.   Anthropologists should avoid any contact with an imperial government

11.   What is the postwar baby boom of the late 1940s and 1950s responsible for?

    a.   It fueled the general expansion of the American educational system, including academic anthropology.
    b.   It promoted renewed interest in applied anthropology during the 1950s and 1960s.
    c.   It brought anthropology into most high school curricula.
    d.   It produced a new interest in ethnic diversity.
    e.   It worked to shrink the world system.

12. Where are most anthropologists employed today?

   a.   the business sector
   b.   international organizations
   c.   universities and colleges
   d.   NGO's
   e.   government

13. Who was studied "at a distance" during the 1940s?

   a.   Germany and Japan
   b.   the Yanomami and Betsileo
   c.   India and Madagascar
   d.   Canada and Mexico
   e.   Brazil and Indonesia

14. According to the results of cross-cultural study, which of the following is *not* culturally constructed?

   a.   perceptions of good and bad health
   b.   gender
   c.   kinship
   d.   average intellectual capacity
   e.   sexuality

15. What does Robert Redfield argue about the relations between urban and rural communities?

   a.   Peasants were culturally isolated from cities
   b.   Cities were centers from which cultural innovations are spread to rural and tribal areas
   c.   Innovation tends to move from rural to urban areas
   d.   There are so many connections between rural and urban areas that it is not useful to distinguish between the two, within one cultural context
   e.   Urban centers have more in common with each other, even across national boundaries, than they do with rural areas in the same country

16. What is the Latin American illness caused by fright?

   a.   *latah*
   b.   *jai alai*
   c.   *susto*
   d.   *terrorismo*
   e.   *coronario*

17. Shamans and other magico-religious specialists are effective curers with regard to what kind of disease theory?

   a.   emotionalistic
   b.   personalistic
   c.   naturalistic
   d.   ritualistic
   e.   scientific

18. What term refers to the beliefs, customs, specialists, and techniques aimed at ensuring health and curing illness?

   a. a disease theory
   b. medical anthropology
   c. health-care system
   d. shaman
   e. psychosemantics

19. What is a disease?

   a. a consequence of foraging
   b. an artificial product of biomedicine
   c. a scientifically described health threat
   d. a health problem, as it is experienced by the one affected
   e. all of the above

20. What is an illness?

   a. a nonexistent ailment; only "diseases" are real
   b. an artificial product of biomedicine
   c. a scientifically described health threat
   d. a purely psychosomatic problem
   e. a health problem as it is experienced by the one affected

21. What did Hill-Burnett's study of a Midwestern American urban school discover about Puerto Rican seventh graders?

   a. They came from a background that placed less value on education than did that of white students
   b. They had parents who did not value achievement
   c. They benefited from the "English as a foreign language" program
   d. They generally learned to speak fluent B.E.V. by the time they reached seventh grade
   e. Puerto Rican students' education was being affected by their teachers' misconceptions

22. What kind of disease theory would attribute a person's disease is to the effects of someone's "evil eye?"

   a. a personalistic disease theory
   b. a naturalistic disease theory
   c. a biomedical disease theory
   d. a indigenous disease theory
   e. a tribal disease theory

23. Anthropology may help the progress of education by enabling educators to avoid

   a. ethnic stereotyping
   b. sociolinguistic discrimination
   c. incorrect application of labels (for example, "learning impaired")
   d. indiscriminate assignment of nonnative speakers of English to the same classrooms as children with "behavior problems"
   e. all of the above

24. In the text, what is the suggested solution for sociolinguistic discrimination?

    a. Black children should be allowed to speak and write BEV in the classroom.
    b. Black students should be sent to separate classrooms where only BEV is spoken.
    c. Teachers should be taught BEV with subsequent instruction being done in SE and BEV according to the percentage of speakers of each dialect in the class.
    d. Teachers should be educated about linguistic and cultural differences.
    e. B.E.V. should be taught as a foreign language in schools.

25. The example of the Samoan *matai* system being used when a policeman in Los Angeles killed two Samoans shows _____.

    a. that primitives do not stop being primitive, even in big cities
    b. that non-Western immigrants have difficulty adjusting to modern city life
    c. that tribal peoples use their traditional systems to adapt to urban life
    d. some tribal systems contribute disproportionately to homelessness
    e. that the "clan mentality" is excessively violent in urban settings

26. What is the world's oldest profession besides forager?

    a. curer
    b. chief
    c. prostitute
    d. big man
    e. soldier

27. What is microenculturation?

    a. A condition that exists in large, industrialized states, wherein most of the population has only a small amount of real culture
    b. The process whereby particular roles are learned within a limited social system (for example, a business)
    c. The process whereby enculturation is accomplished by advanced media technology
    d. What happens among foraging and tribal communities of the periphery
    e. Enculturation based on a focused interest, for example reruns of the TV show, *Star Trek*

28. Which of the following can anthropology contribute to business?

    a. ethnographic inquiry
    b. a cross-cultural, multinational perspective
    c. a systemic view
    d. knowledge of the social context of production
    e. all of the above

29. What did Robert Redfield study?

    a. differences between core and periphery nations
    b. differences between health-care systems in foragers and agriculturalists
    c. differences between urban and rural communities
    d. differences between core and semi-periphery nations
    e. differences between illnesses and diseases

30.   Which of the following is a feature of urban life?

        a.   high population density
        b.   geographic mobility
        c.   social heterogeneity
        d.   economic differentiation
        e.   all of the above

31.   Which of the following should be part of an applied anthropological approach to urban programs?

        a.   identify key social groups in the urban context
        b.   elicit wishes from the target community
        c.   translate the needs and desires of the community to funding agencies
        d.   work with the community to ensure that the change is implemented correctly
        e.   all of the above

32.   The use of anthropological findings, concepts, and methods to accomplish a desired end is known as _____.

        a.   applied anthropology
        b.   economic anthropology
        c.   conceptual anthropology
        d.   sociobiology
        e.   participant observation

33.   What did the judge rule in the lawsuit against the Ann Arbor Board of Education?

        a.   The black students were not facing linguistic discrimination
        b.   The school had to begin teaching B.E.V as a foreign language
        c.   The teachers had to attend a full-year course to improve their understanding of B.E.V
        d.   The white students were facing linguistic discrimination because they did not speak B.E.V
        e.   The Ann Arbor School System had to pay the private school tuition for the black students

34.   What does the American Anthropological Association code of ethics state?

        a.   An anthropologist's primary responsibility is to the host government
        b.   An anthropologist's primary responsibility is to the people studied
        c.   Anthropologists should concentrate on value-free research
        d.   Anthropologists should accept funding only from host governments to avoid conflicts of interest
        e.   all of the above

35. Which of the following defines the advocacy position concerning anthropologists' involvement in practical matters?

   a. Anthropologists should avoid practical matters and concentrate on research, publication, and teaching
   b. Anthropologists should collect facts related to carrying out policy and report their findings to the organization that has commissioned the study
   c. Anthropologists should neither make nor criticize policy, because this would be based on their personal value judgments, which should be kept strictly separate from scientific investigation
   d. Anthropologists should take an active role in creating policies affecting human beings
   e. none of the above

36. What term does Kottak use for the attitude that suggests that anthropologists should avoid practical matters and concentrate on teaching, research, and publication?

   a. an etic approach
   b. the schizoid interpretation
   c. ethical anthropology
   d. the ivory tower approach
   e. apathetic anthropology

37. What is the schizoid view of anthropology?

   a. Anthropologists should confine themselves to teaching, research, and publication, avoiding practical and political issues
   b. Anthropologists should help carry out, but not make or criticize policy
   c. Anthropologists should actively seek to influence government positions and policies, but they should participate only in those projects, which they approve
   d. Value judgments and scientific investigation should not be kept separate
   e. all of the above

ESSAY QUESTIONS

38. Discuss the relevance of the ethnographic method for modern society, contemporary problems, and applied anthropology.

39. Indicate the reasons that many anthropologists have turned from academic to applied work.

40. Discuss ways in which anthropology is relevant to business.

41. What is the relevance of anthropological training to employment opportunities abroad?

42. What (if any) is the difference between an anthropologist consulting on a development project in Indonesia last year and an anthropologist conducting research in support of the British colonial government's efforts to subdue African natives in the 1930s?

43. Identify government, international, and private organizations that concern themselves with socioeconomic change abroad and hire anthropologists to help meet their goals.

44. How might a premedical student apply some of the knowledge learned through anthropology as a physician? What is the value of studying the curing and belief systems of patients' ethnic groups?

45. Indicate your career plans if known and describe how you might apply the knowledge learned through introductory anthropology in your future vocation. If you have not yet chosen a career, pick one of the following: economist, engineer diplomat, architect, and elementary schoolteacher. Why is it important to understand the culture and social organization of the people who will be affected by your work?

46. Discuss the major advantages and disadvantages of scientific and traditional medicine (be careful to distinguish between scientific medicine and Western medicine per se).

47. There is considerable debate today over whether or not governments should require schools to provide bilingual education for students (and to what extent this should be carried). Pretend you are an anthropologist who has been asked to provide some guidance on this issue by a school board in a bilingual community. What can you tell these people about the nature of ethnicity, language, and enculturation that will help them solve their problems?

48. Any of the above multiple choice questions may be converted to an essay question by requiring students to choose the correct answer and justify their selection in essay form. Such justifications should include explanations as to why the chosen answer is correct and why those responses not chosen are incorrect.

49. Discuss ethical dilemmas and possible solutions with respect to the kinds of applied anthropology discussed in this chapter.

50. What is the relationship between theory and practice in anthropology? Do you agree that applied anthropology should be recognized as a separate subdiscipline? How is it logically different from the traditional subdisciplines?

51. Discuss the three viewpoints concerning the anthropologist's role in practical affairs, indicating which one you support and why.

52. Define applied anthropology. What distinguishes the old from the new applied anthropology?

TRUE OR FALSE QUESTIONS

53. True or **False**   The Ivory Tower view of applying anthropology asserts that anthropologists should not leave the security of the university to conduct field work.

54. True or **False**   The Schizoid view of applying anthropology asserts that anthropologist should help create policies, but they should not assist in implementing them.

55. **True** or False   During World War II, the U.S. government recruited anthropologists to study Japanese and German cultures.

56. True or **False**   Colonial anthropology is the branch of applied anthropology that assists groups resisting the hegemonic domination of colonial powers.

57. **True** or False   Although its roots extend farther back in time, the real boom for applied anthropology began in the 1970s.

58. **True** or False   Academic and applied anthropology have a symbiotic relationship as theory aids practice and application fuels theory.

59. True or **False**   Cultural resource management (CRM) refers to the efforts of peripheral nations to develop tourism that focuses on a countries cultural heritage, past and present.

60. **True** or False   Sociolinguists and cultural anthropologists studying Puerto Rican communities in the Midwestern U.S. found that Puerto Rican parents valued education more than non-Hispanics.

61. True or **False**   The fastest population growth rates are found in semiperipheral nations of the Second World.

62. **True** or False   In his comparison of rural versus urban communities, Redfield found that cultural innovations spread from urban areas to rural ones.

63. **True** or False   The Samoan community living in Los Angeles uses the *matai* system to deal with modern urban problems.

64. True or **False**   Medical anthropology is strictly and applied field within anthropology.

65. True or **False**   An illness is a scientifically identified health threat caused by a bacterium, virus, fungus, parasite, or other pathogen.

66. True or **False**   Epidemic diseases are commonly found in band-level foraging societies.

67. **True** or False   Biomedicine which aims to link illness to scientifically demonstrated agents that bear no personal malice toward their victims is an example of naturalistic medicine.

68. True or **False**   Health care-systems refer to the nationalized health-care services that only exist in core industrial nations.

69. **True** or False   In many non-Western societies, mental illnesses are diagnosed and treated in cohesive groups with the support of their kin.

70. **True** or False   Non-Western medicine does not maintain a sharp distinction between biological and psychological illnesses.

71. **True** or False   Non-Western medicine treats illnesses symptomatically seeking an immediate cure.

72. True or **False**   A bachelor's degree in anthropology is of little value in the corporate world.

APPENDIX A
AMERICAN POPULAR CULTURE

LECTURE TOPICS

1.   As the end of the millenium approaches, it becomes increasingly apparent that the
      predictions of the end of religiosity (particularly as applied to complex industrialized
      societies) are not coming to pass. The United States has been as heavily touched by the
      growing strength of evangelical Christianity. Also interesting is the spread of religious
      movements such as New Age-ism. These movements and trends throw into question the
      older anthropological explanations of religion (such as cosmological explanation) and
      reveal the fascinatingly complex interplay between religions and history, identity politics,
      nationalism, environmentalism, and the like.

2.   Discuss the conflict between individualism and cooperation in American culture, and its
      present manifestations. Discuss it in terms of more enduring Western values or
      worldview.

3.   Do a structural or content analysis of current or popular television programs and movies.

4.   Discuss the manner in which popular cultural discourse figures ideas of gender.
      Depictions of femininity in movies is fertile ground (the recent spate of successful
      Disney animated movies work well as examples). There is also an increasingly public
      component of the "subaltern" voice in some movies (e.g., Native American consultants
      for films such as *Dances with Wolves* and *Thunderheart*) and television programs. Is
      popular culture now a stronger arbiter of culture than it was in earlier eras?

5.   Get your students to question the existence of an American popular culture. Is there
      anything out there coherent enough to support such a label? If so, does it consist of mass
      media products, common practices and experiences, or something else? An open debate
      on what it means to feel "American" and how one gets that way might be productive.

SUGGESTED FILMS

The gist of Kottak's analysis is the extent to which extremely popular films shape and are shaped
by popular culture, in general. In keeping with this, you may wish to show one of the more
recent blockbusters and compare it to Kottak's analysis of Star Wars in Chapter 20.

APPENDIX B

Test Bank for
Culture Sketches: Case Studies in Anthropology, Second Edition

By Holly Peters-Golden
The University of Michigan

CHAPTER 1
THE AZANDE

1.   Witchcraft among the Azande:

   a.   is particularly efficient because of its long-range capabilities.
   b.   is encapsulated solely within ritual activity, separated from daily life.
   c.   employs an especially rich assemblage of charms and spells.
   d.   includes the role of a shaman, who serves as the 'tattletale'.
   e.   **serves as an explanation for events that others might define as accidental or coincidental.**

2.   Azande women who wished to formalize their relationship into a permanent bond could do so through a ritual ceremony. This formalized union afforded Azande women all of the following benefits *except*:

   a.   **access to sacred burial ground**
   b.   emotional support
   c.   economic support
   d.   a widened trade network
   e.   enhanced status in the community

3.   The best known trickster tales among the Azande describe the adventures of a character named:

   a.   Pasompe
   b.   Caprice
   c.   Pomo
   d.   **Ture**
   e.   Aadent

4.   In recent years, the Zande have been encouraged to participate in industry which is profitable to Europeans. The introduction of money and wage labor has:

   a.   resulted in a dramatic increase of witchcraft accusations
   b.   been successful because it took into account the Azande's desire for flexible living arrangements
   c.   **weakened kin ties, as individuals no longer need to cooperate in working together outside the household**
   d.   had no discernible impact, so far
   e.   encouraged the formation of new tribal hierarchies

CHAPTER 2
THE AZTEC

1.   Which of the following is *not* true of Mexica (Aztec) migration into the Valley of Mexico?

   a.   Their journey began some two hundred years before their eventual arrival.
   b.   Their travel was marked by internal rebellion.
   c.   **The founding of Tenochtitlan in 1325 finally ended the sociopolitical struggles of the Mexica people.**
   d.   Human sacrifices performed along the way may have been a device to eliminate dissenters who did not wish to continue on the journey.
   e.   The Mexica found elaborate states with complex technologies already in place in the Valley of Mexico, but were unwelcome in their attempt to settle among these peoples.

2.   Human sacrifice and cannibalism were central features of Aztec culture. All of the following have been offered as explanations for these practices *except*:

   a.   human sacrifice insured the movement of the sun and thus the continuation of the universe
   b.   eating the flesh of sacrifice victims bestowed divinity on the consumers
   c.   cannibalism was a response to protein deficiency
   d.   **early Aztecs were forced into cannibalism by the Triple Alliance**
   e.   human sacrifice was a method of population control

3.   The Aztec empire was a complex, stratified society. Economic and political differences between classes:

   a.   **influenced land ownership, access to political office, and control over resources**
   b.   began to disappear after the Toltec line of nobility lost power
   c.   rendered upward social mobility impossible
   d.   were notably absent in the judicial system, the only egalitarian feature of the empire
   e.   were eventually replaced by the 'calpulli' system

4.   Spanish conquest of the Aztec empire:

    a.   resulted in increased social stratification
    b.   decimated the native population
    c.   was accomplished largely through the sheer number of Cortes' forces
    d.   revitalized the Mexica economy by doubling the land devoted to maize cultivation
    e.   could not eradicate the centuries-old practices of human sacrifice and cannibalism

CHAPTER 3
THE BASSERI

1.   The Basseri are a pastoral nomadic society in southern Iran. Which of the following is *not* linked to the nomadic lifestyle of the Basseri people?

    a.   The Basseri's constant movement from place to place puts them at a disadvantage in disputes with sedentary neighbors.
    b.   Many necessities, such as flour, must be obtained through trade with other groups.
    c.   The sedentary chiefs serve as mediators between the nomadic tribespeople and the state government.
    d.   Herd animals are the primary source of wealth for the Basseri.
    e.   The individualistic, wandering nature of the Basseri is demonstrated in their inability to travel in stable groups for longer than two or three weeks.

2.   The common occurrence of marriage between close kin in a Basseri camp is owing to:

    a.   fear of outsiders and their cultural influence
    b.   the matrilineal structure of nomadic peoples
    c.   the tenets of the 'il-rah'
    d.   the fact that this bestows special access to trade routes
    e.   the desire to maintain ties which will foster consensus and solidarity in migratory decisions

3.   Maintaining a sense of community among nomadic peoples, such as the Basseri, is uniquely challenging, because:

    a.   there is no single chief with the authority to unite the Basseri as a tribe
    b.   the fact that unanimous decisions are never necessary results in a less cohesive group
    c.   nomadic camps bear no resemblance to the small villages of sedentary village communities
    d.   the maintenance of the camp as a social unit must be negotiated daily
    e.   they have no formal kinship system

4. The most important feature of the Basseri economy is their herds. As an individual herd increases, and the owner amasses more wealth:

    a. his capital is more secure
    b. he is eligible to assume the role of chief
    c. he must share this wealth by purchasing livestock for others
    d. he is often a source of disruption in the community, as witchcraft allegations are aimed at the wealthiest tribal members
    e. **he becomes vulnerable to his shepherd's theft, and converts livestock to other form of capital**

CHAPTER 4
THE BETSILEO

1. Betsileo subsistence can best be described as:

    a. foraging
    b. light industry
    c. hunting, but not gathering
    d. horticulture
    e. **agriculture**

2. The most important ceremonial event among the Betsileo is:

    a. the *hasina*, or wedding feast
    b. **the *famadihana*, the rewrapping of corpses**
    c. the *fady*, a ceremony where baby boys are circumcised
    d. the *ambiroa*, the ceremonial slaughter of cattle
    e. the *angady*, which blesses rice

3. Among the Betsileo, a baby:

    a. is believed to be bewitched, until ceremonially 'cleansed' on the fifth day of life
    b. is killed if it is the third child of the same sex
    c. is indulged and praised until puberty, when stricter social responsibilities result in more formality between parents and children
    d. **is not deemed 'fully human' for the first few years of life**
    e. is a member of its mother's clan, but not its father's clan

4. The Betsileo believe that witches and dead ancestors:

    a. control the success of their rice farming
    b. inhabit the bodies of cattle
    c. **are 'real people,' who play an important role in daily life**
    d. protect them on the hunt
    e. do not exist

CHAPTER 5
THE KALULI

1. Kaluli songs:

   a.   have been influenced by New Age and World music
   b.   incorporate the sounds of dogs and other domesticated animals
   c.   **make references to place names and sorrowful events to elicit audience emotions**
   d.   use melodies, but no rhythms
   e.   are exclusively performed by women

2. The fact that Kaluli may mourn for a dead relative by speaking in terms of lost goods or labor suggests that:

   a.   the extension of the world capitalist system has so permeated the Kaluli social structure that they regard people as commodities.
   b.   the Kaluli think that a *sei* has killed the person in order to steal the future labor of that person in the spirit world.
   c.   the Kaluli's poverty-ridden existence forces them to subordinate emotional attachments to subsistence needs.
   d.   according to structuralist analysis, the Kaluli think of people and objects as a binary opposition.
   e.   **the Kaluli identify emotional and social closeness with reciprocal sharing of labor and gifts.**

3. Gender roles among the Kaluli:

   a.   are taught exclusively by fathers or grandfathers.
   b.   **are characterized by boys' neediness, and girls' early assignment to physical labor such as carrying water and firewood.**
   c.   ensure that girls learn the skills of wheedling and whining, and boys remain aloof.
   d.   are, for all intents and purposes, non-existent.
   e.   are assigned based on physical characteristics.

4. The most fundamental theme in Kaluli interpersonal relations is:

   a.   the concept of 'nafa'.
   b.   the 'hardening' of language.
   c.   the exchange of plows in harvest seasons.
   d.   **the giving and sharing of food.**
   e.   the elaborate exchange ceremonies which enhance status.

CHAPTER 6
THE KAPAUKA

1. Kapauku ceremonies stand in contrast to those of lowland New Guinea peoples in that they:

    a. are concerned more with magic and the supernatural, and less directed towards exchange of good.
    b. are far less frequent.
    c. are far more frequent.
    d. **are focused on the secular, and are more economic than religious.**
    e. never last more than a single day.

2. Leopold Posposil asserts that one of the most striking features of Kapauku culture is:

    a. the extreme attention paid to music and dance, sometimes to the detriment of providing food for their children.
    b. their communal gardening, found nowhere else in the New Guinea highlands.
    c. **their overriding emphasis on the individual.**
    d. their lack of a concept of telling time.
    e. their unique concept of death and the afterworld.

3. All of the following are true of the Kapauku tonowi *except*:

    a. his position is an informal one, without the power to enforce his will.
    b. he possesses superior verbal skills.
    c. his wealth is dependent upon successful pig breeding, and thus is not secure.
    d. his position is as dependent upon his generosity as it is on his wealth.
    e. **because of his wealth, he need not depend upon his kin for political support.**

4. The Kapauku pursue wealth in the form of cowrie shell money, base status distinctions on this wealth, and espouse an ethic of individualism. Because of this, they have been referred to as:

    a. the most 'Western' of New Guinea tribes.
    b. more economically complex than most post-colonial peoples.
    c. 'rugged individualists'.
    d. **'primitive capitalists'.**
    e. none of the above

CHAPTER 7
THE !KUNG SAN

1. If a !Kung man returns from the hunt with meat to distribute, other members of the band may comment that the meat is of poor quality. This is an expression of:

    a.   endemic intra-band hostility.
    b.   bad manners.
    c.   the poor quality of game in the Kalahari.
    d.   balanced reciprocity.
    e.   **an egalitarian distaste for bragging.**

2. When Richard Lee bought an ox for the !Kung, they:

    a.   were very excited and appreciative for weeks afterward.
    b.   exhibited the rudeness and ingratitude he found typical of their culture.
    c.   **denigrated the ox to prevent him from being too proud.**
    d.   refused to accept it, because it was too expensive and they could never adequately reciprocate.
    e.   also bought oxen so that he would not be the only one to provide for the feast.

3. Which of the following is *not* true of the !Kung San hxaro exchange?

    a.   Hxaro ties with other groups allow relocation to a richer environment when food becomes scarce.
    b.   **The essence of hxaro is the immediacy of returning a gift, and ties are often broken if reciprocity is delayed.**
    c.   Hxaro can diffuse conflicts, providing an occasion for people to go off on an exchange visit when they are embroiled in dissension at home.
    d.   The exact nature of the gift is of less importance than the fact that an exchange is performed.
    e.   All !Kung are eligible to enter into hxaro exchange with one another.

4. Foraging, as a subsistence strategy among the !Kung San:

    a.   is a relatively recent addition to their cultural practices.
    a.   routinely yields enough food, in one foray, to last six weeks.
    b.   is highly successful, despite lack of knowledge regarding the environment.
    c.   must be supplemented by trading for food with outsiders.
    d.   **provides a plentiful and varied diet.**
    e.   is responsible for many of the nutritional ills cured by the !kia ceremony.

CHAPTER 8
THE NUER

1. The Nuer economy is mixed, including:

    a.   both hunting and gathering.
    b.   both pastoralism and horticulture.
    c.   both horticulture and intensive agriculture.
    d.   both cash crops and manufacturing.
    e.   both agriculture and fishing.

2. Among the Nuer, segmentary lineage organization:

    a.   has been replaced with a matrilineal system.
    b.   is believed to afford protection against witchcraft.
    c.   allows the temporary mobilization of forces against outsiders.
    d.   has come under attack by Christian missionaries.
    e.   affords the security of an unchanging group of allies upon whom one can depend.

3. All of the following are true about the Nuer leopard skin chief *except*:

    a.   his most important role is as the mediator of disputes.
    b.   he relies on his powers of persuasion.
    c.   he remains neutral in his mediation, offering refuge in his village to either party.
    d.   his identity is signified by the leopard skin he wears over his shoulders.
    e.   the only dispute which is exempt from his mediating power is the blood feud.

4. A Nuer man who owns many cattle:

    a.   is elevated in status, and enjoys many privileges owing to this position.
    b.   is the only individual eligible for the chiefdom.
    c.   belongs to a different lineage than men who do not.
    d.   is envied, but not treated differently than a man with few cattle.
    e.   is expected to provide more animals for the monthly ritual slaughtering than men with smaller herds.

CHAPTER 9
THE OJIBWA

1. All of the following are distinctive features of Ojibwa religion *except*:

    a.   relationships with 'the grandfathers'.
    b.   visions.
    c.   fasting.
    d.   the natural/supernatural dichotomy.
    e.   dreaming.

2. The consequences of contact, to Ojibwan culture, beginning with the earliest days of fur trading, included all of the following except:

   a. **inability to gain access to iron tools, which might result in advanced hunting techniques.**
   b. the instigation of intertribal conflict.
   c. scattering and relocation of indigenous populations.
   d. dependence on trade goods without the technology to produce or repair such goods on their own.
   e. the introduction of an unfamiliar system of debt.

3. Central to the traditional Ojibwan belief system was:

   a. the sharp division between 'dreaming' and 'waking'.
   b. **the important relationship between people and those who are other-than-people.**
   c. the rivalry between the Great Frogs clan and the Big Turtles clan.
   d. the power of 'sympathetic' magic.
   e. the accumulation of excess goods, to please 'the grandfathers'.

4. Ojibwa in modern times:

   a. have become a homogeneous group.
   b. rarely engage in hunting, gathering and fishing.
   c. **continue to pass along traditions such as art, language and craft to new generations.**
   d. have rejected harsh government policies which would mandate learning the Ojibwan language.
   e. have benefited from the increased diversion of funds from the military to domestic programs.

CHAPTER 10
THE SAMOANS

1. Samoans living in the United States employ their traditional system of *matai*:

   a. **to resolve problems of modern urban living.**
   b. to actively demarcate their neighborhoods from those of other ethnic groups.
   c. as an alternative to Christianity.
   d. to maintain trade relations with kin living elsewhere.
   e. only during major Samoan holidays or festivals.

2. An advantage of ambilineal descent, such as is found among Samoans, is:

   a. the potential provision of exemption from taboos.
   b. the ability to avoid paying bride price.
   c. the expectation of greater income once ambilineal debts are repaid.
   d. **the flexibility of affiliating with either one's mother's or father's descent group.**
   e. the decreased likelihood of restrictive gender roles in such a system.

3. Samoan's 'casual' horticultural behavior was interpreted by early travelers to the island as laziness. In fact, it is due to:

   a. their ignorance of subsistence techniques.
   b. the dictates of their elaborate religious beliefs, which state that over-attention to crops will bring envy from neighbors.
   c. the fact that cultivation is practiced after nightfall, which rendered it unseen by most transient visitors to the island.
   d. the centrality of kinship to horticultural practice, mandating that only the matriline can work the gardens.
   e. **the fact that infrequent weeding of gardens prevents the poor soil from washing away in the rains.**

4. Mead expected to find support, among Samoan adolescents, for the assumption that:

   a. the adolescent period was a universally stressful one, biologically determined.
   b. **different enculturation would result in a different adolescent personality.**
   c. repressive sexuality was physically harmful.
   d. race is biologically determined.
   e. despite their size, Samoan girls behaved in a stereotypically 'feminine' way.

CHAPTER 11
THE TIWI

1. Among the traditional Tiwi, women's labor is crucial to amassing food surplus, and thus essential to acquiring 'big man' status. This demonstrates that:

   a. **Tiwi women's labor power translates into their indirect attainment of political power.**
   b. the old adage 'behind every great man there is a woman' is indeed an ethnographic truth.
   c. Tiwi gender roles maximize the exploitation of women for economic profit.
   d. the Tiwi lack a clear domestic-public dichotomy because gender roles are relatively interdependent and entwined.
   e. Tiwi women lack power and prestige.

2.	Contemporary Tiwi:

	a.	**are very much a part of the modern world system.**
	b.	no longer hold the traditional kulama and pukamani ceremonies.
	c.	have successsfully stayed as they were in older times, primarily by restricting tourism.
	d.	are using modern political strategies to lobby for the return of their land.
	e.	have refused to expand their economic base by selling their indigenous art, a practice common among other indigenous peopels.

3.	The traditional customs surrounding Tiwi marriages:

	a.	stipulate that an individual can marry only once in his or her lifetime.
	b.	follow rules of polyandry in this matrilineal society.
	c.	**ensure that all women are married.**
	d.	have not undergone many changes since contact with Catholic missionaries.
	e.	arose because of the higher proportion of females in Tiwi society.

4.	Which of the following is *not* true, regarding the Tiwi concept of pukamani?

	a.	A person's close family becomes 'pukamani' at his or her death.
	b.	Those who are pukamani have a period of circumscribed behavior which may last for months.
	c.	**It is the mourners, and not the individual who has died, who are the focus of the pukamani funeral ceremony.**
	d.	The name of the deceased, surviving spouse, and any names the deceased has bestowed on anyone else, become taboo.
	e.	During the pukamani funeral ceremony, dancers can sometimes injure themselves in their frenzy of grief.

CHAPTER 12
THE TROBRIANDERS

1.	Malinowski proposed that Trobriand Islanders used magic when sailing because:

	a.	they are naturally fearful of water.
	b.	**magic is employed most in dangerous, uncontrollable situations.**
	c.	magic allowed them to control yam growth even when at sea.
	d.	they were unskilled boat-builders, and magic afforded them security.
	e.	they believed their ancestral spirits dwelled in the water.

2.	Pregnancy, for the Trobrianders:

	a.	**is unconnected to sexual intercourse.**
	b.	is not publicly acknowledged until only weeks before birth.
	c.	is believed to occur as punishment for sins.
	d.	cannot be spoken about by males.
	e.	is 'guided' by ancestral shades, and marked by monthly rituals involving these spirits.

3. The Trobriand kula ring can be described as all of the following *except*:

   a. an elaborate practice of trade with inhabitants of nearby islands.
   b. trade which involves shell ornaments.
   c. **the only form of exchange found among the Trobrianders.**
   d. a way to balance the islands' differing needs, dispersing surplus and providing items where they are lacking.
   e. a practice that persists even in modern times.

4. According to Weiner, women's importance among the Trobriand Islanders:

   a. was erroneously overstated by earlier ethnographers.
   b. **was believed, by earlier ethnographers, to derive from the fact that they are matrilineal.**
   c. revolves around their central role in manufacturing kula shells.
   d. is unattached from their productive activities.
   e. has declined in modern times.

CHAPTER 13
THE YANOMAMO

1. Among the Yanomamo, trading and feasting are two important activities because they:

   a. are a form of ritual worship to the Jaguar god.
   b. allow women to gain equal or even superior status to men.
   c. allow the Yanomamo to share water, a scarce resource in their desert environment.
   d. **create important ties and alliances between villages.**
   e. have replaced raiding and intertribal warfare as the traditional means of revenge.

2. Which of the following statements about the Yanamamo is *false*?

   a. They are an indigenous people whose traditions are threatened by outside cultural and governmental intervention.
   b. **They are hunters and gatherers, organized in small, mobile bands.**
   c. They are a well-studied tribal people settled in villages.
   d. They have an elaborate belief system, which describes the universe as being constructed of four layers which hover atop each other.
   e. Despite no tradition of written texts, the Yanomami are eloquent speakers among whom verbal skills in story-telling are greatly prized.

3. The hekura spirits, as described by the Yanomamo:

   a. are lured to a shaman by his sexual activities.
   b. cause illness by consuming part of the victim's soul.
   c. can be prevented from entering the shaman's body by the use of powerful hallucinogenic drugs.
   d. **appear in the form of beautiful women to male shamans, but as hideously ugly men to female shamans.**
   e. dwell in yams, and thus are most greatly feared during yam feasts.

4.   Currently, the Yanomamo:

    a.   are the fastest growing indigenous population in the world.
    b.   have been prevented from intertribal warfare by the Brazilian government, in an
          attempt to aid in their preservation.
    c.   **are threatened by outside development and introduced diseases.**
    d.   are making the transition from hunting and gathering to plow agriculture.
    e.   have begun to be relocated from South America to other continents, in order to
          protect their traditional culture.

INSTRUCTOR'S RESOURCE FOR:
Through the Looking Glass: Readings in Anthropology

edited by David L. Carlson and Vaughn M. Bryant, Jr.
Texas A & M University

CHAPTER 1
THE SCOPE OF ANTHROPOLOGY

Summary

Linton, Ralph. 1937. One Hundred Percent American. *The American Mercury* 40.

Ralph Linton notes that contrary to belief, most of the things Americans use on a daily basis are really ideas imported from other cultures. He demonstrates this through an analysis of a person waking up, eating breakfast, and going to work. He also notes, with some humor, only one purely American invention. Linton wrote the article in 1937 before World War II. With the development of a global economy since the article was written, not only the ideas and the inventions, but the products themselves come from outside the country. Try following Linton's "One Hundred Percent American" from wake-up alarms through breakfast today. Where are the products that touch our lives each day manufactured?

MULTIPLE CHOICE QUESTIONS

1. The *only* purely American contribution mentioned in Ralph Linton's article "One Hundred Percent American" is:

   a. soap.
   b. the pressed felt hat.
   c. the steam radiator.
   d. necktie.
   e. umbrella.

2. The major point of Linton's article "One Hundred Percent American" is that:

   a. anthropologists are concerned about the harmful effects of cultural blending.
   b. American society has borrowed ideas and inventions from all over the world.
   c. new genetic fingerprinting techniques allow accurate determination of ethnic affiliation.
   d. American society is more culturally diverse now than it was before World War II.
   e. none of the above.

CHAPTER 2
FIELD METHODS

Summary
Bourgois, Philippe. 1989. "Just Another Night on Crack Street." *New York Times Magazine*, November 12, 1989.

Philippe Bourgois has done what few of us would be willing to do. As an anthropologist, he has lived in the slums of Harlem and watched how and why illegal drugs have become the focal point for violence, wealth, prestige and power. He also examines the question of how and why young children in Harlem are drawn into this downward spiral of life when many of them try so hard to escape from their lives of pain and crime. Urban anthropologists study cultural groups within a larger society. Give some examples of other cultural groups within American society that anthropologists could study. What techniques of investigation does Bourgois use in his study?

MULTIPLE CHOICE QUESTIONS

3. In the article "Just Another Night on Crack Street," Philippe Bourgois uses which ethnographic technique?

    a. participatory observation by selling crack at the botanica.
    b. passing out survey forms.
    c. conducting telephone interviews.
    d. recording life-history interviews of crack dealers.
    e. posing as an undercover detective.

4. According to Bourgois in "Just Another Night on Crack Street," violence on crack street:

    a. helps to pass the time.
    b. is mostly caused by the police.
    c. is necessary to be a respected drug dealer.
    d. is the unintended result of being high on drugs.
    e. is much less common than most people think.

5. In the article "Just Another Night on Crack Street," the author says that the concept of conjugated oppression, defined as _____ begins to explain why so many living in poverty tend to "fry" their brains on crack.

    a. having a "rush" that provides instant gratification
    b. perception of being victims of inescapable oppression
    c. loss of moral values
    d. distrust of authority
    e. the perception that one has the "power"

Summary
Gmelch, George. 1990. Caught in the Middle. Natural History 9/90: 32-37.

Juggling the conflicting needs of fishermen, trappers, and big game hunters in a part of Glacier Bay National Park is a challenge. To better understand the potential problems and the needs of the local inhabitants, the National Park Service hires George Gmelch to study traditional subsistence activities in the area. While studying Tlingit and white fishermen in southeast Alaska, he learns as much about developing rapport as he does about the economics of fishing.

MULTIPLE CHOICE QUESTIONS

6. In the article "Caught in the Middle," the anthropologist who studied the fishing habits of the Tlingit Indians of Alaska was treated as an outsider and given little information by them until they "accepted" him as being an "OK-type of guy." What did he do to gain their acceptance?

   a. **Played softball with them.**
   b. Lived with them in their homes and ate the same food they did.
   c. Went fishing with them and worked as hard as they did.
   d. Married one of the girls of the tribe.
   e. Held a beer-bust and big party for the fishermen of the tribe.

7. In the article "Caught in the Middle," Gmelch was hired to study salmon fishing practices by:

   a. Tlingit Indians bringing a lawsuit.
   b. **the National Park Service.**
   c. the white fishermen who believed that Tlingit fishing practices were wasteful.
   d. the National Salmon Fisheries Board.
   e. the Japanese government.

8. The ultimate irony for Gmelch in "Caught in the Middle" was:

   a. learning more about baseball than about salmon fishing.
   b. testifying for the white fishermen in court as an expert in traditional fishing practices.
   c. **testifying for the Tlingit in court as an expert in traditional fishing practices.**
   d. catching more fish than anyone else.
   e. discovering that everything he had been told about fishing was a lie.

CHAPTER 3
CULTURE

Summary
Konner, Melvin. 1988. Everyman. *The Sciences* Nov/Dec: 6-8.

As Konner notes, anthropologists love to poke holes in simplistic assumptions about human nature. In fact, some basic characteristics and capacities are common to human societies everywhere. Understanding the uniqueness of human culture requires an appreciation for both its common and variable features. How does Konner's essay relate to the "nature versus nurture" controversy? Which universals of human behavior does Konner identify?

MULTIPLE CHOICE QUESTIONS

9. In Konner's article "Everyman," Darwin's study of facial expressions is an example of:

   a. differences between cultures.
   b. differences between humans and other animals.
   c. **similarities among humans and other animals.**
   d. Darwin's desire to avoid controversy after publication of the Origin of Species.
   e. Darwin never studied facial expressions.

10.   In Konner's article "Everyman," the problem with most anthropologists is that:

a.   **they are uninterested in universal behaviors.**
b.   they are too interested in universal behaviors.
c.   they don't take the time to learn the language of the culture they are studying.
d.   they assume the culture they are studying is the norm against which all other cultures should be compared.
e.   Konner does not criticize anthropologists.

CHAPTER 4
ETHNICITY AND ETHNIC RELATIONS

Summary

Gmelch, George and Sharon Gmelch. 1988. Nomads in the Cities. *Natural History* 2/88: 50-61.

Forsaking wagons for trailers and handicrafts for recyclables, modern Gypsies in England have retained their distinctive social identity. George and Sharon Gmelch show that attitudes toward Gypsies have also been very stable. Despite efforts to drive them out or settle them down, Gypsies show little desire to settle down and become "respectable." What social groups in the U.S. are similar to England's Gypsies? How are migrant workers in the U.S. different from England's Gypsies?

MULTIPLE CHOICE QUESTIONS

11.   According to the article "Nomads in the Cities," which of the following is *not* a reason why Gypsies tend to be constantly on the move?

a.   boredom
b.   economic need to earn a livelihood
c.   travel is considered good for health and brings good luck
d.   **it is the women, not the men, who refuse to settle down**
e.   fear of being attacked by other ethnic groups if they don't stay on the move

12.   In "Nomads in the Cities," Gypsy families in England:

a.   are now settling down.
b.   are putting their children in school.
c.   are taking permanent jobs.
d.   all of the above.
e.   **none of the above.**

13.   In "Nomads in the Cities," most Gypsy families in England:

a.   live in rural areas, but work in the city.
b.   work and live mostly in the country.
c.   **work and live mostly in the city.**
d.   work mostly with traveling carnival shows.
e.   none of the above.

CHAPTER 5
HUMAN BIOLOGICAL DIVERSITY AND THE RACE CONCEPT

Summary

Rensberger, Boyce. 1981. Racial Odyssey. *Science Digest* Jan/Feb.

Boyce Rensberger questions the usefulness of racial classification by asking what criteria we should use. He explores skin, eye and hair color to see if these are good clues to the origin of races. He also looks at other features like noses, blood groupings, and body size to see what genetic processes may have caused existing differences and asks if these traits are useful clues in the search for pure races. What three major conclusions about race have most scientists reached? What are the two steps of evolution? What were Coon's five races?

MULTIPLE CHOICE QUESTIONS

14.   In the article "Racial Odyssey," Boyce Rensberger argues that racial classifications:

      a.   are a legitimate means of partitioning the complex and diverse human species into simpler, easier to understand, components.
      b.   are useful and biologically sound.
      c.   can be used to identify four distinct races.
      d.   are most useful for those who need to divide the human species into different groups.
      e.   are based mainly on bigotry and hatred.

15.   In the article "Racial Odyssey" by Rensberger, the author argues that:

      a.   races represent distinct subspecies of humans.
      b.   no one has ever discovered a reliable way of distinguishing one race from another.
      c.   only skin color, hair texture, and nose shape should be used to identify races.
      d.   genetic tracing provides the most reliable way to identify race.
      e.   none of the above.

16.   According to Boyce Rensberger's article "Racial Odyssey," what are the **best** categories on which to define true races?

      a.   skin color
      b.   blood groups
      c.   body size
      d.   all of the above
      e.   none of the above

17.   According to Boyce Rensberger's article "Racial Odyssey," a system of racial classification based on the features of a given population is inappropriate because the species *Homo sapiens* is:

      a.   already racially separated.
      b.   isolated and subject to little change.
      c.   an ever-changing species with much gene flow and blending.
      d.   separated socially as well as biologically.
      e.   more diverse than other human species.

CHAPTER 6
EVOLUTION, GENETICS, AND BIOLOGICAL ADAPTATION

Summary
Diamond, Jared. 1988. Founding Fathers and Mothers. *Natural History* 6/88: 10-15.

What happens when an island is colonized by a small group? Jared Diamond explores the role of the founder effect in producing human genetic variability. While the most striking examples of the founder effect involve bizarre genetic conditions, the geographic distribution of many neutral traits can also be explained. What does Diamond say happened in the last 8,000 years that makes founder effects important?

MULTIPLE CHOICE QUESTIONS

18.   In the article "Founding Fathers and Mothers," Jared Diamond describes the founder effect as:

   a.   a cultural phenomenon in which a nuclear family moves into a new area and has sole influence over what customs are taught their offspring.
   b.   a political phenomenon that occurs when a single family colonizes a new area and remains in power for a long time.
   c.   a social phenomenon that occurs when a small, tightly knit band of people migrate to a new area and take control.
   d.   a genetic phenomenon that can occur when a comparatively large population arises from a small group of immigrants.
   e.   an economic phenomenon that occurs when a small group migrates into an uninhabited region that is very rich in natural resources, and prospers.

19.   According to Jared Diamond's article "Founding Fathers and Mothers," the disease, hereditary tyrosinemia, affects less than one individual in 100,000. However, in the Chicoutimi area of Canada, the disease affects 1 in 685 individuals. This difference is primarily due to:

   a.   gene flow.
   b.   natural selection.
   c.   the founder effect.
   d.   all of the above.
   e.   a and b only.

20.   In Diamond's article "Founding Fathers and Mothers," fingerprints are an example of:

   a.   a deleterious trait.
   b.   a neutral trait.
   c.   a beneficial trait.
   d.   a recessive trait.
   e.   a dominant trait.

CHAPTER 7
THE PRIMATES

Summary
Smuts, Barbara. 1987. What Are Friends For? *Natural History*. 2/87: 36-44.

Barbara Smuts challenges the long-held idea that before the development of sexual division of labor, human males and females had little to do with each other except for sex. Her studies of baboons reveal new ideas about the origin of "friendship" between males and females and show how essential non-sexually motivated friendships are to the well being of female and infant baboons. She found that in some cases female baboons and their infants' survival depends on which males they selected as friends and how long friendships lasted. What benefits do male baboons obtain through their friendships with female baboons? What implications does this study have for the evolution of male-female relationships?

MULTIPLE CHOICE QUESTIONS

21. In her article "What Are Friends For?", Barbara Smuts studied baboon behavior and found that:

a. **nonsexual male-female friendships were prevalent among baboons, and that these friendships made an important contribution to the survivability of certain infants in the baboon troop.**
b. all male-female friendships were based on sexual intercourse.
c. jealousy, flirtation, friendship, and rivalry were limited to the lead male, termed the alpha male, who dictated the behavior of the baboon troop.
d. females were passive objects of male competition, and that the most aggressive male always succeeded in mating with the female of his choice.
e. baboons sometimes establish friendships with animals that are normally predators.

22. In the article "What Are Friends For?", Barbara Smuts analyzes the role of friendship:

a. in American business.
b. among early hominids.
c. among chimpanzees.
d. among modern hunter-gatherers.
e. **none of the above.**

23. In the article "What Are Friends For?", Barbara Smuts points out that jealousy is:

a. a uniquely human characteristic.
b. culturally determined.
c. **apparently present among at least some nonhuman primates.**
d. always one-sided.
e. she doesn't talk about jealousy at all.

24. In her article "What Are Friends For?", Barbara Smuts challenges the old idea that the nuclear family developed once females became economically dependent on males. The nonhuman primate evidence she presents challenges this story by claiming:

a. long-term bonds between the sexes can evolve in the absence of a sexual division of labor or food sharing.
b. highly differentiated, emotionally intense male-female relationships can occur without sexual exclusivity.
c. among our closest primate relatives, males clearly provide mothers and infants with social benefits even when they are not the fathers of these infants.
d. **all of the above.**
e. a and b only.

CHAPTER 8
EARLY HOMINIDS

Summary

Fagan, Brian. 1992. Aping the Apes. *Archaeology* 45(3): 16-19, 67.

Our picture of early hominid society is changing rapidly. Once thought to be killer apes with a society much like modern hunter-gatherers, we now know that our ancestors were very different. Fagan describes recent re-analyses of the archaeological materials from Olduvai Gorge which paint a more ape-like picture of *Homo habilis*, the scavenger. What are site formation processes? How has recent research changed our understanding of early hominids?

MULTIPLE CHOICE QUESTIONS

25.   In Fagan's "Aping the Apes" article, he describes the research of Richard Potts. Potts believes that the "living floors" at Olduvai Gorge represent:

     a.   natural accumulations of bone and stone over hundreds of years.
     b.   campsites where hunters brought their kills for cooking.
     c.   places where hominids cached stone tools.
     d.   kill sites representing an "instant-in-time."
     e.   permanent structures.

26.   New research on *Homo habilis* described by Fagan in "Aping the Apes" makes it clear that early hominids:

     a.   scavenged the kills of other predators.
     b.   hunted large animals.
     c.   established sedentary campsites.
     d.   were very similar to modern hunter-gatherers.
     e.   were entirely vegetarian.

27.   In the article "Aping the Apes," Fagan makes which of the following important points?

     a.   What we now consider to be human characteristics may well have developed relatively recently, rather than in the early hominids.
     b.   Australopithecines were much more human-like than ape-like, which is contrary to what we have believed for years.
     c.   Evidence now suggests that before the emergence of *Homo habilis*, hominids were ape-like, but that *Homo habilis* was the first of the very human-like hominids.
     d.   Evidence now suggests that today's humans are much more ape-like than any of us have ever wanted to admit.
     e.   Ape behavior is much more human-like than we have wanted to believe in the past.

CHAPTER 9
THE EMERGENCE OF MODERN HUMANS

Summary

Trinkhaus, Erik and Pat Shipman. 1993. Neanderthals: Images of Ourselves. *Evolutionary Anthropology* 1(6): 194-201.

As we learn more about what makes humanity unique, our interpretations of the place of Neanderthals within our family tree changes. First cast out as too primitive, Neanderthals were later adopted as only slightly different from modern humans. Now their position is again being reconsidered as physical anthropologists explore their basic assumptions regarding the emergence of modern humanity. Why do the authors say that their view of paleoanthropology is not a deconstructionist one?

MULTIPLE CHOICE QUESTIONS

28.   According to the article "Neanderthals: Images of Ourselves," the authors note that the issue of where Neanderthals belong in the tree of hominid evolution is not resolved. The reason why this issue seems to be so "hotly" debated is mainly because:

    a.   as it turns out, the Neanderthals had larger brains than any of the earlier fossil hominid groups and they were even larger than ours.

    b.   nobody can fully agree on how well Neanderthals could speak.

    c.   Neanderthals now seem to have first evolved in areas separate from where major sites of *Homo erectus* or *Homo sapiens sapiens* are found.

    d.   many anthropologists are guilty of basing their view of the Neanderthals' place in human evolution more on suspected behavior patterns than on actual anatomical realities.

    e.   too little skeletal information still remains, much of it was destroyed during the Second World War.

29.   The central issues in the Neanderthal debate, as described in the article "Neanderthals: Images of Ourselves," include all of the following except:

    a.   a dichotomy between traditional morphological approaches and population biology approaches.

    b.   single versus diffuse emergence.

    c.   the role of gene flow.

    d.   the relationships between modern humans and Neanderthals, e.g., the role of mutation.

    e.   the role of mutation.

30.   In the article, "Neanderthals: Images of Ourselves," the authors are primarily interested in:

    a.   our understanding the relationships between Neanderthals and modern humans.

    b.   Neanderthal art and religion.

    c.   a history of Neanderthal finds.

    d.   the sophistication of Neanderthal tools and weapons.

    e.   none of the above.

Summary
Harris, Marvin. 1986. "The 100,000 Year Hunt: Man was not made for a Diet of High Fiber, Meatless Meals." The Sciences Jan/Feb: 22-32.

Marvin Harris discusses the role of meat in human diets past and present. He explores an apparently universal desire for meat among human societies and even cites some comparative data on nonhuman primates. Given the health risks associated with high fat diets, he makes recommendations for sensible eating habits, which do not deny our heritage as hunter-gatherers. Harris makes his argument on nutritional grounds. How would animal rights activists respond to his claims?

MULTIPLE CHOICE QUESTIONS

31. According to Harris in "The 100,000 Year Hunt," foods of animal origin:

   a. **are essential because they are "complete protein sources."**
   b. are inferior to foods of plant origin because they lack high caloric content (starch and sugars).
   c. provided no more than 10% of the total caloric intake of most prehistoric hunter-gatherer populations.
   d. are not essential in human diets; instead they are a luxury.
   e. are inferior to foods of plant origin because they lack fiber.

32. The major conclusion of Marvin Harris in "The 100,000 Year Hunt" is that:

   a. on ethical grounds, humans should be vegetarian.
   b. life expectancy would be increased if humans could end their addiction to meat.
   c. scavenging was more important to humans than hunting 100,000 years ago.
   d. all of the above.
   e. **none of the above.**

33. In "The 100,000 Year Hunt," Marvin Harris concludes that the foodstuff that is most highly valued cross-culturally is:

   a. potatoes.
   b. chocolate.
   c. **meat.**
   d. nuts.
   e. there is no foodstuff that is universally desired.

34. According to the article "The 100,000 Year Hunt," our species-given physiology and digestive processes predispose us to learn to prefer animal foods because:

   a. animal foods are lower in fat and calories than plant foods.
   b. animal foods are more readily available than plant foods.
   c. **animal foods are higher in protein than are plant foods.**
   d. animal foods taste better than plant foods.
   e. it is more fun to kill a deer than it is to kill a carrot.

35. According to the article "The 100,000 Year Hunt," which of the following is not a meat-eater?

   a. humans
   b. chimpanzees
   c. baboons
   d. lions
   e. **all are meat-eaters**

CHAPTER 10
THE ORIGIN AND SPREAD OF FOOD PRODUCTION

Summary
Lewin, Roger. 1988. A Revolution of Ideas in Agricultural Origins. Science 240: 984-6.

Why humankind changed their economic base from foraging to farming is a mystery that many scientists have tried to solve. In this article, Roger Lewin explores some of our most cherished views about "why" agriculture may have begun and then offers some new insights, based on current archaeological research, that are worth considering. What is the revolution in ideas about agricultural origins?

MULTIPLE CHOICE QUESTIONS

36.   In the article "A Revolution of Ideas in Agricultural Origins," Lewin admits that there does not seem to be a unified agreement as to why agriculture and animal domestication first began. Nevertheless, he says that he suspects an important reason it occurred when it did, around 10,000 years ago, was in response to:

   a.   drought and reduced grazing lands for wild animals.
   b.   need to establish secure trading routes.
   c.   discovery that the seeds of cereal plants could be "farmed" as easy as they could be gathered.
   d.   the local herds of wild animals disappeared.
   e.   **over population of humans.**

37.   The main site discussed by Lewin in "A Revolution of Ideas in Agricultural Origins" is:

   a.   Catal Ionescue
   b.   **Abu Hureyra**
   c.   Ali Kosh
   d.   Jarmo
   e.   Jericho

38.   The model of a rich steppe flora exploited by settlers along the Euphrates River in 9500 B.C. that is discussed in "A Revolution of Ideas in Agricultural Origins" is:

   a.   the Foraging Revolution.
   b.   the Post-Pleistocene Overkill.
   c.   **the Lawnmower Hypothesis.**
   d.   the Mass Harvesting Model.
   e.   none of the above.

Summary
Bryant, Vaughn M., Jr. 1992. In Search of the First Americans. *1993 Yearbook of Science and the Future*, pp. 8-27. Encyclopedia Britannica, Inc.

Vaughn Bryant examines the hotly debated topic of "when and how" the first migrations of humans reached the New World. His discussions focus on the key archaeological sites that are being debated, and mentions the strengths and weaknesses of each piece of evidence.

MULTIPLE CHOICE QUESTIONS

39.   The first archaeological site that finally "proved" people had been living in the New World for more than 4,000 years was the _____ site.

   a.   Monte Verde
   b.   **Folsom**
   c.   Old Crow Flats
   d.   El Bosque
   e.   Calico

40. Scientists argue that for an archaeological site to be accepted as confirming the very "early" arrival of human populations in the New World three essential criteria will be needed. These are: 1) evidence dated by accurate methods, 2) finding artifacts that are clearly made by humans, and 3):

    a. a site located in a well-known region of the Arctic.
    b. a site where all materials were excavated and recorded by professional archaeologists.
    c. a site where the artifacts are officially recognized by the Smithsonian Institution.
    d. a site containing human skeletal remains.
    e. **a site where human-made artifacts are found in undisturbed levels.**

41. One of the more important archaeological sites in South America that has attracted much attention, and might eventually prove to be one of the earliest records of humans in the New World is:

    a. **Monte Verde.**
    b. Tulum.
    c. Orogrande.
    d. Valsequillo.
    e. El Grande.

CHAPTER 11
ADAPTIVE STRATEGIES AND ECONOMIC SYSTEMS

Summary
Bryant, Vaughn M., Jr. 1995. The Paleolithic Health Club. *1995 Yearbook of Science and the Future,* pp. 114-133. Encyclopedia Britannica, Inc.

Our most ancient human ancestors may have lived shortened lives, but it wasn't their diets that killed them. In this article Dr. Bryant examines our modern diets and explains why many of today's foods are a causative factor in a number of health problems including cancer, hypertension, obesity, diabetes, and tooth decay. He also suggests how we can improve our health by applying lessons learned by our earliest ancestors nearly five million years ago.

MULTIPLE CHOICE QUESTIONS

42. A medical study of English workers in the year 1900 revealed the alarming fact that 70%:

    a. had some form of cancer.
    b. had high blood pressure.
    c. were malnourished.
    d. had tuberculosis.
    e. **had teeth that were decayed.**

43. Prior to the advent of agriculture, which of the following food items was most often considered the "hardest" to find?

    a. Carbohydrates
    b. Protein
    c. **Fat**
    d. Fiber
    e. Potassium

44. Eating which of the following foods in our modern diet is most likely to increase the level of our serum cholesterol?

   a. **Saturated fats**
   b. Cholesterol
   c. Olive oil
   d. Salt
   e. Sugar

Summary

Cronk, Lee. 1989. Strings Attached. The Sciences. May/June: 2-4.

Reciprocity or gift-giving is important in nonstate societies as a means of exchange and as a way of cementing social relationships. Lee Cronk explores the ways in which gifts create future obligations. Under some circumstances, gift-giving can become a form of competition in which the goal is to demonstrate one's wealth and generosity in public. As Cronk shows, even gifts given in our own society often come with strings attached. Where does the term "Indian Giver" come from? Is gift-giving on the way out in modern society?

MULTIPLE CHOICE QUESTIONS

45. In Cronk's article "Strings Attached," the system of gift-giving, called "reciprocity," is common throughout the peoples of the world. One of the most elaborate systems of reciprocal gift-giving is called:

   a. **the kula, in which shell necklaces and armbands are exchanged by people living on the islands off New Guinea.**
   b. the hxaro, in which different items are not assigned a particular value.
   c. the niffag, a word used to designate the circulation of pearls through the trade network of the Truk Islands.
   d. the potlatch, a word used to designate the gift-giving ceremony of the Kwaikutl of northwestern North America.
   e. swapping, as practiced in modern urban ghettos.

46. The article "Strings Attached" by Lee Cronk discusses:

   a. **the concept of reciprocity.**
   b. the rights and responsibilities found in unilineal descent groups.
   c. the spheres of exchange among the west African Tiv.
   d. the technology of the Pygmy net hunters.
   e. none of the above.

47. According to Lee Cronk's article "Strings Attached," reciprocity or gift-giving is important in nonstate societies as:

   a. a means of exchange.
   b. a way of cementing social relationships.
   c. a means of creating future obligations.
   d. **all of the above.**
   e. both a and b.

48. In "Strings Attached," Cronk makes the point that giving-with-strings-attached is not unique to primitive societies. Which three modern industrial state-level societies, mentioned in his article, are currently practicing such "gift-giving"?

   a. **The United States, Russia, and Japan**
   b. Germany, the United States, and Great Britain
   c. The United States, Russia, and Great Britain
   d. France, Japan, and Germany
   e. China, Korea and Japan

CHAPTER 12
THE POLITICAL SYSTEMS OF BANDS AND TRIBES

Summary
Gorman, Peter. 1991. A People at Risk. The World and I, December, 1991, pp. 678-689.

What is happening to the few remaining indigenous Indians living in remote regions of South America? According to Peter Gorman, their numbers are decreasing alarmingly. Exploitation, the greed of immigrant farmers searching for new lands to till, gold miners illegally searching for riches, and those searching for new oil and gas deposits are all contributing to the demise of native peoples. Can anything be done to curb this tragedy? The author offers his opinion of what the future will hold for them and us.

MULTIPLE CHOICE QUESTIONS

49. In the article "People at Risk," the author points out many reasons why the indigenous Indians of South America are rapidly becoming extinct. Two of the tribes that he mentions as already being in danger of near extinction are the:

   a. **Cueva and Yanomami.**
   b. Yaghan and Ona.
   c. Simque and Queca.
   d. Nunquag and Jivaro.
   e. Aguaruna and Funai.

50. In the article "People at Risk," the director of Cultural Survival compares the frontier areas of South America to:

   a. colonial west Africa.
   b. **the American West.**
   c. Nazi Germany.
   d. the plight of the Palestinians.
   e. the Vietnamese Boat People.

51. In the article "People at Risk," the defense used by ranchers accused of killing Cueva Indians in Columbia was that:

   a. they were acting in self defense.
   b. they were high on drugs.
   c. they were 'just following orders.'
   d. **the Indians were just animals.**
   e. no defense, they took a plea bargain.

CHAPTER 13
CHIEFDOMS AND STATES

Summary

Harris, Marvin. 1989. Life without Chiefs. In: Our Kind, by Marvin Harris, pp. 343-360, 377-395. Harper Perennial, New York.

How can society survive without someone in charge? Marvin Harris traces the development of political authority and leadership. Coercive power is not found in all human societies. Instead, it emerges as a response to specific conditions. As Harris illustrates, life without chiefs is not necessarily "nasty, brutish, and short." What factors does Harris say are necessary for a chiefdom to become a kingdom? What is the role of competitive feasting in tribal society?

MULTIPLE CHOICE QUESTIONS

52. In "Life without Chiefs," the author discusses the important role of apolitical officer called a mumi and about the problems associated with "mumihood." In what type of society would one tend to find people who function as a mumi?

     a. a band-level society.
     b. a tribal-level society.
     c. a chiefdom-level society.
     d. a city-state type society.
     e. an industrial type society.

53. According to Harris in "Life Without Chiefs," societies with big men or chiefs:

     a. can be very violent and warlike.
     b. live in harmony with the environment.
     c. live at peace with their neighbors.
     d. maintain their power with claims of supernatural power.
     e. have a surprising amount of leisure time.

54. According to Harris in "Life without Chiefs," the reason that Hawaii never supported a stable kingdom was that:

     a. its chiefs were not ruthless enough.
     b. Hawaiian gardens were not productive enough.
     c. the weather was too unpredictable.
     d. the population density was not high enough.
     e. none of the above.

CHAPTER 14
KINSHIP AND DESCENT

Summary

Chagnon, Napoleon. 1992. Prying Into Yanomamo Secrets. In *Yanomamo: The Last Days of Eden*, pp. 23-33, 164-170, Harcourt Brace Jovanovich, Inc. New York.

Sometimes the most innocent questions cause the most trouble. While studying the Yanomamo, Chagnon thought that genealogical studies would be an obvious way to learn the language and develop rapport. As this article shows, he greatly misjudged the significance of one's ancestors in the Venezuelan rainforest. How does he circumvent the stringent name taboo?

MULTIPLE CHOICE QUESTIONS

55. In the article "Prying into Yanomamo Secrets," the author talks about the problems he had in trying to determine kinship and descent systems among this tribe of Indians. What was his greatest problem in his effort to get the information?

   a.   inability to speak their language.
   b.   **being misled during his interviews with informants.**
   c.   not being able to unravel the complexities of their patrilineal kinship system.
   d.   being told by informants that they had "no kin."
   e.   trying to determine who the fathers of children really were.

56. In the article "Prying into Yanomamo Secrets," the Yanomamo name taboo involves which group of people?

   a.   **Everyone in the village.**
   b.   Only the deceased.
   c.   Only adult males.
   d.   Only supernatural spirits.
   e.   Only children until they marry.

57. In the article "Prying into Yanomamo Secrets," why are the Yanomamo so interested in the photograph of Chagnon hugging his mother-in-law?

   a.   They also have close, cordial relationships with their mothers-in-law.
   b.   They thought the photograph had captured her spirit.
   c.   **They considered his behavior incestuous.**
   d.   She reminded them of a character in a Yanomamo myth.
   e.   Chagnon did not have a photograph of his mother-in-law, but the Yanomamo often asked to see one.

CHAPTER 15
MARRIAGE

Summary
Bryant, Vaughn and Sylvia Grider. 1991. To Kiss. The World and I, December 1991, pp. 612-619.

Have you ever wondered why many of us kiss under the mistletoe at Christmas, or why we knock on wood for good luck? Where did this odd habit begin and what original significance did it have? These are just a few of the questions that Drs. Bryant and Grider explore in this examination of fact and folklore associated with kissing, Christmas and mistletoe.

MULTIPLE CHOICE QUESTIONS

58. In the article entitled "To Kiss," the authors claim that people in ancient cultures once wore sprigs of mistletoe and hung mistletoe over their doors because it was considered sacred. Later, during the Middle Ages it became a symbol under which we now kiss. In which culture did this custom begin?

    a. **Celtic**
    b. Roman
    c. Turkish
    d. Greek
    e. Jewish

59. Based on reading the article "To Kiss," which of the following cultures would you say was the most "kiss oriented"?

    a. Chinese
    b. Japanese
    c. Greeks
    d. **Romans**
    e. Egyptians

59. In the article "To Kiss," the authors claim that our Christmas tradition of kissing under the mistletoe comes to us from traditions involving mistletoe and kissing that first emerged among the:

    a. French.
    b. Scots.
    c. **Celts.**
    d. Greeks.
    e. Germans.

60. The earliest records describing kissing, as mentioned in the article "To Kiss," seem to have been oral verses that were passed down for centuries in the region now known as:

    a. Italy.
    b. **India.**
    c. Greece.
    d. Turkey.
    e. Middle East.

Summary
Goldstein, Melvyn. 1987. When Brothers Share a Wife. Natural History. 3/87: 39-48.

Melvyn Goldstein explores why many Tibetan cultures prefer fraternal polyandry marriages--several brothers sharing one wife. Is it because there is a scarcity of females, or is it necessary to keep population levels low in a barren and bleak environment? He also shows why fraternal polyandry insures its participants of living the "good life" and why the custom is self-perpetuating.

MULTIPLE CHOICE QUESTIONS

61. According to Goldstein in "When Brothers Share A Wife," fraternal polyandry is on the decline in Tibet because:

    a.   the modern system of range management instituted by the Chinese has allowed the Tibetan herders to increase the carrying capacity of this land.

    b.   the governments now ruling Tibet have outlawed the practice.

    c.   **new opportunities for business and employment have reduced the economic necessity of fraternal polyandry.**

    d.   climatic changes in the region, caused by global warming have forced a change in subsistence patterns that now favors monogamy.

    e.   the practice of polyandry, once viewed by its participants as a core family value, is declining because of changing attitudes regarding sex, love and marriage.

62. Goldstein argues in "When Brothers Share a Wife" that the practice of fraternal polyandry in Tibet is:

    a.   motivated by female promiscuity.

    b.   found only among poor, landless peasants.

    c.   made necessary by the practice of systematic female infanticide.

    d.   helps protect the family from the threat of incessant warfare and raiding.

    e.   **none of the above.**

63. According to the article "When Brothers Share a Wife," the most plausible reason for Tibetan brothers to share a wife is:

    a.   because of the Tibetan practice of female infanticide.

    b.   **to maintain a high standard of living and keep the land within the family.**

    c.   to prevent starvation due to the harsh environment.

    d.   to enable an easier division of the land among the brothers.

    e.   most females become Buddhist nuns.

CHAPTER 16
GENDER

Summary
Diamond, Jared. 1993. What Are Men Good For? Natural History 5/93: 24-29.

Are men really needed anymore? Any woman can buy sperm at a sperm bank and have children without the need for a man. Yet, is there still a vital role played by men in our society? Jared Diamond looks at this question and argues that men still do have a role in society, but it isn't for the reasons many of us believe.

MULTIPLE CHOICE QUESTIONS

64.   In the article "What are Men Good For?", what important observations does the author make about the roles of men in the Ach tribe of South America?

   a.   The society depends on the men hunting to provide most of the food for the band.
   b.   The men are responsible for clearing the lands, planting the maize, and harvesting the crops.
   c.   Most of the women have three or four husbands, which is how they can ensure they get enough food to feed themselves and their children.
   d.   Men who are the best hunters get the most sex from their wife or wives.
   e.   **Successful hunters generally have ample opportunities for adulterous sex.**

65.   In the article "What are Men Good For?", Diamond contrasts what two male strategies?

   a.   hunters versus gatherers.
   b.   trappers versus spear hunters.
   c.   heterosexual versus homosexual.
   d.   **showoffs versus providers.**
   e.   solitary versus cooperative hunters.

66.   In the article "What are Men Good For?", among the Ach foragers, males spend much time:

   a.   processing palm starch.
   b.   caring for their children.
   c.   gathering firewood and constructing temporary housing.
   d.   trapping rodents and lizards.
   e.   **none of the above.**

Summary
Layng, Anthony. 1989. What Keeps Women "In Their Place?" USA Today Magazine (Society for the Advancement of Education) May.

Anthony Layng explores the history of how gender-oriented economic roles developed. These are traditionally: man the hunter and provider, woman the gatherer and child guardian. He points out why these conceptions are archaic and how gender roles are still reinforced in modern cultures. Finally, he explores what changes need to be carried out before true gender equality becomes a reality.

MULTIPLE CHOICE QUESTIONS

67.   According to the article by Layng, "What Keeps Women in Their Place?", the primary force that perpetuates male domination in our modern society is:

   a.   the economic necessity of sexual division of labor.
   b.   **the firm system of beliefs and customs, which have developed since humans, lived at the tribal level of social organization.**
   c.   the requirements of child bearing and child raising by humans.
   d.   the high level of technology that requires increased training and specialization.
   e.   warfare, which requires the conscription of males into the specialized role of warrior.

68. According to Layng in "What Keeps Women in Their Place?", if women are to achieve total equality in our modern society, what needs to happen?

   a. The Equal Rights Amendment must be passed. Equality can be achieved only by changing the U.S. Constitution.
   b. Women must quit cooperating with the system and allowing themselves to be subjugated by males.
   c. Women must gain control of political power in our country.
   d. More women must become actively involved in the feminist movement.
   e. **All must recognize that sexual inequality is a cultural product based only on our own behavior and attitudes.**

69. According to the article "What Keeps Women in Their Place?", division of labor by gender may have originally developed because:

   a. **prolonged helplessness of infants created a need for mothers to depend on others.**
   b. women are biologically unclean and need to be separated.
   c. women are "weaker" than men and are therefore better suited to gathering than to hunting.
   d. women allowed themselves to be subjugated for the betterment of the society.
   e. men are more important socially and more skillful politically.

70. "What," according to Layng's article, "Keeps Women in Their Place?" The answer is that beliefs and customs of many societies act to separate men and women by such means as mythology, veneration of female virginity, and:

   a. segregation of male domains.
   b. preference for male children.
   c. exclusion from military combat.
   d. **all of the above.**
   e. only a and c.

CHAPTER 17
RELIGION

Summary

Saitoti, Tepilit Ole. 1986. My Circumcision. The Worlds of a Maasai Warrior, pp. 66-76. Random House, New York.

Tepilit Saitoti says that for a Maasai male the rite of circumcision "is everything." Though painful and traumatic, he shows why young Maasai boys look towards this event with both fear and joy. He then explores the social significance of being a Maasai warrior.

MULTIPLE CHOICE QUESTIONS

71. As described in the article "My Circumcision," what is the purpose of circumcision in the Maasai culture?

   a. It is performed for health reasons.
   b. It is a custom for which the people have no real explanation, they say it has always been done.
   c. It is performed on infants for cosmetic reasons.
   d. **It is performed on boys after puberty to symbolize the break between childhood and adulthood.**
   e. It is performed only on the elite young men who will become warriors.

72. As described in the article "My Circumcision," during the Maasai circumcision ritual, the person being circumcised is expected to behave in the following manner.

    a. He is supposed to kick the circumciser.
    b. He is expected to remain motionless.
    c. He is expected to stand during the entire ceremony.
    d. He is expected to joke about there being no pain.
    e. He is expected to leave after the ceremony without help, and to give gifts to each of his male relatives.

73. According to the article "My Circumcision," prior to being circumcised, the boys would shave their heads and discard all of their belongings. Which phase of a rite of passage would this be part of?

    a. margin
    b. separation
    c. graduation
    d. aggregation
    e. none of the above

74. According to the article "My Circumcision," if a man moves during his circumcision he would be:

    a. considered a coward.
    b. killed.
    c. thrown out of the village.
    d. become a warrior instead of a chief.
    e. injured severely.

75. According to the article "My Circumcision," when a Maasai girl is being circumcised, she is allowed to:

    a. have her father present.
    b. become a warrior.
    c. have the operation performed by the same person doing the male circumcisions.
    d. cry and kick as long as she does not hinder the operation.
    e. the article does not discuss girls being circumcised.

CHAPTER 18
PERSONALITY AND WORLDVIEW

Summary
Whiting, Robert. 1979. You've Gotta Have Wa. Sports Illustrated, September 24.

Robert Whiting examines the basic differences between American and Japanese cultures through an analysis of baseball. He notes that the most essential goal on a Japanese baseball team is wa. This, he shows is quite different from the goals of American baseball teams.

MULTIPLE CHOICE QUESTIONS

76. According to the article "You've Gotta Have Wa," what is the major difference between the North American version and the Japanese version of baseball?

   a. The Japanese don't train as hard as the North Americans.
   b. The Japanese game is played faster, resulting in a shorter time period.
   c. **In the Japanese game, the primary emphasis is on the good of the entire team.**
   d. The North American team places more emphasis on the powers of the coaches, rather than on the initiative of the individual.
   e. The Japanese place more emphasis on personal initiative.

77. According to Whiting in the article "You've Gotta Have Wa," exactly what is wa?

   a. Wa is that inner sense of personal harmony an individual player achieves after long periods of meditation and relaxation.
   b. Wa is the spiritual belief that you will win.
   c. Wa is the belief that the manager is king, and the individual is supposed to follow him uncomplainingly.
   d. **Wa is the concept and practice of group harmony.**
   e. Wa refers to the subservient attitude the players should have toward the coaches.

78. In the article "You've Gotta Have Wa," wa is:

   a. good fortune on the playing field.
   b. being a star player.
   c. playing with a multi-national team.
   d. being able to throw no-hitters.
   e. **none of the above.**

CHAPTER 19
LANGUAGE AND COMMUNICATION

Summary
Diamond, Jared. 1991. Reinventions of Human Language. Natural History 5/91: 22-28.

How was language invented? Jared Diamond explores this question by looking at pidgins and creoles, simplified mixtures of two languages. Although these simple languages may sound like baby-talk to our ears, they are vastly more complex than the call systems used by nonhuman primates.

MULTIPLE CHOICE QUESTIONS

79. In the article "Reinventions of Human Language," Diamond discusses two different types of human language mixtures. These were:

   a. pidgin and patois.
   b. patois and creole.
   c. **pidgin and creole.**
   d. romance and patois.
   e. PNG patois and Neo-Melanesian.

80. According to Jared Diamond in the article "Reinventions of Human Language,":

   a.   creoles first arise as a second language for colonists and workers who speak different languages and need to communicate with each other.
   b.   creoles evolve rapidly into pidgins whenever the pidgin is adopted as a native (first) language.
   c.   all languages evolve through two stages of development, first creole and then pidgin.
   d.   pidgins represent the first, crude common language between colonists and workers; later creoles develop from pidgin.
   e.   the terms "pidgin" and "creole" describe basically the same language dialect.

81. In the article "Reinventions of Human Language," Jared Diamond looks at:

   a.   the creation of pidgin and creole languages.
   b.   mechanical translation programs based on Chomsky's transformational grammar.
   c.   computer programs which try to evolve natural languages.
   d.   experiments to train chimps to speak.
   e.   none of the above

CHAPTER 20
THE WORLD SYSTEM, INDUSTRIALISM, AND STRATIFICATION

Summary
Bodley, John. 1990. The Price of Progress. In: Victims of Progress (3rd. ed.) by John Bodley, pp. 137-151. Mayfield Publishing Company, Mountain View, California.

Should everyone have a car, and a TV? Is it really a good idea to "help" native populations by exposing them to the affluence of the civilized world? Dr. Bodley takes a long and hard look at what has happened to aboriginal cultures that become exposed to the trappings of Western Civilization. For the most part these contacts have ended in disaster for the native populations. What are the hazards of development?

MULTIPLE CHOICE QUESTIONS

82. In the article "The Price of Progress," which one of the following statements is not true about native populations?

   a.   Progress has brought disease.
   b.   Progress has been chosen by most natives as something they desire.
   c.   Progress has caused high amounts of tooth decay.
   d.   Progress has created many cases of malnutrition.
   e.   Progress has forced ecocide on groups who have no other choice.

83. In "The Price of Progress," John Bodley concludes that economic development and progress for tribal societies:

   a.   create short-term problems, but long-term benefits.
   b.   reduce leisure time, but improve nutrition.
   c.   are overwhelmingly beneficial.
   d.   both a and b.
   e.   result in a lower standard of living and poorer health.

84. In "The Price of Progress," which of the following is not a price of progress?

   a. **Loss of their innocent, childlike demeanor.**
   b. Ecocide.
   c. Disease.
   d. Deprivation.
   e. Discrimination.

CHAPTER 21
APPLIED ANTHROPOLOGY

Summary

Straughan, Baird. 1991. The Secrets of Ancient Tiwanaku are Benefiting Today's Bolivia. Smithsonian 21(11): 38-49.

Archaeological investigations are revealing details about ancient agricultural techniques that have long been forgotten in Bolivia. Baird Straughan describes the efforts of Alan Kolata to reintroduce those techniques. His research is also providing the first detailed picture of a complex society that reached its climax over 1200 years ago.

MULTIPLE CHOICE QUESTIONS

85. In the article "The Secrets of Ancient Tiwanaku are Benefiting Today's Bolivia," the discovery made by archaeologists was that this ancient culture prospered and supported a large population density by:

   a. raising thousands of llamas as pack animals and as food.
   b. using guinea pigs as their main source of protein.
   c. growing many fields of corn on the hillsides of the altiplano.
   d. using floating gardens on Lake Titicaca (similar to the ones once used near Mexico City by the Aztecs).
   e. **a type of farming using water-filled canals and ridges to grow potatoes.**

86. In the article "The Secrets of Ancient Tiwanaku are Benefiting Today's Bolivia," how do the modern Aymara Indians feel about the archaeologists at first?

   a. They believe archaeologists are stealing their cultural heritage.
   b. **They believe archaeologists are responsible for causing a drought.**
   c. They welcome the archaeologists and their theories about their ancient ancestors.
   d. They ridicule the archaeologists for their interest in sherds and bones.
   e. None of the above.

87. In the article "The Secrets of Ancient Tiwanaku are Benefiting Today's Bolivia," Tiwanaku is the name of:

   a. a great supernatural being.
   b. the river that flows through the valley.
   c. **a large, ancient city.**
   d. a particular agricultural practice involving canals.
   e. an ancient book produced by the Inca.

CHAPTER 22
DEVELOPMENT AND INNOVATION

Summary
Lappe, Frances Moore and Joseph Collins. 1977. Why Can't People Feed Themselves? From Food First: Beyond the Myth of Scarcity, pp. 75-85. Houghton Mifflin Co., Boston.

Frances Lappe and Joseph Collins search for the underlying causes of famine in many of the world's Third World nations. They look at the development of these nations and explore how events in the past have destroyed the original cultural patterns of food production capacity of these cultural systems.

MULTIPLE CHOICE QUESTIONS

88. According to the article "Why Can't People Feed Themselves?", the primary reason that famine exists in some Third World countries is:

    a. these people have always been hungry.
    b. the agriculture of the Third World has not kept pace with the changing technologies of the rest of the world.
    c. **colonial rule destroyed the original patterns of food production in these cultural systems.**
    d. the Third World people have rejected the superior European approach to food production.
    e. the cash crop approach to agriculture never caught on in the Third World; therefore, the people could not generate enough money to buy food.

89. The article "Why Can't People Feed Themselves?" explains that colonialism was the answer to the title question. How did colonialism keep people from feeding themselves?

    a. It forced peasants to replace food crops with cash crops.
    b. It took over the best agricultural land and took the best workers as slaves.
    c. It blocked native peasant cash crop production from competing with cash crops produced by settlers or foreign firms.
    d. It encouraged a dependence on imported food.
    e. **all of the above**

CHAPTER 23
CULTURAL EXCHANGE AND SURVIVAL

Summary
Fernea, Elizabeth Warnock. 1993. Cuisine of Survival. Natural History 4/93: 6-11.

Thirty-five years ago, the Ferneas left Iraq after spending two years conducting ethnographic studies. Elizabeth Fernea discusses the adaptive nature of Iraqi cooking and its unique blending of many cultural influences in the context of the destruction and scarcity produced by the Persian Gulf war.

MULTIPLE CHOICE QUESTIONS

90. In the article "Cuisine of Survival," the author notes that in Iraq, by tradition, the women prepare the food, but the order in which the food is served to family members is:

   a. children and women eat first, the men eat whatever is left.
   b. grandparents and other older members are served first, then the children, wives and husbands eat next, at the same time.
   c. the wives and husbands eat first, then their children, and then the older members of the family.
   d. **the men eat first, then the older members, then the children, then the wives.**
   e. as in the United States, all members are served at the same time.

91. In the article "Cuisine of Survival," when the author describes an American hamburger to Selma, the sheik's youngest wife, her response is:

   a. **"Ridiculous, it's not good for you."**
   b. "But ground lamb is so much better."
   c. "I would give anything to try one."
   d. "It sounds just like kubba."
   e. "Pork is unclean."

92. In the article "Cuisine of Survival," what is the author's conclusion about Iraqi cuisine?

   a. It is overly dependent on expensive, imported ingredients.
   b. It is almost entirely vegetarian.
   c. In the rural areas, it is very bland and tedious.
   d. Since the war, the necessary ingredients are impossible to find.
   e. **It is one of creative survival and adaptability.**

Summary

Sung, Betty Lee. 1989. Bicultural Conflict. The World and I, August, 1989.

Betty Lee Sung takes a close look at the acculturation problems experienced by the children of recent Chinese immigrants. She looks at the differences between the values Chinese children are taught at home and compares them with the "norms" of American children. Finally, she looks at what happens to these Chinese children when forced to choose between their home-taught cultural values and those of the America they now call home.

MULTIPLE CHOICE QUESTIONS

93. In the article "Bicultural Conflict," the author discusses who the heroes are in Chinese and American cultures. In China, for example, their heroes tend to be:

   a. military leaders.
   b. political leaders.
   c. famous sports players.
   d. **self-sacrificing workers or mothers.**
   e. movie and TV stars.

94. In the article "Bicultural Conflict," the term "bicultural conflict" refers to:

   a. families in which the parents are from different ethnic groups.
   b. **immigrant families adapting to a new culture.**
   c. violence directed at immigrants.
   d. the influence of American media around the world.
   e. dating between members of different ethnic groups.

95. The tone of the article "Bicultural Conflict" suggests that the author:

    a.   finds American and Chinese norms different, but equally attractive.
    b.   prefers American norms.
    c.   prefers Chinese norms.
    d.   wishes her parents had been more understanding.
    e.   none of the above; she is completely objective in comparing American and Chinese norms.

APPENDIX
AMERICAN POPULAR CULTURE

Summary

Mucha, Janusz L. 1993. An Outsider's View of American Culture. In Distant Mirrors: American as a Foreign Culture, edited by Philip R. DeVita and James D. Armstrong, pp. 21-28. Wadsworth Publishing Co. Belmont, CA.

Dr. Mucha is from Poland but visited America as an exchange professor. His observations of us give an inside look at parts of our culture most of us take for granted. When we smile and say, "please come see us again," do we really mean it? How do others interpret our "potluck" dinners? What do we, as native Americans, think of a man who gives flowers to someone else's wife? These are just some of the interesting points the author examines in this essay.

MULTIPLE CHOICE QUESTIONS

96. In the article "An Outsider's View of American Culture," the author says that he believes our cultural practices lead to a great degree of ethnocentrism. Examples of these practices that the author cites included all of the following except:

    a.   friendly arrogance, which he says, comes from an emphasis on schools to be parochial in their teaching.
    b.   emphasis of couples to marry only others who are Americans.
    c.   wide use of flags and other national symbols.
    d.   news as it is explained on U.S. TV.
    e.   U.S. newspapers.

97. In the article "An Outsider's View of American Culture," the author was totally confused by what American social gathering?

    a.   contract Bridge parties
    b.   gatherings to watch sporting events
    c.   men's service clubs (e.g., Rotary, Lions clubs)
    d.   block parties
    e.   potluck dinners

98. In the article "An Outsider's View of American Culture," the author attributes Americans' 'friendly arrogance' to all of the following except:

    a.   the dogmatism of American Protestantism.
    b.   American news media (with a few exceptions).
    c.   a failure of the educational system to promote knowledge of the rest of the world.
    d.   the diversity and size of the United States itself.
    e.   American ethnocentrism.